The Third Sector in Europe

The role of the third sector within European society is an extremely topical subject, as both governments and the EU continue to consider the role these organizations can play in providing essential public services. This book presents contemporary research into this emerging area, exploring the contribution of this important sector to European society as well as the key challenges that the sector and its components organizations face in making this contribution.

This volume brings together for the first time a range of challenging perspectives upon the role and import of the third sector for European society from a variety of disciplines – including economics, sociology, political science, management and public policy. Areas covered include the third sector, civil society and democracy, relationships with government, its impact on social and public policy, the growth of social enterprise and of hybrid organizations as key elements of the sector and the future challenges for the sector in Europe.

This book will be of great interest to students and researchers engaged with Public Policy, Public Administrations, Public Services Management, Social Policy and Non-Profit Studies.

Stephen P. Osborne is Professor of International Public Management at the University of Edinburgh.

Routledge studies in the management of voluntary and non-profit organizations

Series Editor: Stephen P. Osborne

The Third Sector in Europe

Prospects and challenges

Edited by Stephen P. Osborne

Routledge
Taylor & Francis Group

LONDON AND NEW YORK

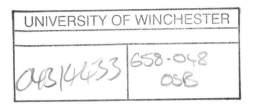
First published 2008
by Routledge
2 Park Square, Milton Park, Abingdon, Oxon OX14 4RN

Simultaneously published in the USA and Canada
by Routledge
711 Third Avenue, New York, NY 10017

Routledge is an imprint of the Taylor & Francis Group, an informa business

First issued in paperback 2012

Typeset in Times by Wearset Ltd, Boldon, Tyne and Wear

British Library Cataloguing in Publication Data
A catalogue record for this book is available from the British Library

Library of Congress Cataloging in Publication Data
A catalog record for this book has been requested

ISBN13: 978-0-415-42339-7 (hbk)
ISBN13: 978-0-203-93282-7 (ebk)
ISBN13: 978-0-415-62033-8 (pbk)

Contents

Illustrations

Contributors

Marton Balogh is Assistant Professor in the Faculty of Political, Administrative and Communication Science, Babes-Bolyai University, Romania.

Thomas P. Boje is Professor in the Department of Society and Globalization at Roskilde University, Denmark.

Taco Brandsen is Associate Professor at Radboud University Nijmegen, the Netherlands.

Celine Chew is Lecturer in Marketing at Cardiff Business School, Cardiff University, Wales.

Adalbert Evers is Professor of Comparative Health and Social Policy at the Justus-Liebig-University, Germany.

Pavel Frič is Senior Researcher at the Centre for Social and Economic Strategies, Charles University of Prague, Czech Republic.

Korel Göymen is Professor of Political Science at Sabanci University, Turkey.

Lars Skov Henriksen is Associate Professor in the Department of Sociology, Aalborg University, Denmark.

Marlies Honingh is a doctoral candidate at the University of Amsterdam, Netherlands.

Bjarne Ibsen is Director of the Centre for Sports, Health and Civil Society at the University of Southern Denmark, Denmark.

Marc Jegers is Professor of Managerial Economics at the Vrije Universiteit Brussels, Belgium.

Inger Koch-Nielsen is a former Senior Researcher at the Danish Centre for Social Research, Denmark.

György Jenei is Professor of Public Administration at Corvinus University, Budapest, Hungary.

Markku Kiviniemi is Research Manager in the Department of Political Science, University of Helsinki, Finland.

Eva Kuti is a Professor of Non-profit Studies in the Budapest School of Management, Hungary.

Ülle Lepp is a PhD student at the University of Tartu, Estonia.

Daimar Liiv is a PhD student at the University of Tartu, Estonia.

Kate McLaughlin is Senior Lecturer in Public Management of the University of Birmingham, England.

Mirella Maffei is Assistant Professor of Public and Non-profit Management at Lum Jean Monnet University, Italy.

Francesco Manfredi is Associate Professor of Public and Non-profit Management at Lum Jean Monnet and Bocconi Universities, Italy.

Juraj Nemec is a Professor the Faculty of Economics, Matej Bel University Banska Bystrica, Slovakia.

Marthe Nyssens is Professor of Economics at the Catholic University of Louvain, Belgium.

Stephen P. Osborne (Editor) is Professor of International Public Management in the Management School and Economics at the University of Edinburgh, Scotland.

Victor Pestoff is Professor of Political Science in the Department of Social Science, Mid-Sweden University, Sweden.

Tiina Randma-Liiv is Professor of Public Management and Policy at Tallinn University of Technology, Estonia.

Per Selle is Professor in the Department of Comparative Politics, University of Bergen, Norway.

Isabel Vidal is a Professor in the Department of Economic Theory at the University of Barcelona, and President of the Research Centre in Economics and Society (CIES), Spain.

Dag Wollebaek is a doctorate student in the Department of Comparative Politics, University of Bergen, Norway.

Dimitris Ziomas is a Researcher in the Institute of Social Policy, National Centre for Social Research, Greece.

Part I
Introduction

1 Key issues for the third sector in Europe

Stephen P. Osborne

Introduction

The third sector[1] is an ever more important element of the institutional mix in Europe. It has been famously described elsewhere as 'a loose and baggy monster' (Knapp and Kendal 1995). Over the past decade its significance in European nations has been heightened considerably and its import now stretches across a number of significant elements of European society. *Inter alia*, it has implications for:

- the creation and sustenance of civil society;
- the efficient and effective delivery of public services;
- the development of socially responsible businesses and social enterprises;
- the promotion of social inclusion and the regeneration of deprived communities and;
- democratic culture and accountability.

Because of this growing importance, social scientists across Europe have turned their attention to the study of this sector. This has generated a range of research networks dedicated to the third sector. These include, but are not limited to:

- the EMES network of researchers on social enterprise;
- the EGPA workshop on the impact of the third sector on public administration;
- at an international level, the International Society for Third Sector Research (ISTR) and the Association for Research on Non-profit and Voluntary Action (ARNOVA) and;
- at a national level, such networks as the Voluntary Sector Studies Network (VSSN) in the UK.

These are all important research networks, but they do have limitations. The EMES and EGPA networks are unequivocally dedicated to the study of a specific issue, the international networks by their nature have a focus beyond Europe, whilst the national networks are explicitly sub-European in their focus.

The third sector in Europe

This book is intended to be the first stage in the creation of a genuinely pan-European body of research and theory that will explore and analyse the third sector from a manifestly European perspective. This is important for three reasons. First, there is a distinctive institutional arena for the third sector within Europe, and especially within the European Union (EU). Second, many pre-existing models of the sector and its relationship to the state have developed in the US. Whilst many of these are valuable, European society and institutions are distinctive and it is important to develop theory and research that addresses this distinctiveness. Third, the sector exists at the cusp of a number of key issues for European society over the coming decade. As identified above these include the promotion of social inclusion, the enlargement of the EU, the creation and/or sustenance of civil society, and the delivery of public services to local communities. The study of the sector itself will thus also contribute to our understanding of these other issues.

Within this broad area, a number of themes have particular importance:

- Do the concepts of civil society and social capital help us to understand the relationships of third sector organizations to society – or rather do they obfuscate it? Can and does the third sector have a role in democratization in Europe?
- What are the implications of the growth of the third sector in Europe for public policy in general and for issues of social inclusion in particular?
- What role(s) do/should third sector organizations play in the provision of public services – and are social enterprise a core element of this role, or a distraction?
- What are the implications of the *New Public Governance* (Osborne 2006) for the third sector – and does it have implications for the role of the third sector in the co-production and co-governance of public services?
- What is the pattern and import of relationships between third sector organizations and local/central government – and particularly as the latter is engaged in a period of profound reform across Europe?
- Are new forms of hybrid organizations emerging from the third sector as a result of their increasing interpenetration of and by the public and private sectors?
- What is the role of social enterprise in Europe – can it combine a contribution to social policy with one of economic regeneration?
- What are the implications of the growth of the EU for third sector organizations in Europe and especially in the new accession states?
- Does *Voluntary Sector Modernization* (Osborne and McLaughlin 2004) have implications for the resources, internal structure, management and governance of third sector organizations?

In addressing theses themes this volume is thus intended to:

* challenge and test existing models and paradigms concerning the third sector in Europe;
* stimulate the emergence of new evidence and theory about the third sector in Europe;
* encourage the inter-disciplinary study of the sector and;
* provide a critique of existing institutional arrangements across Europe for the interface between the state, the market and the third sector.

In drawing together this collection it is important to highlight three points. First there has been no attempt to impose one definitive definition of the 'third sector' or 'third sector organizations'. A distinctive element of European experience is its diversity and this is reflected here, offering the reader the opportunity to draw their own conclusions. Second, inevitably the chapters below address cross-cutting themes, if from slightly different perspectives. This allows some triangulation of our knowledge of the third sector in Europe. Finally this volume is intended as a starting point for the development of a distinctive European body of theory and knowledge on the third sector. It is intended to stimulate debate rather than to provide the final or ultimate statement.

Following on from this introductory chapter, therefore, this collection is grouped around eight themes arising from the above discussion. The first three chapters address the relationship between the third sector and civil society, social capital and democracy. Jenei and Kuti examine the nature of 'civil society', its relationship to the third sector and place this relationship at the heart of the development of the transitional nations of Eastern and Central Europe. Wollebaek and Selle then provide a critique of the concept of 'social capital' in European experience, contrasting the socialization perspective on it with one from institutional theory. Finally in this section, Balogh offers an important empirical exploration of the role of the third sector in the democratization process in Romania.

In the Part III, attention is turned to the third sector and public policy. Lars Skov Hendriksen and his colleagues offer a detailed empirical examination of the capacity of the sector to engage in public policy objectives in Denmark. Marthe Nyssens then introduces the concept of 'social enterprise' and asks what contribution such organizations can make to the social inclusion agenda in Europe. The concept of social enterprise is returned to below.

Part IV of this book follows on to deepen our understanding of the important role of the sector in delivering public services. Brandsen provides a meta-theoretical perspective on this role. Nemec then offers empirical evidence about trends in Slovakia before Osborne and Chew dissect one classically espoused attribute of the third sector in providing public services: their innovative capacity.

Part V develops this debate, by an examination of the concept of co-production. Pestoff provides a Scandinavian perspective on this, based on

Swedish experience, whilst Manfredi and Maffei offer a Mediterranean one, rooted in Italian experience.

Part VI moves on to the perennially significant and over-arching issue of relationships between the third sector and government, in its widest sense. Göymen, Fric and Randma-Liiv and her colleagues offer three perspectives on this relationship, from a Turkish, Czech and Estonian perspective.

Part VII presents a further emerging concept that is being used to make sense of the third sector in European society – that of 'hybrid organizations' where the third sector interacts at an organizational level with the public and private sectors. Evers introduces this concept and explores the challenges it offers to third sector theory in Europe. Honingh then provides a contrasting empirical analysis, exploring the impact of hybridity upon managerial roles in the third sector in the Netherlands.

Part VIII returns to the social enterprise perspective introduced earlier, with Vidal and Ziomas offering contrasting experiences from Spain and Greece, respectively.

The concluding section contains two papers. First, Jegers considers the implications of this changing European context for the third sector for their internal management, from a distinctively economic perspective. Finally Kiviniemi draws together the state of our knowledge and sets out some key research questions to develop further our knowledge of the third sector in Europe.

Notes

1 A range of terms are used to describe this sector, including the third sector, the voluntary and community sector, the non-profit sector, the social enterprise sector and civil society. Each of these has a distinctive conception of the sector which will be explored in this volume. In this introductory chapter, the term 'the third sector' will be used to describe the subject matter of this volume, without prejudice.

References

Knapp, M. and Kendall, J. (1995) 'A loose and baggy monster: boundaries, definitions and typologies' in J. Davis Smith, C. Rochester, and R. Hedley (eds) *An Introduction to the Voluntary Sector*, London: Routledge.

Osborne, S. (2006) 'The new public governance?' in *Public Management Review* (8, 3) pp. 377–388.

Osborne, S. and McLaughlin, K. (2004) 'The cross-cutting review of the voluntary sector: where next for local government – voluntary sector relationships?' in *Regional Studies* (38, 5) pp. 573–582.

Part II
Civil society, social capital and democracy

2 The third sector and civil society

György Jenei and Éva Kuti

The definition of civil society

The very essence of the modern usage of the term "civil society" was to demarcate a clear distinction of state and society and was conceptualized by the German philosopher, Georg Wilhelm Friedrich Hegel in his *Elements of the Philosophy of Right*. In his "triad" concept, civil society was distinguished from the macro community of the state and the micro community of the family. The term civil society, however, has a long history. It is definitely older than the modern world. In ancient Greece, for instance, "civil society" was closely connected with the Aristotelian notion of an ideal way of life.

Today, there are many definitions of civil society. Perhaps the working definition from the London School of Economics Centre for Civil Society provides a relevant orientation:

> Civil society refers to the arena of uncoerced collective action around shared interests, purposes and values. In theory, its institutional forms are distinct from those of the state, family and market, though in practice, the boundaries between state, civil society, family and market are often complex, blurred and negotiated. Civil society commonly embraces a diversity of spaces, actors and institutional forms, varying in their degree of formality, autonomy and power. Civil societies are often populated by organizations such as registered charities, development non-governmental organizations, community groups, women's organizations, faith-based organizations, professional associations, trade unions, self-help groups, social movements, business associations, coalitions, and advocacy groups.
>   (http://pages.britishlibrary.net/blwww3/3way/civilsoc.htm)

Moreover, in the EU member countries, the current definition has two types of historical background. On the one hand, in Central and Eastern Europe (CEE) in the 1970s and 1980s the term was used by oppositional movements and their intellectual leaders (Havel, 1985; Konrád, 1984; Michnik, 1985) in order to express their criticism of the ruling totalitarian or authoritarian political system. In this context, the very existence of horizontal social structures, or "small circles of freedom" (Bibó, 1986), was an expression of society's antagonism towards autocratic political regimes. This moral resistance to totalitarian oppression had potential for important civil society initiatives, even under the conditions of limited political freedom. In the longer run, horizontal social structures were supposed to develop to the detriment of vertical social structures, thus creating a society built from the bottom up, and in which some control could be gained over policy makers. This vision of the development of civil society had an impact on political thinking far beyond the borders of the Soviet bloc.

Ostensibly, in the state socialist system a third sector simply could not exist independently of the ruling state ideology. Despite this ostensible pre-condition, numerous groups, including mainly membership groups, closely related to so-called "mass organizations" existed. There were many member-serving clubs that fulfilled functions similar to those of voluntary associations in market economies, particularly in the fields of sports, culture and recreation (Jagasics, 1992). These organizations provided goods and services for their members as well as for a limited public. The same holds true for quite a number of clubs funded and run by state-owned enterprises.

After the collapse of the state socialist system a new phase in civil society activism began. In the new political system, local activists used their newly won freedom and the number of clubs and voluntary organizations mushroomed, particularly in those fields which had not previously been tolerated by state ideology (Kuti, 1996). Cases in point are activities associated with formerly unmet specific needs for educational, health or social services, and with new social movements such as environmental, pacifist and solidarity groups. Besides the member-serving organizations and clubs engaged mainly in recreation, sports and culture (e.g. hunting associations, football clubs, folk art associations, etc.), there also emerged service-providing nonprofit organizations (e.g. foundation schools and kindergartens, nursing homes, etc.) and advocacy groups principally pursuing political objectives (e.g. organizations protecting and representing the interests of ethnic minorities, the physically disabled, victims of political oppression, etc.).

The motivation behind the establishment of the numerous nonprofit organizations in the early 1990s was mainly the citizens' desire to actively influence the development of the new economic and political system, to participate in the decision-making process, to ensure some autonomy, to strengthen the local identity, to control and influence the local authorities, to promote cultural, ethnic, religious and linguistic diversity, to develop local information networks, to educate citizens and to encourage them to behave as citizens. These civil society functions have become all the more important because political transition brought about fundamental changes in all parts of society and the economy, causing a lot of people to lose orientation and feel endangered in the early 1990s. Voluntary organizations and the additional resources (donations, government support, tax advantages) available through them served as lifebelts for numerous individuals. Whether they wanted to protect themselves or to seize new opportunities, citizens had to form alliances, action groups and advocacy organizations.

Voluntary organizations have also played an important role in the process of social restructuring. People changing their social and economic positions often feel that they have to leave their old organizations and find (or establish) new ones where they can meet the members of their new class. Membership in voluntary associations, participation and volunteering are essential elements of their status-seeking behavior (Collins and Hickman, 1991).

In the traditional EU member countries on the other hand, the term "civil society" has had a different and more complex historical background. The origin of the term can be found in the early liberal writings of the nineteenth century, such as those of Alexis de Tocqueville. He emphasized that the role of civil society in a democratic political system is crucial. Moreover, he pointed out that the stability of democracy is dependent on the strength and dominant impact of civil society.

The dominant role of civil society was reinforced from the 1970s onwards and was connected to the shift from representative democracy to a new wave of democratization closely linked to various forms of participatory democracy. Later, the social capital approach emphasized the importance of social coordination. Robert Putnam (1993) stated that the existence of social capital makes democracy work. He brought to the fore the role of social trust, societal networks and civicness in the associational involvement and participatory behavior of the citizenry.

In the 1960s and 1970s a series of movements and intentional communities mushroomed in the traditional EU countries and all around the modern world. They built up alternative housing systems (organized squatting, tipi making, house-sharing "crash pad networks" which were supported by information centers) and alternative travel services were created by car-sharing networks or by hitching. Similarly, alternative social structures were established in a bottom-up way (alternative soup kitchens, free bookshops). For example, in the 1970s a partially self-governing neighborhood was established in Copenhagen. The independent community, with semi-legal status, called "Christiana" emerged when a group of hippies took over an area of abandoned military barracks. The community is still alive today.

Religious and pseudo-religious groups represent special types of societies for alternatives. They provide a framework for the emergence of alternative lifestyles all around the world in the form of ashrams, kibbutzim, Buddhist monasteries, Rastafarians, Hare Krishna movements, Shaker and Amish movements.

All the above enlisted forms of alternative societies and societies of alternatives have one thing in common: they provide special solutions for the political empowerment of civil society. In this form of empowerment, citizens look for tools and methods of taking control of their own lives, turning against the political power of the state and the public sector and against the economic power, the market-type mechanism dominating the private sector.

The definition of the third sector

The term "third sector" covers a lot of different types of organizations. These organizations differ from each other by their founding origins, by their funding resources and by their functions. Generally, they do not like to consider themselves as "third sector organizations". They prefer to be identified more closely with their particular character: i.e. we are a charity or voluntary organization or we have service provision or advocacy functions.

The term "third sector" also has different meanings. In Japan, for example, since the 1980s, the third sector (known as the Daisan sector in Japan) refers to joint corporations created by a joint investment of the public and private sectors. In the United Kingdom, the third sector is considered to be a place between the public and private sectors. Another approach (Evers and Laville, 2004) puts a greater emphasis on the intermediary nature of third sector organizations within welfare pluralism and on the process of "hybridization", the emergence of multi-stakeholder arrangements in the provision of welfare services.

There is tremendous diversity among the third sector organizations and this diversity

> is reflected in many terms used for its description. Each one of the commonly used terms points out a certain aspect of its character: "third sector" (as a sector active between the state and the market), "nonprofit sector", "voluntary sector", "public-service sector", "non-governmental organizations" (internationally referred to as NGOs), "non-state organizations" (i.e. organizations of a non-state character), "charity (humanitarian, philanthropic) organizations", "self-help groups, clubs, organizations", the British term "non-statutory sector" (i.e. not required by law, non-compulsory), or "informal sector", the American term "tax-exempt sector", the French term "économie sociale" (used in France and Belgium, and increasingly, in European Union institutions), or German terms such as "gemeinnützige Organizationen" and "gemeinwirtschafliche Unternehmen".
>
> (Anheier and Seibel, 1990, quoted in Fric and Bútora, 2003, p. 146)

In spite of the diversity of its organizations, some general statements on the third sector can be made. First, the term "third sector" was coined by Etzioni (1973) and it meant a third alternative sector between the state and the market. According to Etzioni, the main advantage of these organizations is in their combination of the entrepreneurial spirit and organizational effectiveness of the business firm with the common-good orientation of the public sector.

Third sector organizations have an "intermediary role" between state and market and they constitute a very specific segment of modern societies. Their special features can be summarized as follows: they obey the non-distribution constraint that exclusively allows re-investment of profits but not their distribution among the members and/or the employees of the organization; they are private organizations, albeit operating within the public sphere and for the common wealth; voluntary participation is a key feature of third sector organizations. Thus, there is a clear distinction between third sector and communitarian entities, such as families or clans (Priller and Zimmer, 2001).

The incentives and motives of the establishment of these organizations are also different from the motivation behind the creation of public sector and private sector organizations. The central value basis of third sector organizations is reflected in their willingness to serve as vehicles for participation and social integration.

Different disciplines (economics, sociology, political sciences) have different primary foci on third sector organizations. For economists, the non-distribution constraint is the most interesting feature. In accordance with the institutional choice approach, third sector organizations offer an institutional alternative to social service provision by private enterprises or government entities. Sociologists are interested in the potential of third sector organizations to provide avenues for societal integration. They perceive these organizations as bedrocks of social milieus and societal communities and, therefore, as transmitters of values and norms. Political scientists are also primarily interested in the service delivery function of third sector organizations, perceiving them as actors within public–private partnerships, particularly in the welfare domain.

Third sector organizations (TSOs) are also called non-governmental organizations (NGOs). This is justified mainly in the case of different social groups or associations pursuing matters of interest to their members or to certain social groups by lobbying, persuasion or direct action.

Many NGOs – considering the label too broad for them – prefer the term "private voluntary organization" (PVO) or private development organization (PDO). A 1995 UN report noted that there were nearly 29,000 international NGOs. Among those is the International Red Cross, founded in 1863 and the world's largest humanitarian NGO. In terms of the number of national and local organizations, the United States and India were the forerunners with an estimated two million NGOs.

Non-governmental organizations form a heterogeneous group. As a result, very different typologies have been created in order to classify them. The typology of the World Bank, for example, divides them into *operational* and *advocacy* groups.

The primary purpose of an operational NGO, however, is the design and implementation of development-related projects. One categorization that is frequently used is the division into "relief-oriented" or "development-oriented" organizations. Operational NGOs can also be classified according to whether they stress service delivery or participation; whether they are religious or secular; and whether they are more public or more private-oriented. They can be divided into the groups of community-based, national and international organizations as well.

The primary purpose of an advocacy NGO is to defend or promote a specific cause. As opposed to operational project management, these organizations typically try to raise awareness, acceptance and knowledge by lobbying, press work and activist events.

According to a more detailed typology, the following types of NGOs exist:

- INGO, or international NGO, such as CARE, RESPECT Refugiados, International Alert, ADFA-India and Mercy Corps;
- BINGO, business-oriented international NGO;
- RINGO, religious international NGO such as Catholic Relief-Services. RINGO is also an abbreviation for Research and Independent Non-governmental Organization;
- ENGO, environmental NGO, such as Global 2000;
- GONGOs are government-operated NGOs, which may have been set up by governments to look like NGOs in order to qualify for foreign aid;
- QUANGOs are quasi-autonomous non-governmental organizations, such as the International Organization for Standardization (ISO), which is not purely an NGO, since its membership is by nation, and each nation is represented by what the ISO Council determines to be the "most broadly representative" standardization body of a nation. Now, such a body might or might not be a non-governmental organization. For example, the United States is represented in ISO by the American National Standards Institute, which is independent of the federal government. However, other countries can be represented by national governmental agencies – this is the trend in Europe.

Duality in the third sector

As we have already noted, third sector organizations – backed and supported by the civil society – have an intermediary position between the state and the market, and between the state and society. But this intermediary position is often threatened by the actions and policies of government and by the private sector as well.

Market type organizations have two kinds of relationships with TSOs: public–private partnership (PPP) and/or sponsoring relationships. In this context, we use the term in its widest sense: sponsoring embraces both disinterested, generous corporate donations to third sector organizations and sponsors' payments related to business interests (e.g. investment in prestige, cause related marketing, etc.).

The main differences between PPP and sponsoring are:

- In a sponsoring relationship, the private donor is not directly involved in policy making.
- Sponsoring is generally connected to special programs with financial needs additional to the already available resources.
- Sponsoring is a direct contact between service providers and foundations established by private enterprises.

(Strünck and Heinze, 2001)

In a sponsoring relationship, the independent position of TSOs is sometimes limited by the influence of the donor enterprises. There are even more chances for such an influence (though, ideally, mutual) in the public–private partnerships. This collaboration between the public and private sectors whose purpose is to support or provide public services has developed a wide variety of different structures. The actual forms of co-operation and the division of labor between the partners determine whether third sector organizations can play a significant role in developing welfare policy or whether they are simply treated as vehicles of policy implementation.

Governmental policies also can decrease or increase the independence of TSOs. For example, when US President Ronald Reagan cut back government spending on welfare issues, top civil servants pressured TSOs to deliver more social services. The consequence was that large private independent foundations came together to take action against the neo-liberal revolution and tried to protect at least the bare minimum of the welfare state (Anheier, 2005, p. 301–327).

Third sector organizations have to face similar challenges in the CEE countries as well. Not having strong and large independent foundations, CEE third sectors are quite vulnerable (Osborne *et al.*, 2005). Their problem is not simply how they can resist if the government makes efforts to limit their independence. TSOs also need to convince the government that their contribution to the development of democracy and service provision is crucial, and thus they deserve public support.

Nowadays, two competing views are of similar importance – especially in CEE. One view sees the third sector as an expression of civil society, rooted in democratic culture (in CEE, an emerging democratic culture) and based on social participation (in CEE, a broadening social participation). According to the other approach, the third sector is basically an extension of the central and local governments; third sector organizations play an important role in the provision of public services (Jenei and Kuti, 2003). A number of country reports (Salamon *et al.*, 1999) confirm that this duality can be found among third sector organizations all over the world.

The duality issue becomes much more complicated when the multifunctional character of third sector organizations is taken into consideration. The service provision and civil society functions can be combined even at the level of individual organizations. Non-govermental service providers can also carry out lobbying activities for the interests of their members or of a larger social group. Besides providing their members with some services, voluntary associations can also serve the broader public interest. Even the member-serving non-governmental organizations can be important actors of empowerment, social inclusion and fostering solidarity.

This multifunctionality raises the question of potential conflicts between the different functions and also between the TSOs and their supporters. Donors financing non-governmental service provision are not necessarily enthusiastic about the advocacy work of the supported organizations, especially not if these TSOs are outspoken critics of their supporters' political and business activities or initiators of alternative modernization efforts.

This problem has emerged, quite sharply, in CEE countries, thus a detailed exploration of the financial aspects of duality seems to be necessary.

Financial aspects of duality

Based on the limited statistical data available,[1] Figure 2.1, even in its simplicity, clearly displays that there is a close connection between the third sector organizations' main function and their major revenue sources.

Member-serving civil society organizations (leisure and sport clubs, professional advocacy groups, small local voluntary associations which are not registered as "public benefit" organizations) can mainly rely on membership fees and service income. This means that they are more or less dependent on their members' purchasing power. Neither private donors nor government authorities consider them an important target group.

The service fees, sales and dues can only increase if member serving TSOs manage to significantly widen the scope and variety of their activities and they are able to offer what their members are ready and able to buy. This financial constraint on their activities, along with their need for attracting additional fee income, may easily result in neglecting their civil society functions and moving toward professional service provision, thus attracting less and less donations.

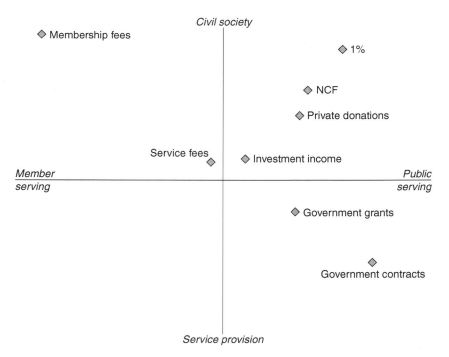

Figure 2.1 Relationships between third sector functions and financing.

By contrast, the most important recipients of private donations are civil society organizations serving public interest (voluntary associations and foundations registered as "charitable" or "public benefit" organizations, not involved in large scale service provision, operating mainly in the fields of culture, education, science, social and health care, environment, etc.). Due to the cyclical nature of private contributions, they have some funds to be invested, thus they also have access to a considerable amount of investment income.

Private giving, however, operates from a small domestic base in the CEE countries. Both individual and corporate donors suffer from a very similar problem, that of limited resources. Though surveys of giving (Czike and Kuti, 2006; Kuti, 2005) confirm that the majority of private people and corporate managers are willing to help voluntary organizations and contribute to the solution of social problems, the same surveys and statistical data also show that the actual individual donations are rather small. Consequently, despite its high proportion, the volume of private donations flowing to public-serving civil society organizations is still a relatively low amount of money. It does not cover the costs of activities which, in an ideal case, would let these TSOs fulfill their civil society functions.

This shortage of private contributions raises the question of whether the concentration of government funding in the service-providing segment of the third sector is acceptable. Civil society organizations argue that decades of state socialism did as much harm to organized civil society as to nonprofit service providers, thus CSOs should also be entitled to claim some "recovery assistance" from the government. While this claim is generally considered legitimate, nevertheless, the public-serving nonprofit service providers (nonprofit schools, kindergartens, hospitals, nurseries, theatres, culture centers, etc.) remain the single most important beneficiaries of state funding.

The actual forms of government support to service-providing TSOs are manifold and their system is quite complicated. Beneficiaries can receive state support in many different forms, from several different government agencies and through various mechanisms of distribution. The most important forms of support are:

- Government grants which can be either lump sum subsidies or project-related grants. These grants may come directly from state budgets on the decision of the Parliament, from the central government or ministries, from special government funds (e.g. National Fund for Vocational Training, Labor Force Fund, National Cultural Fund, National Fund for the Protection of Environment, etc.) or from local governments. They can be distributed at the discretion of government bodies, with the help of special boards or expert committees, and through an open competition.
- Per capita government support which relates directly to the number of clients. Its amount can be guaranteed by the budget law but it can also depend on the donor's decision. Per capita state support can be transferred to service providers through the ministries, through public authorities and

through local governments. It can be received (after eligibility has been determined) in the form of contracting out services, and as a result of the decision of government authorities.

Though most forms of government support already existed in the early 1990s, there have been some important changes in recent years. First, project-related grants have become the dominant form of government support, while lump sum subsidies to TSOs have almost disappeared. The shift from general funding to specific project grants has made government support a bit more transparent and more easily available for nonprofit service providers. Second, the importance of service-related per capita subsidies and contracting out services has noticeably developed. Third, competitive bidding has become an important mechanism in the distribution of all kinds of state support. A large part of government grants and contracts are now available through open competition, and thus are mainly available for those larger and stronger TSOs which can prove that they are important partners in the provision of welfare services.

As a consequence, the distribution of public support to TSOs is highly concentrated. The beneficiaries are significantly larger and much more "affluent" than other institutions of the third sector. The government clearly prefers supporting a limited number of organizations which are strong enough to play important roles in meeting public needs, and can be relatively easily held accountable.

This service-providing segment of the third sector is not far from "being propelled to a role as:

- an agent of modernization, able to exert pressure for change over government institutions, and particularly local government, and towards itself being
- a subject of modernization, with consequent challenges for its own governance arrangements and performance management regimes".

(McLaughlin, 2004, p. 557)

This is a serious danger all over Europe, but it is especially important in the CEE region. CEE countries still have to cope with a series of modernization and democratization challenges. They can hardly afford to lose or to weaken civil society actors. If these latter do not get enough private donations and therefore require government support, they have to receive it in a way which does not create dependence on the state. This reasoning has led to the development of two innovative methods of financing: the "1% system" and the "National Civil Fund" (NCF).

These methods, as shown in Figure 2.1, have proved to be quite efficient in channeling government support to civil society organizations without making them dependent on public authorities.

Support but not dependence from the state

The first of the two new support schemes, the 1% system, was originally introduced in Hungary in 1997 with the aim of strengthening civil society, helping its institutionalization and supporting the everyday operation of CSOs without gaining control over them and endangering their independence. The 1% system became well known in the CEE region very quickly. Since then, similar supporting schemes have been developed in Lithuania, Poland, Romania and Slovakia. The idea of the 1% system is to let private citizens decide on the distribution of government support. This new financing scheme[2] permits the transfer of one percent of personal income tax payments to TSOs. Taxpayers are authorized to choose a civil society organization to which they want their funds allocated.

Several different kinds of third sector organizations are eligible for the 1 percent designation. Namely, TSOs which are engaged in preventive medicine, health care, social services, culture, education, research, public safety, human rights, environmental protection, protection of cultural heritage, sports and leisure time activities for the youth and the disabled, care for the elderly, the poor, the handicapped, children, national and ethnic minorities can all get 1 percent support if they have been in existence for a considerable period, are independent of political parties and do not support candidates for political office, and they are not in arrears with tax and duties, or they agree that the amount they would receive from the personal income tax is used to pay or decrease their debt.

The 1 percent designation is part of the individual's tax declaration. The financial transfer itself is made by the tax authority. If the taxpayer does not name a recipient organization or makes some formal mistake when preparing the designation declaration, the 1 percent transfer is negated and the entirety of the individual's tax payment remains part of the central budget. Similarly, the transfer is not made if the designated organization is not eligible, cannot get the necessary certificates within the established deadline or thinks that the costs of meeting all the application and reporting requirements would be higher than the amount it could receive.

Public authorities play only administrative roles in the process; they do not have any influence on the actual distribution of the 1 percent support. The decisions are made by taxpayers who seem to prefer public-serving civil society organizations to both nonprofit service providers and member-serving voluntary associations. As a result, TSOs performing civil society functions can receive public funds through the 1 percent mechanism without becoming dependent on public authorities.

Obviously, TSOs work hard in order to acquire as much of this kind of support as possible. Nevertheless, a large number of the taxpayers still do not make their designation. Consequently, a significant part of the potential 1 percent support remained in the central budget until 2003. Finding a way of distributing this non-designated 1 percent among voluntary organizations became a subject of heated debates right after the introduction of the 1% system. This debate resulted in the creation of another innovative funding scheme, the

National Civil Fund (NCF) (Jenei *et al.*, 2005). The NCF budget depends on the size of the 1 percent designations. In a given year, it can only distribute exactly the same amount of money that the taxpayers' gave to designated recipients in their tax declarations earlier that year.[3]

The NCF's main goal is to support the operating costs of civil society organizations. At least 60 percent of its money must be spent to this purpose. Besides operating costs, another 30 percent of the fund may be devoted to a variety of purposes, including the public benefit activities of civic organizations, domestic and cross-border events, membership and participation in international civic networks, research, education, advisory work and publications about civil society. The NCF may also offer matching grants and there is a possibility to allocate funds to re-granting organizations. The remaining 10 percent of the fund balance covers the administration costs of the NCF itself. Eighty percent of the NCF's sources are mandated to be distributed either as non-refundable or as refundable grants through open application schemes.

Civil society organizations, such as associations, societies and foundations, are eligible to receive support from the NCF. Parties, trade unions, employers' federations, mutual insurance associations, churches, public benefit companies, and public law foundations established by state or municipal institutions are explicitly excluded. Organizations must be at least one year old and active (i.e. operating) to be eligible.

The National Civil Fund is composed of two types of decision-making bodies: the Council and the Colleges.[4] The Council makes the strategic decisions, sets the NCF's priorities, divides its resources among the various purposes and develops its other rules. The Colleges are operative grant-makers: they accept or reject the applications for NCF grants.

The overwhelming majority of the members of both decision-making bodies are civil society representatives. They are selected through a sophisticated open electoral system which is supposed to ensure that TSO representatives have a decisive voice in the distribution of NCF funds. While the 1% system delegates decision-making rights to the citizens themselves, elected representatives of TSOs are the key actors in the redistribution through the National Civil Fund. Figure 2.1 shows that this arrangement is advantageous for the TSOs performing civil society functions and brings government funding closer to the support of the interests of the civil society. At this point the question can be raised: what is the impact of the duality in service provision to the other functions of TSOs?

Governance, civil society and the third sector

The ongoing shift from government to governance in the European Union (van Kersbergen and van Waarden, 2004) has changed the role of the third sector organizations and the civil society. Indeed, civil society was among the initiators of the shift to governance, with its expectations and higher demands. In the course of the shift, governance arrangements have emerged in the EU – at European, national and subnational levels – involving different actors, diverse stake-holders (not only state actors anymore) such as business associations, lobby groups, public interest groups and service providers. The role of civil society has thus become twofold, as:

- a constant external pressure, requiring a shift toward governance;
- an increasing role in the governance of public service networks, and with growing influence on the bargaining and deliberation processes of the regulatory state in the policy arenas – and with an increasing role in social distributive policies both in terms of services provision and also the decision-making processes.

In the EU member countries in the past decades essential reform steps have been taken in public governance and management. These reform steps were triggered by a changing (civil) society with new and different expectations, and by the demand of third sector organizations for more involvement in service provision, for more empowerment in public policy making, and for a more efficient, open and transparent, more customer oriented, more flexible, accessible and consultative government, more focused on performance.

The expectations of civil society and the demands of third sector organizations are of essential importance in the shift from government to governance in general and in the strengthening of openness and transparency, in enhancing public sector performance, in modernizing accountability and control in the creation of new organizational settings, in the use of market type mechanism in particular. It is not a completed process yet, of course. We are in the middle of the creation of essential new relationships between government and civil society, and among market type, public, and third sector organizations.

It has been demonstrated elsewhere during the last decades that the same reform steps produced quite diverse results in different EU member countries (Pollitt and Bouckaert, 2000). The modernization process is hence context dependent, and the influence of the following factors is significant:

- the strength of civil society;
- the capabilities of civil society in articulating, expressing and implementing the interests of different social groups;
- the level of social capital, encompassing social trust;
- the level of vertical and horizontal value orientation in creating networks;
- the service provision power of third sector organizations; and
- the strength of the demand of civil society for making a shift from the "input legitimacy" of modern democracies to the "output legitimacy", which means to a "participatory democracy".

In 2005 the role of civil society and its organizations was evaluated in detail by the OECD, in the context of basic European administrative principles (OECD, 2005). The main conclusions of this report, which have relevance here, are:

- Openness and transparency – the two basic values of governance – are strongly emphasized as requirements of a civil society. Increasing openness and transparency brings third sector and civil society organizations closer together.
- When civil society receives relevant and understandable information on governance activities it means that TSO activities can also become open and transparent to the public. Relevant and understandable information enhances citizens' access to services and the opportunity to participate in decision making. The lack of relevant and understandable information triggers falling levels of social trust. Citizens' trust in TSOs is reduced when they are not informed as to their specific activities. Therefore, TSOs are required to raise their own standards of openness and transparency – even accountability – in order to maintain their creditability and legitimacy toward civil society.
- The credibility of TSOs depends on their public watchdog function as well. In many EU countries, across many public policy areas, this function has been strengthened because TSOs are not amateur lobbyists anymore. They have evolved into highly professional organizations and they can monitor government performance and provide comprehensible information for the public.

While there are traditional sources of independent monitoring of government performance (e.g. media, international organizations, rating agencies), TSOs have to become new, influential actors in monitoring activities, because they can significantly increase the power and vocal demands of the civil society for openness, transparency and accountability. Openness and transparency strengthen participatory democracy by providing civil society with opportunities to take an active role in society, by exposing abuse of power and corruption, offering greater protection against mismanagement and providing greater opportunities for full range participation in decision making and in service provision.

Civil society has higher demands for an accessible and responsive decision making and public service provision. This can be required not only from the public agencies but from the TSOs as well. In some EU member countries, citizen's access is enhanced through customer charters, which can establish appropriate redress mechanisms for citizens from public services.

Enhancing the performance level of TSOs is also an essential requirement and across the EU, many member states have introduced performance-oriented budgeting and performance management. Many TSOs already link expenditures to specific targets. The key issue is to what extent, in the future, performance results will determine budget allocations and whether the structure of expenditures is dependent upon outcome targets as well.

TSOs are challenged by public agencies and private enterprises in implementing performance management reforms. It is strongly recommended for TSOs to use performance results to set the priorities of projects and different activities, to allocate resources within the projects. A regular improvement of the decision-making process is also needed based on monitoring the type of project evaluation. More autonomy is to be given to the managers of TSOs in using resources for achieving results and improving performance.

In this context, accountability to the citizens has to be improved. TSOs have to be accountable toward their members and toward their target groups in order to increase public trust. Because of scandals, public trust has declined toward TSOs in some areas. Therefore improvement of transparency and accountability is crucially important. It has to include reforms in the application of techniques of performance budgeting and management but also changes in the behavior of TSO employees.

A final challenge for TSOs is the reorganization of their internal processes and activities as a consequence of their strategic partnership relationships with public agencies and the private sector. TSOs now have to compete with organizations from both sectors. In the process of such competition new challenges can emerge for their management systems and reporting mechanisms. Reorganization of TSOs creates new relationships with their members, with their new stakeholders and with other citizen groups. These differing demands need to be balanced by TSOs.

Conclusions

In the EU member countries – depending on differences in their economic, social and cultural context and on historical traditions – a diversity exists in the empowerment of civil society and in the involvement of their organizations in the public sphere. However, some general conclusions can still be drawn:

- The level of the empowerment can be related to the potential shift from representative (output) democracy to the participatory (input) democracy in some parts of the EU.
- The bargaining and lobby power of civil society and its organizations has been increasing in the area of regulatory policy making.
- The service provision function of TSOs in different policy areas has grown significantly, mainly services provision but with commensurate development in the decision making processes of the distributive policies as well.
- Civic participation has been strengthening through the emergence of a "civil dialogue", which implies a shift from consultation by government to co-decision making with it.
- Civil society organizations are accepted by many EU governments and, accordingly, supported as having important economic and social roles in democratic societies.
- The multifunctional character of these organizations is differentiated at the EU level by distinguishing between operational organizations with service delivery function and advocacy organizations aiming to have an impact on the policies of the government, on the behavior of public agencies and on

public opinion. It means that civil society has the potential to contribute not only to the improvement of the input, but also to the output, of the legitimacy of democratic societies in Europe.

Notes

1 These statistical data come from Hungary (Nonprofit szervezetek Magyarországon, 2005) because these are the only ones which are detailed enough and easily available for the authors. However, we would probably find a similar pattern in other countries of the CEE region. It is also possible that the pattern would be not too different in the more developed parts of Europe, either.
2 There are several differences between the national versions of the 1% system. Since these are not important in the context of the present discussion, we limit ourselves to a short overview of the original Hungarian scheme.
3 However, the law guarantees that this amount cannot be less than 0.5 percent of the personal income tax, even if taxpayers' 1 percent designations prove to be extremely low.
4 "College" is a rough translation of the Latin-based Hungarian word "kollégium". Its actual meaning is a decision-making board.

References

Anheier, H.K. (2005). *Nonprofit Organizations. Theory, Management, Policy*. London: Routledge.
Anheier, H.K. and Seibel, W. (eds.) (1990). *The Third Sector: Comparative Studies of Nonprofit Organizations*. Berlin and New York: De Gruyter.
Bibó, I. (1986). *Válogatott tanulmányok* (Selected Essays). Budapest: Magvetö.
Collins, R. and Hickman, N. (1991). "Altruism and culture as social products", *Voluntas*, 2(2). Available online: http://pages.britishlibrary.net/blwww3/3way/civilsoc.htm.
Czike, K. and Kuti, É. (2006). *Önkéntesség, jótékonyság, társadalmi integráció* (Volunteering, Charity, Social Integration). Budapest: Nonprofit Kutatócsoport – Önkéntes Központ Alapítvány.
Etzioni, A. (1973). "The third sector and domestic missions", *Public Administration Review*, 33: 314–323.
Evers, A. and Laville, J.-L. (2004). "Social services by social enterprises: on the possible contribution of hybrid organizations and a civil society", in: Evers, A. and Laville, J.-L. (eds.). *The Third Sector in Europe*, Cheltenham, UK and Northampton, MA: Edward Elgar, pp. 237–255.
Fric, P. and Bútora, M. (2003). "The role of the nonprofit sector in public policy", in: *Public Policy Process in Central and Eastern Europe*, Bratislava: NISPAcee, pp. 143–177.
Havel, V. (1985). *The Power of the Powerless: Citizens Against the State in Central-Eastern Europe*, London: Hutchinson.
Jagasics, B. (1992). "A zalai alapítványok és egyesületek fejlödéséröl" (About the development of foundations and voluntary associations in Zala County), in : Kuti, E. (ed). *A nonprofit szektor Magyarországon*. Budapest: Nonprofit Kutatócsoport.
Jenei, Gy. and Kuti, É. (2003). "Duality in the third sector: the Hungarian Case", *The Asian Journal of Public Administration*, 25(1): 133–157.
Jenei, Gy. *et al.* (2005). "Local governments, civil society organizations and private

enterprises: partnerships in providing social services", *Journal of Comparative Policy Analysis: Research and Practice*, 1: 73–94.

van Kersbergen, K. and van Waarden, F. (2004). "Politics and the transformation of governance: issues of legitimacy, accountability, and governance in political science", *European Journal of Political Research*, 43: 143–171.

Konrád, Gy. (1984). *Anti-Politics*, London: Quartet Books.

Kuti, É. (1996). *The nonprofit sector in Hungary*. Manchester: Manchester University Press.

Kuti, É. (2005). "A magyarországi vállalatok társadalmi felelösségvállalása" (Corporate social responsibility in Hungary), in: Kuti, E. (ed) *A jótékonyság vállalati stratégiája*, Budapest: Nonprofit Kutatócsoport.

McLaughlin, K. (2004). "Toward a 'modernized' voluntary and community sector? Emerging lessons from government: voluntary and community sector relationships in the UK", *Public Management Review*, 4: 555–562.

Michnik, A. (1985). *Letters from Prison and Other Essays*, London and Berkeley, CA: California University Press.

Nonprofit szervezetek Magyarországon (Nonprofit organizations in Hungary) (2005). Budapest: Central Statistical Office.

OECD (2005). *Modernising Government: the Way Forward*, OECD.

Osborne, S.P. *et al.* (2005). "Government/non-profit partnerships, public services delivery, and civil society in the transitional countries of Eastern Europe: lessons from the Hungarian experience", *International Journal of Public Administration*, 28: 767–786.

Pollitt, C. and Bouckaert, G. (2000). *Public Management Reform. A Comparative Analysis*, Oxford: Oxford University Press.

Priller, E. and Zimmer, A. (2001). "Wachstum und Wandel des Dritten Sektors in Deutschland", in: Priller, E. and Zimmer, A. (eds.). *Der Dritte Sektor internacional. Mehr Markt – weniger Staat?*, Berlin: Edition Sigma, pp. 199–228.

Putnam, R. (1993). *Making Democracy Work*, Princeton: Princeton University Press.

Salamon, L. *et al.* (1999). *Global Civil Society. Dimensions of the Non-Profit Sector*, Baltimore: The Johns Hopkins Center for Civil Society Studies.

Strünck, Chr. and Heinze, R.G. (2001). "Public Private Partnership", in: Blanke, B., von Bandemer, S., Nullmeier, F. and Wewer, G. (eds.), *Handbuch zur Verwaltungsreform 2.*Opladen: Auflage Leske and Budrich.

3 Where does social capital come from?*

Dag Wollebæk and Per Selle

Introduction

The present study re-examines the face to face hypothesis in the social capital literature by comparing Putnam's socialization perspective with institutionally oriented perspectives in a cross-national context. There are main differences between the perspectives. Both perspectives agree that organizational affiliation does have an impact on individual levels of social capital. In a socialization perspective, only active members and volunteers develop social capital through organizational activity, as only they experience face to face interaction. On aggregate, members should therefore display higher levels of social capital than non-members, but active members and volunteers should score even higher on such measures. There should, however, be no difference between passive members and non-members. In an institutional perspective, members will tend to have somewhat higher levels of social capital than non-members as their linkages to organizations provide them with direct representation by the organization, loyalty to a system of collective action and more direct knowledge about what the organization does by means of newsletters or emails. Social interaction with other members is not crucial in this perspective. In contrast to the socialization perspective, therefore, there is no hypothesized effect of active over passive affiliations.

Rather than the intensity of the involvement, an institutional perspective stresses its *scope:* the more linkages, the better. Thus, a passive member of two associations should have higher social capital than an active member of one. More important than the individual effects, however, is the impact overlapping memberships has for society. The number of memberships held in a population should be a stronger predictor of social capital than the proportion of the population which is active. By contrast, the face to face hypothesis asserts that the number of passive memberships does not compensate for the lack of direct involvement. Thus, intensity is more important than scope, and active members of one association should have higher social capital than passive members of several. Furthermore, societies characterized by numerous passive members should display *lower* levels of social capital than societies with fewer, more active members.

According to Robert Putnam (1993, 1995a, 2000a; Putnam and Feldstein 2003), social capital is generated through repeated face to face interaction in "horizontal" networks. Voluntary organizations are seen as the most pervasive type of such networks, and as such a productive source of social capital. In Putnam's recent work (2000a), even more informal types of interactions (e.g. card games, picnics and dinner parties) are emphasized alongside organizational involvement, thus reaffirming the prominence of direct social interaction as the main process through which social capital is created.

However, empirical support for such claims is scant. Stolle (2001) found no effect of active organizational involvement on trust over time. Wollebæk and Selle (2002b) found no relationship between the extent of face to face inter-action in organizations and social capital, a finding recently vindicated by a French (Mayer 2003) and a Swiss (Freitag 2003) study. Similarly, Dekker and van den Broek (1998) found no differences between trust levels of volunteering and non-volunteering members in the US, the Netherlands and Italy. The tenuous relationship between active participation in organizations and social capital has led some to conclude that the importance of associations in generat-ing trust is exaggerated (Stolle 2003). Instead, it is claimed, we should divert our attention towards the role of public policy and how institutions function (Roth-stein 2002, 2004; Rothstein and Stolle 2003a, 2003b).

We test the above propositions. While the results confirm that the emphasis on face to face interaction and socialization is indeed misplaced, they do not support dismissing or even downplaying the role of voluntary organizations. Rather, it will be argued, in line with an institutional perspective, that volun-tary organizations are crucial to the sustenance of social capital – not mainly as agents of socialization, but as institutions within which social capital is embedded.

Socialization versus institutional approaches

Putnam (1995b) defines social capital as "features of social life – networks, norms and trust – that enable participants to act together more effectively to pursue shared objectives" (p. 665). Thus, social capital is thought to facilitate concerted action, which in turn enhances democratic vitality, reduces transaction costs in economic relations, as well as a wide array of other desirable outcomes.[1]

In the context of democracy, the concept may be deconstructed into three main components, namely social networks, generalized trust, and civic engage-ment (Wollebæk and Selle 2002b). Social networks are individual resources that facilitate goal attainment (Bourdieu 1985), and catalysts and vehicles for trust and civic engagement (Putnam 1993). Generalized trust, i.e. the attitude that most people are trustworthy and act in the common interest, is necessary to overcome collective dilemmas in interaction with strangers (Putnam 1993, pp. 163–164). Civic engagement, a relatively politically active, interested and knowledgeable citizenry, is a precondition for transforming trust into the type of collective action that matters for a democracy (Wollebæk and Selle 2002b). In the present study, we focus on the second of these components, trust, which represents the main attitudinal (as opposed to structural) component of social capital (Hooghe and Stolle 2003), and which is present in any contemporary definition of the concept.

The concept of generalized trust corresponds to *thin* trust, as opposed *thick* trust, which is embedded in personal relations or restricted to certain subgroups (Newton 1997; Putnam 2000a). While the latter constitutes a form of *bonding* (or exclusive) social capital, the former represents *bridging* (or inclusive) social capital (Woolcock 1998). The two are not interchangeable, and may even be inversely related (Putnam 2000a): strong within-group ties are often coupled with suspicion of outsiders and may affect collective action outside the group adversely. While both types of social capital are useful to individuals, bridging social capital and generalized trust are seen as more beneficial to democracy and social integration than bonding social capital and particularized trust (Putnam and Feldstein 2003). Thus, in the following, we deal with only the former type.

As social capital, according to Putnam, is generated through social interaction, voluntary organizations contribute to the pool of these resources primarily by virtue of facilitating such contacts. This entails that certain types of affiliations and associations are seen as more beneficial to social capital than others. First, the value of passive memberships and the organizations relying primarily on their support is dismissed altogether, as they are devoid of face to face contact.[2] Second, broad scope of participation, i.e. several affiliations, does not compensate for low intensity, i.e. passivity:

> An individual who "belongs to" half a dozen community groups may actually be active in none. What really matters from the point of view of social capital and civic engagement is not merely nominal membership, but active and involved membership.
>
> (Putnam 2000a, 58)

Third, associations that are "horizontal" and cut across social cleavages are seen as more valuable sources of "bridging" social capital than more politically oriented associations, which tend to be organized along such cleavages. In practice, this means that non-political and humanitarian associations are seen as more valuable to social capital formation than, for example, political parties, interest groups or unions.

In Putnam's approach, well-functioning institutions are but a result of such individually generated resources: "institutional reform will not work – indeed it will not happen – unless you and I, along with our fellow citizens, resolve to become reconnected with our friends and neighbours" (Putnam 2000a, p. 414). Although Putnam dismisses the "bottom-up" vs. "top-down"-dispute as a "false debate" (Putnam 2000a, p. 413), there is no question that individual change precedes institutional change in his perspective.

However, the opposite direction of causality is equally plausible: trust in other individuals may emanate from observing that the institutions that administer and regulate society function fairly and efficiently (Rothstein 2002, 2004; Rothstein and Stolle 2003a, 2003b). This applies first and foremost to the institutions at the "output" side of public policy, such as the police, the judiciary and welfare agencies. Thus, this argument differs from perspectives emphasizing trust in authorities in general, or trust in general entities such as "the government" or "politicians". Such attitudes may reflect agreement or disagreement with partisan politics more than attitudes towards other people (Rothstein 2004, p. 134).

The argument for institutional trust rests on two pillars. First, people infer from their personal experiences with civil servants and public institutions (Rothstein and Stolle 2003b): if even the officials that are entrusted the responsibility of guarding common interests are corrupt, then most people are almost certainly also dishonest (Rothstein 2004; Stolle 2004). If the rules of public institutions are divisive, unclear and easy to manipulate, people are more likely to believe that others cheat or otherwise abuse the system to maximize their advantages. An extension of this argument is that universal welfare arrangements where everyone enjoys equal rights are less likely to create distrust than selective or conservative welfare models based on means-testing (Rothstein and Stolle 2003b). Second, well-functioning legal institutions increase people's confidence that treacherous behavior will be sanctioned, and people therefore expect others to act in compliance with the common interest.

However, as Rothstein and Stolle emphasize (2003b, p. 192), institutions within the public sector are not the only ones that matter. Civil society institutions may also embed trust (Wollebæk and Selle 2004a). The dynamics through which this may occur are similar to the above. First, *cognitive inference* applies to organizations as much as governmental institutions. Experiences of how such associations function, be they personal or mediated, influence our view of the cooperative spirit of others. If organizations are successful and visible in a society, it proves the rationality, normality and utility of cooperation for the common good.

Second, many organizations act as *intermediary structures* linking individuals to society and citizens to the political system. Like other types of infrastructure, such as roads or telephone lines, they do not need to be used by everyone all the time in order to be useful; as the benefits of roads are not limited to the people who at a given time drive them, nor are the benefits of organizations limited to those who at a given time are active. In a strong organizational society, non-members are aware of the opportunity to get involved in organizational activity, or to contact organizations for assistance, should the need arise. Thus, it is acknowledged that institutionalized collective action is not only rational, normal and useful, but also generally available.

Third, dense, overlapping and interlocking organizational networks create cross-pressures which have a *moderating* effect on tension and conflict (Rokkan 1967). Cross-cutting networks have been found to increase tolerance and understanding for the argument of others (Mutz 2002). If tensions are reduced between those affiliated, it is likely to benefit people on the outside of organizational society. Obviously, all these arguments presume democracy and de facto freedom of organization and are only valid in societies with these characteristics.[3]

The arguments for an institutional perspective on the contributions of voluntary associations are closely linked to classical theories of pluralism and representative democracy. Such influences are definitely present in Putnam's early work (1993), and corresponds with Putnam's (2000b) concept of *rainmaker effects* of organizational activity, which appears in one book chapter. Yet it breaks radically with the socialization approach in his later work, which is influenced by theories of participatory democracy (Macpherson 1977; Pateman 1970), particularly the works of Tocqueville (1968), some aspects of communitarianism and social psychological assumptions. These traditions emphasize quite other qualities of organizations than pluralist approaches. Thus, while associations are seen as crucial in both a socialization and an institutional approach, they are so for different reasons, and the relative value that they place on various types of associations and modes of participation varies. In the following, these differences are spelled out as conflicting hypotheses that will be tested empirically further on.

Specification of hypotheses

Table 3.1 summarizes the diverging views of a socialization and an institutional approach on the role of organizations in the formation of social capital. Fundamentally, both perspectives agree that organizational affiliation does have an impact on individual levels of social capital. In a socialization perspective, however, only active members and volunteers develop social capital through organizational activity, as passive members are not exposed to face to face interaction. Active members should therefore display higher levels of social capital than those with passive or no affiliations, but there should be less of a difference between the latter two groups. In an institutional perspective, members will tend to have somewhat higher levels of social capital than non-members as their linkages to organizations provide them with direct representation by the organization, moderated views resulting from cross-pressures and more direct knowledge about what the organization does by means of newsletters or emails.[4] The main distinction is between the organized and the non-organized, not between those exposed to social contact and those who participate by proxy. Consequently, active and passive affiliations should yield similar levels of social capital (research question (2) in the table).

Rather than the *intensity* of the involvement, an institutional perspective stresses its *scope* ((3) in Table 3.1): the more linkages, the better. Thus, a passive member of two associations should have higher social capital than an active member of one. More important than the individual effects, however, is the impact overlapping memberships has for society. The proportion holding multiple memberships in a population should be a stronger predictor of social capital than the proportion of the population which is active. By contrast,

Table 3.1 A socialization and an institutional approach to the association-social capital relationship: hypotheses for empirical examination

	Socialization perspective	*Institutional perspective*
Research question		
1 Effect of organizational affiliation?	Yes	Yes
2 *Intensity:* Active members higher levels of social capital than passive?	Yes	No
3 *Intensity vs. scope:* High intensity more important than broad scope of participation?	Yes	No
4 *Type:* Nonpolitical, horizontal groups more valuable than conflict-oriented, "vertical" groups?	Yes	No
5 Does trust in public sector institutions increase generalized trust?	No	Yes
6 Stronger effects at micro- or macro level?	Equal	Macro level
7 Perception of value of organizations or participation in organizations?	Participation	Both (interplay): the fewer the personal links to organizations, the more important perception becomes

Putnam (2000a, p. 58) asserts that the number of passive memberships does not compensate for the lack of direct involvement. Intensity is in this view more important than scope, and active members of one association should have higher social capital than passive members of several. Furthermore, societies characterized by numerous passive members should display *lower* levels of social capital than societies with fewer, more active members.

Putnam also attributes particular importance to non-political, "horizontal" associations (4), as they provide plenty of opportunities for social interaction, and recruit across societal divisions. By contrast, interest groups, unions and political organizations are seen as divisive and their role for social capital formation is frequently downplayed (Foley and Edwards 1996, 2001). Thus, from Putnam's perspective, we expect those affiliated with non-political associations to possess higher levels of social capital than members of other types of groups. Furthermore, societies characterized by many non-political organizations should score particularly high on social capital in aggregate terms, as Putnam strongly emphasized in his study of Italy (Putnam 1993).

However, numerous writers in an institutionalist vein have contested the claim that bowling clubs and music choirs can fill any central role in a democracy, whether as intermediary institutions or counterweights against state dominance (Berman 1997; Foley and Edwards 1996; Quigley 1996; Rueschemeyer *et al.* 1998). Furthermore, their frequently largely localist nature, in a sense, their very "horizontality", make them less visible and less useful as a civic infrastructure and intermediary institutions than federated, hierarchical groups (Skocpol 2003). Moreover, pluralists would assert that the supposedly negative effect of memberships in conflict-oriented groups is reduced if memberships are multiple and overlapping. From an institutional perspective, therefore, we would expect that non-political "Putnam groups" (Knack and Keefer 1997) are *less* productive sources of social capital than organizations that are more conflict oriented and outward reaching.

As shown above, a strong case has been made for the relationship between trust in institutions at the output-side of government and social capital. We would expect from this that trust in the institutions of law and order, which in previous studies have been found to correlate the strongest with generalized trust (Rothstein 2004, pp. 130–131), is an independent source of social capital (research question (5) in Table 3.1). By contrast, trust in public institutions is neither a source nor a type of social capital in Putnam's (1995b, p. 665) work: "I might well trust my neighbours without trusting city hall, or vice versa".[5] Thus, from this perspective there is no reason to expect any effect of trust in institutions and law and order on generalized trust.

In a socialization perspective, social capital is developed at the individual level and mirrored at the aggregate level (cf. Putnam 1993,; 2000a). Consequently, similar effects should emerge at the micro- and macro-level at comparable magnitudes. In an institutional perspective, by contrast, variations between communities should be much larger than within communities (research question (6) in Table 3.1). As personal experiences are secondary to the prevalence of organizations in a society, non-members in communities with encompassing voluntary sectors should display higher levels of social capital than members in weak organizational societies.

Stronger effects at the macro- than the micro-level would give support to an institutional perspective. However, such results would not give direct information about the causal link at the micro-level. In order to get at this relationship, we introduce one additional test (research question (7) in Table 3.1): if the main contribution of organizations to social capital lies in demonstrating the value of collective action and providing the infrastructure for such pursuits, it should be *sufficient* for individuals to be *convinced* that organizations fulfill these functions in order to develop the desired values. This implies, first, that belief in the efficacy of organizations is an independent path to generalized trust, which is more important if personal linkages to organizational society are weak. Second, assuming the sufficiency of perceptions, personal participation is not necessary for trust levels among those who do believe in the efficacy of organizations. In statistical terms, we expect interplay between scope of participation and perceptions of the usefulness of organizations on generalized trust. By contrast, from a socialization perspective, if a correlation between perceptions of organizations and social trust exists, this is a spurious effect of the fact that those intensely involved in organizations hold more positive views of their efficacy. As the relevant questions are not included in the cross-national data set, these propositions are tested on Norwegian data only.

Data and operationalizations

The main data source of the present study, however, is the European Social Survey (ESS). This is a cross-national individual survey undertaken in 2002/2003 (Jowell and Central Co-ordinating Team 2003).[6] The 19 European countries (the former EU-15 plus Norway, Poland, Slovenia and Hungary) which included reliable questions about associational activity and qualify as democracies were selected for the analysis.[7] Face to face interviews were the main mode of data collection. Response rates varied from 43.7 (Italy) to 80 percent (Greece), with an average of 62.4 percent (NSD 2003). For the aggregate analyses, the 19 countries were divided into 141 regions, following the regional classifications made by ESS local associates which was based on the NUTS taxonomy.[8] Regions with fewer than 100 unweighted responses were merged with adjacent regions.[9] For the final analysis concerning perceptions of the efficacy of organizations, the Norwegian *Fellow Citizen Survey* (2001) was utilized (Strømsnes 2003). This was conducted as a mailed survey, with a response rate of 46 percent and a net sample size of 2,297.

The *independent variables* are, first, measurements of the scope, intensity, and type of association involvement. Scope is operationalized as the number of associations with which each individual is affiliated. The scope of involvement includes both memberships, volunteering and participation in activities. If a person has reported several modes of participation for the same type of association, this is only counted once. The intensity of the involvement is measured as whether the respondent has participated in activities or volunteered for the organization over the past 12 months. For cross-tabulations, a composite variable representing four different modes of participation is utilized, based on scope and intensity. Scope is dichotomized between those with singular vs. multiple affiliations, while activity level distinguishes those who have taken part in activities or volunteered in any of the organizations from those who have not.

The intensity measure is a less accurate proxy for degree of face to face contact than the number of hours one has spent in associations, which was employed in a previous study (Wollebæk and Selle 2002b), although it serves the purpose of distinguishing those who have not been exposed to *any* face to face contact from those who have experienced some or a lot. Moreover, one could argue that collapsing "volunteers" (people doing voluntary work for organizations) and "participants" (people taking actively part in organizational activities, but not necessarily doing voluntary *work*) into one group of "actives" conflates two degrees of involvement. In order to test the robustness of this classification, all of the analyses below have been carried out contrasting only volunteers and non-volunteers. This did not influence any of the conclusions, and the original classification was retained. Furthermore, a "time spent in associations"-measure *was* available in the Norwegian data set, and is included in the final analysis of this paper.

The type of affiliations is classified into three groups, more or less following Knack and Keefer's (1997) distinction between horizontal, non-political "Putnam groups" and more politically oriented "Olson groups", the latter with reference to Mancur Olson's (1982) work on interest organizations. The Putnam groups include cultural/hobby activities, social clubs, sports and outdoors activities and humanitarian organizations. Olson groups include science/education/teacher's organizations, trade unions, professional organizations, consumer's organizations and political parties. Political parties are grouped together with the Olson groups. The classification deviates from Knack and Keefer on one point, as they, under doubt, include religious associations among the "Putnam groups". However, while Putnam (2000a, p. 67) sees religiosity as a factor contributing to civic engagement, he also states that religious organizations in some contexts (e.g. southern Italy) may be counterproductive to social capital (Putnam 1993). Consequently, this group is kept apart as a separate third category.

The second main independent variable, trust in law-and-order institutions is represented by a simple additive two-item index consisting of trust in the police and the legal system, ranging from 0 (no trust) to 10 (very high trust) (Cronbach's alpha=0.75 for entire 19-country sample, 0.76 for Norwegian data).

The main *dependent* variable is a three-item index measuring generalized trust based on saved scores from a factor analysis requesting a one-factor solution. The trust index includes the following three items (measured by 11-point self-placement scales): "Most people can be trusted vs. you cannot be careful enough", "Most people try to be helpful vs. mostly looking out for themselves", and "Most people try to be fair vs. try to take advantage of me" (Cronbach's alpha=0.77 19-country sample, 0.81 for Norwegian sample).

The *control variables* in the micro-level analysis include standard sociodemographic variables (age, education, gender, marital status and population density). For the macro-analysis, we have included a number of other potential sources of social capital which only apply at the aggregate level. First, the *ethnic diversity* of a community is often linked to low social capital, as it may be generally easier to express trust when surrounded mostly by people like oneself (Putnam 2002). Furthermore, if organizations are constructed along ethnic lines they may produce bonding (within-group) rather than bridging (inter-group) social capital. Knack and Keefer's (1997) cross-national study indicates that ethnic diversity and trust are indeed negatively related. At the regional level, we measure diversity with an additive three-item index aggregated from the survey data: the percentage speaking another language than the majority language at home, the percentage belonging to other religious denominations than the majority religion, and the percentage who reported that they or one of their parents were born in a different country from where they currently reside.

Social and economic *inequality* is thought by some to be the main mechanism through which social capital is destroyed (Uslaner 2003). Social polarization creates distance between people's preferences and increases incentives to defect from cooperative arrangement in order to defend self-interest (Knack and Keefer 1997). Using World Values Survey data, Knack and Keefer (1997) and Uslaner (2003) find negative effects of inequality on trust. To measure economic inequality within European regions, we use data collected by the University of Texas Inequality Project (Galbraith and Garcilazo 2005).[10] Within-region inequality is captured by Theil's t-coefficients representing pay disparities between 16 economic sectors.

High levels of *religiosity* are commonly assumed to be positively related to social capital, due to the theological emphasis of most religions on the duty to serve fellow human beings (Offe and Fuchs 2002). According to Putnam (2000a, p. 67): "religiosity rivals education as a powerful correlate of most forms of civic engagement". This is measured by average scores on self-placement scale (1–10) on which the respondents were asked to assess their own religiosity. Furthermore, *education* is consistently found to influence social capital positively at the individual level (Putnam 2000a), although the relationship at aggregate level appears more tenuous (Haddad 2004). The educational level of each region was aggregated from the survey data and operationalized as the percentage of 25 to 59-year-olds in the sample who had finished at least upper secondary level education. Finally, urbanization and metropolitan sprawl is seen by Putnam (2000a, p. 284) as one of the four main reasons for the alleged slump in social capital in America. Putnam (2000a, p. 205) asserts that "residents of small towns and rural areas are more altruistic, honest, and trusting than other Americans". Therefore, we expect the proportion of respondents living in large cities or suburbs to yield a negative effect on a region's social capital.

Empirical analysis: individual level data

The propositions presented above are now put to the test. Are joiners more trusting than non-joiners? Is face to face contact really as important as the socialization approach would have it? Table 3.2 gives a preliminary positive answer to the former question, and a relatively clear-cut negative one to the latter.

Organizational members and volunteers are more trusting than outsiders in 17 of the 19 countries. Spain and Portugal represent the only exceptions. Comparing only those who are affiliated, scope matters (either among active or passive members) in nine of the countries, but none of the effects are very strong. In only five countries does active involvement play any positive role, while it is *negatively* related to trust levels in Spain and Italy.

Furthermore, variations between countries are much larger than within-country variation. Non-members in Norway, Finland and Denmark are more trusting than active members of several associations in any country outside Scandinavia. The Eastern European countries constitute the mirror image of the Scandinavian countries. Although organizational affiliations do play a role here, too, they cannot begin to compensate for decades of repressive political cultures. As Uslaner (2003, p. 177) comments:

Table 3.2 Intensity, scope and generalized trust. Average scores and differences on generalized trust index by organizational involvement

| | Means | | | | | | Differences | | | | | |
| | Affiliated | | Passive | | Active | | Impact of affiliation | | Impact of intensity | | Impact of scope | |
	No M0	Yes M1	1 P1	≥2 P2	1 A1	≥2 A2	diff M1-M0	diff A1-P1	diff A2-P2	diff P2-P1	diff A2-A1	N
East Europe												
Poland	-0.62	-0.43	-0.65	-0.06	-0.33	-0.33	0.19**	0.32**	-0.27	0.59**	0.00	2,040
Slovenia	-0.44	-0.21	-0.27	-0.11	-0.24	-0.19	0.23**	0.03	-0.08	0.16	0.05	1,494
Hungary	-0.37	-0.21	-0.34	-0.15	-0.20	-0.12	0.16**	0.14	0.03	0.19	0.08	1,654
Nordic countries												
Norway	0.78	0.92	0.76	0.94	0.87	0.96	0.14**	0.11	0.02	0.18**	0.09	2,031
Sweden	0.42	0.75	0.57	0.76	0.63	0.80	0.33**	0.06	0.04	0.19**	0.17*	1,981
Denmark	0.76	1.04	0.96	1.04	0.86	1.09	0.28**	-0.10	0.05	0.08	0.23*	1,489
Finland	0.65	0.80	0.71	0.82	0.84	0.82	0.15**	0.13	0.00	0.11	-0.02	1,991
South Europe												
Greece	-0.79	-0.69	-0.84	-0.39	-0.76	-0.54	0.10*	0.08	-0.15	0.45**	0.22	2,539
Spain	-0.06	0.02	0.05	0.14	-0.27	0.11	0.08	-0.32**	-0.03	0.09	0.38**	1,683
Italy	-0.45	-0.07	-0.01	-0.04	-0.29	-0.03	0.38**	-0.28*	0.01	-0.03	0.26*	1,192
Portugal	-0.27	-0.19	-0.23	-0.05	-0.23	-0.15	0.08	0.00	-0.10	0.18	0.08	1,481
Central Europe												
Germany	-0.08	0.17	0.01	0.15	0.22	0.23	0.25**	0.21**	0.08	0.14*	0.01	2,902
France	-0.14	0.03	-0.17	0.28	-0.00	0.07	0.17**	0.17	-0.21	0.45**	0.07	1,489
Austria	0.12	0.25	0.10	0.22	0.28	0.32	0.13*	0.18	0.10	0.12	0.04	2,205
West Europe												
UK	0.05	0.30	0.15	0.13	0.23	0.40	0.25**	0.08	0.27**	-0.02	0.17**	2,040
Netherlands	0.27	0.47	0.34	0.44	0.35	0.55	0.20**	0.01	0.11*	0.10	0.20**	2,352
Belgium	-0.12	0.08	0.03	-0.06	0.05	0.15	0.20**	0.02	0.21**	-0.09	0.10	1,865
Ireland	0.34	0.53	0.52	0.53	0.48	0.55	0.19**	-0.04	0.02	0.01	0.07	2,008
Luxembourg	-0.10	0.14	0.08	0.13	0.04	0.22	0.24**	-0.04	0.09	0.05	0.18	1,492
Total (weighted by population)	-0.27	0.17	0.00	0.23	0.01	0.27	0.44**	0.01	0.04*	0.23**	0.26**	35,103

Notes

Differences on right hand side of figure may deviate from differences between scores to the left side of figure because of rounding. Results are weighted by design weight.

$* p \leq 0.05$; $** p \leq 0.01$.

When people feel compelled to turn on their friends lest the state turn on them, generalized trust may become too risky. In such a world, you really cannot be too careful in dealing with people, even if everyone would strongly prefer to treat others as if they were trustworthy.

It takes more than a little face to face interaction to erase decades of deeply entrenched and institutionalized distrust.

As the same countries score high on participation as well as trust, the effects of being affiliated is higher when analyzing Europe as a whole than any single country. However, even at the European level, intensity of involvement remains irrelevant.[11]

Table 3.3 does not reveal any clear-cut variations between supporters of different types of associations beyond those resulting from the effects of membership and scope that have already been established. There is a weak tendency towards higher levels of distrust among members of politicized organizations in recent democracies such as Greece, Portugal, Poland and Slovenia. Other than this, knowledge about the type of the organization adds nothing to the relatively weak effects established above.

The regression analyses, undertaken at the regional as well as the European level, confirm weak, but statistically significant effects of affiliation. Its explanatory power increases when the analysis is extended to the whole of Europe, thus including the highest and lowest ranking countries on both trust and participation. Knowing the different modes of participation does not add much to our understanding of how trust is generated. The face to face hypothesis is rejected in Southern Europe, where active members are slightly *less* trusting than their passive counterparts. Only in Western Europe do we find a weak, positive effect of intensity. However, scope and type ("Putnam group") do not fare much better. Both show weakly positive effects at the European level, which are significant because of the gigantic sample size. Both are irrelevant in Eastern Europe and the Nordic countries. Except for the weaker effect of scope, these results are consistent with the findings of Wollebæk and Selle's (2002b) study of organizational participation and the development of social capital in Norway.

Institutional trust is by far the most important predictor of social trust emanating from the regression analysis. This gives empirical credence to the claims of Rothstein (2004) and Rothstein and Stolle (2003b). We are not able to resolve here whether their proposed direction of causality – that trusting the impartiality of the law makes us trust other people more – is correct or not. A "Putnamian" response would be that pervasive generalized trust in a society, which is generated through face to face interaction, creates well-functioning institutions, which people in turn are more likely to trust. So far, this proposed causal mechanism remains little more than a postulate pending empirical evidence. In any case, a crucial part of this argument, namely the link between face to face interaction and social trust, is weakened for every new empirical test.

Table 3.3 Type and trust. average scores on generalized trust index by type of association

	X. Not affiliated	A. Putnam groups	B. Olson/ politic. groups	C. Relig. groups	D. Putnam + Olson	E. Putnam + relig.	F. Olson + Relig.	G. All three	Net effect of Putnam group[1]	Net effect of Olson group[2]	Net effect of relig. group[3]
East Europe											
Poland	−0.62	−0.41	−0.53	−0.40	−0.37	0.16	−0.39	−0.05	0.11	−0.22	0.11
Slovenia	−0.44	−0.19	−0.28	−0.45	−0.18	0.31	−0.23	−0.18	0.16	−0.16	0.01
Hungary	−0.37	−0.19	−0.30	−0.28	−0.05	−0.42	−0.40	0.22	0.09	0.05	−0.13
Nordic											
Norway	0.78	0.88	0.81	0.58	0.94	0.98	0.91	1.06	0.08	0.00	−0.09
Sweden	0.42	0.70	0.57	0.80	0.80	0.68	0.81	0.96	−0.02	−0.02	0.04
Finland	0.65	0.70	0.77	0.90	0.82	0.77	0.74	0.88	−0.03	−0.01	0.03
Denmark	0.76	0.98	1.00	0.99	1.07	1.02	0.90	1.12	0.05	0.00	−0.03
South Europe											
Greece	−0.79	−0.69	−0.77	−0.63	−0.56	−0.36	−0.41	−0.34	−0.01	−0.08	0.09
Italy	−0.45	−0.10	−0.07	−0.09	−0.07	−0.10	0.00	0.10	−0.03	0.03	0.00
Spain	−0.06	−0.05	−0.10	−0.03	0.16	−0.11	0.47	0.07	−0.14	0.13	0.02
Portugal	−0.27	−0.11	−0.23	−0.43	−0.01	−0.06	−0.60	0.12	0.27	−0.07	−0.19
Central Europe											
France	−0.14	0.01	−0.07	−0.17	0.14	0.14	0.26	0.13	0.00	0.02	−0.03
Germany	−0.08	0.13	0.00	0.20	0.18	0.30	0.23	0.39	0.01	−0.09	0.07
Austria	0.12	0.32	0.03	0.04	0.31	0.31	0.04	0.39	0.18	−0.10	−0.09
West Europe											
Belgium	−0.12	0.11	−0.08	−0.04	0.11	0.32	0.07	0.10	0.11	−0.11	0.01
UK	0.05	0.28	0.10	0.24	0.36	0.15	0.20	0.55	0.07	0.00	−0.03
Ireland	0.34	0.52	0.53	0.65	0.50	0.45	0.59	0.55	−0.06	0.02	0.05
Netherlands	0.27	0.39	0.40	0.29	0.50	0.43	0.44	0.63	0.02	0.03	−0.05
Luxembourg	−0.10	0.18	−0.05	0.27	0.22	−0.19	−0.38	0.30	0.16	−0.05	−0.10
All countries (weighted by population)	−0.27	0.09	0.01	0.04	0.27	0.22	0.27	0.44	0.01	0.00	−0.01

Notes

Weighted by design weight.

1 Net effect of Putnam groups: $Y = (((A − X) + ((D − B) + (E − C) + (G − F)/3) − (((G − (F + E + D)) + ((F + E + D) − (A + B + C)) + ((A + B + C) − X))/3$.

2 Net effect of Olson groups: $Y = (((B − X) + ((D − A) + (F − C)) + (G − E)/3) − (((G − (F + E + D)) + ((F + E + D) − (A + B + C)) + ((A + B + C) − X))/3$.

3 Net effect of religious groups: $Y = (((C − X) + ((E − A) + (F − B)) + (G − D))/3) − (((G − (F + E + D)) + ((F + E + D) − (A + B + C)) + ((A + B + C) − X))/3$.

Table 3.4 OLS Regression analysis of generalized trust. Unstandardized coefficients

	Eastern Europe		Nordic countries		Southern Europe		Western Europe		Central Europe		All	
	Model		Model		Model		Model		Model		Model	
	1	2	1	2	1	2	1	2	1	2	1	2
Affiliated	0.07**		0.05*		0.09**		0.07**		0.07**		0.15**	
Intensity		0.04		0.01		−0.05**		0.06**		0.003		0.001
Scope		0.02		0.04		0.05**		0.01		0.03*		0.06**
Type (P-group)		0.05		0.02		0.02		0.04**		0.04**		0.04**
Institutional trust	0.26**	0.29**	0.34**	0.33**	0.19**	0.22**	0.34**	0.34**	0.29**	0.29**	0.28**	0.31**
Education	0.10**	0.09**	0.09**	0.08**	0.12**	0.13**	0.07**	0.06**	0.10**	0.10**	0.12**	0.10**
Female	0.04**	0.05	0.09**	0.10**	0.01	−0.01	0.01	0.04**	0.03**	0.05**	0.03**	0.04**
Year of birth	0.04*	0.05	−0.08**	−0.09**	−0.01	−0.01	−0.12**	−0.14**	−0.01	0.004	−0.05**	−0.05**
Urban-rural	−0.04*	0.01	0.02	0.02	0.05**	0.01	0.06**	0.04**	0.02*	−0.01	0.03**	0.03**
Married	−0.05**	0.05	0.02	0.01	−0.01	−0.02	0.02	0.02	−0.01	−0.02	−0.03**	−0.02**
R² adj.	0.10	0.11	0.15	0.15	0.07	0.07	0.15	0.15	0.11	0.11	0.14	0.13

Notes
Weighted by population size and design weight. Model 1 includes all respondents, model 2 only those affiliated with organizations.
* $p \leq 0.05$; ** $p \leq 0.01$.

Aggregate data

Above, we saw that the effects of organizational affiliations were much stronger at the European than at the national and regional level; variations between countries were much larger than the individual variations within each country. On the one hand, this may suggest the European level analysis exaggerates the importance of affiliations, as other variations between countries are affecting the individual-level relationship between participation and trust. On the other hand, it may imply that organizations are important, not as socialization agents, but as institutions, and that the international variations observed above reflect variations in the strength of organizational society between European countries.

In the following section, we assess these claims empirically by analyzing how variations in organizational life affect levels of social capital at the aggregate level (141 European regions). As mentioned above, aggregate measures of social trust serve as operationalizations of social capital. Table 3.5 operationalizes types of organizational societies by estimating the proportion of the population holding memberships of different types (multiple, active and "Putnamian"). Bivariate as well as partial correlation coefficients, showing the unique contribution of each of the three modes of participation by controlling for the membership percentage in the region, are presented.

Table 3.5 shows that extensive multiple memberships, a high number of active affiliations and numerous Putnam group memberships are all positively related to social capital. The bivariate correlations between the vigor of organizational society and generalized trust are strong – ranging from 0.66 to 0.87.

The partial correlation coefficients display the *unique* contributions of multiple, active and non-political affiliations over other types of affiliations. Contrary to the expectations of the socialization school, highly active organizational societies do not stand out with higher social capital than others. It is primarily organizational societies with multiple memberships and passive affiliations along with the more active ones, what Dekker and van den Broek (1998) label *broad* organizational societies, that are conducive to high levels of social capital.

In addition, it appears that establishing apolitical "Putnam groups" only is insufficient for social capital formation at the aggregate level. A high number of Putnam groups relative to other types yield an insignificant negative partial correlation with trust. Thus, it does not seem plausible that the effect of non-political organizations is a product of characteristics unique to such associations. To the contrary, the more politically directed "Olson groups" fare better. This strengthens the institutionalist notion that societies with organizations that are more visible in the public sphere possess higher social capital. Religious groups contribute neither more nor less than other groups to social capital formation at the aggregate level.

The relationship between generalized trust and the scope of organizational life is visualized in Figure 3.1. The figure shows that the Nordic regions rank highest on both measures, followed by Western and Central Europe and finally Eastern and Southern Europe. The main outlier is Alentejo and Algarve in southern Portugal,

Table 3.5 Bivariate and partial correlations between dimensions of organizational society and social capital. European regions

	Generalized trust	
	Bivariate correlations	Partial correlations
		Controlling for percentage who are members
Scope (percentage of population affiliated with two or more organizations)	0.88***	0.24***
Intensity (percentage of population who are active in organizations)	0.75***	−0.13
Type (pct. of population affiliated with group)		
Putnam groups	0.83***	−0.10
Olson groups/political	0.86***	0.21**
Religious groups	0.66***	0.11
N = 141		

Notes
* $p \leq 0.10$, ** $p \leq 0.05$, *** $p \leq 0.01$.

where trust is much higher than organizational participation should suggest. As an example of the opposite, the two Belgian regions of Wallonia and Brussels display lower than average values of trust, while organizational life is strong. One reasonable explanation for this deviation is the strong cultural divide between the Flemish and French-speaking groups in Belgian society, divisions which are reproduced and reinforced through economic disparities and separate organizational societies (Lijphart 1984).[12] Thus, Belgian society may be weak on "bridging" social capital partly because of the "bonding" character of their organizations. Overall, however, scope of organizational activity and generalized trust are intimately related, at least at the bivariate level.

What then about our other main independent variable, institutional trust? Figure 3.2 shows that, generally speaking, regions wherein law and order institutions are trusted also enjoy extensive interpersonal trust. Thus, the results generally support the basic tenet of the theory. To some extent, Germans and Austrians are disproportionately more prone to trust authorities than individuals, while the Dutch display the opposite tendency.

While these are minor deviances from a general pattern, Southern Europe points in an entirely different direction: here, regions with high trust in the police and the judiciary tend to have low interpersonal trust. This is particularly evident in Greece and southern Italy, where clientilism is prevalent. In such contexts, strong "vertical" patron-client relationships may undermine and replace strong "horizontal" linkages (Putnam 1993). Furthermore, as Putnam (2000a, p. 345) observes with reference to southern Italy, demands for sterner discipline are borne out of fear of the lawlessness of others rather than a deeply felt respect

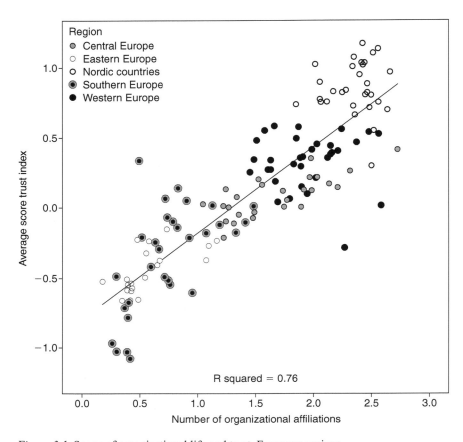

Figure 3.1 Scope of organizational life and trust. European regions.

of the law. In these regions high institutional trust may reflect absence of trust in others rather than social capital (Uslaner 2003).

Thus, while the results support the general notion that high institutional trust in a society may foster high generalized, interpersonal trust, there are clearly also situations where it has the exact opposite effect. The relationship between institutional trust and interpersonal trust is context sensitive, and the theory needs to specify in more detail the conditions under which it is applicable.

Do the above relationships hold in multivariate analysis? Table 3.6 shows regression analyses of the two indicators of social capital at the regional level, comparing and adjusting the effects on society with the impact of other commonly cited sources of social capital at the aggregate level. Model 1 includes only the control variables, which combined explain 56 percent of the variance. When institutional trust is included in model 2, r^2 increases to 70 percent, while the introduction of the organizational participation data elevates the explained

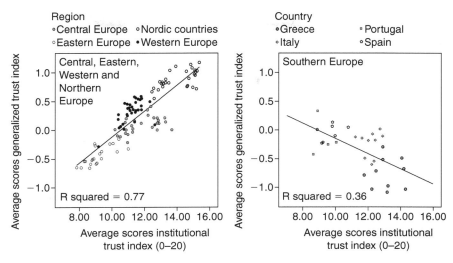

Figure 3.2 Institutional and generalized trust. European regions.

variance even further, to 82 percent. The impact of institutional trust is then reduced somewhat, but it is still clear and significant.

The analysis confirms the existence of an intimate relationship between the strength of organizational society and social capital; even when controlling for a wide array of factors the proportion of the population holding membership in organizations represents the single most powerful predictor of social trust. The activity level of the sector and the proportion of affiliations that were "Putnam groups" proved once again to be more or less irrelevant, while extensive multiple memberships has a slight positive effect on trust. Thus, the institutional interpretation of the role of organizations in social capital construction is strengthened, while the socialization approach is weakened. The institutional approach is further strengthened by the emergence of an overall, positive effect of institutional trust on both variables.

Among the control variables, ethnic diversity surfaced as expected with a significant negative effect in the multivariate analysis of trust. Educational levels did play a role in the initial model, but the effect disappeared when strength of organizational society entered the equation. Urbanized regions did not emerge with the expected negative effect on social trust, and the data do not support the commonly held notion that there is more social capital in rural areas than in cities. Thus, urban life may not be as bad as some would have it, and rural idylls have their limitations.

Strong religiosity in a region is associated with low levels of trust.[13] This is somewhat surprising, given the celebratory tone adopted by many writers in the social capital tradition when embracing religion as a cornerstone of social integration and civic engagement. The analysis show that among the 20 most

Table 3.6 OLS regression analysis of social capital at the regional level. Standardized coefficients

	Trust		
	Model 1	*Model 2*	*Model 3*
Pct. of population who are members			0.56***
Scope[a]			0.15*
Intensity[b]			0.008
Type (Putnam)[c]			−0.08*
Institutional trust		0.44***	0.17***
Diversity	−0.14**	−0.08	−0.19***
Educational levels	0.28***	0.27***	0.05
Inequality[d]	−0.43***	−0.15*	−0.02
Urbanization	−0.07	−0.12**	−0.04
Religiosity	−0.22***	−0.36***	−0.19***
R^2 adj.			
N = 140 regions. [e]	0.56	0.70	0.82

Notes
* $p \le 0.10$, ** $p \le 0.05$, *** $p \le 0.01$.
a Scope: per cent of affiliations which are multiple.
b Intensity: per cent of affiliations which are active.
c Type (Putnam): per cent of affiliations which are "Putnam group"-memberships.
d Regional Theil's t-statistic on pay inequalities between sectors. Source: Galbraith and Garcilazo (2005).
e Luxembourg excluded because of lack of inequality data.

religious regions in Europe, 19 are also among the least trusting.[14] By contrast, only four of the 20 least religious regions are among the 25 most trusting. Thus, a relatively secularized society is a necessary, but insufficient condition for high trust. A frequent claim, emphasizing the hierarchical character of Catholic societies, is that Protestantism is more conducive to social capital than Catholicism and Orthodoxy (Fukuyama 1995; Inglehart 1990; Knack and Keefer 1997; Uslaner 2003), and a stronger intensity of faith among the latter two groups may be the cause of the observed relationship. While it is true that Protestant regions are more trusting, there is considerable variation even within purely Catholic and Orthodox areas: in the 47 regions with fewer than 1 percent Protestants, the correlation between religiosity and trust is −0.74.[15] Thus, strict religious societies seem to foster cultures that are not only God-fearing, but also people-fearing.

With regard to inequality, we find a relatively strong negative effect on trust in model 1, which is very much weakened when institutional trust is entered in model 2.[16] This indicates that the frequently found negative effect of inequality can be partially accounted for by the fact that people generally place less trust in institutions in unequal societies.[17] We may make the relatively safe assumption that this is not coincidental; people in unequal settings probably have more reason to express distrust, as institutions are more likely to mirror and reproduce inequalities in societies characterized by inequality. In this perspective, inequality is not exonerated as a factor potentially destructive to social capital, despite the isolated insignificance of the effect, but should rather be interpreted in light of Rothstein and Stolle's argument concerning the beneficial effect of fair and impartial institutions for the development of social trust.

In summary, a broad organizational society emerges as the main explanation for variations in generalized trust across regions, followed by trust in institutions. The effects of pervasive organizational life are much stronger at the aggregate than at the individual level. This indicates that organizations contribute to the formation of social capital, not mainly through socialization of individuals, but as institutions entrenching in a population the value and rationality of cooperation.

Testing the causal link at the micro-level

Establishing an empirical connection at the aggregate level does not prove anything in terms of underlying causal mechanisms. As mentioned above, the finding that perceptions of the effectiveness of organizations have an independent effect on social trust would strengthen the case for an institutional theory of social capital formation through organizations. Table 3.7 shows that this is indeed the case: those who believe that one can influence decisions effectively in society by working in voluntary organizations are also more trusting than others, independent of individual participation pattern.

In addition, we find the anticipated interaction effect between personal attachments to organizations and perceptions of the efficacy of organizations, as illustrated in the figure in Table 3.7. Among those who are attached to organizational society with several links, perceptions of the utility of organizations hardly matter at all. However, for those who have weaker ties to organizational life, believing that organizations are effective tools of collective action is highly important for levels of social trust. Those who have faith in the available organizational infrastructure are more trusting, irrespective of personal linkages to or experiences with organizations. This belief comes from organizations demonstrating their utility in society. Once again, intensity of involvement, measured as time spent in the association, proves to be irrelevant to social trust. Thus, the impact of individual behaviour is at best secondary to the role organizations play as institutions in the development of social capital.

Discussion and conclusion

Table 3.8 summarizes the main findings of the above analyses. Except for the overall effect of being affiliated to organizations, a hypothesis shared by the socialization and institutional perspectives, none of the assertions of the socialization perspective were backed by the data. Active members did not display higher levels of social capital than their passive counterparts. Activity level was not more important than scope of affiliations, although the effect of the latter at the micro-level was admittedly modest. Members of non-political organizations

Table 3.7 Assessment of organizations as intermediary structures and generalized trust. OLS regression, standardized coefficients

Intermediary (assessment of org.'s as intermediary structures)[1]	0.20**
Scope	0.22**
Scope*intermediary	−0.20**
Intensity	0.004
Type (Putnam group)	0.03
Institutional trust (police, judiciary)	0.25**
Education	0.07**
Female	0.14**
Year of birth	−0.17**
Married/co-habitant	0.09**
Urban–rural	−0.007
R^2 adj.	0.21
N	1,607

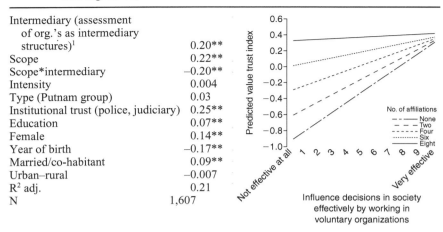

Source: Norwegion survey data, 2001.

Notes

1 Agreement with statement "Influence decisions in society effectively by: Working in voluntary organizations" (self-placement scale (0) Not effective at all, (10) Very effective).

Intensity: Categorized measure of time spent participating in voluntary associations over past year: (1) 0–1 hours, (2) 1–4 hours, (3) 5–10 hours, (4) 11–20 hours, (5) 20 hours or more. Type: Affiliated with "Putnam group" (dummy). Education: Years of full time schooling. Urban-rural: 9-value ordinal measure.

* $p \le 0.05$, ** $p \le 0.01$.

were no more trusting than members of other types of organizations, and trust in public institutions mattered a great deal to the development of social trust.

As predicted by the institutional perspective, the same effects that were found at the micro-level surfaced at the macro-level as well, but in greater magnitude. Here as well, activity levels and type of associations were unrelated to social capital formation, while the scope of organizational life in a region proved to be a crucial explanatory variable. Finally, perceiving organizations as useful tools of collective action was sufficient to raise levels of social trust, irrespective of organizational behavior. In accordance with expectations, this effect was amplified among those with non-existent or few ties to organizational life.

Thus, there is nothing in the data to suggest that the relationship between organizations and social capital has anything to do with the face to face social interaction that takes place within such organizations. As Hooghe (2003) argues, the theoretical basis for this claim was thin to begin with: it is not self-evident that we would generalize from trust in people we know within a group to people in general. The social psychological literature on group interaction does not support the idea that repeated interaction increases general trust in outsiders, rather, experiments point in the opposite direction (Hooghe 2003, p. 92). If

Table 3.8 Summary of findings

Research question	Socialization perspective	Institutional perspective	Empirical result
1 Effect of organizational affiliation?	Yes	Yes	Yes
2 *Intensity*: active members higher levels of social capital than passive?	Yes	No	No
3 *Intensity vs. scope*: high intensity more important than broad scope of participation?	Yes	No	No
4 *Type*: non-political, horizontal groups more valuable than conflict-oriented, "vertical" groups?	Yes	No	No
5 Does trust in public sector institutions increase generalized trust?	No	Yes	Yes
6 Stronger effects at micro- or macro level?	Equal	Macro level	Macro level
7 Perception of value of organizations or participation in organizations?	Participation	Both/interplay	Both/interplay

repeated interaction in fact *did* generate trust, it would be tough to defend the view that organizations represent a more important sphere than the workplace, schools, neighborhoods etc., where we spend a much larger proportion of our time.

The present study, along with others (Mayer 2003; Wollebæk and Selle 2002b), point in the direction that the socialization perspective on the formation of trust is a dead end. However, the present study indicates that the role of organizations is misconstrued rather than exaggerated. We need to reconceptualize a relationship which the present analysis shows is unquestionably present, but insufficiently understood.

This is a pressing task, as misapprehensions of how organizations create social capital may lead us to focus on the wrong types of organizations and activities and prescribe wrong or even "harmful remedies" (Skocpol 2003, p. 255) for civic revitalization. There is nothing in the data to suggest that a revival of locally oriented, social clubs offering plenty of face to face interaction and social contact, will help. They do not seem to make their members more trusting over time. Furthermore, Eliasoph's (2003) account of how localist, non-political volunteering organizations may foster a culture of civic apathy and delegitimize and curtail political discussion is a timely reminder that laying the burden of maintaining democracy on the shoulders of such groups may not be such a good idea.

The present results indicate that if social capital is to be sustained, what a society needs is extrovert, visible organizations that act as real intermediary institutions between citizen and polity, and individual and society. In order to fulfill these functions, associations need to provide translocal links reaching beyond local communities and into the political system (Skocpol 1996, 2003; Wollebæk and Selle 2002a). They would also need to do more than providing arenas for social interaction, but actually get involved in political life.

The preoccupation with whether organizational members are meeting face to face or not, appears increasingly irrelevant. Needless to say, this does not mean that people should be encouraged to be passive. Most organizational societies rely on the time and efforts of activists, without whom organizations would be weakened as institutions. What the above analyses show is simply that the externalities of the efforts they are putting in are incomparably greater than the effect the activity has on them personally.

A shift from a socialization to an institutional perspective implies changing the focus from looking for catalysts or vehicles of social capital, to analyzing how social capital is conserved and strengthened, and how it is destructed. The findings above suggest that fair and impartial public institutions are highly consequential, but clearly so is also the prominence of visible institutions in civil society. Such institutions are not shaped by social encounters, but by history, social context and politics. This is the realm within which the study of social capital in the context of democracy should remain.

Notes

* This chapter extensively overlaps with the article Origins of Social Capital. Socialization and Institutionalization Approaches Compared, published in the *Journal of Civil Society* 3(1): 1–24, June 2007.
1 For overviews, see Foley and Edwards (1999) and Stolle and Rochon (1999).
2 For arguments to the contrary, see Selle and Strømsnes (2001) and Wollebæk and Selle (2004a). The absence of socialization effects of passive memberships is usually simply assumed, and has not been tested empirically.
3 The conditions for voluntary activity varies greatly among authoritarian and totalitarian states. In many cases, the organizations that are likely to be tolerated by an authoritarian state are either instruments of the state apparatus, pure leisure or cultural activities or small-scale community projects (Juknevicius and Savicha 2003; Booth and Richard 2001). In such situations, it is unlikely that organizations are the main source of social capital, whether through socialization or institutionalization.
4 Voluntary organizations represent extensive information systems. A Norwegian study concluded that nationwide organizations publish more than five journals and newsletters per person in the adult population annually (Hallenstvedt and Trollvik 1993). In addition to this, 14 percent of the local chapters, of which there is approximately one for every 30 inhabitants in Norway (Wollebæk and Selle 2004b), published their own newsletters (Wollebæk and Selle 2002a). The increasing contact between organizations and members over email and Internet can be added to this.
5 Trust in government is however sometimes mentioned as a *consequence* of social trust (Putnam 2000a, pp. 347–349), or as circumstantial evidence for civic disengagement and declining social capital (Putnam 1995a, p. 68).
6 The data has been made available by the Norwegian Social Science Data Services (NSD). Neither NSD nor the Central co-ordinating team of the European Social Survey bear any responsibility for the analyses and the inferences from the analyses made here.
7 The Czech Republic and Switzerland are excluded because of errors in the questionnaire design with regard to questions on organizational participation (NSD 2003).
8 NUTS – Nomenclature of territorial units for statistics. http://europa.eu.int/comm/eurostat/nuts/splash_regions.html.
9 Exceptions were made for Sardinia (Italy), Northern Ireland (UK), The Canary Islands (Spain) and Bornholm (Denmark) to which there are no adjacent regions.
10 http://utip.gov.utexas.edu.
11 The extremely weak, but significant effect of activity level among multiple members does not alter this conclusion – at 35,000 respondents even the shadow of a relationship will be statistically significant.
12 The reason why the Flemish regions score higher on social capital may be that they are more internally homogeneous ethnically speaking, and economic conditions are better than in Wallonia.
13 The differences are evident among countries with comparable levels of economic and social development: the strongly religious Greek are much less trusting than the more secularized Portuguese and the religious Polish regions display lower levels of trust than more secular Hungary and Slovenia.
14 The 20th region, Crete, ranks 30 on the least trusting list.
15 The relationship between religiosity and distrusts holds even when percentage Protestants is introduced in the model (not shown).
16 An analysis using GINI coefficients (only available at the national level) as the measure of inequality instead of Theil's t produced similar results.
17 The correlation between inequality and institutional trust is –0.42. As noted in Figure 3.2, southern Italy and Greece, in which high institutional trust coexists with extensive social inequality and low social trust, deviate from the general pattern.

References

Berman, Sheri. 1997. Civil society and the collapse of the Weimar Republic. *World Politics* 49 (3): 401–429.

Booth, John A. and Richard, Patricia B. 2001. Civil society and political context in Central America. In *Beyond Tocqueville. Civil society and the social capital debate in comparative perspective*, edited by M.W. Foley, B. Edwards and M. Diani. Hanover: University Press of New England.

Bourdieu, Pierre. 1985. The forms of capital. In *Handbook of theory and research for the sociology of education*, edited by J. G. Richardson. New York: Greenwood.

Dekker, Paul, and Andries van den Broek. 1998. Civil society in comparative perspective: involvement in voluntary associations in North America and Western Europe. *Voluntas* 9 (1): 11–38.

Eliasoph, Nina. 2003. Cultivating apathy in voluntary associations. In *The values of volunteering. Cross-cultural perspectives*, edited by P. Dekker and L. Halman. New York: Kluwer Academic/Plenum Publishers.

Foley, Michael W. and Bob Edwards. 1996. The paradox of civil society. *Journal of Democracy* 7 (3): 38–52.

Foley, Michael W. and Bob Edwards. 1999. Is it time to disinvest in social capital? *Journal of Public Policy* 19 (2): 141–173.

Foley, Michael W. and Bob Edwards. 2001. Civil society and social capital: a primer. In *Beyond Tocqueville. Civil society and the social capital debate in comparative perspective*, edited by M. W. Foley, B. Edwards and M. Diani. Hanover: University Press of New England.

Foley, Michael W., Bob Edwards and Mario Diani. 2001. Social capital reconsidered. In *Beyond Tocqueville. Civil society and the social capital debate in comparative perspective*, edited by B. Edwards, M. W. Foley and M. Diani. Hanover: University Press of New England.

Freitag, Markus. 2003. Social capital in (dis)similar democracies. The development of generalized trust in Japan and Switzerland. *Comparative Political Studies* 36 (8): 936–966.

Fukuyama, Francis. 1995. *Trust: the social virtues and the creation of prosperity*. New York: Free Press.

Galbraith, James and Enrique Garcilazo. 2005. Pay inequality in Europe 1995–2000: convergence between countries and stabilities inside. UTIP Working Paper no. 30. URL: http://utip.gov.utexas.edu/papers/utip_30.pdf (first accessed November 9, 2005).

Haddad, Mary Alice. 2004. Community determinates of volunteer participation and the promotion of civic health: the case of Japan. *Nonprofit and Voluntary Sector Quarterly* 33 (Supplement to no. 3): 8S–31S.

Hallenstvedt, Abraham and Jan Trollvik. 1993. *Norske organisasjoner [Norwegian organizations]*. Oslo: Fabritius Forlag.

Hooghe, Marc. 2003. Voluntary associations and democratic attitudes: value congruence as a causal mechanism. In *Generating social capital. Civil society and institutions in comparative perspective*, edited by M. Hooghe and D. Stolle. New York: Palgrave Macmillan.

Hooghe, Marc and Dietlind Stolle. 2003. Introduction: generating social capital. In *Generating social capital.*, edited by M. Hooghe and D. Stolle. New York: Palgrave Macmillan.

Inglehart, Ronald. 1990. *Culture shift in advanced industrial society*. Princeton: Princeton University Press.

Jowell, J. and Central Co-ordinating Team. 2003. European Social Survey 2002–2003: technical report. London: Centre for Comparative Social Surveys, City University.

Juknevicius, S. and A. Savicha. 2003. From restitution to innovation: volunteering in postcommunist countries. In *The values of volunteering: cross-cultural perspectives*, edited by P. Dekker and L. Halman. New York: Kluwer Academic/Plenum Publishers.

Knack, Stephen and Philip Keefer. 1997. Does social capital have an economic payoff? A cross-country investigation. *The Quarterly Journal of Economics* 112: 1251–1288.

Lijphart, Arend. 1984. *Democracies. Patterns of majoritarian and consensus government in twenty-one countries*. New Haven and London: Yale University Press.

Macpherson, C. B. 1977. *The life and times of liberal democracy*. Oxford: Oxford University Press.

Mayer, Nonna. 2003. Democracy in France: do associations matter? In *Generating social capital*, edited by M. Hooghe and D. Stolle. New York: Palgrave Macmillan.

Mutz, Diana C. 2002. Cross-cutting social networks: testing democratic theory in practice. *American Political Science Review* 96 (1): 111–126.

Newton, Kenneth. 1997. Social capital and democracy. *American Behavioral Scientist* 40 (5): 575–586.

NSD, ESS data team at. 2003. ESS documentation report 2002/2003, 5th edition. Bergen: Norwegian Social Science Data Services.

Offe, Claus and Susanne Fuchs. 2002. A decline in social capital? The German case. In *Democracies in flux*, edited by R. D. Putnam. New York: Oxford University Press.

Olson, Mancur. 1982. *The rise and decline of nations*. New Haven: Yale University Press.

Pateman, Carole. 1970. *Participation and democratic theory*. Cambridge: Cambridge University Press.

Putnam, Robert D. 1993. *Making democracy work: civic traditions in modern Italy*. Princeton: Princeton University Press.

Putnam, Robert D. 1995a. Bowling alone: America's declining social capital. *Journal of Democracy* 6: 65–78.

Putnam, Robert D. 1995b. Tuning in, tuning out: the strange disappearance of social capital in America. *Political Science & Politics* 28 (4): 664–683.

Putnam, Robert D. 2000a. *Bowling alone. The collapse and revival of American community*. New York: Simon & Schuster.

Putnam, Robert D. 2000b. Introduction: what's troubling the trilateral democracies? In *Disaffected democracies*, edited by S. Pharr and R. D. Putnam. Princeton: Princeton University Press.

Putnam, Robert D. 2002. Conclusion. In *Democracies in flux. The evolution of social capital in contemporary society*, edited by R. D. Putnam and K. Goss. New York: Oxford University Press.

Putnam, Robert D. and Lewis M. Feldstein. 2003. *Better together. Restoring the American community*. New York: Simon & Schuster.

Quigley, Kevin F. F. 1996. Human bonds and social capital. *Orbis* 40 (2): 333–343.

Rokkan, Stein. 1967. Geography, religion and social class: crosscutting cleavages in Norwegian politics. In *Party systems and voter alignments. Cross-national perspectives*, edited by S. M. Lipset and S. Rokkan. New York: The Free Press.

Rothstein, Bo. 2002. Social capital in the social democratic state. In *Democracies in flux. The evolution of social capital in contemporary society*, edited by R. D. Putnam and K. Goss. New York: Oxford University Press.

Rothstein, Bo. 2004. Social capital and institutional legitimacy: the Corleone connection.

In *Investigating social capital*, edited by S. Prakash and P. Selle. New Delhi/Thousand Oaks/London: SAGE.

Rothstein, Bo and Dietlind Stolle. 2003a. Introduction: social capital in Scandinavia. *Scandinavian Political Studies* 26 (1): 1–26.

Rothstein, Bo and Dietlind Stolle. 2003b. Social capital, impartiality and the welfare state: an institutional approach. In *Generating social capital*, edited by M. Hooghe and D. Stolle. New York: Palgrave Macmillan.

Rueschemeyer, Dietrich, Marilyn Rueschemeyer and Björn Wittrock, eds. 1998. *Participation and democracy East and West: comparisons and interpretations*. Armonk: M. E. Sharpe.

Selle, Per and Kristin Strømsnes. 2001. Membership and democracy. In *Social capital and participation in everyday life*, edited by P. Dekker and E. Uslaner. London: Routledge.

Skocpol, Theda. 1996. Unravelling from above. *The American Prospect* (no. 25, March-April).

Skocpol, Theda. 2003. *Diminished democracy. From membership to management in American civic life*. Norman: University of Oklahoma Press.

Stolle, Dietlind. 2001. Clubs and congregations: the benefits of joining an association. In *Trust in society*, edited by K. Cook. New York: Russel Sage Foundation.

Stolle, Dietlind. 2003. The sources of social capital. In *Generating social capital*, edited by M. Hooghe and D. Stolle. New York: Palgrave Macmillan.

Stolle, Dietlind. 2004. Communities, social capital and local government: generalized trust in regional settings. In *Investigating social capital*, edited by S. Prakash and P. Selle. New Delhi/Thousand Oaks/London: SAGE.

Stolle, Dietlind and Thomas R. Rochon. 1999. The myth of American exceptionalism. A three-nation comparison of associational membership and social capital. In *Social capital and European democracy*, edited by J. van Deth, M. Maraffi, K. Newton and P. F. Whiteley. London and New York: Routledge.

Strømsnes, Kristin. 2003. *Folkets makt*. Oslo: Gyldendal Akademisk.

Tocqueville, Alexis de. 1968. *Democracy in America/Alexis de Tocqueville; edited by J. P. Mayer and Max Lerner; a new translation by George Lawrence*. Edited by J. P. Mayer and M. Lernar. London: Collins.

Uslaner, Eric. 2003. Trust, democracy and governance: can government policies influence generalized trust? In *Generating social capital*, edited by M. Hooghe and D. Stolle. New York: Palgrave Macmillan.

Wollebæk, Dag and Per Selle. 2002a. *Det nye organisasjonssamfunnet. Demokrati i omforming*. Bergen: Fagbokforlaget.

Wollebæk, Dag and Per Selle. 2002b. Does participation in voluntary associations contribute to social capital? The impact of intensity, scope, and type. *Nonprofit and Voluntary Sector Quarterly* 30 (1): 32–61.

Wollebæk, Dag and Per Selle. 2004a. Passive membership in voluntary organizations: implications for civil society, integration and democracy. In *Investigating social capital*, edited by S. Prakash and P. Selle. New Delhi/Thousand Oaks/London: SAGE.

Wollebæk, Dag and Per Selle. 2004b. The role of women in the transformation of the voluntary sector in Norway. *Nonprofit and Voluntary Sector Quarterly* 33 (3 (supplemental issue)): 120–144.

Woolcock, Michael. 1998. Social capital and economic development: toward a theoretical synthesis and policy framework. *Theory and Society* 27: 151–208.

4 The role of Romanian NGOs in the democratization process of the society after 1990

Márton Balogh

Introduction

This chapter strives to critically discuss the role that NGOs[1] played in the democratization process of the Romanian society after the changes from 1990. In the transition process from a dictatorial system to a democratic one, NGOs functioning is absolutely necessary. There is a variety of ways in which the civil society can contribute to the democratization of a country. To some, the very proliferation of civil society organizations – no matter what their type, agenda, or influence– builds the infrastructure of democracy, because according to the supporters of this view an active associational life is a precursor of democracy. The right to free elections, the freedom of speech, and citizens' participation to governance (including free access to public interest information) represent only few aspects whose evolution is worth studying in this paper.

Also, the existence of a strong NGO sector provides a great opportunity in a society, mainly because its involvement in community development is thought to build skills and foster democratic values and attitudes in individuals that will eventually spread to the broader society. They also enhance the prospects for democratization because they foster associational life, empower individuals, and provide them with the skills and attitudes that are useful for democratization.

Definitions

This section is meant to critically assess the role played by the Romanian NGOs towards the democratization of the society after the collapse of the communist regime in 1989. In this chapter the concept of "non-profit sector" is used in a manner that is consistent with the definition provided by Salamon and Anheier[2] (1992, 1996) who consider that there are five features that describe a non-profit organization:

1 *Organized, i.e., institutionalized to some extent.* What is important is that the organizations have some institutional reality to them.
2 *Private, i.e., institutionally separate from government.* Non-profit organizations are not part of the apparatus of government. They are

"non-governmental" in the sense of being structurally separate from the instrumentalities of government.

3   *Self-governing, i.e., equipped to control their own activities.* Some organizations that are private and non-governmental may nevertheless be so tightly controlled either by governmental agencies or private businesses that they essentially function as parts of these other institutions even though they are structurally separate. To meet this criterion, organizations must be in a position to control their own activities to a significant extent.

4   *Non-profit-distributing, i.e., not returning profits generated to their owners or directors.* Non-profit organizations may accumulate profits in a given year, but the profits must be plowed back into the basic mission of the agency, not distributed to the organizations' owners, members, founders or governing board.

5   *Voluntary, i.e., involving some meaningful degree of voluntary participation.* To be included in the non-profit sector, organizations must embody the concept of voluntarism to a meaningful extent. This involves two different, but related, considerations: first, the organization must engage volunteers in its operations and management, either on its board or through the use of volunteer staff and voluntary contributions. Second, "voluntary" also carries the meaning of "non-compulsory".

The other major theoretical concept employed in the analysis within this paper is democracy. Defining democracy is a very difficult task since the term that we currently use in a variety of contexts has a very long theoretical history and its meaning is still evolving. *Democracy* (literally "rule by the people", from the Greek *demos*, "people", and *kratos*, "rule") as defined by Abraham Lincoln, is a government "of the people, by the people, and for the people". The author does not agree with definitions that define democracy only in terms of free, open and rightfully held elections (Huntington, 1991). This approach portrays free, open and rightfully held elections as the core values of a democracy. The reason why the author does not support this view is because the governments that emerge from such elections can be inefficient, corrupt, and governed by individual interests and without a strategic view with regard to the public good. Such features can determine some governments/regimes to be undesirable but not undemocratic. Democracy should be considered a public virtue among others and the relationship between democracies and other ills or virtues can be understood only if democracy is clearly separated from other characteristics of the political systems.

The concept of democracy is defined in this paper based on the "strong democracy" literature (Barber, 1984) which assumes that: the democracy depends, for its existence, on actively involved members who have a commitment to individual freedom and to the rights and responsibilities of participating in a democracy. Democracy gives to ordinary citizens the greatest opportunity of influencing public decisions.

The NGOs role in society

Democratic society presumes the existence of active and responsible citizens, a multiparty political system, a competitive economic market and a strong non-profit sector.

The third sector is proved to be the most efficient in the enhancement of moral codes and individual conduct responsibilities. Non-governmental organizations are characterized by a large mobility considering the manner and the course of their actions. This mobility represents a prerequisite for survival since their functioning depends on the proper identification of communities' needs and the attraction of the necessary resources to meet these needs.

In a democratic society, the generic function of non-governmental organizations is to meet those needs of the community that cannot be completely covered by other types of institutions (belonging to the public sector or the business environment). This view has its roots in the economic theories that explain the development of the third sector. A different set of theories – the political theories – consider that NGOs emerged in order to offer the possibility of a wide participation of citizens in the public life (Walter W. Powell, ed. 1987). In this sense non-governmental organizations may undertake different functions. Bădilă *et al.* (2002) argue that NGOs assume the following functions:

- mediating the relationship between citizens and authorities;
- facilitating the social and political integration of citizens (organizations represent a framework for civil participation);
- delivering goods and services to the community;
- representing the interests of different groups from within the society.

One should note that at the functional level NGOs have a very important role in taking over responsibilities directed towards the development of democracy in a country. The ways in which relationships between citizens and authorities are mediated, in which citizens' participation and representation is facilitated, influence to a significant extent the democratic character of a country.

NGOs as main actors in the democratization process

The main hypothesis of the chapter is that the role of the NGOs in the Romanian democratization process is connected to the development of a partnership between NGOs and government, and the development of governance capacity as a necessity for a modern governing system.

Based on the study of the evolution of the associative sector, the right to free elections, freedom of speech, citizens' participation in governance, and transparency of governmental activity, the author strives to explore the relationship in the remainder of this chapter. As documentary groundwork the analysis discussing the evolution of the non-governmental sector in Romania from 1990 to 2005 is used. This analysis is based on documents published by different NGO leaders from Romania as well as the evaluations elaborated by different international organizations: the European Commission, World Bank or other private entities like Freedom House (Nations in Transition).

This analysis can prove to be relevant mainly because there are scholars and political analysts who currently examine the Romanian context as a possible source of solutions for other emerging democracies: for example, politicians such as Paul Wolfowitz argued that the establishment of a Romanian type of democratic system should be considered in Iraq (*The New Yorker*, November 1, 2004). However, this view is not singular in the American media and literature. Fareed Zakaria (1997) argued that the Romanian democracy could be described as non-liberal, along with other democracies such as Belarus or Bangladesh. The non-liberal feature had been present in Romania according to Zakaria during the first two terms of the Iliescu regime. According to the literature that supports this view (Brâncoveanu, 2006), the Romanian non-liberal democracy implies that the alternation of various parties to power is possible and keeping appearances is essential; the alternation of various parties to power was limited by means of a weak enforcement and reinterpretation of the existing laws (the best example stems from the debate with regard to how many terms former president Iliescu was entitled according to the existing laws) or simply by political schemes and populism. However, the consequences of this so-called non-liberal democracy were not as severe as in the case of Belarus or Russia or in other countries from the ex-Soviet space. As opposed to these countries the non-liberal democratic system in Romania does not seem to progress toward an autocratic government, rather it can be described as a non-liberal system that allows for changes in the political leadership.

The analysis of the sector between 1990–2005

If one examines the socialist period in the Eastern European states through the lens of a historian it seems to be a voluntarily enforced, unfortunate deviation from the natural course of evolution (Bucur, 1998).

This is the reason why, after the collapse of the socialist system, this part of the world faces the necessity of thoughtful economic and social reconstruction in order to re-enter the natural track of development.

Practically, the comeback to normality of the states affected by the socialism presumes a wide economic, institutional, legal, cultural, and human construction work, all in all the remodeling of the structural components of the society that had been altered in their façade and function during the socialist age.

The implication of the communist regime for the evolution of the associative sector after the post-Decembrist period can be explained through several factors. First of all the communist regime in Romania was the most refractory with regard to the altering of the totalitarian project in comparison to the corresponding regimes from the states that were members in the communist bloc – mainly Hungary and Poland. The Romanian Communist Party suppressed any internal change that might have given birth to an organized dissidence. The Security –

Political Police – (*Securitatea* in Romanian) was the main instrument of control imposed by terror and mass disinformation. Security left a bitter memory regarding the faith in the governing machine and state institutions. Politically or economically influential personalities were looked at with skepticism and considered to have connections with the Security. This heritage stands at the origins of the mistrust most people have in NGOs after 1989. Non-governmental organizations were suspected to promote unstated political interests.

Another characteristic of the Romanian communist regime after 1965 that influenced the associative sector is connected to the personality cult. In the period between 1965–1989, Nicolae Ceauşescu initiated and controlled the construction of a complicated network of institutions, public policies and symbols that served to enforce his power and authority. As a consequence, many people identify civic participation with this kind of false participation, lacking any kind of personal implication. Shortly after 1989 many people began to associate freedom and democracy with the right to not participate in the public sphere.

The third characteristic that derives from the communist period, and considered to have an influence upon the evolution of the associative sector and the role it has in society, is connected to the partnership between NGOs and public administration that is meant to provide some services mostly in the social department.

Ironically, although a sentiment of rejection and mistrust still exists towards the public sphere, at the same time there is a general perception that the state should undertake the responsibility of providing the majority of the social services. Most people, despite their feelings toward the government, saw the state as a primary provider of social services.

In Romania, following the collapse of the communist regime in 1989, mistrust towards the political and public life have started to emerge. Volunteering was already compromised by the restriction policies of the Ceauşescu regime so the majority of the public came to identify the "liberalization" with the withdrawing from activities with public character.

We can analyze the evolution of the role that non-governmental organizations had in the democratization of the Romanian society dividing the period between 1990–2004 in three different periods: 1990–1996, 1997–2000, and 2001–2004. This division in historical periods is made after the election cycles and changes in political leadership.

The period 1990–1996

After 1989 in Romania, as well as in the rest of the Central and Eastern European countries, the number of registered NGOs increased. This can be interpreted as an expression of the newly gained freedom of association, as well as a result of the available foreign funds for the non-profit sector. In this period, the main regulation concerning the organization and functioning of the non-governmental organizations was Law Marzescu (Law No. 21/1924), which was incapable of assuring the efficient functioning of the non-governmental sector from a registration point of view and also from the fundraising perspective. In 1990 the number of registered non-governmental organizations reached 400 per month (Vamesu and Constantinescu, 1996). At the end of the first period (1996) it is estimated that 12,000 NGOs were officially registered (Şăulean and Epure, 1998).

While the non-profit sector and associative behavior have developed relatively rapidly, a number of problems and obstacles still remain. Among these are the outdated legal framework and the weak development of relations between government and non-governmental sectors. However, probably one of the most significant problems is caused by the limited access to financial resources and the weak economic capacity of NGOs. Financial dependence on foreign financers and their strategies can be considered as an important characteristic of the associative sector of this period. The outdated legal framework means that several of the provisions of Law No. 21/1924 were still in place; however, they were not able to respond to contemporary issues and problems faced by the non-profit sector. One of the most important problems posed by these outdated regulations refers to the incorporation procedure that was extremely tedious and lengthy. Prior to their incorporation, NGOs had to consult with administrative authorities and obtain their permission. The law also created a rather restrictive framework for their organization and functioning. Also, access to funding was low and a distinction was made in this respect between associations and foundations (the latter were not allowed to conduct any sort of economic activity).

The relationship between the government and the NGOs in this period cannot be characterized as a prolific one. In this period the administration of the country was made up of people who previously belonged to the Communist Party/regime, and had, different ideological convictions to the ones promoted by the non-governmental sector. Often during the first six years of democracy we could encounter non-governmental organizations working side by side with "historical parties" (by this it is meant the National Liberal Party and the National Peasant Party that continued the traditions of their ancestors from the interwar period) fighting against the authoritarian practices that existed at government level. This is why we can find in Romania at the beginning of the 1990s the concept of "anti-governmental" instead of "non-governmental organization" (Bădilă *et al.*, 2002). Many charismatic NGO leaders from that period were active members or supporters of the political opposition and some even took part in the elections held in 1996 (for example the Civic Alliance – conceived as an associative structure although it participated in the 1996 elections beside the coalition of the forces in opposition).

It is the immediate period after the 1989 revolution when different important objectives are accomplished regarding the democratic development. In this period the first democratic – after the collapse of the communist regime – Romanian constitution is adopted; in it the freedom of association, and freedom of speech are regulated. Also the first democratic elections are organized in this period. This new fundamental law – the constitution – was an issue that presumed that basic elements of democratic development should be understood and internalized and not only regulated at formal level as had been previously the case.

Regarding the partnerships between the NGOs and the government during 1990–1996 there is a limited number of examples mainly because a lack of rules governing this field.

The 1996–2000 period

During this period a total of 27,000 NGOs were created (Dakova *et al.*, 2000). However their increasing number and rapid evolution is not necessarily the best indicator with regard to the role played by NGOs in the development of the civil society. Studies conducted during this period prove that of the 27,000 registered NGOs merely 1,500–2,000 organizations were active, by this meaning they had a place/location from where activities were run and they hired personnel.[3] This discrepancy between the number of registered NGOs and the number of active NGOs can be explained by two main reasons:

1   a lack of financial resources available to NGOs which forced many of them to cease their operation;
2   the possibility of creating an NGO purely in order to derive personal gain from this status.

This latter situation stems from the fact that after 1995, several laws allowed for vehicles older than eight years to be registered only by non-profit organizations. The aim of the law was to support NGOs and to allow them to function while having very few resources available. However, these provisions spurred the creation of a huge number of fictitious NGOs. Many of them were created and registered by individuals for the mere reason of buying and bringing into the country cars that were older than eight years. For example, during this time-frame, numerous NGOs were created for this sole purpose, especially in rural areas. It was widely known, however, that the creation of NGOs, especially in the rural area, was solely a consequence of the aforementioned regulations.

According to the statistical data compiled in the Catalogue of Associations and Foundations in 1999 the main fields of activity for NGOs are shown in Table 4.1.

Data presented in Table 4.1 show that more than 50 percent of the Romanian NGOs operate within three main fields of activity: culture, social and educational services. Other areas such as health, environmental protection, and human rights are much less likely to represent the main field of activity many non-profits in Romania.

The author argues that it is relevant to closely scrutinize the field of activities for NGOs as this endeavor clearly shows that one of the most significant problems NGOs are confronted with has to do with a lack of clarity and specification with regard to how the mission and their goals are defined and also with a weak visibility of the activities undertaken by them. As with activity levels, these figures on fields of activity do not really enlighten understanding of the sector or

Table 4.1 Fields of activity for Romanian NGOs

Field	Percent
1 Culture	26
2 Social services	18
3 Education, research	16
4 Health	8
5 Human rights	7
6 Environmental protection	5
7 Social and economic development	5
8 Professional associations/unions	4
9 International cooperation	3
10 Philanthropy and voluntaries	3
11 Religion	3
12 Others	2

Source: Associations and Foundations Catalogue, 1999.

the role it is playing. The review has confirmed earlier research that showed most NGOs (90 percent) do not have a focused mission. Some operate more as private businesses (for example, the majority of their income comes from fees from private sector clients) and many others change their focus depending on the availability of funds.

Most NGOs are not visible at all in society; however the non-profits that operate in the social field benefit from press coverage more often and are therefore more visible. This happens because they respond to daily needs such as healthcare, social protection of children and the elderly as opposed to those organizations who operate in the field of ethnic minorities, for example. The latter are not well known either by the society or by the sector.

With regard to the evolution of the non-profit sector legislation during this period there are several aspects that are worth mentioning. First the election of a new government determined a change in the official attitude towards NGOs as compared with the attitude of the former governments. The parliament debated more than once different drafts of the NGO framework law and as a result in May 2000 the government decided to adopt via a Governmental Ordinance (No. 26/2000) the new law of the NGOs. The new law brought several changes that were considered to foster the development of the third sector. The main changes included:

- establishing an easier registration procedure;
- allowing associations and foundations to undertake economic activities;
- forcing local authorities to collaborate with NGOs – they have to provide NGOs with public interest information, a location from where NGOs can run their activities, and consult NGOs with regard to issues that are of interest to the community;
- granting the status of public utility to NGOs that work towards the achieving of the public interest/good.

With regard to the changes in the legislative framework that regulates the activity of NGOs, there is no consensus regarding the actors involved:

- According to one opinion, it is considered that these changes were the result of the government's "good will" and a very good personal relationship between actors from the two sectors rather than a strong lobbying process on the behalf of the non-profit sector.
- According to a second opinion, it is argued that NGOs were actively involved in the process of legislative change; however, the experts rather than representatives of the non-profit sector played a greater role.

This period is also characterized by an enhancing of the relationships between the government and the NGOs. There are different reasons for this change (Dakova *et al.*, 2000). The main reason is related to the change in political leadership that took place at the end of 1996. The new government established mechanisms and structures that would allow for a real dialogue with the associative sector at both the central and local level. At the central level two such organizational structures were created – one in close connection with the president (The Bureau for Civil Society) and the other one functioning in connection with the government (The Bureau for the Relationship with NGOs). The Bureau for Civil Society had among other tasks the obligation to maintain the flow of information and the dialog between the non-profit sector and the government, to consult with the NGOs with regard to relevant problems, and provide the NGOs with the opportunity to voice their opinions to the government. The Bureau for the Relationship with NGOs was meant to coordinate the legislative efforts in the field of NGOs and to support the national network comprised of those responsible for the relationship with the NGOs. During this period the framework law that regulates the organization and the functioning of the non-profit sector was adopted. This law made compulsory the existence of an organizational structure that would facilitate cooperation. This law did not, however, produce visible effects until 2001.

With regard to the financing of the non-profit sector the dependence of NGOs on external donors is still a main feature of this period (Dakova *et al.*, 2000). Dakova *et al.* argue that at the end of this stage the external funds accounted for 55 percent of the financial resources employed by the non-profit sector in Romania. With regard to how NGOs are financed during this period two important aspects have to be mentioned: first, the financial crisis from 1996 to 1998, caused by the exit of several big donors from Romania, forced numerous NGOs to cut down on the number of projects implemented; second, this was for the first time that the central public administration – the Ministry of Sports, the Ministry of Labor, the Department for Interethnic Relations –allocated money for the financing of various projects undertaken by NGOs.

The 2001–2004 period

During this stage the strengthening of the NGO sector took place – the number of organizations gradually increased, the sources of finance diversified, and the implication and the impact of the third sector's activities on the community grew. The number of NGOs in this period increased until it reached 40,000. The big number of inactive organizations continued, however, to represent a big problem for the non-profit sector (Donors Forum).

From the political standpoint this period can be characterized as stable. The Social Democratic Party was in power during this period. This party was also the leading party during the 1990–1996 period (the Social Democratic Party was also known during the previous years as the Social National Movement, and the Romanian Democratic and Social Party). With regard to the relationship between the government and the NGOs there was an important change in attitude, mainly concerning the domineering tendency of the government. For example, the organizational structures in charge of the management of the government-NGO relationships continued, however, several attempts were made towards limiting the independence of the third sector. A relevant example stems from the adoption of a new Governmental Ordinance – (37/2003) – that was amending the framework law of NGOs. A provision that was interpreted as a restriction with regard to the independence of NGOs refers to the obligation of NGOs that are in the process of incorporation to ask for the approval of the central government structure under which jurisdiction its activity takes place (ministries in different fields of activities). Also numerous debates were generated by the drafting and adoption of the strategy for the development of the civil society. Numerous NGOs' representatives considered that several of its provisions were meant to limit the autonomy of the non-profit sector vis-à-vis the government.

Two important legislative endeavors are worth mentioning during this stage:

- the modification of the 1991 Constitution in 2003, and;
- the issuing of the Governmental Ordinance No. 37/2003 that modifies the Governmental Ordinance No. 26/2000 that used to regulate the functioning of NGOs.

An important law for the functioning of the third sector – Law No. 52/2003 regulating the transparency in the decision-making in public administration was also adopted in 2003. The law was mainly a result of the pressures exercised by international organizations (the European Union) as well as by NGOs. The necessity of adopting such a law stems from the following reasons (Stefan and Georgescu, 2003):

- There was no coherence or consistency with regard to the government's obligation of involving the civil society in the decision-making process, including the process of drafting and adopting new legislative acts.

- Even though there were situations when cooperation between the governmental organizations and NGOs was successful, there was mainly a lack of transparency.
- Governmental institutions who were not open to dialogue with the civil society were able to take advantage of a limited legal framework that did not make transparency a compulsory obligation.
- The participation of NGOs in the decision-making process mainly took place as a result of their own initiatives. The success of such endeavors was further enhanced by the openness of certain public institutions mainly due to open-minded people in leadership positions.
- The necessity of a dialog between public institutions – NGOs tend to be agreed upon by the governmental structures involved mostly at the level of principle rather than in practice when decisions need to be made.
- The techniques used to consult with the civil society are still in their infancy and they are merely tentatively used by the government despite the existence of a very broad array of such techniques. The use of such techniques by the public institutions seems to be a purpose in itself and not a means. The practical aspects that would further their efficiency are not taken into consideration. Also the input gathered during consultation is rarely used towards the drafting of the final decision/document.

All these legislative efforts have an important role in the evolution of the non-profit sector as well as in the democratization process of Romanian society.

This period is characterized by an increased diversity in the types of financial resources available to NGOs; other resources became available besides the "traditional ones", namely external donations, both public and private and domestic governmental funds. The first locally financed programs for NGOs occur during this period. The local public authorities that were financing such programs include the city halls in Cluj Napoca, Oradea, etc.

With regard to enhancing the public visibility of NGOs several initiatives were undertaken during this period, all of them related to the development/enhancement of democratic practices. An important effort in this sense is represented by the NGOs' involvement in the adoption of the Transparency Law (see p. 62). The Coalition for a Corruption Free Parliament was also created (a coalition among several NGOs whose main task was to monitor the correctness of the election process). Within this context it is important to highlight the occurrence of several policy nuclei/centers whose main focus is on the studying of public policy issues and on the initiation of several debates on issues of public interest.

Based on all these evolutions one can argue that the Romanian NGO sector remained diverse and influential during this period, leaving its imprint on various laws and policies.

Conclusions

The democratization wave in Europe started in 1974 in Portugal. At that point in time there were only 40 democratic countries. However the number of democratic regimes today is above 120. A clear definition of democracy is needed not in order to count how many democratic countries exist today worldwide, but rather because it may prove a useful instrument that could guide us through the complicated web of political and geo-strategic processes that are taking place right now and through the globalization process. The peak of the democratization process that started in 1974 was represented without any doubt by the collapse of communism. Its demise represents in a way a success of democracy mainly because communism seemed to be so entrenched in these countries. Thus, in this new century, the democratization effort is not only a political but also a military endeavor. The war in Iraq has to be understood in the context of a military effort that is necessary in order to further the democratization process. This dichotomy war – democracy is not necessarily unrelated to the issue of establishing democratic regimes.

The support of the Romanian NGOs for the development of the democratic regime was often inconsistent. Democratic changes were implemented generally due to external pressures from international organizations and/or international donors. NGOs were frequently acting as intermediaries for their interests.

Specific elements that influence the development of democracy can be noted in the relationship between NGOs and public authorities for each of the analyzed sub-periods in the interval of 1990–2005. First sub-period 1990–1996 is characterized by a conflict approach. The legislation was then passed that guaranteed the necessary rights for the democratic evolution, such as the right to associate, to freedom of expression, to elect and to be elected, free election, etc. Therefore one can say that during this period the fundamentals of a democratic society were settled.

The second sub-period is characterized by partnership – solutions for current issues were searched based upon the openness from the government. There were attempts to build solutions using the basic elements already laid out during the previous interval. Entities/institutions that would implement these basic elements were established.

The third sub-period consisted of the transition to elements that are more specific to democratic development such as transparency and involvement in decision-making. Democratic development was meant both in terms of governmental activity and political activity and agenda.

NGOs had an important role in the democratic evolution of Romania in each of the three sub-periods of the studied interval. However, additional issues to be investigated are:

1   who establishes the goals and objectives;
2   the extent of their impact in the development of the society after these goals and objectives were internalized by the NGOs.

For the Romanian situation, goal setting depended to a large extent on donor agendas and to a lesser extent on the wishes/needs of beneficiaries and the impact of these activities was influenced not only by the power of the NGOs but also by governmental openness.

Notes

1 Non-governmental organizations.
2 The author employs in this chapter the following concepts interchangeably: non-profit or non-governmental organizations.
3 Civil Society Development Foundation – Associations and Foundations Catalogue from Romania, 1999.

References

Bădilă, A., Lisetchi, M., Olteanu, I., and Ticiu, R. (2002) *Organizaţii neguvernamentale. Ghid practic*, Agentia pentru Informarea si Dezvoltarea Organizatiilor Neguvernamentale, Editura Brumar, Timişoara.

Barber, B. (1984) *Strong Democracy*, Berkeley and Los Angeles: University of California Press.

Brâncoveanu, Romulus (2006) "Democraţia românească teorie şi metodă", in *Sfera Politicii*, Bucuresti.

Bucur, Maria (1998) "Philanthropy, Nationalism, and the Growth of Civil Society in Romania", in Lester M. Salamon and Hemut K. Anheier (eds) *Working Papers of the Johns Hopkins Comparative Nonprofit Sector Project*, Baltimore: The Johns Hopkins Institute for Policy Studies.

Catalogul Asociaţiilor şi Fundaţiilor, Editura FDSC, 1999.

Dakova, V. (coord.), Dreossi, B., Hyatt, J., and Socolovschi, A. (2000) *O prezentare a sectorului neguvernamental din România*, Editura FDSC, Bucureşti.

Huntington, Samuel P. (1991) *The Third Wave: Democratization in the Late Twentieth Century*, Oklahoma: University of Oklahoma Press.

Powell, Walter W. (ed.) (1987) *The Nonprofit Sector: A Research Handbook*, New Haven: Yale University Press.

Salamon, Lester M. and Helmut K. Anheier (1992) *In Search of the Nonprofit Sector II: The Problem of Classification. Voluntas. International Journal of Voluntary and Non-profit Organizations*, Vol. 3, No. 30.

Salamon, Lester M. and Helmut K. Anheier, eds (1996) *Defining the Nonprofit Sector: A Cross-national Analysis*, Manchester: Manchester University Press.

Şăulean, Daniel and Epure, Carmen (1998) "Defining the Nonprofit Sector: Romania", in Lester M. Salamon and Helmut K. Anheier (eds) *Working Papers Of The Johns Hopkins Comparative Nonprofit Sector Project*, Baltimore: The Johns Hopkins Institute for Policy Studies.

Stefan, Laura and Georgescu, Ion (2003) *Transparenta decizionala in administratia publica – ghid pentru cetateni si administratie*, Bucuresti: Transparency International.

Strategia de dezvoltare a societăţii civile 2003–2007, Guvernul României.

Vameşu, A. and Constantinescu, L. (coordinators) (1994) *Nongovernmental Organizations Directory Romania*, Bucharest: Soros Foundation for an Open Society.

Zakaria, Fareed (1997) "The Rise of Illiberal Democracy", Foreign Affairs, Nov./Dec. Vol. 76, No. 6, pp. 22–43.

Laws

Constituţia României din 1991.
Constituţia României din 1993.
Ordonanţa 26/2000 – legea Asociaţiilor şi Fundaţiilor.
Ordonanţa 37/2003 – privind modificarea ordonanţei 26/200 – Legea Asociaţiilor şi Fundaţiilor.
Legea 21/1924.
Legea 246/2005.

Part III

The third sector and public policy

5 Welfare architecture and voluntarism

Or why 'changing the welfare mix' means different things in different contexts

Lars Skov Henriksen, Thomas P. Boje, Bjarne Ibsen and Inger Koch-Nielsen

Introduction

Historically, voluntary associations and popular movements have played an important role in the making of the Scandinavian democracies and welfare states (Klausen and Selle 1996). Within the welfare fields, a remarkable upsurge of interest in these institutions has been observable since the early 1980s in many European welfare states. Growing scepticism and criticism of state and professional monopoly in the welfare fields, together with mounting concerns over 'new' social problems like social exclusion, have paved the way for more 'ideological space' for voluntary organizations. A strong political consensus that ageing populations and globalization set limits to taxation (Goul Andersen 2006) has also been central to the argument that alternative partners will be needed in social policy in future. Even in social-democratic welfare states like the Scandinavian, strong public and political trust in the voluntary or non-profit sector as a partner in a 'new welfare mix' has been voiced over the last 15–20 years. In Denmark this has been evident in symbolic political expressions such as a 'charter for the mutual cooperation between associations and government' in 2001, as well as in changes in various laws and legal frameworks, e.g. the 'Social Services Act' of 1998, in which it was made compulsory for local government to cooperate with voluntary social organizations.

However, such efforts to promote civic engagement and voluntary organized provision of help and services are seldom followed by close empirical research into the actual problem-solving capacity of the voluntary sector. Too often it is merely taken for granted that it is possible to rely more on volunteers and their organizations, and too often it is simply assumed that the voluntary sector, by virtue of its alleged independence and autonomy, is able to perform critical functions. The aim of this chapter is twofold: first, to carefully describe and evaluate the capacity of the Danish voluntary sector by measuring its absolute and relative size and importance within different sub-sectors of society. And second, to characterize the function and role of the voluntary sector in Denmark by analysing, among other things, its financial relations with the government. We do so by summarizing the information available on three interdependent dimensions, which are too often treated separately:

1   the individual level of volunteering;
2   the organizational level of voluntary organizations and associations, and;
3   economic and labour market indicators of the size and impact of the voluntary sector.

We think an empirically based close investigation of the actual size, composition and operation of the voluntary sector is necessary, because the more general and popular 'civil society talk' leaves too little room for taking into consideration the specific 'division of labour' between state, market and voluntary sectors that characterize different welfare systems; a fact that, as we will demonstrate, is highly consequential for not only the capacity but also for the role played by the voluntary sector. In this chapter we will refer to data covering voluntary work and voluntary organizations in a wide array of sub-fields, but our main focus will be on the welfare fields (social services, health, and education) where policy attention has been most intense recently. All data derive from the Danish part of the Johns Hopkins Comparative Non-profit Sector Project carried out from 2004 to 2006.

Concepts and definitions

In this chapter we use the terms 'volunteering', 'voluntary organization' and 'voluntary sector'. At the most general level, *volunteering* can be defined as 'the contribution of services, goods, or money to help accomplish some desired end, without substantial coercion or direct remuneration' (Smith 1981: 33). Most definitions stress that volunteer work is non-obligatory, unpaid, and takes place in an organized context; often in an association but this need not be the case. Often volunteer work is treated as a leisure activity which mostly benefits the participants themselves. But the fact that volunteer work is undertaken freely, uncommodified and unpaid does not make it unproductive (Wilson and Musick 1997: 694). Plenty of work done by volunteers would have to be paid for, if not provided by volunteers. This is true of activities such as coaching the local soccer team, visiting old people, auditing the accounts of the local girl scout association, advocating human rights, conducting the church choir or raising funds for the local chapter of the Red Cross. In all of these instances, volunteers are producing collective goods which can be consumed by either fellow members or people in general (Wilson 2000: 216). In this chapter, we will concentrate on formal volunteering, leaving aside more informal voluntary activities such as helping friends and neighbours.

The *voluntary sector* consists of a host of *organizations* which, according to the widely accepted 'structural/operational definition' of the non-profit sector, share the following characteristics, in that they are:

Organized, i.e., they have some structure and regularity to their operations, whether or not they are formally constituted or legally registered. [...] *Private*, i.e., they are not part of the apparatus of the state, even though they may receive support from governmental sources. [...] *Not profit-distribution*, i.e., they are not primarily commercial in purpose and do not distribute profits to a set of directors, stockholders, or managers. [...] *Self-governing*, i.e. they have their own mechanisms for internal governance. [...] *Voluntary*, i.e., membership or participation in them is not legally required or otherwise compulsory.

(Salamon *et al.* 2004: 9, 10)

In a Danish context, this definition includes three different forms of organization in particular: the traditional voluntary association, the so-called independent or self-governing institution, and the charitable foundation (Ibsen and Habermann 2006). Space limitations do not allow a detailed discussion of the many problems regarding inclusion and exclusion of particular organizations; suffice to say that the 'empirical reality' of the voluntary sector cannot be constructed in any final and unambiguous way. Mapping the scope and size of the voluntary sector, therefore, depends on how 'strictly' the above criteria are applied to cases falling into the 'grey zone'. In the Danish Johns Hopkins study, rather strict application procedures have been pursued (for a detailed discussion, see Ibsen and Habermann 2006).

Included in the Danish voluntary sector is a set of diverse organizations in a wide range of fields. At a more general level, we can distinguish between:

1   activity-oriented voluntary organizations within the fields of sports, culture and recreation;
2   welfare-oriented organizations within the fields of social services, health and education, and;
3   societal-oriented organizations[1] such as political parties, trade unions, international, environmental and community organizations.

These organizations perform a variety of functions and roles. Some supply human *services*, while others play an *advocacy* role, identifying problems and bringing them to public attention. Others are vehicles of cultural *expression and activities* in arts, music or sports, while still others *build communities* (Salamon *et al.* 2004: 23). Organizations may perform several of these functions at the same time.

Data

As mentioned, our data are derived from the Danish part of the Johns Hopkins Comparative Non-profit Sector Project. *Individual level data* is based on a random sample of 4,200 persons aged 16–85, drawn from the Central Population Register. Interviews were conducted as telephone interviews, and the response rate was 75 per cent. The pre-coded questionnaire applied was constructed in accordance with the Johns Hopkins manual.[2] A comparison of the characteristics of the 3,134 persons in the final database with the characteristics of the Danish adult population in general suggests that the sample is representative as regards gender, age, and geographical dispersion. However, respondents with non-ethnic Danish backgrounds from non-western countries are under-represented in the study. In the survey respondents were probed about formal volunteering within 14 different fields (culture, sports, hobby, education, health, social services, the environment, housing and community, trade unions and work organizations, advice and legal assistance, political parties, international organizations, religion, and other). Respondents were asked if they volunteered within each field; if the reply was affirmative, they were asked about the number of hours volunteered, the type of volunteer work done, and whether they were members of the organization or association for which they volunteered. It should be noted that in some cases volunteering took place in an organization which is not voluntary – for instance a public school or kindergarten.

Organizational level data are based on a comprehensive mapping of all *local and regional* organizations, associations and foundations found in one representative region in Denmark (the island of Funen). A total of 5,764 local and regional associations were registered together with 600 self-governing institutions and 582 foundations. 4,047 of the local and regional associations were sent a questionnaire asking about members, activities, financing, cooperation with the government etc. The response rate was 49 per cent (Ibsen 2006). A questionnaire was sent to all local and regional self-governing institutions and foundations as well (response rate 44 per cent and 41 per cent respectively). Similarly, 2,992 *national* organizations were mapped and sent a questionnaire. Whereas identification of local and regional organizations can be assumed to be close to total, this ambition proved far more difficult to achieve at the national level. There are several reasons for that: an official register or directory of national organizations does not exist, and it is often quite difficult to distinguish a national organization from a local or a regional organization. The questionnaire for the national organizations was sent to 1,661 registered organizations, of which 39 per cent responded.

The *economic and labour market impact of the voluntary sector* is estimated based on figures from the population survey of individuals, and on information and data from the Danish National Account database. A special survey was carried out by Statistics Denmark in spring 2004, interviewing a sample of 670 non-profit institutions out of a total population of about 37,000 non-profit institutions registered in the Danish National Account. From this survey, we have information on the value added by the non-profit institutions, capital assets held by the sector, economic transfers to the voluntary sector from the welfare state, donations and membership fees, and the number of individuals gainfully employed in the voluntary sector. Several of these data have been complemented with data from the population survey in order to produce estimates of the amount of work – paid and unpaid – carried out in the voluntary sector, and the economic resources available for activities to be carried out by the voluntary sector (see Boje 2006 for more detailed information).

Findings

Below we report on our findings for the individual level data, organizational level data, and economic and labour market data.

Formal volunteering

According to our findings, about 35 per cent of the Danish adult population reported having done some form of organized voluntary work within the last year. This finding is roughly equivalent to findings obtained in the Danish part of the European Values Study from 1999, in which 37 per cent reported having carried out volunteer work (Koch-Nielsen and Clausen 2002, 2004), and to the Danish study on cultural and leisure activities from 1998, where 34 per cent reported having spent time volunteering (Fridberg 2000). Combined with the fact that our survey is based on a large random sample, these findings suggest that our data are robust.

Comparing rates of volunteering across countries presents researchers with numerous methodological problems. Evidence is mixed and contested, and some times enormous differences are found for the same country from one study to another. Some of the differences are caused by definitional variation while others are due to methodological problems; it is especially important to note the exact wording of the questions, and whether respondents were prompted or not (Rooney *et al.* 2004; Toppe 2005). We do not intend to go into detail with this topic; but compared with our neighbouring countries, Norway and Sweden, it seems that they consistently report somewhat higher rates of volunteering than Denmark. Depending on the particular study in question, volunteering rates go up to, or even above, 50 per cent in Norway and Sweden (Wollebæk *et al.*, 2000; Sivesind 2005; Hodgkinson 2003). These figures are probably among the highest in Europe. However, compared with other European countries, Denmark is not doing badly at all. Several studies have found Danish volunteering rates to be on the same level as the UK and the Netherlands, and there is reasonable evidence suggesting that volunteering is more widespread in Denmark than in Germany, Belgium, Ireland and other European countries as well (Gaskin and Smith 1995; Hodgkinson 2003; Salamon *et al.* 2004; Dekker and van den Broek 2005).

An important aspect to bear in mind in the case of Denmark (and probably more important than these hazardous cross-country comparisons) is that formal volunteering seems to have been on the increase since the early 1990s. At that time, two separate studies, from 1990 and 1993 respectively, found that only about 25 per cent of the Danish population was volunteering (Gundelach and Riis 1992; Anker and Koch-Nielsen 1995).

Volunteering also accounts for a significant number of work hours. If we

Table 5.1 Percentage of Danish population reporting volunteering last year by field of activity. (Men, women, and all, 2004)

Fields	Men	Women	All
Leisure: culture, sports, recreation and hobby	21	15	18
Housing and local community	8	4	6
Social services and health, including advice	4	7	6
Politics: Vocational, political parties, and international	6	4	5
Teaching and education	3	4	3
Other: the environment, religion, and other	5	5	5
Total	38	32	35
N	1,502	1,632	3,134

Source: Koch-Nielsen *et al.* (2005).

limit our focus to the 25 per cent in the data set reporting to have volunteered within the last month,[3] they worked on average 17 hours a month. That is equivalent to 4.5 weeks of full-time work a year, worked by about 25 per cent of the adult population. This is a substantial contribution, which would amount to a considerable payroll, were these activities and services to be provided by the state or the market. Of course, it must be remembered that the mean masks great variations between individuals.

Overall rates of formal volunteering and hours volunteered, though, may not be the most important indicator of civic engagement. More important may be the distribution of volunteers within fields of activity. While the aggregate data give us some broad idea about the level of volunteering and voluntary work, it does not tell us anything about where we find the volunteers.

Our findings follow a general pattern which is also found in the other Scandinavian countries (Helander and Sivesind 2001): most volunteers are found within sports, culture, recreation and hobby, where 18 per cent of the population reported volunteering; 6 per cent reported volunteering within housing and local community; 6 per cent within social work or health; 5 per cent within some form of political organization (including international organizations), and 3 per cent within teaching and education. Very small numbers were found in the fields of religion and the environment. There are some statistically significant gender differences. Men tend to be over-represented compared to women within the leisure field and housing and the community, whereas we find the opposite pattern within social services and health.

Organizational ecology

Our individual level data findings are complemented by findings from the mapping of *local and regional and national organizations*. Table 5.2 below on the distribution of local and regional associations, where we find the majority of the volunteers, seems to mirror the patterns of individual volunteering. Our data seem to support the idea that the population ecology of voluntary organizations

Table 5.2 Distribution of Danish local and regional voluntary associations, 'self-governing institutions', and national voluntary organizations by field of activity. (2004, percentage)

	Local and regional associations		Local and regional non-profit institutions ('self governing institutions')*		National associations and organizations	
	N	%	N	%	N	%
Leisure: culture, sports, recreation and hobby	3,007	52.2	138	23.2	859	28.7
Education and research	274	4.8	123	20.6	64	2.1
Social services and health	499	8.7	197	33	395	13.2
Local community and housing	619	10.7	126	21.1	18	0.6
Political parties, legal advice and international organizations	497	8.7	5	0.8	225	7.5
Work organizations: unions, business and professional	682	11.8	–	–	1,245	41.6
Other: religious, the environment and other	185	3.2	7	1.8	186	6.2
Total	5,763	100	596	100	2,992	100

Source: Ibsen (2006).

Notes

* For reasons of conceptual clarity, 'foundations' have been excluded from the category of non-profit institutions.

makes a difference to the opportunity structure of volunteering. That is, the particular institutional setting in which the individual volunteer finds himself is important, as some forms of voluntary action are enabled while others are constrained.

More than half (52 per cent) of all *local and regional* voluntary associations are found within the fields of sports, hobbies, and arts and culture. Other important fields are housing and local community (11 per cent), professional work organizations, business organizations and trade unions (12 per cent), and social services and health organizations (9 per cent). Political organizations (together with legal advice and international organizations) constitute 9 per cent, whereas organizations for education and research hold about 5 per cent. Environmental protection and religious organizations represent very small numbers.

What further characterizes the population of local and regional voluntary organizations in Denmark is the fact that the bulk of them are membership-based associations. More than 80 per cent of all local organizations were classified as membership-based associations (Ibsen 2006). This is also reflected in the individual level data on formal volunteering, where 79 per cent of all volunteers said their volunteer work was carried out for an organization or association of which they were also a member. The organizational reliance on volunteers is further reflected in the fact that 80 per cent of the local and regional organizations had no paid staff on their payroll (Ibsen 2006). Based on the organizational data, it is estimated that the total number of voluntary organizations in Denmark is about 70,000–100,000 – or about one association for every 80–100 citizens. Many of these organizations are quite small: only 20 per cent had more than 250 members and 60 per cent had less than 100 (Ibsen 2006).

The distribution of organizations on the *national level* is somewhat different from the local level. The most important relative differences are found within the fields of leisure, and community and housing organizations, which are all mainly found on the local level. The share of health and social services organizations is higher at the national level, which is mainly due to the fact that Denmark has a large number of quite small membership-based interest organizations working for a variety of different types of illnesses and handicaps. Work organizations such as trade unions, business organizations and associations for professionals are also mainly national.

The *self-governing non-profit institutions* have a strong position within social services and education and research. Within social services there is a long-established tradition, dating back to the Christian philanthropy of the latter part of the nineteenth century, for public-private partnerships. Historically, self-governing non-profit institutions have played an important role as complementary and alternative service providers within child welfare, eldercare, and in relation to marginalized groups (juvenile homes, rehabilitation centres for abusers, homeless shelters, refugee centres, etc.) (Henriksen and Bundesen 2004). Within education and research, the private and so-called 'free schools', 'free boarding schools' and the 'folk high schools', dating back to the famous social movement of farmers and smallholders also in the latter part of the nineteenth century,[4] have played an important role in primary and continuing education. Within these two sub-fields, we see strong social movements which have over time built non-profit institutions that continue to shape Danish society. These institutions are important welfare providers and important components in the Danish welfare architecture, although their role as an alternative institutional device might not be that pronounced anymore: today most self-governing non-profit institutions have become part and parcel of the societal fabric and few would consider themselves in opposition to society. They rely heavily on public funding, and many of them are essentially contract partners functioning as vehicles for implementation of public policies.

The Danish voluntary-sector economy and labour market: size and importance

A final aspect of describing the importance of the voluntary sector in Denmark involves estimating its size and economic impact, and the composition of its voluntary workforce; i.e. paid as well as unpaid work activities carried out in the sector. We start with an estimate of the work carried out in the voluntary sector. We distinguish between paid work performed in the voluntary sector and unpaid work carried out in non-profit and voluntary organizations (formal volunteering). In Table 5.3 the size of the two types of work is estimated.

For comparative reasons, we calculated the estimates in full-time equivalents (FTE) for both types of work. The total number of individuals doing unpaid work in the voluntary sector is close to 1.5 million but, as we have seen, most of these individuals only work a couple of hours per week. Therefore, in order to compare the figure for unpaid work and the amount of paid work, we have to estimate the full-time equivalents for both. As can be seen in Table 5.3, unpaid work done by volunteers in Denmark is equivalent to 110,041 full-time workers or 3.0 per cent of the active Danish working population in 2004. This is only slightly less than the paid work carried out in the voluntary sector, which is calculated to 140,620 full-time workers or 3.8 per cent of the active Danish working population.

Table 5.3 Size of the Danish voluntary sector, measured by the workforce. (Paid and unpaid work, 2004)

	Total workforce in the Danish voluntary sector (FTE)*	*Share of active working population – aged 16–66 (3,677 million persons) (%)*
Paid work in the voluntary sector	140,620	3.8
Unpaid work in the voluntary sector	110,041	3.0

Sources: calculated from the Danish Johns Hopkins Population Survey, 2004, and the Danish National Account survey of non-profit institutions, 2004.

Notes
* Full-time equivalent (FTE) is defined as 1,650 hours per year.

As touched upon earlier, the level of formal volunteering is lower in Denmark than in Norway and Sweden. However, the Danish voluntary sector is characterized by a higher level of paid work than our Scandinavian neighbours – as can be seen in Table 5.4. The main explanation for this higher level of paid work in the Danish voluntary sector is the relatively large number of self-governing non-profit institutions within education and social services described above. By definition, they are part of the voluntary sector, despite the fact that they are strongly regulated by the state and financially dependent on public finance.

Looking outside Scandinavia, we find that the economic impact of the voluntary sector in Denmark is lower than in the Netherlands and the UK. In the Netherlands, the voluntary sector has a significant economic impact, measured by the sector's total expenditure as a share of the Gross Domestic Product (GDP) and also by the proportion of paid work in the sector. Denmark is closer to the UK in terms of the voluntary sector's share of GDP, whereas the proportion of paid work is considerably lower in Denmark. The differences are most likely due to the importance of voluntary and non-profit organizations as service providers in the UK and the Netherlands. Though the proportion of the population in Denmark doing voluntary work is approximately at the same level as in the Netherlands and the UK, volunteers apparently work more hours in these two countries, which would explain why they seem to be adding more value. However, caution is called for here, as methodological variations – rather than empirical – might account for these differences.

Differentiating between sub-sectors of the Danish voluntary sector, we find huge differences in both the amount of paid work and voluntary work. In Table 5.5 we have calculated the number of paid employees and volunteers within 11 different sub-sectors of the Danish voluntary sector.

When analysing the voluntary sector's contribution to welfare provision, it is important to note that the largest share of paid employment is found within two welfare fields: education and research, and social services. Approximately 36 per cent of total paid work within the voluntary sector is found in education and research, and 28 per cent in social services. Together, these two non-profit sub-sectors account for about two-thirds of total employment in the voluntary sector. They are also the most formalized and professionalized, measured by the share of paid work in relation to the total workforce in each of the two fields (as shown in the right column of Table 5.5). This is also what we would expect, given the role played by self-governing non-profit institutions in these fields. By comparison, the field of health has a very low share of paid work in the sector, only about 2 per cent, and hence also a lower degree of professionalization.

However, when we look at the distribution of unpaid voluntary work, the picture is completely different. Close to half of the voluntary work calculated in full-time equivalents is carried out in the sector for sports, cultural and recreational activities, while voluntary work in education and social services only

Table 5.4 Economic impact of the voluntary sector and the size of the workforce (paid and unpaid) in Denmark (2004) and selected European countries

	Denmark	Norway	Sweden	United Kingdom	The Netherlands
Total expenditure in the voluntary sector in per cent of total GDP	6.6	3.7	4.1	6.8	15.5
Paid work in the voluntary sector in per cent of total active population	3.8	3.0	2.6	6.2	9.3
Unpaid work in the voluntary sector in per cent of total active population	3.0	5.1	7.4	4.4	5.8
Proportion of the population volunteering. Per cent	35	59	51	30	32

Sources: Salamon *et al.* (2004) and Johns Hopkins University (2004) *Global Civil Society At-a-Glance*. Sivesind: data for Norway, 2004; Svedberg and Grassmann: Data for Sweden, 2002; Dekker: data for the Netherlands, 2001.

Table 5.5 Number of paid employees and volunteers (full-time equivalents, FTE*) in the voluntary sector in Denmark by sub-sectors. Paid work as a share of total workforce. (2004, percentage)

	Number of paid employees in the voluntary sector (FTE)	Number of volunteers in the voluntary sector (FTE)	Paid work as a share of total workforce in each sub-sector (%)
1 Education and research	50,909	4,999	91.1
2 Social services	39,748	8,342	82.7
3 Work and professional organisations	20,370	6,890	74.7
4 Housing and community	9,743	6,446	60.2
5 Health	2,616	3,667	41.6
6 Other	2,820	7,810	26.5
7 Politics, legal advice, advocacy	1,839	5,851	23.9
8 International	1,274	4,205	23.3
9 Sports, culture and recreation	9,675	53,968	15.2
10 The environment	213	1,396	13.2
11 Religion	944	6,489	12.7
Total	140,620	110,041	56.1

Source: figures calculated from the Danish Johns Hopkins Population Survey, 2004, and the Danish National Account survey of non-profit institutions, 2004.

Notes

* Full-time equivalent is counted as 1,650 hours per year.

represents 5 per cent and 8 per cent of the total amount of voluntary work respectively. Welfare services are thus an important source of employment in the voluntary sector. Within education and research, the 'free schools', the 'free boarding schools' and the 'folk high schools' are the main agencies, and within social services it is kindergartens, nursing homes, juvenile homes, homeless shelters and rehabilitation centres for alcohol and drug addicts. These non-profit institutions are important welfare providers, and it seems there is some institutional capacity for problem solution here. Compared to Norway and Sweden, it also seems that there is more scope for these non-public providers of welfare in the Danish welfare system. Still, in general, the Danish voluntary sector's contribution is relatively small compared to the public-sector welfare provision. Only in a few cases does voluntary organized service provision account for a considerable part of the services provided. On the other hand, the universalistic welfare path followed by Denmark does not exclude a mix of public, voluntary and non-profit providers.

Another very important feature to consider when characterizing the voluntary and non-profit sector is its *financial composition*. As regards the *local* organizational society, financial autonomy must be said to be the main characteristic. On average, about 50 per cent of all financial resources of the local and regional associations derives from membership fees. Adding to this another 25 per cent derived from associational activities and arrangements, a total of 75 per cent of all revenue is generated from fees and charges. The remaining 25 per cent consists mainly, but not exclusively, of public-sector support (Boje and Ibsen 2006: 60, 61). In the social services field, public subsidies to local and regional associations amount to 36 per cent, whereas the corresponding figure in the field of health is 27 per cent.

However, when taking the *self-governing non-profit institutions* into account, the picture changes. Now, almost 44 per cent of total income in the voluntary and non-profit sector comes from government sources (Boje and Ibsen 2006: 215). This is close to the average of 48 per cent that Salamon, Sokolowski and Associates (2004: 33) find for developed countries, which would actually put Denmark in the group of 'government-dominant' countries, together with e.g. the UK (47 per cent), France (58 per cent), the Netherlands (59 per cent), and Germany (64 per cent). Denmark seems to hold a middle position between the fee-dominant Scandinavian countries, Norway and Sweden, where 35 per cent and 29 per cent of total revenue respectively come from government sources, and some of the continental and liberal European welfare states.

However, it is important to note that the Danish voluntary and non-profit sector is split into a large majority of locally based membership associations with a low degree of public support, and a relatively small number of self-governing non-profit institutions, which are important both in terms of service provision and economic impact, within the welfare fields; especially social services and education (but not health).

Basic structures

We would like to conclude the descriptive part of the chapter with some remarks on the connection between the type of welfare regime and the type of organizational society. Adequate empirical evidence seems to suggest that the Scandinavian organizational societies form a particular sub-group (Sivesind and Selle 2005). However, to some extent Denmark differs from Norway and Sweden, in spite of the similarities in basic structures and division of labour between government and voluntary sector. Based on our results from the Danish Johns Hopkins study, we would like to point out the following distinctive characteristics of the Danish voluntary sector:

1   Based on the quantitative indicators of formal volunteering in our study, it is difficult to find support for the often-held pessimistic view that we are witnessing a decrease in people's support for and involvement in associational life and social networks in Denmark, and more generally in Scandinavia. On the contrary, our data seem to confirm prior studies finding a strong mobilization of volunteers and civic engagement in the Scandinavian countries (Lundström and Wijkström 1997; Wollebæk *et al.* 2000; Oorshoot and Arts 2005) – although Denmark in this respect is lagging somewhat behind both Norway and Sweden. In all the Scandinavian countries, volunteering and voluntary work seem to unfold on the foundations of a large public sector which takes the main responsibility for social assistance and investment in culture and leisure facilities. There is no evidence that the generous welfare states of these countries have crowded out people's engagement in civil society organizations. Individual volunteering is, however, predominantly directed towards sports and recreational activities, where local voluntary associations are the prime vehicles for expressing a variety of sentiments and impulses. In all the Scandinavian countries, it is within these fields that we find close to half of all volunteers and voluntary organizations.

2   To a very large extent, the political debate about changing the welfare mix and more prominent roles for voluntary organizations and volunteers is driven by the perception that these phenomena should be considered part of a 'cluster of helping behaviors' (Wilson 2000: 215) and an essential part of what has been called 'the culture of benevolence' (Wilson and Musick 1997: 697). But the very notion of volunteering as synonymous with 'helping and caring' might be misleading in a context like the Scandinavian one. Here volunteering is much more about facilitating leisure activities and organizing political interests (in the widest meaning of the term) than about taking care of the needy. Because of the strong tradition for public provision of welfare services, volunteering is only to a very limited extent inclined towards helping and caring in the Scandinavian countries. Even though there is room in the welfare fields – and more so in Denmark than in Norway and Sweden – for service provision by non-profit institutions, the

welfare field is relatively small, and many social services and health organizations have an essentially representational role, advocating the interests of particular groups such as the elderly, the mentally ill, the handicapped etc. In fact, it is among the specialized interest groups that we find the most rapid growth in the present organizational society – close to half of all present organizations within the field of health have, for example, been established after 1990 (Boje and Ibsen 2006).

3   Volunteering mainly takes place within membership-based local and regional organizations. This underlines the importance of the 'associational foundation' of the Scandinavian organizational societies. However, the bulk of these organizations have a limited membership base and they depend to a very large extent on volunteers. With the exception of the self-governing institutions within social services and education, we are far from the 'professional non-profit service institutions' much more prevalent in continental and liberal welfare societies. The Scandinavian countries have a comparatively small share of what David Horton Smith (1997: 120) has called 'formal program volunteering' (as opposed to 'associational volunteering'): i.e. non-profit organizations providing services such as hospital care, higher education, cultural entertainment etc. In such institutional arrangements, volunteers play only a supplementary role to the predominantly paid staff.

Discussion

In the debate about future welfare arrangements, it is often claimed that actors other than state and local governments will have to play a more active part. A typical argument is that changes in the division of labour are necessary in order to 'cut costs and enable states to concentrate on core activities' (Kangas and Palme 2005: 5).

This is a compelling argument, and the ideological space thus opening for actors other than the core governmental ones in providing welfare has indeed paved the way for voluntary and non-profit institutions across most Western countries. In general, however, 'third way' rhetoric does not leave much scope for taking into consideration the specific institutional arrangements characterizing different welfare states; a fact that is highly consequential for not only the capacity but also for the role played by voluntary and non-profit institutions in different settings.

As outlined above, the voluntary sector in the Scandinavian countries has a size and composition which to some extent matches the social-democratic welfare regime of these countries (Helander and Sivesind 2001; Sivesind *et al.* 2002; Sivesind and Selle 2005). Measured by employment, the voluntary sector is relatively small compared to other European countries; but measured by the number of volunteers and the amount of volunteering the sector is relatively large. When it comes to the core areas of welfare provision (social services, health, education), however, the contribution of volunteers is relatively small. In Denmark only 6 per cent of the population volunteers within the fields of health and social services, and only 3 per cent within the field of teaching and education. Yet, there seems to be some capacity for welfare provision within the fields of teaching and social services, where we find the majority of the sector's employees. Whether these non-profit services are in fact a distinct alternative to those provided by the government is open to question. There is no doubt, however, that the 'free schools', 'free boarding schools' and 'folk high schools' are important, not only as supplementary providers of basic and continuing education, but also to some extent as institutionalized spaces in Danish society where 'deliberative democratic processes' are being practised and learned. Similarly, it is a fact that the voluntary social services organizations and non-profit institutions can and do deliver important social services, especially to those in greatest need, and that they often address inequalities and unmet needs in Danish society which would not otherwise be raised.

Having said that, the fact remains that by far the largest share of volunteers, associations and voluntary activities in Denmark are found within the recreational areas of sports, leisure and culture. Adding to this picture is also the fact that most voluntary organizations are relatively small and autonomous membership-based associations strongly dependent on volunteers. Ironically, in many ways these structural characteristics are in accordance with the ideal-type understanding of civil society as, in the words of Michael Walzer (1991: 293), 'the space of uncoerced human association'. The institutional arrangement of the Scandinavian countries has neither led to a crowding-out of civic engagement nor a decline in social capital – rather, the contrary seems to be true. But the hard fact still remains that the voluntary sector in Denmark, like the Scandinavian countries in general, seems to lack both the volunteers and the institutional capacity to generate the resources needed to become a significant actor in the welfare fields. Apart from a few exceptions, the universalistic path followed by these countries has led to a voluntary sector with a comparatively weak problem-solving capacity within the welfare fields.

What we have seen during the past 20–25 years is first and foremost a change taking place at the level of discourse. By and large, the basic structures of the Danish voluntary sector have remained unchanged. A relevant question therefore seems to be to what extent a new welfare mix relying more on voluntary organized provision of welfare is realistic. To what extent this will change in the future is difficult to predict. At present, it seems questionable whether voluntary organizations and non-profit institutions within the welfare fields will be able to compete with the much more professionalized public and for-profit providers in the new contract culture. Thus the discourse on 'civil society' may have the paradoxical consequence that in future we will see more for-profit provision of welfare, because many non-profit welfare providers are less well-equipped to compete for funds (Selle 2001). Trends in that direction have been emerging in the US, where increased competition has resulted in an almost quadrupling of for-profit employment within social services over a 20-year period from 1979 to 1997. Non-profit employment also increased over that period, but the relative growth was slower (Smith 2002: 157).

Notes

1 It might be considered to divide this third category into two sub-categories:

    1 political or ideological organizations or movements such as political parties, religious organizations, human rights and environmental movements, and;

    2 interest organizations working to improve the conditions of their own members, such as trade unions, business organizations, homeowners' organizations, etc.

2 The Johns Hopkins Comparative Non-profit Sector Project: Key Population Survey Module on Giving and Volunteering.

3 Instead of 'within the last year'. We use this measure here because we expect to get a more reliable picture in this way.

4 Consisting mainly of village halls ('forsamlingshuse'); the many self-governing institutions within the sub-field of local community and housing belong to the same peasants' social movement tradition.

References

Anker, J. and Koch-Nielsen, I. (1995) *Det Frivillige Arbejde*, København: Socialforskningsinstituttet. Rapport 95: 3.

Boje, T. P. (2006) Metode for den Samfundsøkonomiske og Beskæftigelsesmæssige Analyse, in T. P. Boje and B. Ibsen *Frivillighed og Nonprofit i Danmark – Omfang, Organisation, Økonomi og Beskæftigelse*, København: Socialforskningsinstituttet. Rapport 06: 18.

Boje, T. P. and Ibsen, B. (2006) *Frivillighed og Nonprofit i Danmark – Omfang, Organisation, Økonomi og Beskæftigelse*, København: Socialforskningsinstituttet. Rapport 06: 18.

Dekker, P. and van den Broek, A. (2005) Involvement in Voluntary Associations in North America and Western Europe. *Journal of Civil Society*, 1(1) pp. 45–59.

Fridberg, T. (2000) *Kultur – og Fritidsvaner 1975–1998*, København: Socialforskningsinstituttet.

Gaskin, K, and Smith, J. D. (1995) *A New Civic Europe – A Study of the Extent and Role of Volunteering*, London: The Volunteer Centre.

Goul Andersen, J. (2006) Deconstructing Welfare State Change. Paper presented at CCWS International Conference 'Welfare State Change, Conceptualisation, Measurement and Interpretation', St. Restrup Herregaard, DK, January 13–15.

Gundelach, P. and Riis, O. (1992) *Danskernes Værdier*, København: Forlaget Sociologi.

Helander, V. and Sivesind, K. H. (2001) *Frivilligsektorns Betydelse i Norden*, in L. S. Henriksen and B. Ibsen (eds) *Frivillighedens Udfordringer*. Gylling: Odense Universitetsforlag.

Henriksen, L. and Bundesen, P. (2004) The Moving Frontier in Denmark: Voluntary–State Relationships since 1850. *Journal of Social Policy*, 33(4) pp. 605–625.

Hodgkinson, V. A. (2003) Volunteering in a Global Perspective, in P. Dekker and L. Halman (eds) *The Values of Volunteering, Cross-Cultural Perspectices*. New York: Kluwer Academic.

Ibsen, B. (2006) Foreningerne og de Frivillige Organisationer, in T. P. Boje, T. Fridberg and B. Ibsen (eds) *Den Frivillige Sektor i Danmark – Omfang og Betydning*, København: Socialforskningsinstituttet. Rapport 06: 19.

Ibsen, B. and Habermann, U. (2006) Definition af den Frivillige Sektor i Danmark, in

T. P. Boje, T. Fridberg, and B. Ibsen (eds) *Den Frivillige Sektor i Danmark – Omfang og Betydning*. København: Socialforskningsinstituttet. Rapport 06: 19.

Kangas, O. and Palme, J. (2005) *Social Policy and Economic Development in the Nordic Countries*, London: Palgrave Macmillan.

Klausen, K. K. and Selle, P. (1996) The Third Sector in Scandinavia, *Voluntas*, 7(2) pp. 99–122.

Koch-Nielsen, I., Henriksen, L. S., Fridberg, T., and Rosdahl, D. (2005) *Frivilligt Arbejde. Den Frivillige Indsats i Danmark*, København: Socialforskningsinstituttet. Rapport 05:20.

Koch-Nielsen, I. and Clausen, J. D. (2002) Værdierne i det Frivillige Arbejde, in P. Gundelach (ed.) *Danskernes Værdier 1981–1999*, København: Hans Reitzels Forlag.

Koch-Nielsen, I. and Clausen, J. D. (2004) Frivilligt Arbejde, in P. Gundelach (ed.) *Danskernes Særpræg*, København: Hans Reitzels Forlag.

Lundström, T. and Wijkström, F. (1997) *The Nonprofit Sector in Sweden*, Manchester: Manchester University Press.

Oorshoot, W. v. and Arts, W. (2005) The Social Capital of European Welfare States: The Crowding Out Hypothesis Revisited, *Journal of European Social Policy*, 15(1) pp. 5–26.

Rooney, P., Steinberg, K., and Schervish, P. G. (2004) Methodology is Destiny: The Effect of Survey Prompts on Reported Levels of Giving and Volunteering, *Nonprofit and Voluntary Sector Quarterly*, 33 pp. 628–654.

Salamon, L. M., Sokolowski, W., and Associates (2004) *Global Civil Society: Dimensions of the Nonprofit Sector, Vol. II*, Bloomfield: Kumarian Press.

Selle, P. (2001) Privatisering som Tidsskel, in L. S. Henriksen and B. Ibsen (eds) *Frivillighedens Udfordringer*, Gylling: Odense Universitetsforlag.

Sivesind, K. H. (2005) *Seniorer Deltakelse i Frivillig Arbeid*, Oslo: Institutt for Samfunnsforskning.

Sivesind, K. H., Lorentzen, H., Selle, P., and Wollebæk, D. (2002) *The Voluntary Sector in Norway, Composition, Changes, and Causes*, Oslo: Institutt for Samfunnsforskning. Report 2002: 2.

Sivesind, K. H. and Selle, P. (2005) Is there a Social Democratic Civil Society Regime in the Welfare Field? Paper presented at the 34th annual ARNOVA conference, Washington, DC, November 17–19.

Smith, D. H. (1981) Altruism, Volunteers, and Volunteerism, *Journal of Voluntary Action Research*, 10 pp. 21–36.

Smith, D. H. (1997) The Rest of the Nonproft Sector: Grassroots Associations as the Dark Matter Ignored in Prevailing 'Flat Earth' Maps of the Sector, *Nonprofit and Voluntary Sector Quarterly*, 26(2) pp. 114–131.

Smith, S. R. (2002) Social Services, in L. M. Salamon (ed.) *The State of Nonprofit America*, Washington, DC: Brookings Institution Press.

Toppe, C. (2005) Measuring Volunteering: A Behavioral Approach. Paper presented at the 34th annual ARNOVA conference, Washington, DC, November 17–19.

Walzer, M. (1991) The Idea of Civil Society, *Dissent*, Spring pp. 293–304.

Wilson, J. (2000) Volunteering, *Annual Review of Sociology*, 26 pp. 215–40.

Wilson, J. and Musick, M. (1997) Who Cares? Toward an Integrated Theory of Volunteer Work, *American Sociological Review*, 62 pp. 694–713.

Wollebæk, D., Selle, P., and Lorentzen, H. (2000) *Frivillig Innsats, Sosial Integrasjon, Demokrati og Økonomi*, Bergen: Fagbokforlaget

6 The third sector and the social inclusion agenda

The role of social enterprises in the field of work integration

Marthe Nyssens

The increasing acknowledgement of the third sector in Europe, together with the broader interest in non-conventional entrepreneurial dynamics addressing current challenges, led to the emergence of the new concept of 'social enterprise'. Social enterprises have been defined by the EMES Network as:

> organisations with an explicit aim to benefit the community, initiated by a group of citizens and in which the material interest of capital investors is subject to limits. Social enterprises also place a high value on their autonomy and on economic risk-taking related to ongoing socio-economic activity.
>
> (Defourny and Nyssens 2006: 5)

The persistence of structural unemployment among some groups, the difficulties traditional active labour market policies face in integrating them and the need for more active integration policies have naturally raised questions as to the role that social enterprises can play in combating unemployment and fostering employment growth. Indeed, although the rate of employment varies greatly among European countries (with high rates of participation in the UK and Nordic countries and the lowest ones in Spain, Italy and Belgium), all EU countries are characterised by low rates of employment for some groups, such as women, non-European workers, older people and/or low-skilled workers.

The field of 'work integration' is emblematic of the dynamics of social enterprises and constitutes a major sphere of their activity in Europe. 'The major objective of 'work integration social enterprises' (WISEs) is to help disadvantaged unemployed people, who are at risk of permanent exclusion from the labour market. They integrate them back into work and society, in general through productive acivity' (Defourny and Nyssens 2006: 13).

In this chapter, we will first define more precisely the concept of social enterprise and its relevance for grasping some dynamics inside the third sector. Then, we will analyse the dynamic of institutionalisation of work integration social enterprises in the landscape of public policies and explore how this process influences the identity of these social enterprises. Finally, we will explore the extent to which the hybrid nature of the logics mobilised by social enterprises constitutes a channel to fulfil their multiple-goal mission.

The concept of social enterprise

Whereas a dozen years ago the concept of social enterprise was rarely discussed, it is now making amazing breakthroughs on both sides of the Atlantic (Defourny and Nyssens 2006).

In the European public debate, the concept may have various meanings. One school of thought stresses the social entrepreneurship dynamic exemplified by firms which seek to enhance the social impact of their productive activities. In this area, the literature quite often highlights the innovative approach to tackling social needs which is taken by individuals in fostering business (Grenier 2003), mainly through non-profit organisations, but also in the for-profit sector (Nicholls 2005). In this latter case, this idea has to do, at least partially, with the 'corporate social responsibility' (CSR) debate.

Another stream only uses the concept of social enterprise for organisations belonging to the third sector and therefore builds on the specificities of the latter. According to the European tradition of the social economy (Evers and Laville 2004; Defourny 2001), the third sector brings together cooperatives, associations and mutual societies (and, with increasing frequency, foundations). The third sector is viewed here as the set of organisations whose mission is to benefit either their members or a larger collectivity rather than to generate profits for investors. In such a perspective, the social impact of social enterprises (which are generally organisations of the non-profit or cooperative type) on the community is not only a consequence or a side-effect of their economic activity, but their motivation in itself. The EMES concept of social enterprise belongs to this school.

Theoretically, the EMES concept of social enterprise can be seen as a tool for building bridges between distinct components of the third sector. On the one hand, compared to traditional associations, social enterprises place a higher value on economic risk-taking related to an ongoing productive activity (in the world of non-profit organisations, production-oriented associations are certainly closer to social enterprises than are advocacy organisations and grant-making foundations). On the other hand, in contrast to many traditional co-operatives, social enterprises may be seen as more oriented to the whole community and putting more emphasis on the dimension of general interest. Moreover, social enterprises are said to combine different types of stakeholders in their member-ship, whereas traditional co-operatives have generally been set up as single-stakeholder organisations. These contrasting elements, however, should not be overestimated: while social enterprises as we have defined them are in some cases new organisations, which may be regarded as constituting a new sub-division of the third sector, in other cases, they result from a process at work in older experiences within the third sector. In other words, it can be said that the generic term 'social enterprise' does not represent a conceptual break with institutions of the third sector but, rather, a new dynamic within it – encompassing both newly created organisations and older ones which have undergone an evolution.

Legal forms

The legal form adopted by social enterprises varies from one country to another (Nyssens and Kerlin 2006). In some cases, social enterprises adopt existing legal forms: association, cooperative, company limited by guarantee or other, country-specific forms (such as the Industrial & Provident Societies in the UK). Most social enterprises are associations or cooperatives; social enterprises are more commonly established as associations in those countries where the legal form of association allows a degree of freedom in selling goods and services on the open market, whereas in countries where associations are more limited in this regard, like in the Nordic countries, social enterprises are created, more often, under the legal form of cooperatives.

Besides these traditional legal forms, a number of national governments have created new legal forms specifically for social enterprises, with the goal of promoting their development. In 1991, Italy was the first to create a 'social cooperative' legal form, which has been successful in increasing the number of organisations of this type. The Italian law distinguishes between two types of social cooperative: on the one hand, those delivering social, health and educational services, called 'A-type' social cooperatives and, on the other hand, those providing work integration for disadvantaged people, called 'B-type' social cooperatives. Then, in 2006, an Italian law on social enterprise was enacted which opens this label to various legal forms (and not only social cooperatives) and fields of activities, provided that the organisation complies with the non-distribution constraint and involves certain categories of stakeholders, including workers and beneficiaries. Belgium introduced legislation for a 'social purpose company' in 1995, Portugal created the 'social solidarity cooperative' in 1998, and Greece the 'social cooperative with limited liability' in 1999. France introduced the 'cooperative society of collective interest' in 2002. Most recently, in 2004, the UK approved the creation of the 'community interest company' legal form. All of these legal forms define social enterprise by the social purpose of the company and the limitation imposed on the distribution of profit; all of them, except the UK model, also define a specific governance model regarding the involvement of the various stakeholders and the implementation of a democratic decision-making process within the board.

Institutionalisation of work integration social enterprises[1]

Social missions of social enterprises are various: fight against the structural unemployment of groups excluded from the labour market, provision of social services, urban regeneration, provision of environmental services, etc. As the focus of this chapter is the contribution of social enterprises to the social inclusion agenda, we will now concentrate on work integration social enterprises (WISEs), whose social mission is to help disadvantaged unemployed people, who are at risk of permanent exclusion from the labour market. WISEs integrate them back into work and society, in general through a productive activity: recycling, building and processing industry (wood, clothing, painting, carpentry, metal etc.), running of restaurants, provision of social services (childcare, elderly care, second-hand shops for needy people, etc.).

Pioneering initiatives[2]

In the European Union, the pioneering Work Integration Social Enterprises were launched in the late 1970s–early 1980s, without any specific public scheme to support their objectives. In a context of increasing unemployment and social exclusion, social actors did not find public policy schemes adequate to tackle these problems. Initiatives thus emerged as a protest against established public policies and pointed at the limits of institutional public intervention practices towards those excluded from the labour market: long-term unemployed people, low-qualified people, people with social problems etc.

Most pioneering WISEs were founded by civil society actors: social workers, associative militants, representatives of more traditional third sector organisations, sometimes in cooperation with the excluded workers themselves. Most of these initiatives were launched by persons whose main objective was to help persons excluded from the labour market, i.e. they were created in a perspective of general interest. In some countries with a tradition of cooperative entrepreneurship, some pioneering initiatives were launched by the workers themselves, relying on a self-help dynamic. Sometimes, the groups launching the WISEs were linked to public bodies and, in countries such as Germany or Denmark, the composition of the WISEs' founding groups probably reflected the fact that the third sector and the public sector were closely interwoven.

The key role of active labour market policies

The processes of institutionalisation of WISEs should be studied in the context of the boom in active labour market policies. During the 1980s, public bodies, faced with high rates of unemployment and a crisis in public finances, developed policies which aimed to integrate the unemployed into the labour market (through professional training programmes, job subsidy programmes, etc.), instead of relying only on passive labour market policies based on a system of allocation of cash benefits to the unemployed.

It seems that WISEs have increasingly represented a tool for implementing these active labour market policies – in other words, they constituted a 'conveyor belt' of active labour market policies. Indeed, they were pioneers in promoting the integration of excluded persons through a productive activity; it could even be considered that the first WISEs actually implemented active labour market policies before the latter came into institutional existence.

However, we can observe, at least at the beginning of these processes of public institutionalisation of WISEs, that some countries, such as Sweden and Denmark, which are characterised by a long tradition of social policies, used programmes other than employment programmes to sustain such pioneering initiatives; one example is the 'Social Development Programme' in Denmark. WISEs whose main target groups are disabled people were also recognised through traditional social policies.

In some countries, like the United Kingdom or Spain, where welfare spending in general is low and labour market policies in particular are underdeveloped, pioneering initiatives received little, if any, public support. This also seems to be the case, in all the countries surveyed, for initiatives that rely more on a self-help dynamic. Indeed, public bodies seem to consider that workers developing their own initiatives should be considered as carrying out 'normal business' and do not need to receive any special support, even though they are at risk in the labour market regarding their employability profile.

In some countries, WISEs are officially recognised and a specific public scheme supports their mission at the national level (this is, for example, the case in Portugal, France, Ireland and Finland) or at the regional level (for example in Belgium, Spain and Italy). This legal recognition, by public authorities, of the mission of integration through work performed by WISEs allows, in most cases, a more stable access to public subsidies, but in a very specific way. Most of the time, some temporary subsidies are granted to start the initiative and to make up for the 'temporary unemployability' of the workers. In fact, these public schemes are also considered as a tool of active labour market policies. Public bodies recognise and support the actions of WISEs – and at the same time, they also influence their objectives and target groups, as we will expand on below.

Support to WISEs through public contracts

Another way for public authorities to support the mission of WISEs is through the contracting out of the provision of goods or services. Public bodies can organise their purchases in different ways: as traditional market purchases (when the bid with the lowest price, for the level of quality required, is chosen) or as purchases motivated by social criteria. 'Socially motivated purchases' (Gardin 2006) take into account the social goals of WISEs. Below a certain threshold, these purchases can occur in a discretionary way: when they have to buy a product or service whose price does not exceed a certain amount, set by European law, public bodies (usually at the local level) may simply 'privilege' WISEs they know in order to support them and their social mission. In the case of larger purchases, when the public bodies have to issue public calls for tenders, some social dimensions can be included in the public procurement procedures, for example in the form of social clauses that take into account types of criteria other than market ones, such as the importance of integrating disadvantaged workers. These are ways – formalised or not through regulations – to support both the production and the work integration goals of WISEs.

Competing in the market with for-profit companies solely on the basis of financial criteria often appears difficult for WISEs, and some WISEs thus demand that public authorities take their social dimension into account when awarding public contracts. However, the practice of inserting social criteria in public contracts is not yet very extensive in the European Union. In this region, Italy provides the oldest case of introduction of a social dimension into public purchasing: in 1991, a law was passed which reserved certain public markets to social cooperatives. But this law had to be re-examined, following objections from the European Commission (it is at the level of European legislation that the principal debate in this matter occurs today). This kind of legislation does not exist in countries such as Ireland, Portugal, the UK or Spain; legislation is evolving in other countries (such as Belgium), which are considering introducing social clauses into public tenders. Indeed, national and regional practices in this matter are relatively diverse across the European Union.

WISEs and public policies: a typology

Different kinds of support can coexist within one country. However, the analysis of the general patterns of labour market policy expenditures allows us to construct a typology of the countries surveyed in terms of public support to WISEs.

The first group includes Denmark and Sweden and is characterised by a high level of active labour market policies and of welfare expenditure in general. In these countries, no public schemes specific to WISEs have been developed, but there is an increasing collaboration between WISEs and public bodies to implement 'activate labour market policies' (ALMP). As Stryjan (2004) stresses for Sweden, the current Swedish labour market is, to a significant extent, the product of active labour market policy. In this context, WISEs are not the result of a shortage of active labour market policies but are rather a response to the fact that such facilities either cannot reach significant portions of the population, or are ineffective for certain groups. This is quite a new phenomenon for these countries, where the third sector is traditionally viewed as having an advocacy role, not a role of service provider. This first group corresponds to the 'universalist' group of Esping-Andersen's typology – a group in which welfare has traditionally been delivered by the state (Esping-Andersen 1999). Finally, it has to be noted that even though there is no official accreditation for social enterprises in Sweden and Denmark, there is in these countries a tradition of a cooperative movement; it is thus not surprising to see that there is now a Swedish Minister of the Social Economy, rooted in this cooperative movement, and that there are linkages and lines of communication between the cooperative movement and new social enterprises.

The countries in the second group – Belgium, Germany, France and Ireland – still have relatively high levels of expenditure on active labour market policies (although these levels are lower than in the countries in the first group) and, within the field of active labour market policies, there exists a large 'second labour market programme' offering intermediate forms of employment, within the non-profit sector, between employment policies and social policies. The implementation of these active labour programmes was based on the observation that, on the one hand, a number of unsatisfied social needs existed and, on the other hand, a large number of people were unemployed. These programmes thus tried to encourage the creation of new jobs in the non-profit sector, in areas where they could satisfy social needs, as a mean of both creating jobs for unemployed persons and curbing mainstream social spending.

The first WISEs in these countries relied heavily on these 'second labour market' programmes. All these countries, except Ireland, belong to the 'Bismarckian' tradition or the 'corporatist' group of countries, i.e. in these countries, intermediate bodies are important not only for the management of social insurance but also for the delivery of social services (Esping-Andersen 1999). Indeed these countries (Salomon *et al.* 1999) are characterised by a significant presence of non-profit private organisations, mainly financed by public bodies, in the field of social services. Not surprisingly, it is in these countries that the 'second labour market programmes' emerged; they relied on this kind of organisations. The inclusion of Ireland in this second group may seem rather odd as it does not belong to this Bismarckian tradition. Nevertheless, Ireland has one of the highest shares of employment in the non-profit sector, which relies heavily on public funding. Actually, some research has shown that Ireland is a borderline case between the 'liberal' and the 'corporatist' state (Hicks and Kenworthy 2003).

In the 1990s, the countries in this second group adopted public schemes specific to WISEs; the only exception is Germany – which probably reflects the decline of the cooperative movement in this country. In the other countries, the persistence of a social economy sector or a cooperative sector which still maintains some of its original features influences the environmental perception of WISEs and the building of organisational identities within this tradition (Bode *et al.* 2006).

A third group – bringing together Portugal, Spain, Italy and the UK – is characterised by a low level of expenditure on active labour market policies and by the (near) non-existence of a second labour market programme. Regarding the development of a public scheme specific to WISEs, Italy played a pioneering role in the European Union, thanks to the action of its strong cooperative movement. In the countries of this group that do not have a historical heritage similar to that of Italy, the situation is in rapid evolution at the moment, due among other factors to the increasing number of interactions – and probably a certain homogenisation – between European Union initiatives and national public policies. Portugal and the UK are now experimenting an increase in their ALMP, and public schemes specific to WISEs viewed as an ALMP tool have recently been adopted in these countries.

Multiple-goal WISEs facing institutionalisation

Historical analysis shows that social enterprises have contributed to the development of public policies. Indeed, they were pioneers in promoting the integration of excluded persons through a productive activity. As we have seen, WISEs have increasingly represented, for public bodies in most European countries, a tool for implementing labour market policies.

However, dialogue has not always been smooth. Indeed, the accommodation between the views of WISEs and those of public bodies on the contested nature of WISEs' mission does not seem to be easy. This explains why some pioneering initiatives chose not to use WISE-specific public schemes; this is for example the case of the 'local development' initiatives in Ireland, which did not adopt the 'social economy' framework (O'Shaughnessy 2006). It should be noted too that, if public schemes have encouraged some initiatives, they have also excluded others. In France, for instance, the institutionalisation process recognised and favoured initiatives launched by professional and associative militant actors aiming at the integration through work of disadvantaged populations, whereas the initiatives originating from these populations themselves were in most cases neglected.

Social enterprises are usually viewed as multiple-goal organisations; they mix social goals, connected to their specific mission to benefit the community (for WISEs, the integration of people excluded from the labour market trough productive activity); economic goals, related to their entrepreneurial nature; and socio-political goals, as social enterprises are often rooted in a 'sector' traditionally involved in socio-political action (Campi *et al.* 2006).

The WISE-specific public schemes or the more general activate labour market policies used by WISEs now shape (at least partially) their objectives and practices. But is the extent of this influence sufficient to speak of 'isomorphism' on the part of WISEs – isomorphism being understood as a progressive loss of their inner characteristics under the pressure of legal frameworks or professional norms spilling over from the for-profit private or public sectors? Bode *et al.* (2006) conclude that there is no overall tendency, among European WISEs, towards isomorphism understood as an evolution in which WISEs completely lose their initial identity. This being said, external pressures however generate strained relations between the different goals of WISEs. The simultaneous pursuit of these various goals often constitutes an essential challenge for these organisations.

Social goals

Regarding the social goal of integrating disadvantaged workers through a productive activity, the philosophy of the innovative social enterprise which emerged in the 1980s clearly resided in the empowerment and integration of excluded groups through participation in WISEs whose aim was to offer the disadvantaged workers a chance to reassess the role of work in their lives by supporting them while they gained control over their own personal project. This conception implies not only giving an occupation to these persons but also developing specific values, for example through democratic management structures in which the disadvantaged workers are given a role, and/or through the production of goods and services generating collective benefits (such as social services or services linked to the environment) for the territory in which the WISEs are embedded. Getting workers back into the 'first' labour market was thus not the priority of these pioneering WISEs. But the progressive institution-alisation and professionalisation of the field over the years, through public schemes increasingly linked to active labour market policies, has generated a clear pressure to make the social mission instrumental to the integration of dis-advantaged workers into the first labour market.

As a result, we observe a strained relation between the mission of empower-ing excluded groups and the mission of integrating the beneficiaries into 'normal' jobs. This has implications for the actual implementation of the social mission of WISEs.

First, as showed by Borzaga and Loss (2006), the type of integration pro-vided by a WISE is highly influenced by the type of integration scheme defined by the labour market authorities that this WISE uses. Integration schemes usually consist of temporary public support intended to compensate for the 'tem-porary unemployability' of the disadvantaged workers. But it appears that the length of this temporary subsidy is not sufficiently linked to the actual profiles of the workers. This can lead to a phenomenon of skimming, i.e. there are incen-tives for the enterprises to hire only those workers who are most likely to be 'cost-effective' by the end of the project and to retain only those who have attained this level of 'cost-effectiveness' when the subsidised period ends.

Second, although the pioneering initiatives emphasised the empowerment of participants through participative decision-making processes, nowadays, daily practices are more deeply influenced by other factors, such as the extensive pro-fessionalisation of the organisation and the evolution of production methods towards those of the private sector (Bode *et al.* 2006). As a matter of fact, WISEs sell their products in markets in which they compete with for-profit enterprises; as a result, WISEs can be driven to adopt the norms of these for-profit competitors. Analysis of formal channels of participation such as board membership indeed shows that, on the one hand, the level of participation of dis-advantaged workers is low and that, on the other hand, the staff is one of the more influential categories within the boards of the WISEs surveyed (Campi *et al.* 2006); this could be a consequence of the process of professionalisation, in which participation may suffer. However, deeper investigation is needed regard-ing the participation of disadvantaged groups within WISEs through informal channels potentially linking the social enterprise and its workers.

Economic goals

Regarding the production goal, the first challenge for WISEs is to find a type of production suited to the capacities of the disadvantaged groups they employ while making it possible to train these workers through the production process.

To meet this challenge, developing market niches has proven a successful strategy, but 'WISEs that have successfully entered into niche markets may discover that, from the moment these markets become more stable, private competitors (with fewer social concerns and constraints) are keen to make money in them as well' (Bode *et al.* 2006). The case of recycling is emblematic in this regard: at the European level, WISEs played a pioneering role in developing recycling services, but today, these markets are more secure and WISEs have to compete with new entrants coming from the for-profit sector. Moreover, when choosing a production niche, WISEs sometimes face a trade-off between the type of production and the level of employability of the participants. For example, the building and gardening sectors employ more workers with a weak employability profile, while – unsurprisingly – workers in the field of social services and education are usually more qualified.

If WISEs consider their goal of producing goods and services as important insofar as it supports their integration mission, some of them also develop the production of a specific type of goods because it generates collective benefits and equity[3] (this is for example the case of social services). These WISEs face a second challenge when looking for the necessary resources to support this kind of production. Indeed, while all WISE-specific public schemes emphasise the production goal as the main support for work integration, only a few of them recognise the possibility of producing (quasi-)collective goods. Moreover, when this is the case, this collective dimension is rarely sustained by specific public financing, which makes it more difficult for these WISEs to maintain the concurrent pursuit of different collective goals – namely the integration of their disadvantaged workers and the production of a good or service with a collective dimension – that characterises them. As O'Shaugnessy (2006: 140) explains: 'this presents an enormous challenge to those WISEs which may be serving a disadvantaged community, where the consumers of their services lack the financial means to procure these services from other vendors and where public service provision is inadequate'.

Socio-political goals

Regarding the socio-political goal, we have shown how WISEs have contributed to shaping public policies in the field of work integration. Both public authorities and promoters of WISEs agree on the fact that the hiring and occupational integration of disadvantaged workers are at the very heart of WISEs' mission, but differences arise, as we just explained, regarding the way in which this integration is to be understood. The dominant model of public recognition of WISEs tends to recognise only one kind of benefit – namely those benefits linked to the work-integration goal – in the framework of active labour market policies and with a very specific target – the integration of workers into the normal labour market. This evolution entails a risk of reducing the innovation capacity of WISEs.

Social enterprises at the crossroads of market, public policies and civil society

Social enterprises are often presented as hybrid organisations (on this subject, see Chapter 15 in this book); this hybrid nature is reflected particularly clearly in their mode of governance and sources of income. Does this hybrid character of social enterprises constitute a channel to fulfil their multiple-goal mission and therefore a bulwark against isomorphism, or is it rather a threat for their identity, embedded in different, contradictory logics?

Their mode of governance could be seen as hybrid insofar as it relies on a dynamic of linking people with different backgrounds. Indeed, most WISEs were founded through a partnership among different kinds of civil society actors. Local public bodies were sometimes associated with this dynamic. Fifty-eight per cent of European WISEs have been described as involving more than one category of stakeholder on their board (Campi *et al.* 2006), and the data collected seem to indicate that 'the participation of stakeholders in these WISEs leads to the exercise of a real influence within boards', thanks to the 'balanced governance structure' (see Table 6.1). These features highlight the collective and hybrid dynamic of social entrepreneurship and contrast with the emphasis that social entrepreneurship literature generally places on individual social entrepreneurs (Grenier 2003).

Hybridity is also reflected by the resource mix mobilised by European WISEs (Gardin 2006). The latter indeed show a particular capacity to articulate resources coming from different sources. Moreover, it appears that WISEs do not rely only on a mix of market- and redistribution-based resources; they are the scene of a more complex hybridisation, built upon four types of economic relationship: the market and redistribution, but also the socially embedded market (see above) and reciprocity (an example of a reciprocity-based resource is provided by volunteering). The sales of goods and services represent on average, at the European level, 53 per cent of WISEs' resources – of these 53 per cent, one-third are socially motivated sales. Redistribution resources (direct and indirect subsidies) account for 38.5 per cent of resources. Voluntary resources, which are most probably undervalued, represent on average 8.5 per cent of total resources. This last kind of resource reflects the degree of embeddedness of WISEs in civic networks; social enterprises which are more strongly embedded in civic networks are usually better able to mobilise volunteer resources than social enterprises launched by public bodies. It finally has to be noted that this resource mix varies from one type of WISE to another in accordance with their specific social mission.

Public schemes, though, usually do not recognise this hybrid character of social enterprises. Indeed, one of the most visible effects of the institutionalisation of WISEs in the different European countries is that it pushes them to reduce the variety of their resources mix and to position themselves, most of the time, either in the 'market economy' or, when they employ very disadvantaged workers, in the 'redistributive economy'; as to the role of voluntary resources, it

Table 6.1 Influence of stakeholder categories in multi-stakeholder WISEs

Country/stakeholder category	Users/customers (%)	Volunteers (%)	Staff (%)	Participants (%)	Business (%)	Government (%)	NPOs (%)	Other* (%)	Total (%)
Belgium	1	13	24	10	9	10	19	15	100
Denmark	9	7	17	7	13	25	18	5	100
Finland	0	6	26	21	10	10	15	13	100
France	10	36	10	3	10	10	13	10	100
Germany	0	25	12	18	10	18	18	0	100
Italy	4	29	55	1	3	0	1	6	100
Spain	0	44	28	0	4	0	15	9	100
Sweden	12	6	24	24	9	15	3	8	100
United Kingdom	3	13	4	0	25	19	19	17	100
EU (average)	5	20	21	7	10	13	14	10	100

Source: Campi *et al.* 2006: 40.

Notes

*This category includes: private individuals (other than consumers), local community representatives, private financing bodies, experts, etc.

is in neither case recognised. This type of scheme puts social enterprises in 'boxes', denying one of their fundamental characteristics – namely the fact that they are located in an intermediate space between the market, the state and civil society.

This dynamic has put pressure on the identity of the WISEs which try to preserve:

> their original approach, that is, to provide for the long-term social integration for disadvantaged groups, to solidly establish different sorts of economic activities that are beneficial to the community, to keep relying on strong civic stakeholders, and to empower employees through workplace democracy and broad social support.
>
> (Bode *et al.* 2006: 254)

The presence of various stakeholders constitutes a channel for developing links and trust across different types of stakeholders and can consequently enhance the development of bridging social capital. Analysis tends to show that this multi-stakeholder nature can in turn be a resource for WISEs to pursue their complex set of objectives. The reliance on a variety of resources, both from the point of view of their origin (e.g. from private customers, from the private sector, from the public sector, from the third sector) and from the type of allocation (e.g. the sale of services, public subsidies, gifts and volunteering), also appears to be a key element for WISES to fulfil their multiple-goal missions. Managing hybridity constitutes a daily challenge for social enterprise, but this character also appears to be a part of their identity linked to their multiple-goal mission.

Conclusion – widening the scope of investigation to the service sector

Social enterprises have become associated mainly with work integration. They are not often recognised by public bodies as a viable strategy in other fields of activity. In a context where the sector of services – and more specifically that of personal services – is 'on the rise', the analysis of the specific characteristics of social enterprises must go beyond the field of work integration. Indeed, personal services are provided by a variety of operators (for-profit private enterprises, traditional non-profit bodies, social enterprises and public sector organisations) which have specific organisational forms and modes of governance. The development of these services generates many expectations, based on the collective benefits they can produce (impact in terms of equity regarding the users, creation of high-quality jobs). Therefore, it is important that the question of the value added of the model of social enterprises – which are driven by their explicit aim to benefit the community – be studied more thoroughly. Is the development of social enterprise in this field a sign of a retrenchment of the welfare state or, on the contrary, a way to enhance the collective benefits that may be associated with these services? The answer is obviously complex. The analysis of the work integration field suggest that the response will vary depending on the type of regulation that is developed. If public bodies limit their action to developing quasi-market policies, which place all types of providers on an equal contractual footing, without taking the collective benefits the providers create into account, the risk is that the social innovation role of social enterprises will be curtailed, as most probably will be their capacity to provide specific answers to these collective problems. Conversely, if public bodies recognise the specific characteristics of the social enterprise model and foster its development, social enterprises could, most probably, make their specific contribution to the public good.

Notes

1 All the data regarding WISEs in this paper comes from the PERSE project. PERSE is the acronym of the name of the project in French; a translation of the project's full name would be: 'The Socio-Economic Performance of Social Enterprises in the Field of Integration by Work'. This research project was carried out from September 2001 to March 2004; the project was undertaken within the framework of the 'Key Action Improving the Socio-economic Knowledge Base' programme of the European Commission (Research DG, Fifth Framework Programme). The sample of the project comprised 160 European Social Enterprises across 11 countries: Belgium, Denmark, Finland, France, Germany, Ireland, Italy, Portugal, Spain, Sweden and the UK. Results are presented in Nyssens 2006.
2 This section is based on Laville *et al.* (2006).
3 Such goods can be considered as quasi-collective goods. Their consumption is clearly divisible but it gives rise, besides the private benefits, to collective benefits which affect the whole community.

Bibliography

Bode I., Evers, A. and Schulz, A. (2006) 'Social Enterprises: Can Hybridisation be Sustainable?' in Nyssens, M. *Social enterprises at the crossroads of market, public policies and civil society*, New York and London: Routledge, pp. 237–258.

Borzaga, C. and Loss, M. (2006) 'Profiles and Trajectories of Workers in Work Integration Social Enterprises' in Nyssens, M. *Social enterprises at the crossroads of market, public policies and civil society*, New York and London: Routledge, pp. 169–194.

Campi, S., Defourny, J. and Grégoire, O. (2006) 'Multiple Goals and Multiple Stakeholder Structure: The Governance of Social Enterprises' in Nyssens, M. *Social enterprises at the crossroads of market, public policies and civil society*, New York and London: Routledge, pp. 29–49.

Davister, C., Defourny, J. and Grégoire, O. (2004) 'Work Integration Social Enterprises in the European Union: an Overview of Existing Models', EMES Working Papers Series, 04/04, Liège.

Dees, J. G. (1998) 'Enterprising Nonprofits', *Harvard Business Review*, January–February: 55–67.

Dees, J. G. (2001) 'The Meaning of Social Entrepreneurship' www.fuqua.duke.edu/centers/case/leaders/resources.htm.

Defourny, J. (2001) 'From Third Sector to Social Enterprise' in Borzaga, C. and

Defourny, J. *The emergence of social enterprise*, New York and London: Routledge, pp. 1–28.

Defourny, J. and Nyssens, M. (2006) 'Defining Social Enterprise' in Nyssens, M. *Social enterprises at the crossroads of market, public policies and civil society*, New York and London: Routledge, pp. 3–26.

Esping-Andersen, G. (1999) *Social Foundation of Postindustrial Economies*, New York: Oxford University Press.

Evers, A. (2001) 'The significance of social capital in the multiple goal and resource structure of social enterprises' in Borzaga, C. and Defourny, J. *The emergence of social enterprise*, New York and London: Routledge, pp. 296–311.

Evers, A. and Laville, J.-L. (2004) *The third sector in Europe, globalization and welfare*, Cheltenham and Northampton: Edward Elgar.

Gardin, L. (2006) 'A Variety of Resource Mix inside Social Enterprises' in Nyssens, M. *Social enterprises at the crossroads of market, public policies and civil society*, New York and London: Routledge, pp. 111–136.

Grenier, P. (2003) 'Reclaiming Enterprise for the Social Good: the Political Climate for Social Entrepreneurship in UK' *32nd Annual ARNOVA Conference*, Denver, Colorado.

Hicks, A. and Kenworthy, K. (2003) 'Varieties of welfare capitalism', *Socio-Economic Review* (1): 27–61.

Laville, J.-L., Lemaitre, A. and Nyssens, M. (2006) 'Public policies and Social enterprises in Europe: the challenge of institutionalisation' in Nyssens, M. *Social enterprises at the crossroads of market, public policies and civil society*, New York and London: Routledge, pp. 272–295.

Navez, F. (2005) 'Marchés publics et évolution du droit européen: quelles possibilités de soutien pour les entreprises d'économie sociale' *Première conférence européenne ISTR et EMES*, Paris.

Nicholls, A. (2005) 'Measuring impact in social entrepreneurship: new accountabilities to stakeholders and investors' *Seminar on Social Enterprises*, Milton Keynes University.

Nyssens, M. (2006) *Social enterprises at the crossroads of market, public policies and civil society*, New York and London: Routledge.

Nyssens, M. and Kerlin, J. (forthcoming) 'Social Enterprises in Europe', in *Social enterprise: a global comparison*, Bloomfield CT: Kumarian Press.

O'Shaughnessy, M. (2006) 'Irish Social Enterprises: Challenges in Mobilizing Resources to Meet Multiple Goals' in Nyssens, M. *Social enterprises at the crossroads of market, public policies and civil society*, New York and London: Routledge, pp. 137–143.

Putman, R. (1993) 'The Prosperous Community: Social Capital and Public Life', *The American Prospect* 13: 35–42.

Salomon, L., Anheier, H., List, R., Toepler, S., Sokolowski, S. and associates (1999) *Global civil society: dimension of the nonprofit sector*, Baltimore: Johns Hopkins University.

Stryjan, Y. (2004) 'Work Integration Social Enterprises in Sweden', *EMES Working Papers*, 4(2), Liège.

Part IV
Delivering public services

7 The third sector and the delivery of public services

An evaluation of different meta-theoretical perspectives

Taco Brandsen

Introduction

In many European countries, the third sector has traditionally played a major role in providing public services.[1] Over recent decades, its significance has further increased as governments have contracted out parts of their service delivery duties. Partly as a result of this, research on the sector has also grown exponentially. It has raised the question about useful ways to link theories from the traditional disciplines to this object. There are many interesting academic perspectives out there, but how should they be used? When to choose which perspective?

In this chapter, I will identify different categories of theoretical perspectives and judge how they are useful for the study of public service delivery by the third sector. The perspectives will be illustrated with interesting examples from current literature. The specific way in which I frame them is borrowed from the work of the sociologist Charles Tilly, which I find particularly perceptive. However, the purpose of the chapter is not to argue that his way of framing different types of theories is superior to all others. There are different, equally valid ways to categorise them. The point is that applying such a framework can be a useful exercise for understanding the relative strengths of different theoretical approaches in a particular field of research. The premise is that each perspective highlights certain aspects of reality at the expense of others. Consequently, if the object of an empirical investigation is to examine a specific aspect of a phenomenon, it makes sense to analyse it with a theoretical approach that is likely to deliver the best results. The question posed in the chapter is: how does this work for public service delivery by the third sector?

The structure of my argument will be as follows:

- first, I will argue that the concept of a third "sector" in itself invites normative connotations that are harmful to theoretical development in this field;
- then follows the introduction of three meta-theoretical perspectives (systemic, dispositional and transactional);
- next I will suggest a small set of criteria for assessing the different perspectives;

- each approach will be illustrated with relevant theories on the role of the third sector in public services;
- the chapter ends with a brief assessment of what is necessary for further theoretical development.

Finally, a word on the meaning of key terms. The term "public service" will here be used in a narrow sense, referring to services carried out by the third sector on behalf of the state. This is a choice of convenience and not one that reflects the full meaning of the term as I would normally understand it. The term "the third sector" is notoriously difficult to define, an issue which will be addressed in the next paragraph.

The purity of exploitation

The recent popularity of third sector-specific research was spurred by political developments of the 1980s and 1990s. The US government based its policy on the assumption that a reduction in state expenditure and taxation would allow private initiative to blossom, suggesting a direct trade-off. More generally in the Western world, there were moves towards privatisation and contracting-out that brought the third sector into the spotlight. Finally, the disintegration of the communist regimes in Central and Eastern Europe aroused interest in the movements and organisations that would fill the gap left by a retreating state.

These events not only spurred a continuing interest in voluntary and non-profit organisations, but also reinforced two assumptions that have pervaded some of the research since: first, that these collective actors could be thought of as a "sector"; second, that its relation with the state is essentially an oppositional one. This assumption of opposition has been reinforced by some important sources of inspiration for third sector research. The social movement literature, which gained momentum at a far earlier stage and which is conceptually more coherent, has an oppositional perspective almost by nature. Although there have been various perspectives on social movements, they are generally focused on protest in situations of conflict (Della Porta and Diani, 1999). In political philosophy, the number of illustrious names who have argued in favour of an autonomous civil society is daunting (for an overview, see Hall and Trentmann, 2005).[2] When the focus is on power and democracy, and civil society is recognised as separate from politics, then authors tend to emphasise the need for distance from the state rather than closer integration.

The question is not whether such perspectives are right or wrong, but whether the assumption of a fundamental separation between state and third sector is useful for studying their role in public service delivery. This is highly questionable. To begin with, the empirical evidence does not support such a perspective. In fact, the interdependence between state and third sector in many countries is so high that it is misleading to present their relationship as a zero-sum game. Lester Salamon's well-known study of US non-profits showed that the growth of the state and growth of the third sector went hand in hand, contrary to the "crowding out" assumption at the heart of the Reagan government's policies (Salamon, 1995). The Western European context is no different. Recent efforts to decentralise and to contract out services to voluntary and non-profit organisations have only increased the interdependence further.

It could be argued that the material growth in terms of financial and human resources has led to a loss of the third sector's autonomy and of certain qualities that make it distinctive. Indeed, recent studies show an increasing emergence of hybrid organisations (Brandsen *et al.*, 2005). Be that as it may, the trade-off is too complex for a priori normative assumptions about the nature of the relationship. Indeed, given the overwhelming evidence that the relationship between state and third sector in the public services is symbiotic, one might wonder why the myth of opposition is still worth discussing. The key arguments against it were made some time ago (e.g. Gidron *et al.*, 1992; Kuhnle and Selle, 1992).

If this is the case, why does the notion of opposition continue to be so influential in third sector research? There are various possible explanations. For a start, the position of the third sector in Western industrial democracies is of course different from that in many other countries, especially in dictatorial regimes. But there is a more fundamental reason for the continuing re-emergence of the oppositional perspective. This is because the concept of a "third *sector*" itself implies such a view. The term "third sector" itself is of quite recent origin, but the notion of a third domain next to state and market originated in the political philosophy of the eighteenth century, with an increasing emphasis on its autonomy – especially from the state (Hall and Trentmann, 2005).[3] Previously, civil society and political society were regarded as more or less integrated. In the Aristotelian view of politics, for instance, the only alternative to participation in political life was to withdraw to a secluded existence. There was no public life separate from politics. The word "sector" itself therefore implies a separation between these social phenomena. The symbiosis between sectors must conceptually remain limited when they are defined as separate.

This is not problematic when the term is used only for limited theoretical or for practical purposes. Problems arise when meanings derived from different perspectives (e.g. different disciplines) are made to refer to the same phenomenon. For instance, from a legal perspective, the "third sector" can be used to refer to collections of organisations with certain legal characteristics (e.g. foundations, associations, charities). For practical purposes, this can be used to operationalise the philosophical notion of a third domain in society. When one is trying to collect large-scale survey data on the third sector, this may be the best choice. But the legally defined category is in this respect only a methodological substitute for a philosophically defined category. This becomes most clear when there are debates over entities that are intuitively considered part of the philosophical category, but which fail to fit the criteria of the legal understanding (e.g. because they lack legal form).[4] But they are essentially two very different things. Likewise, the legal category may or may not have meaning in a sociological sense. Research has borne out that in some countries people identify with the notion of such a sector, whereas in others it only exists as an abstraction (see e.g. Dekker, 2001). Kendall and Knapp identified the third sector as a "loose and baggy monster" (Kendall and Knapp, 1995, p. 66), but this is only true if one bundles all the different meanings into one.

Nevertheless, it is convenient to retain the "sector" label for practical purposes. The "third sector" is a useful blanket term and can be more precisely defined in the context of specific projects. Its use as the label for academic fora and networks makes sense because it is socially meaningful to the participants as members of a professional community. There is also a methodological benefit in defining ideal-types of organisations as state or third sector. It means that each move towards the other implies a loss of distinctiveness by definition. For instance, the decision of a non-profit to professionalise in order to meet the standards of state contracts makes it less of a non-profit. This can help to understand how the interaction changes the organisations. But one should remain aware such an ideal-typical approach can be a Trojan horse, smuggling in normative assumptions. For example, if it is noted that organisations ideal-typically defined as third sector shift towards organisations ideal-typically defined as state, this is in itself a neutral observation. But when this same observation is defined in terms of *sectors*, the shift becomes a loss of ground for the third sector, which in turn implies an imbalance. Such a line of reasoning is especially insidious when conceptual assumptions subtly blend with personal beliefs. Many third sector researchers share a personal commitment to the sector or to the values it represents. A shift away from the third sector then becomes a personal loss, even if the shift in question is no more than a conceptual construction.

To some extent, this is unavoidable in the real world of research. If at this point I were to advocate value-free research, it would surely invite (justified) hoots of laughter. Nonetheless, it is important to be wary of the pitfalls of the sector concept. While it is useful to retain state/market/third sector ideal-types (as long as there is no credible alternative), these should be cleansed of normative assumptions inherited from political philosophy, in which it means something essentially different. Such assumptions include the desire to retain an autonomous third sector, independent of the state. These are fine for other discussions. There are all sorts of other reasons why one could favour an autonomous third sector. As a democratically minded citizen, I welcome the thought that there are pockets of diversity and freedom in my society. But that is a democratic argument and irrelevant to an examination of the public services. The removal of such normative connotations can only be achieved by putting the public services at the heart of the analysis. In such an analysis, the cooperation between state and third sector serves only the quality of those services.

In my view, the best way to avoid tangled arguments is to approach the third sector not as a democrat, but as a tyrant. The only pure analytical approach is one of exploitation (even if this is not the reality of state–third sector relationships). If public services are truly at the core of the analysis, then the third sector must analytically be regarded as undiscovered territory that can be subjugated and raided at will, left free only where this is necessary to keep its beneficial qualities intact. If one left the goose with the golden eggs alive, it was probably not out of respect for animal rights, but out of greed.

This is not necessarily at odds with an independent third sector. If the quality of services is better when delivered by organisations with a high degree of self-organisation (e.g. when democratic decision-making is part of the definition of quality) there is an argument in favour of autonomy, but it is one subordinated to the analysis of service delivery. This is the only reliable means of separating different types of arguments. Such an instrumental approach essentially means that the concept of a third *sector* is abandoned, because it has no regard for the balance that a model based on sectors implicitly advocates. If we use the term for convenience, we must make sure that it is an empty shell.

The remainder of the chapter will focus on three types of perspectives that each imply a different conception of what the third sector means. Consequently, they interpret its role in the public services differently. In distinguishing between ontological perspectives, I have refrained from re-inventing the wheel and worked with an existing typology.

Three meta-theoretical perspectives

In his recent book *Identities, Boundaries and Social Ties*, Charles Tilly distinguishes between three different meta-theoretical perspectives on social life (Tilly, 2005b). Each offers a different type of explanation of empirical phenomena. The triple distinction creates an opportunity to review different directions from which to approach the third sector's role in the public services. I have chosen this categorisation because it is lucid and (relatively) easily applicable, the more so because it transcends disciplinary barriers and levels of analysis. Let me start with a general description of each.

Systemic perspectives to social life suggest the existence of a coherent entity. Social phenomena are explained by reference to their location within that entity. Functionalist reasoning is the prime example of such an approach: a social phenomenon is explained with reference to its function for the total system. Suppose that the waiter who brings me my coffee gives me a particularly friendly smile (in the US, where I have written this chapter, it is less hypothetical than in Europe). How can this event be interpreted systemically? It could be argued that these kinds of expressions function to uphold a culture of service that is embedded in a particular variety of capitalism. In another system, a smile might be dysfunctional because it assumes some sort of familiarity. According to Tilly, the advantage of systemic accounts of social life is that they connect small-scale and large-scale events. However, they are less good at bounding systems and at establishing clear causal lines of reasoning.

Dispositional perspectives to social life likewise assume the existence of coherent entities, but usually at a smaller scale (e.g. individuals). They explain what happens on the basis of the orientations of the entity before action occurs. The orientations can be conceptualised as preferences, rationalities, logics or cultural templates, to name but a few. Action then depends on incentives and opportunities related to those orientations. For instance, if I can deduce that two actors have certain preferences, I can explain how they will interact. To return to the example of my friendly waiter, I could analyse his behaviour in terms of his incentive to maximise his tip. His action is informed by his expectation that my disposition is to reward those who are friendly to me. External conditions, such as the setting and the price of the coffee, will co-determine the ultimate action. It is an approach widely used in economics. According to Tilly, these types of accounts relate well to the findings of disciplines such as psychology, but cannot deal well with aggregate properties, nor with properties of the relations among actors.

Transactional perspectives explain events as the result of interactions between social sites. They imply that the characteristics of these "sites" themselves are the result of these interactions. It is also known as a "relational approach". My waiter's smile could be understood as reinforcing the relationship of asymmetric independence that exists between us. His compulsion to smile is bigger than mine. But should I return his expression with an equally friendly smile, the relationship is at least given the illusion of equality. The advantage of these types of accounts is that they put communication at the heart of social science, but they may be counter-intuitive when popular accounts of events tend to stress dispositions.

Tilly notes the advantages and disadvantages of each approach, but in the end comes down firmly in favour of the transactional approach. But what does it mean to favour one of these perspectives? They essentially represent ontological positions that cannot be proven or disproved. Arguments between rival explanations usually take place within such an approach, because it is on the basis of shared assumptions that empirical propositions can be verified. When researchers from different traditions meet, they will have to first reach a compromise over basic assumptions before they get down to theoretical disputes (imagine a neo-classical economist arguing with an economic sociologist). Academic life is often organised to avoid such uncomfortable meetings. The choice for one or another approach will often be determined by socialisation within a particular academic environment rather than by a conscious choice.

That does not mean, however, that it is impossible to evaluate the usefulness of an approach for the study of a particular field at a particular time. Although he does not explicitly state any evaluative criteria, Tilly's reference to the "advantages and disadvantages" of perspectives implies that he has some. They appear to be the following:

1 Methodological validity, especially the ability to clearly identify and bound units of analysis and the ability to establish clear causalities.
2 The ability to explain change.
3 The ability to span boundaries (disciplinary, national).
4 The extent to which an approach reinforces or contradicts "intuitive" explanations of social life.

These criteria are based on the shared background of the three perspectives: commonly accepted beliefs about methodology, institutionalised disciplinary communities and general beliefs about the dynamics of social life. They can be used to assess the strengths and weaknesses of perspectives to our topic, the role of the third sector in the delivery of public services. I hope readers will forgive me if I leave out the final criterion, since I doubt my capacity to judge what is intuitive to most people.

In the remainder of the chapter, each of the three types of perspectives will be assessed on the basis of the first three criteria. In each case, I will use one or two theories to illustrate my argument. It is certainly not meant to be a comprehensive literature review on the topic, but rather an exercise in positioning and judging different perspectives. Again, let me emphasise that this is not an attempt to set up Tilly's categorisation as the one that should replace all others. There are different ways of categorising theories which are equally valid. But I have found this one useful for understanding my own field of study and hope that it will clarify directions in which it could potentially develop.

Systemic perspectives

To reiterate, systemic perspectives explain social phenomena on the basis of their position in a larger whole. Most public services delivered by third sector organisations are "human services" by nature, meaning that they affect the personal attributes of individuals directly (Hasenfeld, 1983). Consequently, it makes sense to discuss them in the context of social policy, even if the mainstream debate on social policy has so far taken little heed of the third sector.

This lack of attention can at least partly be explained by the dominance of welfare regime perspectives during the 1990s, although they currently appear to be going out of fashion. Esping-Andersen's well-known *Three Worlds of Welfare Capitalism* (1990) identified three analytically distinct clusters of countries: liberal (e.g. the UK), corporatist (e.g. Germany) and social democratic (e.g. Sweden). The typology was based on several variables, of which the level of decommodification was the most important. The regimes were regarded as the outcome of historical bargaining processes between capital and labour. The regime typology has been used for an endless range of comparisons between countries with different regimes. A wide variety of criticisms has been levelled at this type of work, most concerning the inclusion of relevant dimensions and the causal assumptions in the model. Although the critique has severely eroded the basis of Esping-Andersen's model, its value in encouraging international comparative research is undeniable (for an overview of the criticism, see Arts and Gelissen, 2002).

The welfare regime concept as defined by Esping-Andersen has certain characteristics that inherently tend to downplay the third sector's significance (Pestoff *et al.*, 2006). It is almost solely based on income transfer, whereas the third sector's role in the welfare state is predominantly one of service provision. In addition, it focuses on national arrangements, while the third sector often tends to rely on local arrangements. It is no coincidence that Esping-Andersen deals with the third sector only in two footnotes. Nonetheless, there have been some attempts to insert the third sector, or parts of it, within this framework. Gidron *et al.* (1992) combined the dimensions of financing/authorising and delivery. Unfortunately, most countries tend to end up in one of the categories, which makes the typology illustrative of similarity rather than of diversity. Kuhnle and Selle (1992) have proposed a typology based on the dimensions of distance (in terms of communication) and dependence. These dimensions are fundamentally different from those of the welfare regimes. The latter explain the present on the basis of institutional reproduction, a product of past forces that have created recurrent patterns. The other typology offers us useful ways of understanding present developments on the basis of dimensions considered relevant to the third sector. However, they arguably allow us to see change without explaining it, as they are not theory-based (at least not ostensibly so). Probably the most elaborate and successful attempt was Salamon and Anheier's "social origins theory" (1998), which distinguishes between four different types of regimes by embedding economic theory in historical context.

There can certainly be benefits in coupling third sector research to the welfare regime debate. It might be a powerful rallying call for cross-national comparative research, as the welfare regime typology was in the broader social policy field. It would provide a shared conceptual framework for a research field where single country case studies still predominate. The drawback of regimes is that they may in a double sense be resistant to change. To begin with, there is a danger that they degenerate into simple categorical tools for comparison, yielding massive empirical data, but little theoretical development. Furthermore, when one starts to tweak at the individual threads, the whole starts to unravel, which means that minor points of criticism cannot easily be incorporated into the whole and the latter tends to become stagnant. When changes are incorporated, they tend to weaken the coherence and appeal of the original rather than strengthen it. It could be argued that the concessions Esping-Andersen has made to his critics have strengthened the validity of the regimes, but weakened their appeal.

Another fundamental criticism of systemic perspectives is that they tend to be weak at explaining change, other than through external and sudden events. The welfare regime theory shows how historical interactions between actors have resulted in particular institutional configurations. However, they have had difficulty in explaining recent welfare reforms since they stress permanence rather than change (Green-Pedersen and Haverland, 2002). Put differently, their contemporary relevance can only be demonstrated insofar as nothing changes. Salamon and Anheier's social origins theory comes closest to incorporating the third sector in welfare regime model and in doing so incorporates its weaknesses. It cannot account adequately for (what appear to be) current changes in the third sector, nor does it cover any changes in the qualitative nature of providers and services.

Summing up, these and other systemic theories tend to be inherently static.

However, they could greatly encourage comparative research on the third sector in the public services. The question is what one regards as the priority of current research. If it is to explain the third sector's role in a larger context, based on a theoretical understanding of historical development, this is the way forward. If it is to explain the third sector's role in welfare reform, it is likely to be unsatisfactory.

Dispositional perspectives

Dispositional perspectives explain social phenomena on the basis of the orientations of actors prior to their actions. It is typical of contemporary economics: an analysis of social phenomena is impossible without an understanding of preferences.

There is a wide variety of economic literature on the third sector, as noted elsewhere in this volume. Yet, when it comes down to applications of this type of theory, they are sometimes not very distinct from those of other types. Some years ago, a volume by Anheier and Ben-Ner (2003) reviewed the state of the art in economic theories of non-profits. Yet on reading how various theories have been refined, the question arises whether some of the theory labelled as "economic" is in fact so monodisciplinary. Especially where relational goods are concerned, the theories deal with issues that are normally associated with the "softer" social sciences: altruistic motivations, the desire for attention and direct interpersonal coordination (see e.g. Ben-Ner and Gui, 2003). It is then more accurate to speak of a rational choice approach that incorporates insights from several disciplines. There is much to be gained from adopting a well-structured theory of agency, in that it will strengthen the methodology of third sector research.[5] Whether that is considered economic theory or not is neither here nor there.

The one thing that makes such theories truly dispositional is the insistence that demand determines supply or, put differently, that preferences determine the shape of institutions; not the other way round. This has been criticised as one of the greatest failures of economics. In one of his lesser-known works, Hirschman has laid down the foundations of a theory of disappointment (Hirschman, 1982). Rather than assuming a fixed set of preferences, he argued that initial preferences could be changed through experience, which led to recurring changes on the demand side without necessarily any changes in supply. Interestingly, he noted that services might be especially prone to disappointment due to their uneven and unpredictable nature. Addressing the question of what consumers expect from the third sector and how experience affects these expectations is one that could make dispositional theories more dynamic and encourage interdisciplinary work.

To conclude, the specific benefit for the study of the third sector would be in strengthening its methodology. However, its strict theoretical tenets can discourage interdisciplinary work. This is a pity because, as the collection by Anheier and Ben-Ner (2003) shows, there is an impressive body of work on the third sector in economics. Unfortunately, it makes little to no attempt to relate its development to insights from other disciplines.

Transactional perspectives

The transactional approach suggests social phenomena must be understood as the result of interactions. Tilly applies it to the concept of trust (Tilly, 2005a). Intuitively, we tend to interpret it as an aspect of how we feel about another actor – in other words, a disposition – but a transactional approach conceives of it as an aspect of the relationship between ourselves and that other actor: the relationship is one of trust.

This approach has informed most of the literature on the role of the third sector in the public services. This is perhaps due to a certain disciplinary bias. Much of the interest in the topic has come from the field of public management, where network theory has steadily gained popularity. In addition, the focus on regime theory in social policy studies may have encouraged third sector researchers to look for alternatives. Whatever the origin, transactional perspectives have taken various forms.[6]

Of particular importance to the study of public services are the network perspectives that became popular in the field of public management and elsewhere in the social sciences over the past decades (e.g. Koppenjan and Klijn, 2004). These have brought home the point that public services are not the exclusive product of governments, but take shape as the joint product of a number of different actors. Not only has this perspective made it easier to include non-profit and voluntary organisations in the equation, but it has also made the relations between those actors the object of systematic empirical investigation, rather than making prior assumptions about the nature of those relations. More so than the other perspectives, it is capable of capturing the dynamics of state–third sector relations.

One risk is that the bigger picture is lost. An analysis of relationships is often built on an understanding of units of analysis or "nodal points" that are conceptually similar. For example, collective units such as organisations are analysed in relation to other collectives, but not to individuals. Likewise, individual clients face bureaucrats, not bureaucracies. It means that developments on other levels of analysis are left external to the analysis, unless specific attempts are made to integrate them. Recently, there has been such an attempt through the use of the "co-production" concept, distinguishing between three types of relationships between state and third sector (Pestoff and Brandsen, 2007). The concept connects activities of third sector organisations at different levels of analysis and at different stages of the policy cycle, which are often studied separately. Bringing them together within one framework could help to signal trade-offs and to allow a more holistic perspective. This is not necessarily limited to the third sector's role in service delivery, although that was what the framework was designed for.

Another risk is that the smaller picture is lost. In a transactional account, attention is not necessarily limited to relationships between actors. Interaction within the relationships changes the actors themselves, e.g. how they look upon the relationship or what they hope to get out of it. This is a crucial difference with dispositional perspectives that tend to take the actor's orientations as fixed. In third sector research, quite some attention has been given to how interaction with the state changes non-profit or voluntary organisations (e.g. Smith and Lipsky, 1993). In that respect, the latter could make a valuable addition to general network analysis, in which the focus tends to be on the interaction and its impact on relationships, but not on its impact on the actors themselves. What has received less attention in third sector research is how the relation between state and third sector has affected the former. Elsewhere, I have argued that the incorporation of non-profits in service delivery has encouraged the integration of service networks, breaking down traditional systems of differentiation (Brandsen and van Hout, 2006). Perhaps this constitutes innovation in the welfare state from the bottom up.

To conclude, transactional perspectives appear to be particularly apt at analysing the dynamics of institutional change. They are therefore especially useful for understanding the role of the third sector in reforms of the public services. They also hold up better to methodological scrutiny than systemic perspectives, although not (yet) as well as dispositional ones. What systemic accounts do show better is how processes at different levels of analysis connect. There is a risk that transactional accounts bound their units of analysis so tightly that the relationships with other levels of analysis are lost from view.

Conclusion

Earlier, I noted that theoretical development in third sector research during the 1990s has been more modest than in the period preceding it, although in recent years there seems to be a revival (see e.g. Evers and Laville, 2004). The slackening of the pace can be partly attributed to the fact that scholars have redirected their efforts towards accumulating empirical knowledge, which has indeed increased significantly. This, in turn, has allowed them to sharpen their theoretical lenses. But my own impression is that other factors have also been at play. In Europe at least, the debate has been insufficiently structured to allow different perspectives to "speak to" each other and to allow for the emergence of common frameworks and cumulative gains. The lack of a sound infrastructure for third sector research at the European level has held back the quality of the debate. Ironically, this has happened at a time when the empirical significance of the topic has been steadily mounting.

The exercise conducted in this chapter has left me with a new optimism about our ability to transcend disciplinary boundaries in this field. My review of the literature has been only illustrative and naturally reflects my personal bias. Nevertheless, it leads me to believe that the demarcations between different types of theoretical perspectives are not as solid as they might appear. In their ideal-typical form, they highlight specific aspects of the third sector's role. However, their applications only tend to lean toward one of the perspectives, without necessarily excluding others. Theoretically innovative work is likely to emerge at the crossroads. One of the ways for third sector research to move forward is to position itself at these crossroads, bringing together insights from various corners of the academic world. Its ambitions would then go beyond those of a specialist subject. Establishing an interdisciplinary forum at the European level would be a first step in realising those ambitions.

Notes

1 An earlier version of this chapter was presented at the ESF exploratory workshop "The Third Sector in a Changing Europe: Key Trends and Challenges" in December 2006 and subsequently published in the February 2007 edition of the bulletin of the *Centro de Investigación de Economía y Sociedad* (CIES, www.grupcies.com). I would like to thank all participants at the workshop and particularly Eva Kuti for their constructive comments.
2 The relationship between the terms "third sector" and "civil society" is contested, but it is clear that in discussions there is often a great deal of overlap.
3 Indeed, ideas of the "state" and the "market" as separate domains date from the same period.
4 The operationalisation of the philosophical in the shape of a legal category has worked best where it could easily be benchmarked against characteristics of the other domains, i.e. in terms of economic indicators.
5 Some may find it upsetting to cast such social phenomena as volunteering and altruism in rational terms, but that is either to confuse normative views with methodology or to deny the possibility of a duality in human motivation.
6 Kuhnle and Selle advocated a "relational approach" (Kuhnle and Selle, 1992), but as I have argued above, theirs is closer to a systemic than a transactional approach.

References

Anheier, H. and A. Ben-Ner (2003) *The Study of the nonprofit enterprise: theories and approaches*. Kluwer Academic/Plenum.

Arts, W. and J. Gelissen (2002) "Three worlds of welfare capitalism or more? A state of the art report", *Journal of European Social Policy*, 12, 2, pp. 137–58.

Ben-Ner, A. and B. Gui (2003) "The theory of nonprofit organizations revisited" in H. Anheier and A. Ben-Ner, *The study of the nonprofit enterprise: theories and approaches*, New York: Kluwer Academic/Plenum, pp. 3–26.

Brandsen, T. and V. Pestoff (2006) "Co-production, the third sector and the delivery of public services: an introduction", *Public Management Review*, 8, 4, pp. 493–501.

Brandsen, T. and E. van Hout (2006) "Co-management in public service networks: the organisational effects", *Public Management Review*, 8, 4, pp. 537–49.

Brandsen, T., W. van de Donk and K. Putters (2005) "Griffins or chameleons? Hybridity as a permanent and inevitable characteristic of the third sector", *International Journal of Public Administration*, 28, 9–10, pp. 749–65.

Dekker, P. (2001) "What crises, what challenges? When nonprofitness makes no difference" in H.K. Anheier and J. Kendall (eds), *Third sector policy at the crossroads: an international non-profit analysis*, London: Routledge, pp. 61–8.

Della Porta, D. and M. Diani (1999) *Social Movements: An Introduction*, Oxford: Blackwell.

Esping-Andersen, G. (1990) *The Three Worlds of Welfare Capitalism*, Cambridge: Polity Press.

Evers, A. and J.-L. Laville (eds) (2004) *The Third Sector in Europe*, Cheltenham: Edward Elgar.

Gidron, B., R.M. Kramer and L.M. Salamon (1992) "Government and the third sector in comparative perspective: allies or adversaries?" in B. Gidron, R.M. Kramer and L.M. Salamon (eds), *Government and the third sector: emerging relationships in welfare states*, San Francisco: Jossey-Bass Publishers, pp. 1–30.

Green-Pedersen, C. and M. Haverland (2002) "The new politics and scholarship of the welfare state", *Journal of European Social Policy*, 12, 1, pp. 43–51.

Hall, J.A. and F. Trentmann (2005) *Civil society: a reader in history, theory and global politics*, Basingstoke: Palgrave Macmillan.

Hasenfeld, Y. (1983) *Human service organizations*, Englewood Cliffs: Prentice Hall.

Hirschman, A.O. (1982) *Shifting involvements: private interest and public action*, Princeton and Oxford: Princeton University Press.

Kendall, J. and M. Knapp (1995) "A loose and baggy monster. Boundaries, definitions and typologies", in J.D. Smith, C. Rochester and R. Hedley (eds) *An introduction to the voluntary sector*, London: Routledge, pp. 66–95.

Koppenjan, J. and E.H. Klijn (2004) *Managing uncertainties in networks: a network approach to problem solving and decision making*, London: Routledge.

Kuhnle, S. and P. Selle (1992) "Government and voluntary organizations: a relational perspective" in S. Kuhnle and P. Selle, *Government and voluntary organizations*, Aldershot: Avebury, pp. 1–33.

Pestoff, V. and T. Brandsen (eds) (2007, forthcoming) *Co-production, the third sector and the delivery of public services*, London: Routledge.

Pestoff, V., S. Osborne and T. Brandsen (2006) "Patterns of co-production in public services: some concluding thoughts", *Public Management Review*, 8, 4, pp. 591–5.

Salamon, L.M. (1995) *Partners in public service: government-nonprofit relations in the modern welfare state*, Baltimore and London: Johns Hopkins University Press.

Salamon, L.M. and H.K. Anheier (1998) "Social origins of civil society: explaining the nonprofit sector cross-nationally", *Voluntas*, 9, 3, pp. 213–48.

Smith, S.R. and M. Lipsky (1993) *nonprofits for hire: the welfare state in the age of contracting*, Cambridge and London: Harvard University Press.

Tilly, C. (2005a) *Trust and rule*, Cambridge: Cambridge University Press.

Tilly, C. (2005b) *Identities, boundaries and social ties*, Boulder/London: Paradigm Publishers.

8 The third sector and the provision of public services in Slovakia

Juraj Nemec

Introduction

The size of the state and the methods of fulfilling its main functions (see for example Musgrave, 1959) have changed significantly in recent decades. After the World War II the role of the state expanded rapidly and public expenditure grew faster than GDP (Stiglitz, 1988). For example in Sweden in the early 1980s government expenditure reached almost 70 percent of GDP. The state delivered most of its activities via public sector bodies and public expenditure. But both countries and experts came to realize that such trends were unsustainable and started "reinventing government" (Osborne and Gaebler, 1993). "New Public Management" (NPM) (Coombes and Verjheijen, 1997) "replaced" the concept of the classical state in the last two decades of the twentieth century. However, after evaluations of the impact and outcomes of NPM it became clear that the use of market forces in the public sector also had noticeable limitations (Pollit and Bouckaert, 2004).

The "new" solutions at the beginning of this century are "modern governance" and public-private-civil sector mix (Finlay and Debicki, 2002).[1] This change brings new challenges for the third sector in all developed countries. The extent of the functions of non-governmental organizations is significantly increasing, and they are becoming increasingly important partners of the state in realizing all its objectives.

In this chapter we investigate the role of the third sector in the processes of delivery of public services in Slovakia. The first part of our paper provides general information about the third sector in the country and relates its trends and situation to respective phases of Slovak public administration reforms. The core part analyzes two different angles of the participation of the third sector in delivery of public services. First we investigate the sectoral level and focus on two crucial public services – education and healthcare. Second we analyze the municipal level – the methods of delivery of selected local public services and the system of allocation of grants to non-profit organizations, using data collected by the author and his research team.

The last parts present a synthesis of our findings and provide some lessons and conclusions.

The third sector in Slovakia

The Slovak Republic was established on January 1, 1993, as the result of an amicable split in the former Czechoslovakia. After the "Velvet Revolution" in 1989, the process of a gradual transition to a pluralistic democratic public administration system began in Czechoslovakia and the result was two independent countries – the Czech Republic and the Slovak Republic. After a successful process of transition in the major areas of political, social and economic life, on May 1, 2004 Slovakia became a member of the European Union.

Slovakia is a relatively small state in the middle of Europe. Its territory covers 49,034 km², the population at the end of 2005 was 5.4 million and the population density is 110 inhabitants/km². In recent years its economy and economic policies have developed the reputation as the most progressive in the region. Most economic indicators have shown significant improvement (Table 8.1) and its growth in 2004 and 2005 was the highest in the region.

The third sector also existed in Slovakia on a mass scale before 1989, with several types of private non-profit organizations (NPOs), playing very different roles in the society. Some "NPOs" were established to support communist ideology, such as the "Association of Women"; some NPOs just focused on the internal interests of their members (for example sport clubs), and few real non-governmental organizations served as small cells of resistance against the ruling regime (most of them as non-legal persons). The most common types of NPOs in the socialist Czechoslovakia were sports clubs and other interest associations.

After 1989 the changes did not bypass the third sector, but significantly amended its character. Bútorová and Bútora (1996) and Kuvikova (2006) characterized the following six phases of transformation of the third sector in Slovakia after the "Velvet Revolution":

Table 8.1 Main economic indicators for Slovakia

Indicator/year	1993	1996	2000	2001	2002	2003	2004
GDP (bil. Sk current prices)	369.9	581.3	936.2	1,010.4	1,091.8	1,189.1	1,325.5
Inflation	23.2	5.8	12.0	7.1	3.3	8.5	7.5
Unemployment rate	12.2	11.1	18.6	19.2	18.5	17.4	18.1*
Foreign trade balance (bil. Sk)	–	–	–0.9	–2.1	–2.1	–0.7	–1.4
Public debt (% GDP)	–	24.6	–	48.7	43.3	42.6	43.6
Public deficit (% GDP)	–	–	–6.1	–6.4	–7.5	–3.6	–3.3

Source: *Statistical Yearbook Slovakia*, 2005.

Note
* But according to the Labor office only 14.3%.

1   Diversification (1989–1992) – newly established NPOs defined their goals and status; many of them were created on the base of former "socialist NPOs", by redefining their goals.
2   Consolidation and professionalization (1992–1993) – the growth in the number of professionals and volunteers in the third sector; differentiation of NPOs starts.
3   Self-confidence (1994–1996) – the third sector begins to understand its importance and role in the modern society. The Meciar government does not cooperate with the third sector and the sector reacts by creating several initiatives to promote itself.
4   Mobilization (1997) – the third sector is actively involved in the pre-election process.
5   Stabilization (1998–2004) – the new Dzurinda government approves a legislative package for the non-profit sector and improves its relations with the sector.
6   Networking (2004 to date) – also as a result of joining the EU, and as a reaction to the increased complexity of daily problems NPOs start to cooperate and create networks.

According to the relevant legislation, the (formal) third sector in Slovakia comprises the following types of organization (Kuvikova, 2006):

- *Associations* – legal persons with physical or legal persons as their members. Associations are established by the decision of the founding group and are registered by the Ministry of the Interior. Associations are not subject to any specific state regulations and have free use of their own funds. Their business activities are not limited.
- *Foundations* – purpose based funds, based on monetary and non-monetary activities that are for the public interest. The existing legislation defines possible areas of the use of foundation resources, like protection of human rights, humanitarian activities, environmental activities, health, and education. The minimum value of a foundation fund must be 200,000 Slovak crowns. Foundations cannot enter entrepreneurial activities. Administrative costs are limited to a maximum 15 percent of total costs. Received grants with a value over 10,000 Slovak crowns must be reported to the tax office. Foundations must publish annual reports.
- *Non-investment funds* – non-profit legal persons associating financial funds that shall be used for public interest activities – namely activities in areas of cultural and human heritage and values, environment, maintenance of natural and cultural values and protection and development of health and education. These funds are registered by the regional state administration offices. Maximum administrative costs are limited to 15 percent of total costs. Entrepreneurial activities are not allowed. Funds must publish their yearly reports.
- *Non-profit organizations delivering public services* – legal persons that

deliver public services in the following areas – cultural and human heritage and values, environment, humanitarian activities, education of children and youth, social and healthcare. This type of NPO is registered by the regional office of the state administration. They can engage in entrepreneurial activities, but administrative costs are set at a maximum of 4 percent of total costs.

The description of types of NPOs in Slovakia clearly indicates that except for associations they are strictly regulated by legislative acts and can only be established for given legally specified purposes. The statistics on the NPO sector reflect this fact.

According to Kuvikova (2006) the central registry of all NPOs included 26,778 registered subjects. Of these, 93 percent were associations, 1.2 percent foundations, 1.9 percent non-investment funds and 3.9 percent were non-profit organizations delivering public services.

According to Filadelfiová *et al.* (2004) in 2002 the NPO sector employed 22,928 full-time employees, 60,574 part-time employees and 91,837 volunteers (2 percent of employment in the service sector, volunteerism not counted). It produced 1.1 percent of GDP. The most frequent NPO activities are described in Table 8.2.

In 2002 the cash revenues of the third sector were 18,103 million Sk (1.7 percent GDP), in kind revenues 13 million Sk. From this the state granted the NPO sector 4, 852 million Sk. State grants were allocated to finance cultural, sport and recreation activities (24.4 percent); professional organizations and unions (14.3 percent); education and research (9.2 percent); social care (3.0 percent); and healthcare (1.9 percent). The situation where the state focused on

Table 8.2 NPO activities in Slovakia

Activity	Total proportion (%)
Education and training	39.9
Social care and social services	32.3
Free tie activities (TIE?)	29.6
Culture and arts	18.9
Defending individual and group rights	17.2
Environment	13.3
Charity	11.7
Health care	9.5
Regional development and housing	9.0
Foundations and funds	9.0
Sport	7.4
Research, analytical studies	7.3
Exchange of volunteers	6.4
Recreation	5.6
Other	6.9

Source: Filadelfiová *et al.*, 2004.

financing of sport clubs and professional organizations (like chambers) changed a bit after 2005 with the transformation of many hospitals to the NPO form – social care expenditures do not include municipal level spending.

Slovak public administration reform and the third sector

Public administration reforms in Slovakia after the breakdown of the totalitarian regime were realized in three main phases:

- creation of self-governing structures (1990);
- "structural" reform (1996);
- "decentralization" reform (2001–2005).

The first important steps in the public administration reform had already been taken in the common Czechoslovak state after the 1989 "Velvet Revolution". The first democratic elections were held in June 1990 and became the basis for most changes. By virtue of the National Council Act 369/1990 self-government of municipalities with a high level of independence was re-established. Under this legislation, local authorities were constituted in municipalities, which are territorial and legal entities with their own budgets and assets.

The creation of municipal self-governments is also an important issue also from the point of view of the existence of NPOs in Slovakia. Municipalities may take decisions independently and act in all matters pertinent to the administration of the municipality and its property, if a special law does not assign such acts to the state or to other legal bodies or natural person. Their decisions and ordinances may be superseded or invalidated only by parliamentary acts or, if illegal, by courts. Already in 1990 municipalities were allocated many responsibilities – namely local public transport in big cities (Bratislava, Košice, Žilina, Prešov, Banská Bystrica), construction, maintenance and management of local roads and parking places, public space, public parks, public lighting, marketplaces, cemeteries, local water resources and wells, water supply networks, sewerage and water cleaning establishments in small municipalities, construction, maintenance and management of local cultural establishments, part of the sport, leisure and tourist establishments, childrens' homes, part of the ambulatory health services establishments, establishment of the basic social services (daily care) the support of following activities – education, nature and heritage protection, culture and artistic hobbies, physical culture and sport, the support of humanity activities and the administration of the municipality including police forces and fire services. The scope and method of discharging those responsibilities are independently decided by municipalities.

Under these conditions and in order to discharge their responsibilities, from the beginning municipalities started to cooperate with the third sector in many different ways – from simple non-monetary cooperation, via the provision of financial grants to the contracting and outsourcing of some services to NPOs. However, as we will show below in some case studies none of these forms of cooperation were undertaken in a fully systematic way.

The second stage of the public administration reform in Slovakia was mainly characterized by the following structural changes:

- the reversion to general local state administration;
- the change to the territorial structure of Slovakia;
- beginning a process to establish regional self-government.

These important changes were reflected in two important laws, Law No. 221/1996 on the territorial and administrative subdivision of the Slovak Republic and Law No. 222/1996 on organization of local state administration. But the noted changes had no significant influence on relations between public administration and the third sector.

After general elections in 1998 the new liberally oriented Dzurinda governments (1998–2006) readdressed the issue of public administration reform, as one of their main goals. The position of Government Appointee for Public Administration Reform was created, outside of formal ministerial structures, and Viktor Nižnanský, a representative of the right-wing political spectrum, was appointed.

The main idea was that decentralization would solve all inefficiencies (Stiglitz, 1999). In 2001 during a very short – probably too short – time all the basic legislation was approved by the parliament. For example the Civil Service Code was approved in June and the Public Service Code, the law on the creation of territorial authorities, and the law on elections of territorial authorities in July. The law on transfer of competencies of the state to the regional and local self-administration was approved in September, the amendment of the law on municipalities, the amendment of the law on municipal property, the law on the property of territorial authorities, an amendment to the law on budgetary rules, and finally the law on financial control and audit were all passed in October. Regional self-governments became operational from 2002.

The important law on transfer of competencies defined the set of competencies to be transferred to regional and local authorities. Following it a very large number of competencies were transferred in 2001–2002. Municipalities got new responsibilities in areas of road communications, water management, birth, marriage and death certificates, social care, environmental protection, education (elementary schools and similar establishments), physical culture, theatres, healthcare (primary and specialized ambulatory care), regional development and tourism. Regional governments became responsible for competencies in areas of road communications, railways, road transportation, civil protection, social care, territorial planning, secondary education, physical culture, theatres, museums, galleries, local culture, libraries, healthcare (polyclinics and local and regional hospitals), pharmacies, regional development, and tourism. A large set of these competencies was re-allocated from direct ministerial responsibility (hospitals, education, etc.). Finally a new fiscal decentralization system was only established in 2005, where the bulk of self-government incomes are from their own revenues, including shared taxes.

Changes in 2001–2005 significantly amended the public administration system and also positively changed several aspects of relations between public administration and the third sector, namely:

- In some sectors, like education (see below) the third sector got the same rights as other ownership forms to deliver public services.
- The third sector, and especially some segments of it, became the partner of the government and many NPOs started to be used as advisors in preparing public policies (e.g. MESA10, INEKO).
- The system of tax assignation (originally 1 percent for physical persons, from 2004 even 2 percent from tax obligation of legal and physical persons) was created. In 2005 almost one billion Slovak crowns were transferred to the third sector via this channel (www.rozhodni.sk).

However in most sectors and especially at a local level the reform did not set any rules or prepare any guidelines for the systematic realization of the public-private-civil sector mix. Thus there is scope for open agreements, for local political preferences, but also for non-transparency and even corruption, as we note below.

In 2006 the liberal government was replaced by a left-wing and populist parties' coalition under Prime Minister Fico. Concrete steps by this government have only just started, but it is apparent that the third sector may lose some of its previous prominence. The original proposal to abolish the system of tax assignation was not passed by parliament when voting on the 2007 state budget, but such a change is still pending. Some NPO tax deductions have already been abolished. The return to a massive state administration is already visible, via proclamations and also concrete actions such as the new law on financing of secondary art schools. It is impossible to assess how far the new government will revert to previous policies but the proposed changes surely cannot improve the efficiency and effectiveness of state service provision.

The third sector and the delivery of public services in Slovakia: sectoral cases

This part of the chapter analyzes the role of the third sector in the delivery of two main public services – education and healthcare.

Education

The financing of primary and secondary schools is a most effective example of the real incorporation of the third sector into the system of delivery of public services. It is based on the law on financing primary schools, of secondary schools and of other educational establishments (597/2003 Z.z.). According to this legislation, all schools delivering "state curricula" have an equal right to public finance. The system is relatively simple (based on the experience, for example, of the UK). The performance indicator is the number of pupils and the norms to calculate the grants are defined annually by the Ministry of Education (see Table 8.3).

Table 8.3 Financial norms for Slovak schools, 2006

School	Norms for salaries	Heating norms minimum	Heating norms maximum	Other running costs norms	Total norms minimum	Total norms maximum
Elementary	18,422	2,321	3,249	2,312	23,055	23,983
Grammar school	23,931	2,321	3,249	2,453	28,705	29,633
Sport grammar school	42,675	2,321	3,249	4,486	49,482	50,410
Professional schools	30,744	2,321	3,249	2,627	35,692	36,620
Secondary business schools	24,972	2,321	3,249	2,480	29,773	30,701
Secondary health care schools	40,792	2,321	3,249	2,884	45,997	46,925
Secondary art schools	56,167	2,321	3,249	3,278	61,766	62,694

Source: www.minedu.sk.

Such an approach might look effective, but as always there are problems. We raise only a few of them.

One hot issue is small schools in rural areas. With a limited number of pupils, but the same norms, their revenues cannot be sufficient to operate the school.[2] There are many arguments whether or not to close such small schools, and also a lot of discussion about this. Are unit costs and perhaps lower quality of education in combined classes for pupils of different ages more important than the factor of local culture, time, safety and transport costs to take pupils to other schools? Who could provide a definite answer?

The second hot issue is "equality" and "competition". Private non-profit schools have much more freedom in fundraising and in some cases they can even charge fees to pupils, though the state grant norms are not reduced by the full level of fees collected. Under these financial conditions the equal norm standard creates important inequalities and unfair competition. Moreover there is only very limited evidence of performance enhancing competition between different types of school.

Surprisingly, compared to primary and secondary levels, the system of tertiary level financing is designed to favor public institutions. Both public and private (for-profit and not-for-profit) universities/high schools can apply for accreditation. However only public schools have the right to public financing, and for most of them public grants, allocated mainly according to the number of students, represent about 90 percent of their total income. We argue that their dependence on the state is too high and the allocation formula does not encourage quality improvements. Public schools cannot collect student fees from full or part-time students.

Private schools, already discriminated against in the accreditation process (Nemec, 2006), can be subsidized from public funds. But the decision is entirely at the discretion of the Ministry of Education, and the level of grants differs widely – from zero to almost that given to public schools – where the school is linked to top politicians. The average annual level of private school fees is about €1,000.

Current proclamations indicate that in future the situation will not improve. The new Minister of Education even wants to exclude private non-profit schools from the system, mainly via accreditation.

Healthcare

The healthcare reform in Slovakia is characterized by the semi-radical shift after 2002 to the limited use of markets. In June 2004 Health Minister Zajac prepared and submitted to the parliament a new set of health laws that were expected to significantly change the system by increasing the level of co-payments, introducing commercial voluntary health insurance, and changing health insurance companies into joint-stock companies. All six draft laws were approved and have been operational from January 1, 2005.

From our point of view the most important was the law on health providers, health professionals and their professional bodies that enlarged the list of types of health providers (for example by including homecare and daycare), set the principles of minimum network and *provided for transformation of all health providers to non-profit or shareholder companies.*

Based on this law all state healthcare providers were transformed. Establishments of national importance were changed into public shareholder companies, and regional and local establishments were or privatized, turned into non-profits, or transferred to self-government.

All providers have the right to apply for reimbursement of their costs to health insurance companies, which are responsible for concluding contracts with healthcare providers. In order to guarantee the transparency of contract decision-making health insurance companies are obliged to publish selection criteria. Based on them, they will set the rank of contracted providers they must stick to. This rule means that all ownership forms are equal, and the service, though not the form of delivery, is the concern of state health policy. Thus a real space was opened up for the non-profit sector.

New legislation significantly influenced the ownership forms involved in the delivery of regional healthcare, but did not change the main principles of providing health to all Slovak citizens. The principle of the universal access remains the main goal, but the new ownership form was expected to improve the quality of services and the economic performance of providers.

The scale and outcomes of the transformation might be described using the example of the Banska Bystrica self-governing region. At the beginning of the reform the region had 16 state-owned hospitals. In 2005 one hospital – the teaching hospital in Banska Bytrica – was converted into a state-owned shareholder company. The other 15 hospitals were first transferred to the region or to municipalities and later most of them were transformed to non-profit organizations. First evaluations show that at least from financial viewpoint the transformation was a success – all 15 transferred hospitals significantly improved their economic performance and decreased deficits. Some of them even started to work with balanced budgets.

The new government already indicated that the "Zajac reform" will be re-evaluated. At a central level nothing has yet happened, but changes have already started at the regional level. For example, in spite of the initial success of the 2006 transformation the new Banska Bystrica regional parliament, led by "left-wing" parties, has started to discuss the future of four major transformed hospitals. The formal argument was about a lack of control over the basic network of in-patient care in the most important regional centers (Zvolen, Lucenec, Rimanska Sobota and Ziar nad Hronom). Unluckily, the discussion about the future ownership form of these hospitals was driven by ideology and not pragmatic policy issues, very much returning to a "socialist" terminology of "state=good", "private/non-profit=bad". The final outcome is re-nationalization. By spring 2007 all four hospitals are expected to be returned to the region. But the region is not even prepared to compensate their non-profit owners for the investments made during their management (www.pravda.sk).

The third sector and the delivery of public services in Slovakia: municipal level

Here we analyze the role of the third sector in the delivery of public services at a municipal level. Two aspects are investigated – the role of the third sector in delivery of local public services and the system of allocation of municipal grants to third subjects.

The third sector and the delivery of local communal services

Our research team has studied the methods of delivery of the local public services for more than five years and the main findings have already been published in comprehensive form in PhD. theses defended at the Matej Bel University in Banska Bystrica (Merickova, 2003; Majlingova, 2006).

According to our findings, all forms of ownership are used to deliver local public services, including third sector capacities. The third sector is represented mainly via two main forms:

* municipalities create NPOs (associations) to deliver the services, for example more than 10 percent from all arrangements for waste collection in small municipalities.
* the service is out-sourced to an independent NPO.

The main problems of these arrangements are connected with the selection of the method of delivery and with efficiency outcomes. In theory, the decision of the municipality to contract – to achieve the "best value" – should be based on careful analysis of all available choices. In our research we did not directly investigate this reality, knowing that under current circumstances this process cannot be systematic, and we focused only on the concrete process of the selection of an external supplier. The data from all our samples show that most municipalities use direct purchase or were not willing to provide information about the procurement method, despite their obligation to do so under the law on free access to information. We did not insist on answers at this stage, as the missing answer alternative is a good indication of two potential problems: municipalities either do not know, or do not want to tell, knowing that the selection was unfair. These both amount to the same thing.

The outcomes from non-systematic, perhaps corrupt selection process are straightforward and can be highlighted by efficiency (cost) figures. The data from different benchmarking samples clearly indicate that, even within the same size category, the costs of service delivery show far too wide a variation. The clearest case was found by Merickova (2003) – Table 8.4.

There are major cost differences. We do not have sufficient information to decide to what extent such differences are caused by objective factors – costs vary with local conditions – and to what extent by more subjective factors – such as a lack of decision-making capacity. They may even be due to corruption.

Table 8.4 Average costs of waste collection and refuse disposal by form of service delivery: Slovakia

Form of delivery	Number of municipalities	Average yearly costs per inhabitant
1 Municipal employees	2	136,29
2 Gross budgetary organization	2	295,34
3 Net budgetary organization	7	420,36
4 Municipal limited company	9	538,35
5 Municipal joint stock company	2	701,35
Average for internal forms	22	398,34
Contracting 1	11	351,14
Contracting 2	9	251,44
Contracting total	20	301,29

Notes
In gross budgetary organizations revenues and costs are separated, revenues cannot be used to cover costs and must be transferred to higher budget.
Contracting 1 – citizens pay fees only to the municipality.
Contracting 2 – citizens pay fees to both municipality and to supplier.

But they are very important, for they clearly indicate that any ownership form (including NPOs) can be effective and the financial and quality outcomes of any arrangement depend on the municipality and its capacity of effective and efficient decision making in favor of citizen interests and not in favor of the pockets of municipal bosses.

Municipal grants

As indicated above, after finishing the processes of transfer of responsibilities and of fiscal decentralization, municipalities are responsible for a really broad spectrum of public services and activities. Some of costs of these services are financed directly, via municipal bodies and organizations, some by contracts (see above), but some also by financial grants provided to legal persons delivering services of public interest.

The system of financial grants to legal persons was the subject of heavy criticism by NPOs, as the decision-making processes were non-transparent and non-systematic (Wright and Nemec, 2002). Such criticism and new budgetary rules, namely the change to medium-term programs and performance budgeting on the national level (www.finance.gov.sk) "motivated" most of the larger municipalities to draft and implement new rules for allocation of financial grants to legal persons in 2005 and 2006. To check the situation, we investigated websites of eight cities that were seats of regional self-government and looked for such regulations. The results are described in Table 8.5.

Our findings show that cities established certain rules on how to finance nongovernmental bodies involved in delivering public functions. But few if any of them created a substantive document that could be used as a rulebook guaranteeing

Table 8.5 The existence of a regulative document defining the rules of providing municipal grants

	The document is available from the web and sets criteria	The document exists but does not set criteria	The document is not available from the web
City	Banska Bystrica	Kosice, Presov, Zilina, Trnava*	Bratislava, Nitra

Note
*Trnava: criteria are not set but should be announced yearly by respective professional commissions.

an impartial, transparent, effective, predictable, reliable and accountable decision-making process when allocating municipal resources. These descriptors are the main values of the "European Administrative Space" – see the "White Paper on European Governance" (European Commission, 2001).

We document the problem of criteria with the example of Banska Bystrica (www.banskabystrica.sk). The main parts of the city legislation concerning the allocation of grants to legal bodies include the following:

1   Financial grants from the municipal budget can be provided to legal persons established by the municipality, and to other legal and natural persons[3] for listed public services.
2   The listed public services are healthcare, social care, humanitarian activities, charity, recreation, maintenance and presentation of human and cultural values, protection of human rights and freedoms, education, physical culture, research and science, environmental activities, regional development and employment and housing.
3   Evaluation of applications:

   •   The administrative bodies of the municipality check all formal aspects of the application.
   •   The professional committees of the municipality evaluate the application and set the proposed level of the grant.
   •   The municipal assembly decides the final structure and level of all grants.

4   Evaluation criteria (examples):

   •   Culture (planned level of grants about one million Slovak crowns in 2006) – history of the applicant, results of the applicant, development of city culture.
   •   Sport (planned level of grants about three million Slovak crowns in 2006) – number of members, results, involvement of citizens.

The shortened text of the municipal regulation concerning the allocation of grants in Banska Bystrica clearly indicates that subjectivism and clientelism have still an "open door". The criteria are not functional criteria to compare applications. The municipal assembly, when approving the budget (including grants), does not have enough detailed information about all applications, thus the main decision-making power is with committees. Those represented on committees, or having links and relations to their members have better chances than those who do not.

Compared to cities most smaller municipalities do not have any stated rules and finance activities purely on the basis of subjective decisions by local deputies and the local council. In sport resources predominantly go to local football clubs.

Findings and conclusions

In the first part of the chapter we clearly showed that the third sector in Slovakia is relatively well developed and has an important capacity to help to develop modern society through the many forms of its activities.

The second part highlighted the main general limits blocking a really comprehensive use of the capacity of the third sector to develop the country, connecting those limits with the character of the government and public sector reform. "Left-wing" coalitions naturally prefer the state and do not accept the third sector as a real partner. This was the case with the Meciar governments. It is also the case with the new Fico government (in power since 2006). This government has already reversed some previous governments' policies for financing the NPO sector and for the delivery of some services, especially education, to favor state production.

As regards "right-wing" coalitions, in spite of the relatively long period of liberal government (Prime Minister Dzurinda) and the liberal character of all public sector reforms from 1998 to 2006, a real plurality and equality of all ownership forms in the delivery of public services was not achieved. Indeed such a goal was not even mentioned in any of that government's final reform documents.

How does this situation impact the third sector in Slovakia? As shown in our selected concrete cases, the level and ways of involving the non-profit sector in the delivery of public services in Slovakia differ significantly between sectors, and between self-governing bodies. In some cases the non-profit sector is accepted as a standard delivery vehicle, e.g. primary and secondary education. In other cases – e.g. universities, and recently also regional healthcare and art schools – it is still discriminated against in spite of the fact that Slovakia has already introduced medium-term programs and performance budgeting systems at all levels. Some local and regional self-governments respect the principle of open competition for delivery of public tasks, others do not.

The outcomes of such a situation are straightforward – lack of transparency, openness, reliability, accountability and predictability when deciding the best delivery method for public services or the allocation of public grants to legal bodies. This results in damage to the efficiency, effectiveness and quality of delivery of public services. It contributes to the high level of corruption in the country, which in turn slows growth and development.

How and when will this situation change? At this point there is no effective answer.

Notes

1 Not all agree that public-private-civil sector mix, competition and cooperation are the optimal solution for the public sector at the beginning of the twenty-first century. Nevertheless this assumption is the normative basis of our paper.
2 To help small schools to adapt to the new system of financing, the concrete level of grant allocation changes in a "step by step" way – the minimum annual allocation is set as 90 percent from previous year's grant.
3 Including NPOs.

Bibliography

Bouckaert, G. (2002) "Renewing Public Leadership: the Context for Service Delivery Reform". *Delivering Public Services in CEE Countries: Trends and Developments*, Bratislava: NISPAcee, pp. 15–26.

Bútora, M. and Fialová, Z. (1995) *Nonprofit Sector and Volunteerism in Slovakia*, Bratislava: SAV.

Bútorová, Z. and Bútora, M. (1996) *Non-governmental Organizations and Volunteers in Slovakia*, Bratislava: SPACE.

Coombes, D. and Verheijen, T. (eds) (1997) *Public Management Reform: Comparative Experiences from East and West*, Bratislava: European Commission.

—— (2002) *Delivering Public Services in CEE Countries: Trends and Developments*, Bratislava: NISPAcee.

Filadelfiová, J., Dluhá, M., Marček, E. and Košičiarová, S. (2004) *Recognition of the Third Sector in Slovakia*, Bratislava: SPACE.

Finlay, J. and Debicki, M. (eds) (2002) Delivering Public Services in CEE Countries: Trends and Developments, Bratislava: NISPAcee.

Frič, P. (2000): *Neziskové organizace a ovlivňovaní veřejné politiky*, Praha: UK.

Korimová, G. (2006) "Moderný sociálny štát a sociálna ekonómia – nástroje novej sociálnej politiky" *Ekonomika a spoločnos_* 2/2006, pp. 35–46.

Kuvíková, H. (2004) *Neziskové organizácie v Európskej Únii*, Banská Bystrica: EF UMB.

—— (2006) *Rozvoj MVO za pomoci zdrojov EÚ*, Banská Bystrica: EF UMB.

Lane, J. E. (2000) *New Public Management*, London: Routledge.

Majlingova, L. (2006) *Spôsoby zabezpečovania služieb odpadového hospodárstva v SR*, Banska Bytrica: EF UMB.

Merickova, B. (2003), *Zabezpecovanie verejnych sluzieb verejnym a sukromnym sektorom*, Banská Bystrica: EF UMB.

Musgrave, R.A. (1959) *The Theory of Public Finance*, New York: McGraw-Hill.

Nemec, J. (2006) "Accreditation, Evaluation and Financing of Universities: Selected Issues". *Theoretical and Practical Aspects of Public Finance*, Praha: VŠE, CD-rom.

Osborne, D. and Gaebler, T. (1993) *Reinventing Government: How the Entrepreneurial Spirit is Transforming the Public Sector*, New York: Penguin Books.

Pollitt, Ch. and Bouckaert, G. (2004) *Public Management Reform. An International Comparison*, Oxford: Oxford University Press.

Salamon, L.M. (1999) *Global Civil Society: Dimensions of the Non-profit Sector*, Baltimore: Johns Hopkins Institute.

—— (2005) *Statistical Yearbook Slovakia 2005*, Bratislava: SSU.
Salamon, L.M. and Anheier, H.K. (1994) *The Emerging Sector. The Nonprofit Sector in Comparative Perspective – An Overview*, Baltimore: Johns Hopkins Institute.
—— (1998) *The Emerging Sector Revisited. A Summary*, Baltimore: John Hopkins Institute.
Stiglitz, J.E. (1988) *Economics of the Public Sector*, New York: W.W. Norton and Company.
—— (1999) *Stratégia decentralizácie a reformy verejnej správy*, Bratislava: Slovak government.
—— (2001) *White Paper on European Governance*, Brussels: European Commission.
Woleková, H., Petrášová, A., Toepler, S. and Salomon, L.M. (2000) *Nonprofit Sector in Slovakia – Economic analysis*, Bratislava: SPACE.
Wright G. and Nemec. J. (eds) (2002) *Public Management in the Central and Eastern European Transition: Concepts and Cases*, Bratislava: NISPAcee.

Websites

www.rozhodni.sk
www.minedu.sk
www.pravda.sk
www.finance.gov.sk
www.banskabystrica.sk

9 The innovative capacity of voluntary and community organizations

Exploring the organizational and environmental contingencies[1]

Stephen P. Osborne, Kate McLaughlin and Celine Chew

Theoretical and empirical background

The innovative capacity of voluntary and community organizations (VCOs) as public service providers has long been a key assertion of the public policy debate in the UK, stretching back for almost 100 years. This ascribed capacity has its basis in historical fact, as VCOs were the prime innovators of social welfare, and other, public services in the nineteenth century (Webb and Webb 1911). Subsequently this perception became embedded as the official view of this capacity (for example Beveridge 1948; Ministry of Health 1959; Home Office 1990; Labour Party 1990). Yet, despite such reification of this innovative capacity, little research has taken place to evaluate this claim. The only study of any substance prior to this current work is the American study of Kramer (1981) – now limited both by its American context and considerable age. Reviewing the literature in 1998, Osborne (1998a) concluded that such studies as there were, were limited by three factors:

1 their reliance on normative argument rather than empirical data;
2 their lack of attention to the mainstream innovation studies literature (for example, Rogers and Shoemaker 1971; Rothwell 1975; Abernathy *et al.* 1983; Van de Ven *et al.* 1989; Herbig 1991) and the potential that this literature has for offering theoretical and empirical insights into the public service context, and;
3 the lack of attention to the possibility of situating this capacity within a contingent framework that recognized the impact of the public policy environment upon innovativeness.

In the broader public services arena, there have also been a limited number of studies of innovation in public services (see Osborne and Brown (2005) for a more extensive literature review). Most notably in this literature, Borins (2001) has explored the public policy – public services delivery interface and its impact on innovation in public services. Despite its importance, this work is hampered in its applicability to the UK by its national specificity within the US public policy system. In a European context, Koch and his colleagues in the EU *Publin* programme (for example, Koch and Hauknes 2005; Malikova and Staroòová 2005; Koch *et al.* 2006) have explored the public policy context of innovation within public service organizations in the European Union. However, whilst this is useful work at the industry level, the issue of the innovative capacity of VCOs is wholly absent from their work.

Finally, much of this work has not been grounded in the 'innovation studies' literature, above, that might give a more robust theoretical, as opposed to normative or empirical, basis to the debate (Osborne and Brown 2005). Consequently the previous work of the lead author of this paper, in the early 1990s (Osborne 1998a), was the first research study in the UK that:

- mapped this innovative capacity of VCOs and developed a contingent model of it, within the field of social welfare in the UK, and;
- drew upon the organization theory and innovation studies literature to inform our understanding of the innovative capacity of VCOs.

Crucially it developed a typology of innovation (Osborne 1998b) in the social sector that differentiated between:

- *the traditional activity of VCOs* in providing specialist services (situated within the 'traditional organizations' in this chapter);
- *the developmental activity of VCOs* involved in the incremental change of their services (situated within the 'developmental organizations' in this chapter), and;
- *the innovative activity of VCOs* that changed the paradigm of their services and/or their skills base (situated within the 'innovative organizations' in this chapter) – and also separated this innovative activity into three distinct modes, as discussed further below.

It is important to note that this differentiation does not suggest any normative difference between these modes of work – they can all have a positive or negative impact upon an organization or its services (for example, Rosner 1967; Kimberly 1981; Mole and Elliot 1987). Nor does it suggest any differentiation in term of longer term impact – over time, a series of smaller, incremental, service developments may produce a much more profound effect upon a service than a single innovation (see, for example, Van de Ven *et al.* 1989). However, as the innovation studies literature makes clear, innovation does pose distinctive organizational and managerial challenges, compared to the other two modes.

Osborne (1998a) argued further that the innovative capacity of VCOs was not a function of their organizational characteristics, such as their structure or culture (as much of the policy literature invariably suggested), but rather it arose out of the interaction of these organizations with their institutional and policy environments. *That is, it was the action and policy context created by central and local government that encouraged innovative activity by VCOs rather than it being an inherent consequence of their organizational structure or culture.* Subsequent work by other researchers has confirmed and developed this model in other fields beyond social care – such as the work of Walker *et al.* (2001) in the field of housing.

The original study by Osborne (1998a) provided a significant empirical study of the organizational and environmental factors that mediated the innovative capacity of VCOs in the provision of social care services. The present chapter reports on a replication of this original study to test if/how this innovative capacity has changed over the past decade and in relation to what contingencies.

Methodology

The 1994 research involved both a postal survey and cross-sectional case studies of VCOs across three localities in England – an urban (Midwell), suburban (Bellebury) and rural (Southshire) locality. The initial intention for the present study had been for an exact replication of this research. However, at a late juncture, the key stakeholder for one of the original research sites (the suburban locus) withdrew involvement because of their own financial crises and subsequently a replacement locality was identified. 'Bellebury' was thus replaced with 'Siliton'.[2] Whilst this does diminish the exact replication of the original research, nonetheless it does provide a robust longitudinal test of the sustainability of the innovative capacity of VCOs.

This chapter first summarizes the first stage of this replication study – the postal survey of all VCOs involved in social care across the three localities. The purpose here was to map the extent of the innovative, developmental and traditional VCOs and to examine any key differences between them. This element of the study is reported in full in Osborne *et al.* (2008). It then explores three cross-sectional case studies conducted across the three research sites, in order to test out four possible hypotheses for the innovative capacity of VCOs. These hypotheses are detailed further below.

These cross-sectional case studies included semi-structured interviews with the chief executives of VCOs and their staff, semi-structured interviews with other key informants in the localizes (such as staff from the local voluntary sector intermediary bodies, governmental officials and other community leaders) and the collation and analysis of key organizational and service policy documents. Twenty-four VCOs were involved in the case studies in 1994–1999: nine (38 per cent) innovative VCOs, seven (29 per cent) developmental VCOs and eight (33 per cent) traditional VCOs. Thirty VCOs were involved in the 2006 case studies – 16 (54 per cent) innovative VCOs, seven (23 per cent) developmental VCOs and seven (23 per cent) traditional VCOs. All were split equally across the three localities.

Mapping the extent of the innovative capacity of VCOs

The initial postal survey was analysed by the use both of Chi-Square tests and Discriminant Analysis, in order to evaluate the significant organizational dimensions of the innovative capacity of VCOs. It explored the extent of the innovative, developmental and traditional work of these organizations, as defined above. The research methodology is detailed further in Osborne *et al.* (2008).

Table 9.1 lays out the profile of the innovative activity in both the 1994 and 2006 surveys. The contrast between the surveys in 1994 and 2006 is stark. Over this period, the innovative activity of VCOs shrank from 37.9 per cent to 19.1 per cent whilst their developmental work increased from 13.9 per cent to 35.7 per cent. The traditional activity has stayed almost constant at 45.2 per cent in 2006 compared to 48.2 per cent in 1994. Far from being a constant element of the organizational activity of VCOs, innovation appears as a variable – and potentially a contingent one. This contrast is shown diagrammatically in Figure 9.1.

The relationship between a group of organizational characteristics and innovative capacity was also explored in both studies through Chi-Square tests and Discriminant Analysis (Eisenbis and Avery 1972; Klecka 1980). In 1994 it proved hard to differentiate the innovative and developmental VCOs on the basis of these characteristics. This was also the case in 2006.

A strong discriminating function[3] did exist in 1994 between the innovative and traditional organizations around the former's receipt of significant government funding,[4] the presence of paid staff and being young (aged under six years) organizations. By 2006, however, the strength of this function had been dissipated – and significantly government funding had been removed from it. This will be returned to below.

Table 9.1 The innovative activity of VCOs

Type of activity	Locality				
	Bellebury	*Siliton*	*Midwell*	*Southshire*	*Overall*
Innovative 1994	*43.1*	*N/A*	*35.0*	*36.5*	*37.9*
Innovative 2006	N/A	18.8	24.2	18.8	19.1
Developmental 1994	*13.8*	*N/A*	*19.0*	*9.5*	*13.9*
Developmental 2006	N/A	33.3	30.3	44.1	35.7
Traditional 1994	*43.1*	*N/A*	*46.0*	*54.0*	*48.2*
Traditional 2006	N/A	47.9	45.5	41.2	45.2
Total	100	100	100	100	100

Notes
A note on response rates. In 1994 376 organizations were surveyed with 196 organizations responding – a response rate of 52.1 per cent (potentially rising to 67.6 per cent allowing for organizational morbity). In 2006 356 organizations were surveyed with 115 responding – a response rate of 32.0 per cent (potentially rising to 42.0 per cent allowing for organizational morbity).

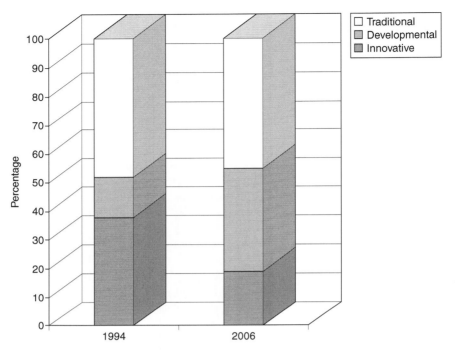

Figure 9.1 The activity of VCOs in 1994 and 2006 (by %).[6]

An important conclusion of the 1994 study was that governmental policy, at a central and local level, was a key contingency in the priming of the innovative capacity of VCOs, rather than any inherent organizational characteristics. Given that this has now disappeared from the analysis in 2006, and that the innovative capacity has shrunk as the developmental capacity has increased, a question raised by this replication study was therefore: *have the policy imperatives of governmental policy changed to lessen the innovative imperative upon VCOs?*

Four hypotheses of the innovative capacity of VCOs

The 1994 study established four hypotheses that might explain the innovative capacity of VCOs. These were derived from an analysis of the existing organizational studies and VCO literatures upon innovation (Osborne 1998a, pp. 62–67). These were that it was a function of:

- their structural organizational characteristics;
- their internal organizational culture;
- their relationship to their external environment, and;
- the institutional framework for their role in delivering public services.

That study found no evidence to support either of the first two hypotheses. Rather it argued that the innovative capacity of VCOs was a result of the confluence of the latter two hypotheses. First, the innovative VCOs had a more proactive strategic intent towards their environment. Second, the innovative VCOs were significantly more dependent upon the government for the main income stream – and this funding was predicated upon public policy that privileged innovative activity above all other activity. *Far from being an inherent characteristic, therefore, the innovative capacity of VCOs arose from their interaction with their environment, and particularly with their public policy environment.* This encouraged them both to pursue innovative activity in preference to developmental or traditional activity, and to portray their organizational activity as innovative, irrespective of its actual nature, in order to secure their income streams from government. The 2006 study thus returned to explore these four hypotheses again, to discover whether this pattern had maintained or not.

The organizational hypothesis

This hypothesis argues that the innovative capacity of VCOs is a function of their formal structural characteristics. The VCO literature has long claimed that innovative capacity of VCOs was a result of the low level of their organizational structure and the consequent flexibility that this gave them (for example Mellor 1985).

The case studies in 1994 and 2006 found little to support this hypothesis. In terms of organizational status, there was no discernable pattern between the three organizational sub-groupings. All the VCOs were either independent organizations or else a part of federated VCOs with significant local independence of organizational activity. Similarly, the majority of the organizations had been founded independently by either an individual or a small group of people. Only five VCOs in 1994, and six in 2006, reported that another organizational has been involved in their foundation.

In terms of organizational decision-making, all the organizations reported that the formal decision-making responsibility lay within the organization (either with the trustees or a paid manager) for five key areas: the allocation of organizational resources; staffing and personnel; capital expenditure; structural change; and organizational policy/procedures.

Some differentiation is found in terms of organizational complexity and this is consistent over the two time periods. Respondents were asked to specify the organizational tiers of their VCOs. The traditional VCOs were the least 'tiered' – two-thirds of these VCOs over the two time periods had only a Management Committee and a volunteer base. In contrast both the developmental and innovative VCOs had at least one paid manger with other staff to manage – and with a striking increase over 1994–2006 from one manager alone to a larger managerial team.

In terms of organizational formalization an interesting, if serendipitous, finding emerges. In 1994, all the VCOs had low levels of organizational

Table 9.2 Levels of organizational structure

		Management committee plus volunteers [1] additional paid staff [2]	[1] plus a paid manager, with/without to them	[2] plus other paid managers with staff responsible
Innovative	1994	1	8	0
VCOs	2006	3	6	7
Developmental	1994	2	4	1
VCOs	2006	1	3	3
Traditional VCOs	1994	5	3	0
	2006	5	2	0
Total	1994	8 (33%)	15 (63.5%)	1 (3.5%)
	2006	9 (30%)	11 (37%)	10 (33%)

formalization and with no discernable pattern across the three organizational modes. Only around one-third had any formal organizational policies, procedures or work schedules, though 46 per cent did have job descriptions. Only 17 per cent reported any formal evaluation of their work.

By 2006 the level of formalization has increased dramatically, particularly for those VCOs involved in innovative or developmental work. Most revealingly the formal evaluation of their work has increased significantly for the innovative and developmental organizations, though it has declined slightly for the traditional ones (Table 9.3). The picture is thus one of a VCO sector that is becoming increasingly formal in its work practices. The level of formalization does differentiate the innovative and developmental VCOs from the traditional ones, but with little to differentiate these former two groups.

Finally VCOs were asked to report the extent to which specialist job roles (where a member of staff specialized in that task alone) existed within them. There are some differences here (Table 9.4). In 1994 the innovative and developmental VCOs had far more specialist posts than the traditional VCOs whilst administrative roles were far more common within the innovative than

Table 9.3 levels of organizational formalization (%)

Type of document	1994 (all VCOs)	2006			
		Innovative	Developmental	Traditional	Total
Organizational policy	33	75	100	43	77
Organizational procedures	37.5	62	86	43	63
Organizational work schedule	33	44	57	29	43
Job description	46	62	86	43	64
Formal evaluation of all/part of organizational work	17	75	71	14	60

Table 9.4 Specialization of organizational roles (%)

Organizational role	Innovative VCOs		Developmental VCOs		Traditional VCOs		Total	
	1994	2006	1994	2006	1994	2006	1994	2006
Service provision	55	75	57	86	25	71	46	66
Administrative	78	87	0	71	25	71	37.5	80
Support services (e.g. training)	22	37	14	86	0	29	12.5	59

the developmental organizations. By 2006, again all the organizations had become more formalized with much greater levels of job specialization for all the organizations (interestingly the developmental VCOs had a much greater level of organizational support roles than the other two modes). Yet overall, no clear pattern emerges to differentiate the VCOs engaged in innovative activity from their developmental or traditional counterparts.

In conclusion there is no significant evidence from either 1994 or 2006 of significant organizational differentiation between the innovative, developmental and traditional VCOs. *There is serendipitous evidence of increasing organizational formalization and specialization across the innovative and developmental VCOs, in particular, that may well indicate isomorphic pressures on the sector as a whole, as it has taken on an increasing role in the provision of public services.* This is deserving of further exploration in the future. However such patterns as there are, are not substantial and there is no support for the organizational hypothesis of the innovative capacity of VCOs.

The cultural hypothesis

In both studies this was explored through organizational and staff group size and managerial style. In terms of organizational size, 1994 presented a picture of VCOs that were predominantly small organizations – two-thirds of them had annual budgets of under £10,000. Of the larger organizations two-thirds were involved in innovative activity. In 2006, by contrast, the VCOs in the study were now much larger – two thirds of them had annual budgets of over £10,000 (four of them had budgets of over £1,000,000) and half of the larger organizations were involved in innovative activity. Conversely all of the developmental VCOs had larger budgets (Tables 9.5 and 9.6). The picture therefore suggests size is a potential differentiator between the traditional VCOs and the innovative and developmental ones but it is by no means clear cut. Nor is it clear whether the larger size is a potential causal factor or consequence of such activity.

In terms of leadership style, the two studies explored these for all the case study organizations. All the organizational leaders were asked to classify themselves across five archetypes of managerial style: administration; line management; delegation; networking; and leadership.[5] Not surprisingly, most

Table 9.5 Organizational size as measured by budget (1994)

Type of VCO	Level of budget		Total
	£10,000 or under	*£10,001 or over*	
Innovative	5	4	9
Developmental	6	1	7
Traditional	7	1	8
Total	18	6	24

Table 9.6 Organizational size as measured by budget (2006)

Type of VCO	Level of budget		Total
	£10,000 or under	*£10,001 or over*	
Innovative	6	10	16
Developmental	0	7	7
Traditional	4	3	7
Total	10	20	30

Table 9.7 Organizational leadership archetypes (1994)

Type of VCO	Managerial archetypes				
	Administration	*Line management*	*Delegation*	*Networking*	*Leadership*
Innovative	4	0	1	2	2
Developmental	1	1	1	2	2
Traditional	5	1	1	1	0
Total	10	2	2	5	4

respondents found this hard, as they often took on multiple roles in an organization, as one of the managers of the innovative VCOs in the original study articulated: 'Even if the [new] idea didn't originate with me, I would have to enthuse others, set up contacts and arrange meetings, carry out administrative functions for weeks, months or even years.'

However, when pressed, all leaders were able to identify most with one of the archetypes (Tables 9.7 and 9.8). In 1994 the picture was very mixed – no one leadership archetype dominated for the innovative organizations (though an administrative role was widespread), the developmental VCOs were mixed and the traditional VCOs tended to adopt a primarily administrative approach. The picture is similar in 2006. The innovative VCOs still displayed a range of managerial styles, though this time with the 'leadership' role predominating, the

Table 9.8 Organizational leadership archetypes (2006)

Type of VCO	Managerial archetypes				
	Administration	Line management	Delegation	Networking	Leadership
Innovative	2	3	2	1	5
Developmental	5	0	0	1	4
Traditional	5	0	0	1	1
Total	12	3	2	3	10

developmental VCOs continued to be mixed and the traditional VCOs adopted a primarily administrative approach.

In terms of organizational culture, therefore some limited differences were noted above between the three modes of organizations. These are significant in terms of the traditional VCOs (they tend to be smaller organizations with an administrative style of leadership), but offer no convincing explanation of either innovative or developmental capacity for VCOs.

The environmental hypothesis

This hypothesis looked at how the case study VCOs related to their environment across two dimensions. These were their mode of service delivery and their strategic orientation.

Mode of service delivery

The 1994 study found little differentiation between any of the organizational modes in terms of the extent to which they provided standard or user-defined services. By 2006 there was a clear move towards more user-defined services – though this was across all three modes of organizations and not solely the innovative ones. In terms of accessibility to service users, the 1994 study found that all the organizations accepted referrals from users themselves and only a minority accepted them through another organization (17 per cent). This remained the case for all the VCOs in 2006.

Strategic orientation

This was explored by classifying the responses of organizational leaders to the external environment using the Miles and Snow (1978) strategic gestalts (Table 9.9). The 1994 study found a striking difference between the innovative and traditional VCOs – the former committed to the prospector and analyser gestalts, with their forward looking orientation, and the latter towards the defensive gestalt, with its commitment to maintaining the status quo. No identifiable pattern was found for the developmental VCOs. This finding was replicated in

Table 9.9 The strategic gestalts of the VCOs

Organizational gestalt	Key features	Year	Organizational mode			Total
			Innovative	Developmental	Traditional	
Defender	Limited service lines with emphasis on efficiency and stability	1994	0	2	7	9
		2006	0	2	6	8
Prospector	Broad service lines with dynamic approach to the environment	1994	4	0	0	4
		2006	7	1	0	8
Analyser	Standard range of services but also searching for new ones	1994	5	3	1	9
		2006	7	2	0	9
Reactor	Makes inconsistent choices – a 'non-strategy'	1994	0	2	0	2
		2006	0	2	1	3

2006. It does seem therefore that the innovative VCOs did and do adopt a more 'hands-on' and responsive strategic approach to their environments whilst the traditional VCOs are significantly more cautious. However this does not offer any explanation of the relationship between the innovative and developmental VCOs. To understand this we must examine the public policy framework and its contingencies in more detail.

The institutional hypothesis

The exploration of this hypothesis requires an understanding of how the public policy framework both for innovation in public services and towards the role of VCOs in public services delivery has shifted over the 1994–2006 period and its impact upon the innovative capacity of these organizations. What is interesting from the earlier examination of the survey data (Osborne *et al.* 2008) is how the balance of government funding has changed over the past decade. In 1994, the innovative organizations accounted for 80 per cent of government funding compared to the developmental VCOs, and for 73.8 per cent compared to the traditional VCOs. In 2006, by contrast, the balance swung. Now the developmental VCOs accounted for 56.6 per cent of governmental funding compared to the innovative ones and the traditional VCOs accounted for 59.3 per cent of such funding compared to their innovative counterparts. The import of government policy has thus swung away from the innovative VCOs and towards their developmental and traditional counterparts. This is particularly interesting when one examines how the public policy terrain has also shifted over this period.

The policy framework in 1994

It is unquestionably true that innovation was seen as a core element of the provision of social care services by VCOs in the early 1990s. At the broadest policy level, the introduction of non-statutory, and especially VCO, service providers was argued to stimulate the development of services that 'met individual needs in a more flexible and innovative way' (Department of Health 1989, para 3.4.3) and the influential Griffiths Report had also argued for the use of VCOs to provide social care services in order 'to widen consumer choice, stimulate innovation and encourage efficiency' (Griffiths 1988, para 1.3.4).

This policy focus on innovation as a normative good was also mirrored in the key professional organizations in social care at the time. The Kings Fund Institute (1987) had previously argued for the centrality of innovation in the impending community care reforms to be stimulated by the Griffiths Report. In a similar vein, Smale and Tuson (1990) at the National Institute of Social Work made a case for innovation to be elevated to the status of a method of social work intervention. Innovation, they argued, should become 'almost synonymous with social work' (p. 158).

A key policy driver at that time was undoubtedly the influential 'New Right' think tank, the Adam Smith Institute, epitomized by the work of its Director,

Madsen Pirie (1988) and which embraced the model of competitive advantage (Porter 1985). This placed innovation at the heart of the effective workings of the market. Its tenets are well summarized by Nelson (1993, p. 364):

> For-profit business firms in rivalous competition with each other are the featured actors [in innovation]. Firms innovate in order to gain competitive advantage over their rivals ... A firm that successfully innovates can profit handsomely.

It has been argued convincingly elsewhere that it was this model of competitive advantage that influenced the public policy models of the Conservative government of the early 1990s, predicated upon assumptions that the introduction of market disciplines to public services would lead to both greater economy and greater efficiency in service delivery. One influential commentator at the time argued that in social care this shift was itself a paradigmatic one from the community development roots of social care (as epitomized by Abrams *et al.* 1989) and towards one of 'market development and market management' (Wistow *et al.* 1994, p. 22; see also Le Grand 1991 and Wistow *et al.* 1996).

As innovation became more ingrained in the public policy agenda of the early 1990s, so did the ascribed role of VCOs in bringing this capacity to the provision of public services. This was embodied both by the then efficiency scrutiny of VCOs by the government (Home Office 1990), that lauded their ability to be 'in the forefront of developing new [public] service approaches' and the pronouncements of both the Labour and Conservative Parties in the run up to the 1992 general election (Labour Party 1990; NCVO 1991). Finally, the VCO sector was itself not slow in heralding its innovative capacity, in its efforts to establish itself as a mainstream public service provider alongside, or instead of, local government (for example Burridge 1990).

This macro-level public policy context influenced profoundly the structure of government funding of VCOs in the early 1990s. Thus the then Department of Health placed innovation firmly at the heart of its funding rules for VCOs. An example of this was funding of these groups under Section 64 of the *Health Services and Public Health Act 1968*. The first page of the application form for these grants in the early 1990s emphasized that for a project to be considered for a grant it 'must be innovatory' – a point emphasized further in the Guidance Notes accompanying these forms. Similar conditions were also found in the *Inner City Partnership Scheme* of the Department of the Environment. Finally the Department of Health, again, adopted the 'outcome funding' model of the Rensselaerville Institute (Williams and Webb 1992) as a means through which to stimulate innovation in relation to the *Drugs and Specific Alcohol Grants 1994–1995* – and engaged the self-styled 'Innovation Group' to administer this scheme.

The 1994 study found this national public policy emphasis upon innovation as key funding parameter of VCOs active at the local level also. All three local authorities in the case study sites had strategic plans on their relationship with the VCO sector and all emphasized the importance of their innovative capacity.

The Bellebury document asserted that they had a 'capacity to innovate, experiment and test new ideas' and explicitly related funding such organizations to their ability to innovate in public services delivery, whilst the Midwell document identified innovation as one of four key funding priorities in relation to the VCO sector (Osborne 1998a, p. 150).

Importantly, as well as being a policy imperative, innovation was also seen as a useful tool through which to allocate scarce resources. One central government policy officer in 1994 explained that they did not actually use a strict definition of innovation but rather used a loose one that 'allowed [us] to support and help [VCOs] to do things that we would like them to do' – a position echoed at the time by the Research Director of one of the large charitable foundations that funded VCO activity.

This approach to innovative as an allocative mechanism invariably drew an angry response from VCO workers, as epitomized by this VCO field worker quoted in the 1994 study:

> Things have to be innovative for the [funding body], whether they are needed or not. It's just dressing things up as innovative to get money. What we want is an appropriate response to an appropriate problem ... but we have to dress it up as innovative for them. The process is tortuous.
>
> (quoted in Osborne 1998a, p. 151)

Finally, as at the national level, VCOs were not slow to ascribe to themselves this innovative capacity, if they thought that it could assist in gaining governmental funding. For example, a leading VCO intermediary body in Southshire in 1994 prefaced its contribution to the Community Plan of the local authority by emphasizing the 'adaptive and innovative' character of VCOs in that area.

The early 1990s thus presented a set of inter-locking factors that all privileged the ascribed innovative capacity of VCOs as a core expectation when they sought governmental funding:

- a government influenced by the market approach to the provision of public services and the centrality of competition and of innovation to this;
- subsequently, government public policy that required innovation as a precondition of governmental funding of VCOs;
- practice at a local level that both reflected these national priorities and that used innovation as a useful tool by which to allocate scarce public resources, and;
- both local and national VCOs actively encouraging the perception of themselves as innovative in order to attract governmental funding and to assert their hegemony over local government as the 'provider of first choice' for public services.

The net result of these factors for those VCOs dependent upon government funding as a prime source of income was twofold. It was *both* to encourage them to engage in innovative activity rather than to provide and/or develop their traditional 'specialist' services *and* to portray their services as innovative, irrespective of their true nature, in order to gain governmental funding within the prevailing rules of the game at the time.

The policy framework in 2006

Analysis of the core policy documents from the contemporary period and the stakeholder interviews from the three longitudinal case sites have revealed three significant changes in the place of innovation in public policy and the role that VCOs can play in it. These are:

- a *reformulation of innovation* not as paradigmatic shift but rather as 'continual improvement';
- a *re-evaluation of the role of the VCO sector in innovation* in public services, and;
- a *changing orientation towards innovation* at the local level, in terms of the operation of funding regimes for public services.

In terms of *the reformulation of innovation*, at the outset it is vital to emphasize that innovation has not disappeared from the public policy environment. This is far from the truth. Innovation has been at the core of the 'modernizing government' agenda of the current Labour government, since the publication of the *Modernizing Government* White Paper in 1999 (Cabinet Office 1999). At the time, the Public Audit Forum emphasized that this White Paper 'encourages public bodies to adopt innovative and flexible approaches to [public] service delivery' (Public Audit Forum 1999). Subsequently national government initiatives such as the *Invest to Save Budget* have been predicated upon the need 'to promote successful innovation and to deliver better public services' (House of Commons Select Committee of Public Accounts 2003, p. 2) whilst the National Endowment for Science, Technology and the Arts (NESTA) has emphasized the links between innovation in public services, public procurement policy and the efficient and effective provision of public services (NESTA 2007).

What has occurred however has been a reformulation of the nature of innovation. As noted, in 1994 that understanding of innovation was rooted in Porter's model of competitive advantage and it emphasized the view of innovation as 'creative destruction' by which existing service paradigms were transformed by discontinuous organizational change. This approach is at the heart of the innovation studies literature and is encapsulated in the definition and classification of innovation used in this study and presented above.

Significantly, the view of innovation employed within the current policy framework is profoundly different – and indeed somewhat at odds with the academic advisors to government who have continued to emphasize the transformational, rather than developmental, nature of innovation (for example, Hartley 2006). Situating its discourse within the organization behaviour discourse, rather than the market economics discourse, the *Modernising Government* White Paper (Cabinet Office 1999) portrays innovation as part of the creation of a culture of organizational learning by public service organizations – and the creation of 'learning organizations' (Argyris and Schon 1978; Senge 1990). In this it identifies innovation as the process of the '*continuous improvement* in central government policy making and service delivery' (para. 4.9, our emphasis).

Such an approach is central of a range of policy documents since the publication of the 1999 White Paper (such as National Audit Office 2005; Prime Minister's Strategy Unit 2006; Museum Libraries Archives Partnership 2007), as well as to the Best Value performance regime for local authorities (for example ODPM 2003). The reformulation is best captured though in the text of a speech by the British Prime Minister, Tony Blair, in 2004. This criticized the 'failed neo-conservative experiment' that relied upon markets and competition to drive forward public services and offered an alternative vision:

> Public services have a crucial role to play in our society.... It is only by truly transferring power to the public through choice, through personalising services, through enhanced accountability, that we can create the drivers for *continuous improvement* in all our services ... Our strategy for *continuous improvement* [in public services] through giving power to people involves greater choice, greater voice and more personalised services.
>
> (Tony Blair 2004, our emphases)

Alongside this re-conceptualization of the nature of innovation in public services as continuous improvement rather than paradigmatic change, there has also been *a re-evaluation of the role that VCOs can play in innovation*. The early part of this paper noted the reification of the innovative capacity of VCOs in public policy from the turn of the twentieth century up to the mid-1990s. Current government policy, whilst not dismissing this, is rather more circumspect. The influential *Cross Cutting Review* of the role of the sector in delivering public services (HM Treasury 2002) noted that, whilst 'at best' VCOs could be 'flexible and innovative' the extent of this was 'difficult to test and ... the empirical evidence was inconsistent'.

In subsequent policy documents, both the VCO and the public sectors are posed as equally innovative, though with problems of sustainability (Office of the Third Sector 2006, para. 93). *Crucially the innovative capacity of VCOs is argued not as something intrinsic to the sector but rather as a capacity that can only be activated in partnership with government*:

> The third sector's potential to improve public services and help deliver better value for money can only be fully realised if there is joint working with local authorities ... to help the sector build its capacity to play a more effective role.
>
> (HM Treasury/Cabinet Office 2006)

From being the pre-eminent source of innovation in public services, the VCO sector has thus become a conditional one – and then only under the hegemony of the government.

Finally there has been *a changing orientation towards funding VCOs at the local level.* An important starting point for understanding the institutional framework for the innovative work of VCOs at the local level is the observed gap between the policy level and actually existing management practice in the delivery of public services. Mulgan and Aubrey (2003), reviewing contemporary practice in the UK have already observed this gap and concluded that in reality innovative is invariably 'an optional extra or an added burden' for public sector organizations, rather than a core activity.

This observation is verified when the commissioning guidance for these organizations in relation to VCOs is examined. A key document here is the guidance issued by the Office of the Third Sector (2006). As noted above, this 57-page document does contain two pages exhorting the importance of innovation by VCOs. Its recommendations, however, are precisely the sort of 'add-ons' noted by Mulgan and Aubrey – an 'Innovation Exchange' and an 'Innovation Team' within the Office of the Third Sector, for example, rather than initiatives at the heart of public services procurement and delivery. When one reviews its detailed guidance on commissioning and procurement (covering 13 pages), for example, there is no mention of how to optimize the innovative activity of VCOs by these processes.

If the reality of government practice in relation to the innovative capacity of VCOs does not seem to match up to the public policy framework, this becomes even more problematic at the local level. Here, the spending targets and assessments of local government set by central government dominate – and no where is innovative activity recognized in these. This was made quite explicit by both the local authority and the VCO staff on the cross sectional case studies, as the following excepts illustrate:

> Everything is funding led of course. It is impossible to make a strategic decision to take a certain direction, like to be innovative and then look for money. You have to follow the money. It's all targets. And innovation is not one of them.
>
> (CVS organiser in Southshire)

> The role [of VCOs] has changed. I'd have given you a different answer in the nineties. Now the ability of the statutory bodies in the Partnership to fund innovation is reduced dramatically. This is because of changes in government policy and funding streams. We no longer fund the sector to innovate. And we are very unhappy to mainstream innovations as well. We just don't have the capacity to do this. So we say 'why bother funding a pilot scheme if we can't afford to mainstream it?' The capacity has gone.
>
> (Local authority representative in Southshire Local Strategic Partnership)

Local Area Agreements? A good idea gone wrong. They are too top down and lack reality at the sharp end. It's all set by above to targets from above *(sic)*. Innovation doesn't figure, I don't think.

(District Authority Service manager in Southshire)

We do need the voluntary sector to innovate. Local government doesn't have the capacity. We are driven by statutory duties. But now so is the voluntary sector through our commissioning. We need to re-create freedom to fail. We've lost it. Risk management and minimisation dominates our commissioning – and this destroys the freedom to fail and the capacity to innovate.

(Local Authority member of Siliton Local Strategic Partnership)

When I first came into the [voluntary] sector it was all innovation. You couldn't get money for anything else. Now the irony is its all changed. Local government doesn't want innovation anymore. You can develop a service, yes. Especially if it helps you to meet a target. But innovation? Not a chance – too risky and it doesn't feature on the targets radar. Maybe it will come around again – who knows?

(Manager of VCO in Siliton)

The strength of voluntary organizations is that they do things differently. They innovate. But our contract specifications don't encourage or reward this. It's lost. It is funding driven. We can only buy services now that fit our specifications and targets – and innovation is not one of these.

(Midwell Social Services Department Service Manager)

Innovation is not a burning issue any more. The key issue for [local government] is the transfer of public services – getting them off their books and onto ours. Its transfer not transformation the government wants!

(Manager of local VCO in Midwell)

Conclusions

This chapter started by noting a shift in the balance of activity of VCOs involved in providing social care services over 1994–2006. The predominance of innovative activity has been replaced by a predominance of developmental activity. Again it is important to emphasize that no normative differentiation is being made between innovative and other modes of organizational activity. It is important both that specialist (traditional) expertise is maintained as well as that new approaches to social care delivery are developed and that these new approaches are developed through both innovation and incremental development. The key issues are twofold: first that innovation requires a specific approach to organizational and change management that needs to be recognized and, second, that a rhetoric of innovation should not be allowed to 'crowd out' other equally important forms of the organizational capacity of VCOs.

This chapter has found little systematic evidence in the way of intrinsic organizational characteristics to explain the changing innovative capacity of VCOs over 1994–2006. Admittedly there are some changes: there is evidence of increasing formalization within the innovative and developmental VCOs, and that these organizations have experienced significant budgetary growth compared to their traditional counterparts. There is no evidence of a direct relationship between these changes and the mode of organizational activity – or whether any mooted role might be a cause or consequence of this mode. The innovative VCOs do maintain a more proactive strategic intent towards their environment compared to their developmental and traditional counterparts. However by itself this is insufficient to explain the pattern of organizational activity. To attempt this, one needs to turn to the important changes in the institutional public policy context that have been identified.

In 1994 this context privileged innovative activity above other types of activity. This led VCOs both to focus more of their activity on innovative work and to portray their other work as innovative, irrespective of its true nature, in order to gain government funding. In 2006, this context has shifted to favour the development and provision of specialist services that enable local authorities to meet their own performance targets from central government. This has been reflected in the changing balance of the income of VCOs from governmental sources – in 1994 this was weighted predominantly towards innovative VCOs but in 2006 the balance has swung towards the developmental and traditional VCOs. Underlying this shift in context and activity have been three policy elements: a re-conceptualization of innovation in public services as 'continuous improvement' rather than transformation; a change in perception of the innovative capacity of VCOs to emphasize the importance of the leadership of, and partnership with, government in producing innovations in public services; and a re-orientation of government performance targets for local public services that emphasize specialization and incremental organizational/service development rather than the 'discontinuity' of innovation.

It could be argued that this is merely a correlation rather than a causal relationship and it must be admitted that the evidence is not conclusive. However the case made is a strong one, with implications for theory and for evidence based policy-making and managerial practice.

At the theoretical level, this emphasizes the need to understand the innovative capacity of VCOs as a variable organizational capacity, with its key contingencies in the institutional environment rather than an inherent element of these organizations 'per se'. This is a significant shift in our understanding of the contribution of VCOs to public services provision.

At a service level, this has implications for policy makers and VCO managers alike – in the UK and elsewhere. First, public policy-makers and managers need to understand and take seriously the impact that that their policy decisions have upon the structure and activity of VCOs. These organizations are not in a 'steady state', with inherent capabilities to bring to public services provision. Public policy makes as much difference to the activities of these organizations as it does to public sector ones.

Second, for VCO managers, it is important to emphasize that *appropriate innovation* is an important activity for VCOs to undertake. *Funding driven innovation*, though, risks skewing the vital role that they can play in the provision of public services – and undermines the, at least, equally important contributions that they can make both by providing specialist services and by the incremental improvement of such services. VCO managers thus have to achieve a difficult balance. On the one hand, they need to be sensitive to the aspirations and requirements of public policy and assess what, if any, contribution they can make to this (and its impact upon them if they are so dependent upon such funding for survival). On the other hand they need to be clear about their distinctive contribution to public services, if they have one, and whether this involves innovative, developmental or specialist services.

Finally, this chapter serves as a warning to VCO managers and staff not to attach too great a significance to the sectoral rhetoric of innovative capacity. In the past it was too easy a rhetoric to adopt in order to establish hegemony over public sector organizations. Yet such rhetoric both is prone to obsolescence and is liable to undermine other equally important capacities that VCOs may possess – such as specialist expertise. The research upon which this paper is based serves as a warning against such easy sophistry.

Notes

1 The research upon which this paper is based was funded by the Economic and Social Research Council (ESRC) in the UK. Responsibility for the views presented in this paper, however, lie with the authors alone.
2 The names 'Midwell', 'Siliton', 'Bellebury' and 'Southshire' are pseudonyms to ensure the anonymity of the organizations and agencies involved in this study.
3 As measured both by the eigenvalue of the function and by Wilkes Lambda.
4 A total of 73.8 per cent of those VCOs citing government funding as their most substantial income stream were engaged in innovative activity.
5 These archetypes are described in more detail in Osborne (1998a) pp. 126–127.
6 See Table 9.1 for the exact percentages.

References

Abernathy, W., K. Clark and J. Utterbach (1983) *Industrial Renaissance*, New York: Basic Books.
Abrams, P., S. Abrams, R. Humphreys and K. Snaith (1989) *Neighbourhood Care and Social Policy*, London: HMSO.
Argyris, C. and D, Schon (1978) *Organizational Learning: a Theory of Action Perspective*, Massachusetts: Addison Wesley.
Beveridge, W. (1948) *Voluntary Action*, London: Allen Unwin.
Blair, A. (2004) 'Speech at the Guardian's Public Services Summit' in *Guardian Unlimited* (http://society.guardian.co.uk/futureforpublicservices/comment/0,,1134531,00. html).
Borins, S. (2001) *The Challenge of Innovating in Government*, Washington: IBM Center for the Business of Government.
Burridge, D. (1990) *What Local Groups Need*, London: NCVO.

Cabinet Office (1999) *Modernising Government*, London: HMSO.

Department of Health (1989) *Caring for People*, London: HMSO.

Eisenbis, R. and R. Avery (1972) *Discriminant Analysis and Classification Procedures*, Lexington: Lexington Books.

Griffiths, R. (1988) *Community Care*, London: HMSO.

Hartley, J. (2006) *Innovation and Its Contribution to Improvement*, London: Department for Communities and Local Government.

Herbig, P. (1991) 'A Cusp Catastrophe Model of the Adoption of Industrial Innovation' in *Journal of Product Innovation Management*, (8, 2) pp. 127–137.

HM Treasury (2002) *The Role of the Voluntary and Community Sector in Service Delivery: A Cross Cutting Review*, London: HM Treasury.

HM Treasury/Cabinet Office (2006) *Local Area Pathfinders – Building Public Service Partnerships*, London: HM Treasury/Cabinet Office.

Home Office (1990) *Efficiency Scrutiny of Government Funding of the Voluntary Sector*, London: HMSO.

House of Commons Select Committee of Public Accounts (2003) *Improving Public Services Through Innovation: the Invest to Save Budget. Sixteenth Report of Session 2002–03*, London: House of Commons.

Kimberley, J. (1981) 'Managerial Innovation' in P. Nystrom and W. Starbuck (eds) *Handbook of Organizational Design*, Oxford: Oxford University Press, pp. 84–104.

Kings Fund Institute (1987) *Promoting Innovation in Community Care*, London: Kings Fund Institute.

Klecka, W. (1980) *Discriminant Analysis*, Beverley Hills: Sage.

Koch, P. and J. Hauknes (2005) *On Innovation in the Public Sector*, Oslo: NIFU STEP.

Koch, P., P. Cunningham, N. Schwabsky and J. Hauknes (2006) *Innovation in the Public Sector, Summary and Policy Recommendations*, Oslo: NIFU STEP.

Kramer, R. (1981) *Voluntary Agencies in the Welfare State*, Berkeley: University of California Press.

Labour Party (1990) *Labour and the Voluntary Sector*, London: Labour Party.

Le Grand, J (1991) 'Quasi Markets and Social Policy' in *The Economic Journal*, (101) pp. 1256–1267.

Malikova, L. and K. Staroòová (2005) *Innovation in the Social Sector – Case Study Analysis*, Oslo: NIFU STEP.

Mellor, M. (1985) *Role of Voluntary Organisations in Social Welfare*, London: Croom Helm.

Miles, R. and C. Snow (1978) *Organization Strategy Structure and Process*, New York: McGraw Hill.

Ministry of Health (1959) *Report of the Working Party on Social Workers in the Local authority Health and Welfare Services*, London: HMSO.

Mole, V. and D. Elliot (1987) *Enterprising Innovation*, London: Frances Pinter.

Mulgan, G. and D. Aubrey (2003) *Innovation in the Public Sector*, London: Cabinet Office.

Museums Libraries Archives Partnership (2007) *A Blueprint for Excellence. Public Libraries 2008–2011*, London: Museums Libraries Archives Partnership.

National Audit Office (2005) *Improving Public Services through Better Construction*, London: HMSO.

National Council for Voluntary Organisations [NCVO] (1991) 'Political Supplement' in *NCVO News* (June).

National Endowment for Science Technology and the Arts [NESTA] (2007) *Driving Innovation through public Procurement*, London: NESTA.

Nelson, R. (1993) 'Technological Innovation: The Role of Non-Profit Organizations' in D. Hammock and D. Young (eds) *Nonprofit Organizations in a Mixed Economy*, Ann Arbor: University of Michigan Press, pp. 363–377.

Office of the Deputy Prime Minister [ODPM] (2003) *Local Government Act 1999: Part I. Best Value and Performance Improvement*. ODPM Circular 03/2002, London: ODPM.

Office of the Third Sector (2006) *Partnership in Public Services. An Action Plan for Third Sector Involvement*, London: Cabinet Office.

Osborne, S. (1998a) *Voluntary Organizations and Innovation in Public Services*, London: Routledge.

Osborne, S. (1998b) 'Naming the Beast. Defining and Classifying Service Innovations in Social Policy' in *Human Relations*, (51, 9) pp. 1133–1154.

Osborne, S. and K. Brown (2005) *Managing Change and Innovation in Public Service Organizations*, London: Routledge.

Osborne, S., McLaughlin, K. and C. Chew (2008) 'The Once and Future Pioneers? The Innovative Capacity of Voluntary Organisations and the Provision of Public Services: a Longitudinal Approach' in *Public Management Review* (10, 1) [in press].

Pirie, M. (1988) *Privatization. Practice and Choice*, Aldershot: Wildwood House.

Porter, M. (1985) *Competitive Advantage*, New York: Free Press.

Prime Minister's Strategy Unit (2006) *The UK Government's Approach to Public Service Reform*, London: Prime Minister's Strategy Unit.

Public Audit Forum (1999) *The Implications of Audit for the Modernising Government Agenda*, London: PAF.

Rogers, E. and F. Shoemaker (1971) *Communication of Innovation*, New York: Free Press.

Rosner, M. (1967) 'Economic Determinants of Organizational Innovation' in *Administrative Science Quarterly*, (12) pp. 614–625.

Rothwell, R. (1975) *Project SAPPHO – Some Hypotheses Tested*, Stockholm: Paper to the Innovation Symposium, Royal Swedish Academy of Engineering Science.

Senge, P. (1990) *The Fifth Discipline. The Art and Practice of the Learning Organization*, London: Random House.

Smale, G. and G. Tuson (1990) 'Community Social Work: Foundations for the 1990s and Beyond' in G. Darvill and G. Smale (eds) *Partners in Empowerment. Networks of Innovation in Social Work*, London: NISW.

Van de Ven, A. (1998) 'Central Problems in the Management of Innovation' in M. Tushman and W. Moore (eds) *Readings in the Management of Innovation*, Cambridge: Ballinger, pp. 103–122.

Van de Ven, A., H. Angle and M. Doole (1989) *Research on the Management of Innovation*, New York: Harper & Row.

Walker, R., E. Jeanes and R. Rowlands (2001) *Managing Public Services Innovation: The Experience of English Housing Associations* Bristol: The Policy Press.

Webb, S. and B. Webb (1911) *The Prevention of Destitution*, London: Longman.

Williams, H. and A. Webb (1992) *Outcome Funding*, New York: Rensselaerville Institute.

Wistow, G., M. Knapp, B. Hardy and C. Allen (1994) *Social Care in a Mixed Economy*, Buckingham: Open University Press.

Wistow, G., M. Knapp, B. Hardy, J. Forder, J. Kendall and R. Manning (1996) *Social Care Markets*, Buckingham: Open University Press.

Part V
Co-production

10 Co-production, the third sector and functional representation in Sweden

Victor Pestoff

Pestoff (2006a) argues that the Swedish welfare state faces three major democratic challenges at the beginning of the twenty-first century that are crucial for its sustainability. The public sector in Sweden suffers from an abysmal work environment due to drastic cutbacks in public finances in the 1990s that also led to deteriorating quality of public services; declining citizen participation in most walks of political life; and permanent austerity in terms of funding welfare services. In order to reverse the situation Sweden must resolve these three interrelated challenges by:

1   improving the service quality and enriching the work environment of those providing welfare services;
2   increasing possibilities for citizen participation in and allowing them more control of the services that they demand and pay for through taxes and user fees;
3   finding new ways to provide public financed universal welfare services without major increases in taxes or user fees.

Unless all three of these challenges are faced and dealt with in a coherent fashion the universal, tax-financed welfare state as we have known it in Scandinavia faces a bleak future.

The common currency of the three democratic challenges is power and influence. They reflect the lack of power and influence of ordinary citizens over some of the most important issues in their daily lives. First is the power of employees to improve the quality of their work life and the welfare services they provide to the public. Second is the power of service users to actively contribute to improving welfare services for themselves and their loved ones. Third is the power of taxpayers to influence the development of the welfare state and to contribute directly to its sustainability in ways other than paying higher taxes or more user fees. The Swedish constitution states that all power comes from the people. Perhaps it should be amended to include that some power should now be returned to them.

This chapter focuses on the role of citizens and the third sector in the provision and governance of social services in Sweden. It begins by noting some of the unique characteristics of the universal welfare state in Sweden and introduces the concept of co-production. It goes on to discuss citizen participation and user influence in the provision and governance of social services of the twenty-first century. Developments in Denmark suggest new ways for promoting partnerships between users and producers in Scandinavia. It then discusses what, if any, is the relationship between citizen participation in the provision of social services and in their governance? This chapter argues that both state and market provision of social services tend to marginalize the role of citizens as co-producers of such services. Greater citizen participation can either be individual or collective.

A comparison of parents' participation in childcare services in eight EU countries provide the basis for concluding that only when the third sector is included can citizens become involved in democratic processes of governing social services at the micro-level. However, this may not be sufficient to guarantee the involvement of citizens in the governance of social services, at the meso-level. Third sector providers of childcare were included in local governing bodies in France and Germany, but not Sweden. Welfare regimes and government policy can facilitate greater citizen participation and a greater role for the third sector both in the provision and governance of social services. Changes in government usually result in either promoting more state or more market solutions, but continue to ignore co-production, citizen participation and the third sector as a provider of welfare services. Only when moving beyond simple black/white alternatives of more state or more market will there be room for greater citizen participation, third sector provision of social services and greater welfare pluralism in Sweden.

Greater citizen participation and third sector provision of social services in Sweden provided the focus of *Beyond the Market and State* (Pestoff, 1998). Here the concept civil democracy was introduced as:

> citizen empowerment through cooperative self-management of personal social services, where the citizens become members in social enterprises, where they participate directly in the production of the local services they demand, as users and producers of such services, and where they therefore become co-producers of these services.

> (ibid., p. 25)

The Swedish welfare state has several unique characteristics that it often shares with its Nordic neighbors. Taken together they comprise a separate welfare model or welfare regime known as the Scandinavian welfare model or social democratic welfare regime (Esping-Andersen, 1996). Among the unique characteristics of such welfare regimes we can note the following: it is universal and provides high quality social services; it has a large tax-financed public sector, with mainly public provision of social services; it is a unitary system based on centrally decided and locally provided, but highly standardized social services; for historical reasons it is closely associated with the dominance of the

Social Democratic Party that ruled Sweden for most of the twentieth century, but was recently replaced by a non-socialist majority in 2006. Citizens and third sector only play a marginal role in the delivery of social services, but this role varies between service sectors and changes with time. Citizens may volunteer to provide some fringe activities, but seldom are involved in producing core services. Childcare, charter schools and handicap care are, however, exceptions to this in Sweden.

Co-production

Co-production or citizen involvement in the provision of public services generated a flurry of interest among public administration scholars in the US in the 1970s and the 1980s (see Parks *et al.* 1981 and 1999, for a good overview). The concept was originally developed by the Workshop in Political Theory and Policy Analysis at Indiana University. During the 1970s they struggled with the dominant theories of urban governance underlying policy recommendations of massive centralization. Scholars and public officials argued that citizens as clients would receive more effective and efficient services delivered by professional staff employed by a large bureaucratic agency. But, they found no empirical support for claims promoting centralization (Ostrom, 1999, p. 358).

However, they stumbled on several myths of public production. One was the notion of a single producer being responsible for urban services within each jurisdiction. In fact, they normally found several agencies, as well as private firms, producing services. More important, they also realized that the production of a service, in contrast to goods, was difficult without the active participation of those receiving the service. They developed the term *co-production* to describe the potential relationship that could exist between the "regular" producer (street-level police officers, schoolteachers, or health workers) and "clients" who want to be transformed by the service into safer, better-educated or healthier persons.

In complex societies there is a division of labor and most persons are engaged in full-time production of goods and services as regular producers. However, individual consumers or groups of consumers may also contribute to the production of goods and services, as consumer-producers. This mixing may occur directly or indirectly. Co-production is, therefore, noted by the mix of activities that both public service agents and citizens contribute to the provision of public services. The former are involved as professionals or "regular producers," while "citizen production" is based on voluntary efforts of individuals or groups to enhance the quality and/or quantity of services they receive (Parks *et al.*, 1981 and 1999; Ostrom, 1999). Co-production is one way that a synergy can occur between what a government does and what citizens do (ibid.).

Co-production differs notably from the traditional model of public service production in which public officials are exclusively charged with responsibility for designing and providing services to citizens, who in turn only demand, consume and evaluate them. The dominant model of public service production was based on two distinct spheres: one of regular (public) producers and a second sphere of goods and service consuming clients or citizens, interest groups, etc. Feedback between these spheres can be problematic. By contrast, the co-production model is based on the assumption of an active, participative populace of consumer producers. When the two spheres overlap to a greater or lesser degree the feedback between them becomes an internal process. This lowers information costs for both the producers and consumers of such services. It may also help to lower other transaction costs. Service delivery becomes a joint venture involving both citizens and government agents. Thus, co-production implies citizen participation in the execution or implementation of public policies.

Co-production is often seen as an approach to the enhancement of municipal productivity and it can lead to cost reductions, higher service quality and expanded opportunities for citizens to participate in decisions concerning public services. The latter can result in greater satisfaction with and support for public services. Thus, co-production becomes an important means of enhancing both the quality and quantity of public services. However, savings to the public budget from co-production are constrained by the amount of substitution that can effectively be undertaken between citizens and service agents or public employees. Citizens normally lack the training and experience to perform services requiring specialized training. Moreover, substituting paid personnel with voluntary efforts means that some of the costs are transferred to the co-producers themselves. These costs are not eliminated, merely shifted to the citizens.

However, citizens may consider the net benefits of their voluntary efforts in terms of fellowship, self-esteem or other intangible benefits stemming from them and/or better service quality. The interface between the government and voluntary sectors is important since voluntary action always takes place in a political context. The individual cost/benefit analysis and the decision to cooperate with voluntary efforts are conditioned by the structure of political institutions. Centralized service delivery tends to make articulation of demands more costly for citizens and to inhibit governmental responsiveness, while citizen participation seems to fare better in decentralized service delivery (Ostrom, 1975).

While co-production initially attracted a lot of attention in the US in the 1970s and 1980s, since then involving people and groups outside the government in producing public services has received more sporadic interest. Alford (2002) argued that in addition to the basic exchange where services are exchanged for money, there is also an exchange of the client's time and efforts for heightening the value the client perceives in certain situations. He noted that material rewards and sanctions are ineffective in eliciting the requisite client contributions of time and effort in all but the most simple of tasks. Rather, many clients are motivated by more complex non-material incentives, such as intrinsic rewards or by social, solidarity and expressive values. These different motivators elicit co-production in different contextual circumstances. The more public the value consumed by clients, the more complex the motivations for them to co-produce. He concludes that: "eliciting co-production is a matter of heightening the value that clients receive from the services by making more explicit their non-material aspects through intrinsic rewards, solidarity incentives or normative appeal." (ibid.).

In Sweden the idea of enhancing the role of citizens in providing welfare services seldom gains attention from scholars and politicians; except perhaps in terms of promoting more volunteering. However, citizens currently contribute much of their time and effort to the production of welfare services, both as parents in relation to childcare or youth sports activities and sports clubs, as well as relatives in terms of eldercare and handicap care. They directly contribute to the realization of the final value of good quality childcare, healthful youth sports activities, and/or good quality eldercare and handicap care, although such services are primarily financed by taxes. A report to the Swedish parliamentary committee, *Ansvarskommittén*, called for a greater role for citizen participation and direct democracy in continued reforms of the Swedish welfare state (Häggroth, 2005). In order to come to grips with the growing democracy deficit and to renew the legitimacy of the welfare state, the report concluded that citizens should play a greater role in the delivery of welfare services. Co-production has been employed in Sweden to refer to the growing involvement of citizens in the production of their own welfare services, where parent participation in providing childcare comprises the main empirical example (Pestoff, 1998; 2006a, 2006b; Vamstad, 2004a, 2004b).

In the UK, co-production has been used to analyze the role of voluntary and community organizations (VCOs) in the provision of public services (Osborne and McLaughlin, 2004). Here it is contrasted with co-management or coordination, and co-governance. However, co-production in the UK context implies a more restricted service delivery role for VCOs in the provision of community services, i.e., simply that of a service agent or provider, with or without member involvement; while co-management refers to a broader role for VCOs in local service management. Co-governance refers to the role of VCOs in policy formulation and community governance, as illustrated by the Voluntary Sector Compact(s), at both the national and local levels. They are expressed as Local Strategic Partnerships to promote local area regeneration (ibid.). Co-production was recently the focus of a special thematic issue of *Public Management Review* (No. 8/4, 2006).

Citizen participation, user influence and its critics

Evers (2006) maintains that there are at least five different approaches to user involvement in welfare services in Europe. They are partially overlapping and partially conflicting. They range from welfarism and professionalism, through consumerism and managerialism to what he calls participationalism. They are based on different values and promote different degrees of user involvement. He states that these approaches will vary among sectors and over time. Their mix will probably differ among countries. They regard service users either as:

1   citizens with entitlements;
2   consumers to be empowered or protected;
3   co-producers who have active civic roles in their communities, in cooperation with authorities, service managers and professionals.

Welfarism and professionalism are closely associated with each other and neither leaves much room for user involvement. Rather clients are viewed as people with little competence of their own. Consumerism and managerialism call for giving users greater choice through more exit options and argue that the public sector needs to learn from the private sector (ibid.). However, they do not facilitate voice.

Participationalism (ibid.) encourages on-site participation by users of welfare services, based on the belief that citizens should engage personally in shaping the welfare services they demand. It emphasizes multi-stakeholder organizations and demands that users become co-producers. This concept is close to the definition of civil democracy presented earlier. Evers warns that at the level of service provision a mix of these approaches may result in "hybrid" organizations containing elements from many of them. However, some may work better together than others and they may, in fact, lead to "mixed up" or disorganized systems where user involvement works badly (2006).

Dahlberg and Vedung (2001) note a growing engagement among the clients or consumers of some public services in Sweden. They argue that representative democracy needs to be complemented, when possible, by other forms of democracy. First and foremost, direct democracy and deliberative democracy are suitable complements to representative democracy. The expansion of the welfare state also meant that the development of new channels of influence became necessary. Citizens are the users of public services like healthcare, education, social care, culture, etc. It is therefore noteworthy that individuals should have access to such services without being able to directly influence their own situation or the quality or composition of the service consumed. They give six main reasons for promoting greater consumer participation in public services:

1   it provides greater *training* in the role as *citizens*;
2   it permits them to express their feelings through discussion and interaction with others;
3   it increases *legitimacy* of public sector services;
4   it results in *greater effectiveness* of service;
5   it promotes an *equalization of power* by giving ordinary citizens a more active role;
6   it facilitates the *adaptation of services* to the needs of the consumers (ibid., pp. 43, 72, italics in the original).

Moreover, political science normally focuses on the input side of the political system (Easton, 1996). We ask how non-governmental organizations (hereafter NGOs) influence decisions; but we say little or nothing about how NGOs influence the outcomes or the output side of the equation, nor how they could if they tried. Yet, it is on the output side of the equation that the state expanded dramatically during the past 50 years. This expansion is seen both in terms of the types and amount of services provided today that were unthinkable 50 years ago and the number of civil servants providing them. How and where do citizens and the third sector fit into this new equation? What new democratic rights have citizens gained in recent years to help them influence, and at times even protect themselves from, the expanding welfare state bureaucracy and growing number of civil servants? Thus, it is on the output side that we must develop a new understanding of the role of citizens as co-producers of welfare services and the potential of the third sector for democratizing the welfare state.

The politics of user participation in the provision of social services helps to shift attention from the input to output side of the political system. In the public sector in general and at the municipal level in particular citizens became viewed as "users" or consumers in the 1980s. This led to discussions about "user democracy," where users participate in and exercise influence on the production of services. However, user democracy refers to "voice" or consumer participation in the production of services, but "freedom of choice" is more a matter of "exit" or voting with your feet (Montin and Elander, 1995). While the latter may be a necessary condition, it is not considered sufficient for insuring greater consumer influence.

Montin (2000) notes that the local popular government model of representative democracy is now challenged by three competing perspectives in Sweden: communitarianism, functionalism and governance. Communitarianism refers to traditional ideas that local government is a territorial community with citizens as responsible members. Functionalism refers to an ideology that local government is mainly a service provider and emphasizes the use of more market models as seen in New Public Management. Citizens are first and foremost consumers or users of services and efficiency constitutes the basis of legitimacy. This is also referred to as "service democracy" (ibid., p. 7). Governance falls somewhere in between the other two. It focuses on how to deal with a situation where politics are defined and implemented within different networks and partnerships, rather than hierarchies or markets. No single actor, public or private, has the knowledge, resources or authority necessary to tackle social problems unilaterally. Hence, several relevant actors are normally involved in governance. Today, local governments are facing a legitimacy crisis which opens up for various renewal programs and projects, and experiments with developing models that complement liberal representative democracy (ibid., p. 22).

Critics of greater citizen participation in the production of municipal services refer to three ideal types or models of influence (Klasson, 2000). They are the citizen participation model, the user influence model and the consumer adjustment model. Klasson assumes that citizens are unlikely to take the general interest into account in the citizen participation model, rather, he argues, they will primarily act in their own self-interest or group interest (ibid., pp. 44–45). They are normally organized according to sectors for providing the public services, like childcare, eldercare, etc. While users may gain influence in a particular sector, this can come into conflict with the territorial principles on which citizens are organized, i.e. residence. Also non-users are excluded from this model. Moreover, political authority is gained from competitive elections, while increased citizen participation, user influence and consumer adjustment can all be seen as a fragmentation of political authority and accountability (ibid., p. 48).

However, it should be kept in mind that when party politics first began to develop in the early 1900s at the local level in Sweden the very word party was synonymous with particularism and considered an unnatural division within the local community. It was also argued that parties failed to take the common good into account or to see the whole picture (Aronsson, 2001, p. 41). This is, of course, a far cry from today, where few could imagine holding elections or convening representative institutions without political parties. Moreover, contrasting the interests of the users of public services with those of representative democracy ignores the disenfranchisement of some public service users due to a growing representation gap in modern society, stemming in part from greater geographical mobility of daily life. This mobility results in some citizens residing in one territory or a "sleeping town," where they can vote and influence political decisions, while they spend much of their daily life and time in adjacent territories, where they work and receive many services. However, they lack influence on political decisions and the services provided there. Nor do they necessarily contribute directly to the financing of such services, as their taxes remain in their home municipality, although they commute on a daily basis and use the services where they spend most of the day. The main reasons for commuting are, of course, the lack of work and/or of local service, like schools, medical facilities, care services, etc., where they reside. Their daily commuting can take them across both municipal and county lines two or more times almost every day (Wiklund, 2004).

Moreover, democracy is not only a matter of electing representatives or majority decisions. In *Associative Democracy* Hirst (1994) presented a model for developing two-way communications between the governors and governed in order to extend the meaning and substance of democracy. He noted that elections and referenda are relatively infrequent and only decide certain salient issues, whereas governance is a continuous process. Not all of its decisions can be subject to majority approval within a given territory. Thus, he proposed large-scale institutional reforms which devolve as many of the functions of the state as possible to civil society, while retaining public funding, in order to restore limited government. The aim would be to separate service provision from supervision at all principal levels of government within a nation state. This would both simplify the role of representative institutions and make them watchdogs of public interests. Service provision would be devolved to self-governing associations whenever possible. Members would elect to join such service providers and the associations would receive public funds proportionate to their membership for providing a specific public service like education or healthcare. Members would then enjoy the option of both exit and voice (Hirst, 2002, pp. 28–29). In this fashion associative self-governance would supplement and extend representative government, not replace it (ibid., p. 30).

Whether users take the general interest into account remains an empirical question, and few scholars have attempted to study it empirically. Some evidence on this question is, however, found in a study of municipal and county boards for user influence (Jarl, 2001). Jarl's questionnaire to all Swedish municipalities and counties had a response rate of 82 percent. Of these, 90 percent employ some organized form(s) for user influence in one or more of the seven areas she surveyed for formal user influence (ibid.). Moreover, seven of ten municipalities claim to promote user influence in four or more of the seven areas studied (ibid., see Table 2 on p. 84 for details). They were: childcare services, elementary and high school education, cultural and leisure activities, eldercare, handicap care, and individual and family services. It was most common to find institutions for user influence in elementary education and childcare services, followed by eldercare and handicap care, then cultural and leisure activities and high school education (ibid., p. 27). The area of individual and family care allowed for the least user influence.

Various forms for user influence were employed by the municipalities. User influence was most often promoted through institutional councils of local users at the site of service provision or through municipal-wide councils of all users of a particular service; while self-administrative bodies were found occasionally. Although user co-ops technically fell outside the scope of her study, they were mentioned occasionally. However, different types of user influence were found in different policy areas, and influence at the meso- or municipal-wide level was greatest for eldercare and handicap care; while self-administrative bodies at the micro-level or site of production were found in elementary education in 42 percent of the municipalities and parent co-op childcare services were found in 54 percent of the municipalities (ibid., see Table 3 on p. 87 for more details). However, Jarl questions whether the most common forms of user influence permit any real influence. The dominant forms are user councils at the institutional level, followed by the same at the municipal level, which allow relatively little room for real user influence. Moreover, municipalities often took the initiative in starting such user councils and users were primarily invited to participate in discussions and consultations, without any decision-making powers or an independent budget (ibid., p. 39). Only parent co-op childcare services were based on user initiatives, allowed for user participation in decision-making and had independent budgets (ibid.).

In summary, the Swedish municipalities and counties' experience of organized user influence was generally positive. The most common form of user influence was some type of consultative council, where various issues were discussed, but no decisions were reached. Fears that increased user influence could pose problems for representative democracy found little support in this report. More than four-fifths of the municipalities did not see any serious consequences of user councils for equality between citizens (ibid., see Table 13 on p. 173 for more details). Nor did the municipalities' experience show that there were any serious infringements or conflicts between promoting greater user influence and representative democracy. On the contrary, most municipalities felt that the creation of user councils had provided them with useful insights into their own activities (ibid., p. 31). Jarl states that a dialogue between the politicians and users is of great importance to avoid conflicts. The report concludes that Swedish municipalities seem concerned about how to improve user influence in municipal services, and some wanted to expand such opportunities. But, most municipalities seemed content with initiating user councils at the site of production for different types of services. At the same time there was little interest to give user councils real influence (ibid., p. 95).

Montin (2006) compared information on political attitudes from a limited local study of 200-plus inhabitants in Västerås municipality and 860 inhabitants in Tillberga township. Social services were provided by service cooperatives in Tillberga. His study showed that active members in childcare co-ops and eldercare co-ops in Tillberga who experienced influence as users of welfare services also tended to be more "active citizens" than others. This was particularly evident in terms of attitudes related to trust in local politicians, interest in local politics, interest in taking responsibility for local affairs, trying to influence municipal politics and political efficacy. This limited local study also shows that user participation in the provision of social services can promote a willingness to become involved in local politics and greater political efficacy among active users, rather than greater particularism and group egoism suggested by critics of user participation. This, in turn, suggests the existence of a cumulative effect of user participation. It can function as the door-opener for greater political participation or first step on the ladder of participation and influence. Thus, user participation in the provision of welfare services can be equated to a school of democracy.

In a service democracy citizens are the passive consumers of publicly financed social services that are either provided by municipal authorities, private companies, or perhaps both. They vote every fourth year and in the meantime they choose between various service providers, public or private. By contrast, in a participative democracy citizens are active in the provision of their own social services, in the development of the welfare state and the renewal of democracy. By including citizens and the third sector in the provision of welfare services the dialogue between the rulers and ruled takes on a new dimension and citizens can choose between more than the two alternatives of more state or more market.

User participation in Denmark

Although Sweden and Denmark are both universal welfare states, a different pattern of citizen participation and user influence is noted in Denmark. Sörensen (1999) discusses users as political actors and underlines the importance of developing new institutions to involve users as political actors, yet complement representative democracy at the same time. She notes the development of three main models in Denmark during the 1990s. They involve:

1   greater freedom of choice;
2   user boards in public institutions;
3   municipal user councils.

Freedom of choice developed in health and education sectors where citizens could choose between family doctors and hospitals as well as between schools. User boards, on the other hand, permitted parents to elect a majority of members to a school board, together with representatives from the children and teachers. Municipal user councils were introduced in 1997, as a central body for governing services to elder persons. They have no formal decision-making rights, but the right to be heard on matters concerning living conditions for elderly persons. Missing in the Danish experience, however, is a model for citizens to co-produce their own services, as witnessed by the rapid development of alternative childcare services in Sweden in the 1980s and 1990s (Pestoff, 1998).

Sörensen refers to Danish politics of today like a play, where the politicians are the actors and citizens are spectators (1999, p. 17). Engaging users can help to make politics concrete again for citizens, rather than something remote and abstract. However, greater user influence poses some democratic problems. Sörensen (1998) notes that while there is general agreement that increasing user influence is an important means of empowering citizens in relation to public authorities, there is some doubt whether it is a democratic form of empowerment. For example, providing citizens with more freedom of choice does not always imply more democracy, but only more market power in the market-like reforms of the public sector in the 1990s.

In Denmark some authors stress the contribution of greater user influence in developing a more participatory democracy than is possible through traditional representative institutions. However, opponents argue that greater user influence both promotes a particularistic perspective on policy-making at the costs of a universalistic perspective and that it undermines the institutional borderline between collective rule and individuality so important to liberal democracy (ibid., p. 129). Danish experience is therefore of special importance, since Denmark has undergone three waves of decentralization involving greater user control over the services produced. The first concerned decentralizing a number of tasks from the central government to the municipalities in the 1970s, known as *Kommunereformen*/Municipal Reform. This mainly involved some areas of social policy and the primary education system. The second wave of decentralization came in the 1980s and involved moving tasks from municipalities to a wide-range of self-governing public institutions. This included preschool, primary schools, housing for the elderly, libraries, etc. They are now run by user boards that are elected by all users of the service or institution. The third wave of decentralization, beginning in the late 1980s, involved increasing cooperation between the state/municipality and civil society organizations, mostly in the social service sector (Sörensen, 1998, p. 129).

Both the second and third wave of decentralization in Denmark changed traditional institutions of liberal democracy in at least three ways. First, it added a new level of influence; second, it introduced a functional rather than territorial basis of representative democracy; and third, it introduced a new form of empowerment. This implies both more freedom of choice between service producers, or more exit and more voice for elected user representatives on the self-governing boards. Moreover, the third wave of decentralization introduces public spending by private or third sector organizations, which limits public control (ibid., p. 130).

The disagreement over the particular vs. the universal in terms of greater user influence is also related to the distinction between territorial and functional forms of democratic empowerment. The territorial form of democratic empowerment has clear strengths. Channels of influence are equally distributed to all citizens through principles of "one member/one vote." This form of empowerment serves to ensure an equal distribution of influence and enhance a holistic perspective on territorial governance; but, it nevertheless faces at least two important problems. First, it institutionalizes a low level of participation by ordinary citizens due to the central role of elections and representation as the main means of democratic empowerment. Second, it turns the political into something very abstract, remote and distant, having to do with principles and ideology, etc., but lacking immediate relevance for the everyday life problems of most citizens (ibid.).

Sörensen also discussed the need to create the right balance between territorial and functional democracy in the Danish primary school system. She analyzed this in terms of achieving an optimal balance between exit and voice. Providing parents with increased voice would facilitate the employment of their resources to improve the quality of schools. Yet, maintaining a limited exit option would provide them with a safety valve if the situation became intolerable (ibid., p. 132). One way would be to institutionalize the balance between exit and voice as forms of democratic empowerment in all areas of social life. This would allow for both user exit and voice within the public sector itself.

She concludes that if functional forms of empowerment were to become democratic then all members of functional units and all functional units within a given territory should have access to the same channels of empowerment. It is also necessary that functional politics be institutionalized in such a way that tight bonds are created between functional and territorial units of societal governance, or between user boards and municipal councils (ibid., p. 141). Danish primary schools comprise a two level system of governance. At the school or institutional level functional forms of empowerment dominate, while territorial forms of empowerment govern at the municipal level. It becomes a problem of achieving the right balance and institutional bonds between these two forms of democracy (ibid., p. 142).

The relationship between providing and governing social services

The concept of governance gained extensive attention recently, becoming a buzz word in the social sciences. It is used in a wide array of contexts with widely divergent meanings. Van Kersbergen and van Waarden (2004) identify nine different definitions of the concept; while Hirst (2002) attributes it five different meanings or contexts. They include economic development, international institutions and regimes, corporate governance, privatized provision of public services in the wake of New Public Management and new practices of coordinating activities through networks, partnerships and deliberative forum (ibid., pp. 18–19). This chapter focuses mainly on the latter context. He argued that the main reason for promoting greater governance is the growth of "organizational society." Big organizations on either side of the public/private divide in advanced post-industrial societies leave little room for democracy or citizen influence. This is due to the lack of local control and democratic processes for internal decision-making in most big organizations. The concept of governance points to the need to rethink democracy and find new methods of control and regulation, ones that do not rely on the state or public sector having a monopoly of such practices (ibid., p. 21). Accordingly, he defines governance as "a means by which an activity or ensemble of activities is controlled or directed, such that it delivers an acceptable range of outcomes according to some established social standards" (ibid., p. 24).

We asked at the outset of this chapter what, if any, was the relationship between greater citizen participation in the production of social services and in their governance? Is it possible for citizens to participate in the one without participating in the other? A comparative European project, the TSFEPS Project,[1] in eight EU countries on family policy and childcare, permitted us to examine the relationship between parent participation in the provision and governance of childcare (Pestoff *et al.*, 2004; Pestoff, 2006b). We found different levels of parent participation in different forms of provision, i.e., public, private for-profit and third sector childcare. The highest levels of parent participation were found in third sector providers like parent associations in France, parent initiatives in Germany, and parent cooperatives in Sweden.

We also noted different kinds or dimensions of participation, i.e., economic, political and social. All three kinds of participation were readily evident in third sector providers of childcare services, while economic and political participation were mostly absent in municipal and private for-profit services included in this study. Moreover, we observed differences in the patterns of participation between countries. Parents participated actively in the provision of third sector childcare services in France, Germany and Sweden, and in their governance in the first two countries, but not in the latter one.

Thus, we concluded that neither the state nor market allow for more than marginal or ad hoc participation by parents in the childcare services. For example, parents may be welcome to make spontaneous suggestions when leaving or picking up their child from a municipal or for-profit childcare facility. They may also be welcome to contribute time and effort to a social event like the annual Christmas party or Spring party at the end of the year. They could bake a cake, prepare a dish or even help in cleaning afterwards. Also discussion groups or "Influence Councils" can be found at some municipal childcare facilities in Sweden, but they provide parents with very limited influence. Parent representatives meet with the staff three or four times per year, exchange information, but make no decisions and have no budget. More substantial and institutional participation in economic or political terms of providing such services can only be achieved when parents organize themselves collectively to obtain better quality or different kinds of childcare services than either the state or market can provide. Thus, only through collective action and the third sector can citizen participation and co-production take on an economic and/or political dimension at the site of service production.

Although there was a high degree of co-production in Sweden, we found no evidence of parent participation in the governance of local childcare services. We wanted to understand why the new entrants to the field failed to gain any influence on or access to the local governance of childcare. The period from the 1970s to the 1990s saw the entry of many new interests in this quickly changing and rapidly expanding field of service provision. How was it possible to maintain a monopoly of political influence shared exclusively by the municipalities and trade unions? Is this perhaps a classical example of collusion between the welfarist and professionalist approaches to user influence discussed by Evers (2006)? It would seem logical for the new entrants like parent or worker co-ops and other types of third sector providers to attempt to gain influence on the development and expansion of this new field.

However, their mere presence, without any representation in policy circles was certainly not enough to provide them with influence. So, Sweden presents a dilemma in terms of citizen participation in governing the field of publicly financed childcare for preschool children. Sweden is the only country in the TSFEPS Project with extensive parent-managed childcare services that completely lacks institutional structures at the municipal level for the representation of third sector providers in the local governance of the field. A consultative body did exist in Stockholm for a few years in order to promote discussions between third sector providers and municipal administrators. But it provided no opportunity for the third sector providers to meet other types of providers on a regular basis or for them to develop common viewpoints on important issues of common interest. By contrast, city-wide structures open to third sector providers of local childcare services were found both in France and Germany, where many third sector providers of childcare services also exist, alongside municipal providers.

Given the long tradition of administrative corporatism in Sweden, in particular during long periods of social democratic dominance, it is difficult to understand why the new providers of important welfare services like childcare, that affect the interests of so many economic, political and social groups, were not able to gain access to important political arenas at the municipal or national level(s) where childcare policies were developed and implemented. It was a cornerstone of Swedish corporatism, until the mid-1990s, to include both the unions and employers in governing labor market policy. Representatives from both the trade unions for blue and white-collar workers and academicians, like LO, TCO and SACO, as well as employer organizations, like SAF, sat for decades on the governing bodies of various labor market agencies, both at the national and regional levels (Pestoff, 2003).

A similar pattern of corporatist representation developed in the area of consumer policy, but there were no natural representatives for consumers, as consumers are notoriously difficult to organize. So the consumer co-ops and trade unions were actively co-opted by the social democratic government to assume the role of consumer representatives on various public consumer bodies; thereby becoming a countervailing power to well-organized business and commercial interests. This was achieved in part by recruiting high-ranking trade union leaders to serve as the General Director of various national consumer agencies in the 1950s and 1960s and in part by having balanced governing boards in the 1970s and 1980s with an equal number of consumer and industry representatives (Pestoff, 1984, 1989).

Why then did a similar pattern of corporatist representation not develop in childcare, one that could help integrate the newcomers providing third sector childcare services? No simple or clear answer is available, but a few might be suggested. First, perhaps in the social and family policy spheres, introducing ideas of corporatist representation and countervailing forces appeared farfetched. The need for promoting the representation of the weaker party was not seen as crucial for achieving the policy goals, as these very individuals were already the subjects or focus of such policies. Second, childcare is provided at the municipal level, not directly by the state. Administrative corporatism was not as prevalent at the municipal level as the central level (Nyhlén, 2007).

Third, since the municipalities were the principal providers of publicly funded childcare services, there was no need to encourage the inclusion of third sector providers in policy-making at the municipal level. The municipalities, after all, represent all citizens or inhabitants in a given geographical area, not just a single group or class of citizens, as was the case with labor market or consumer policy, where two opposing groups or classes were readily identified. Fourth, existing municipal actors may perceive new actors as a threat, both in economic and political terms. The staff of municipal childcare providers may feel threatened in terms of their jobs and financial security; while the politicians and administrators responsible for governing and supervising the municipal childcare service systems may fear the loss of political influence if new actors were recognized and included in local forums of policy deliberation. This corresponds to the welfarist and professionalist approaches to user influence.

Fifth, some municipal and even national actors fail to see any difference between the small social enterprises made up of staff or parents and the large private for-profit corporations operating in several different municipalities. "If you accept one of them then you must accept them all," seems to be their reasoning. Thus, including or legitimizing parent and staff cooperative childcare may serve to breach the outer walls of opposition to private for-profit services. Sixth, Swedish competition law lends some credence to such an interpretation. An organization's social values cannot provide the basis for choosing between providers, only the lowest bid counts. So, political and ideological reasons may weigh heavily in opposing the inclusion of third sector providers. Finally, Sweden's tradition of a unitary rather than a federal pattern of government also leave less room for variation with institutions of local representation in new areas, where new actors emerge, as witnessed by the exclusion of third sector providers of childcare (Vamstad, 2004a and 2004b).

One final reason for the lack of representation and influence by third sector childcare service providers at either meso- or macro-levels in Sweden is the lack of an infrastructure to promote coordination among third sector service providers themselves or between them and public providers of such services. Childcare delivery is provided by small, independent third sector organizations, parent and worker co-ops or voluntary organizations, which do not belong to an intermediary organization designed to promote their common interests within the public system for service provision, nor in any given service sector. Not only is the public system of childcare delivery closed to them, but also their own intermediary organizations are very specific, to the extent that they belong to any. Some third sector childcare providers do belong to the regional cooperative development agencies, now called *Koompanion*. However, the latter focus mainly on promoting the establishment of new cooperatives in their respective regions, not on promoting the interest of third sector providers in any given service sector. So, they lack the necessary infrastructure both for articulating and coordinating their interests as a specific group of service providers. Moreover, there are no public institutions for involving third sector providers in policy development or system governance; particularly not at the sectoral level. However, the mere existence of such public institutions would promote greater collective action by third sector providers of childcare.

Prentice (2006) discusses the negative impact of the lack of formal mechanisms to integrate third sector providers into policy development or service coordination for the overall development, or lack thereof, of childcare policy in Canada. Despite profound reliance on the third sector to provide childcare services it remains a system of mainly individual, stand-alone facilities, governed directly by the users (ibid., p. 19). By contrast, Japan has witnessed, in recent years, the development of local third sector intermediary organizations, often with the help of local governments, in order to promote a more active role for the third sector in the co-governance of important social services (Tsuskamoto and Nishimura, 2006). It would, therefore, appear logical to explore new ways to include third sector providers of childcare services in order to accommodate them in the management and governance of childcare services in Sweden. In addition to public support for establishing intermediary organizations to promote the third sector and the development of models of functional representation might provide a way forward (Pestoff, 2006c).

Sub-municipal politics and functional representation

In modern parliamentary democracies in Scandinavia, with a unitary system, there are usually three levels of decision-making and administration, i.e., the central, county and municipal levels. Each level has its own sources of income and taxation powers in Scandinavia. Sweden is a large, sparsely populated country, about the size of California, but with a population only the size of Los Angeles. Its nine million inhabitants participate in elections every fourth year. In general elections representatives are chosen at the same time to the *Riksdag* or parliament, to the county councils and to municipal councils. All three of these elections take place on the same day and at the same election polling places. This promotes a high level of participation in elections at all three levels. However, participation in *Riksdag* elections has decreased from 91.4 percent of the electorate in 1982 to only 80.1 percent in 2002, while it increased marginally in 2006 to 81.9 percent. Participation rates are only slightly lower in county and municipal council elections and follow the general declining trend. Approximately 80 percent of the population resides in the urban areas. Swedish cities are often sub-divided into administrative wards to promote a feeling of nearness between inhabitants and the city administration. However, few if any Swedish cities allow for direct elections of representatives at the ward level. This means that at the sub-municipal level there are no direct means of electoral representation. This gap in Swedish representative democracy leaves the citizens with no direct influence at the sub-municipal or ward level.

There are also numerous other political and democratic activities found below the municipal level, but nevertheless within their territorial confines. They can be referred to as sub-municipal politics. Here we find various local development groups, municipal wards in urban areas, various user groups, in particular those related to welfare services, etc. There are 4,168 local development groups in Sweden today (Herlitz, 1999). Many urban areas are sub-divided into a number of wards to facilitate their administration and to decrease the distance between them and their voters and the users of their services. However, they lack direct elections to ward councils. Their boards are appointed politically by the municipality. In addition, there are a number of user controlled service providers, like parent cooperatives or third sector childcare, schools, eldercare, handicap care, etc. Here the users are responsible for the management of the service. When they become members, users often have a work obligation and they are represented on the governing bodies of the service. In addition there are numerous local branches of voluntary associations, popular movements, foundations and other non-profit organizations found within the territorial confines of all municipalities. Thus several different types of political actors are found at the sub-municipal level in Sweden. Just as at the global, European or regional levels, these sub-municipal actors do not always have clear political institutions or a forum, nor can they easily find channels of representation. Figure 10.1 illustrates this.

In order to empower citizens as co-producers of welfare services greater use of functional representation at the municipal level could be promoted, especially in the sectoral boards responsible for providing and supervising various kinds of welfare services at the local level. They would function as a supplement to existing representative channels of democracy. So, the voters would continue to vote for their preferred political party in municipal elections and the political majority would continue to form the municipal government, just as today. Also, just as

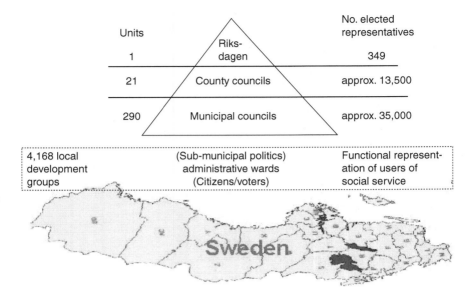

Figure 10.1 Politics at the sub-municipal level in Sweden.

today, the municipal governments would appoint the members of boards to supervise the provision of various municipal welfare services. This top-down selection procedure allows no direct representation of the users of such services. However, functional representation could supplement political representation in the following fashion. Public, private and third sector providers of welfare services would be invited to sit on relevant municipal sector boards.

This type of functional representation could be on a proportional basis in relation to their importance as providers of welfare services in a given territory. If there were numerous providers of a given welfare service in a municipality, like childcare, then a lottery system could insure the rotation among all the providers in any given category, public, private and third sector. This would promote a bottom-up representation of the providers in a given welfare sector. If the sectoral representatives were guaranteed a majority of seats on a municipal board then they would have real influence and a greater interest in participating in its deliberations and decisions. However, it is unlikely that the views of all the functional representatives would be identical in all questions, especially given the prevalence of municipal providers. So there is little chance that they would vote as a block against the positions of the politically appointed representatives of the municipality. However, their dialogue would promote greater understanding and tolerance for their differences.

Functional representation should occur whenever there is a sufficient pluralism of providers of a given welfare service in a given municipality. Functional representation might encourage the spread of co-production to municipal services, since their ideas and organizational models would be shared in the forum provided by sectoral boards. The existence of a sectoral municipal forum for discussion and decision-making would also facilitate the co-management of the sector in a municipality and eventually could also promote the co-governance of the sector nationally, based on the growing collaboration between public, private and third sector providers of welfare services.

This type of functional representation in the management of publicly financed welfare services need not be seen as an alternative to representative territorial democracy. Rather than viewing it as an either/or situation or a zero-sum game, functional democracy should be conceived as a supplement to representative democracy, as Danish experience shows, and it can help to develop and strengthen representative democracy.

Sörensen (1998) also discussed the need to create the right balance between territorial and functional democracy, as well as the right bonds between them. However, if functional forms of empowerment are to become democratic, she then argues, all members of functional units and all functional units within a given territory should have access to the same channels of empowerment. This recommendation is reflected in the proposal made above for representing third sector providers of social services in relevant municipal boards in Sweden. She also states that it is necessary for functional politics to be institutionalized in such a way that tight bonds are created between functional and territorial units of societal governance, or between user boards and municipal councils (ibid., p. 141). Once again, the proposal above for functional representation made here also takes this into consideration.

Summary and conclusions

It was noted that co-production is the mix of activities that both public service agents and citizens contribute to the provision of public services. The former are involved as professionals or "regular producers," while "citizen production" is based on voluntary efforts of individuals or groups to enhance the quality and/or quantity of services they use. In complex societies there is a division of labor and most persons are engaged in full-time production of goods and services as regular producers. However, individual consumers or groups of consumers may also contribute to the production of goods and services, as consumer-producers.

The Swedish welfare state strongly embodies the characteristics of welfarism and professionalism (Evers, 2006) in the production and governance of welfare services. This clearly reflects the dominance of social democratic values of equal services for all citizens everywhere in the country. Guaranteeing equality, however, requires continued public provision of welfare services. This stands in sharp contrast to the non-socialist values of consumerism and managerialism that call for privatization and competition among providers. Absent today in Sweden is what Evers (2006) calls participationism.

His distinction between five different approaches to user involvement in the production of social services has clear implications for citizens' possibilities to participate in the provision and governance of such services. Two of his categories for user influence are more closely associated with public production of social services, while two others are more closely related to market provision. All four of these approaches flourish in the Swedish debate. However, his fifth approach to user influence is largely missing, i.e., greater citizen participation in the provision of social services, i.e., co-production. The Swedish debate about the future of the welfare state is highly polarized and ideologically divided between continued public provision or rapid privatization of social services, where the only options discussed are either more state or more market solutions (Blomqvist and Rothstein, 2000; Blomqvist, 2003). It is difficult, if not impossible, to promote a third alternative, e.g., greater welfare pluralism, more citizen participation or more third sector provision of social services in this highly ideological context (Vamstad, 2007). Thus, citizens are normally faced with simple black/white choices between more state or more market solutions to most problems facing them.

The discourse in Denmark and Sweden on greater user influence was compared. Denmark placed greater emphasis on large-scale experiments with user boards and local user councils, combined with greater choice for service users, while Sweden focused on establishing consultative councils of users at the site of service provision. The Danish experience added a new level of influence, by introducing functional democracy and it provided a new form of empowerment. Swedish experience remained more limited and built on the introduction of new municipal structures that were mainly discussion clubs.

Sub-municipal politics was discussed in relation to functional democracy. One factor contributing to the growing democracy deficit at the local or municipal level is the lack of democratic representative channels at the sub-municipal level. There are no direct representative elections to ward councils found in larger municipalities in Sweden. Rather they are purely administrative bodies, albeit with significant discretionary powers. This stands in sharp contrast to the existence in Sweden of numerous local democratic bodies of citizens that can either take the form of local development groups or a variety of users groups of municipal welfare services at the sub-municipal level.

Functional representation of the latter would promote greater citizen participation, greater flexibility in the delivery of welfare services and greater sustainability of welfare services, as well as greater service legitimacy. Functional representation makes clear the necessary connection between co-production and co-management. It would help facilitate and legitimize the co-management and co-governance of welfare services. Without co-management and co-governance through functional representation, existing examples of co-production in welfare services will remain isolated islands of citizen participation, democracy and legitimacy in the increasing gap between the rulers and ruled and the growing democracy deficit that continues to erode support for the universal welfare state and for representative democracy itself.

Greater user participation in the provision of services refers to the output side of the political system. In the public sector in general and at the municipal level in particular citizens became viewed as "users" or consumers in the 1980s. While, greater "freedom of choice" may be necessary, it is not sufficient for greater consumer influence. "Freedom of choice" is more a matter of voting with your feet, while user democracy refers to "voice" in the production of services. This realization led to discussions about "user democracy," where users particip-ate directly in and exercise influence on the production of public services. However, consumer influence can take different forms. The promotion of greater citizen influence and participatory democracy, requires that consumer influence should be collective, rather than individual. This means that citizens must organ-ize themselves as consumers of public services, or co-producers of such ser-vices, in order to provide a democratic supplement to representative democracy.

This chapter emphasized the importance of the interface between the govern-ment and third sector and noted that co-production always takes place in a polit-ical context. The individual cost/benefit analysis and the decision to cooperate with voluntary efforts are conditioned by the structure of political institutions and the encouragement provided by politicians. Centralized service delivery tends to make articulation of demands more costly for citizens and to inhibit governmental responsiveness, while citizen participation seems to fare better in decentralized service delivery.

Thus, it appears that citizens can at best achieve marginal influence at the site of production of a welfare service as individuals. This is found in childcare through spontaneous interactions between the parents and staff when leaving or picking up their child, by participating in social events and discussion groups. But it is first when parents organize themselves as co-producers and manage the welfare services themselves that they can achieve more substantial economic and/or political influence in the provision of welfare services at the micro-level. However, while organized citizen participation in the provision of welfare ser-vices is necessary, it is clearly not sufficient to achieve user influence in the gov-ernance of welfare services. Parent associations and parent initiatives in France and Germany that provide childcare to their members do participate in local councils for child and youth matters, and they are able to influence the provision of such services in their municipality.

In Sweden, by contrast, systematic and institutional influence at the municipal level has remained beyond the reach of third sector providers of childcare. They are mostly run as parent cooperatives and they enroll between 12–15 percent of all children under seven years old attending institutionalized childcare services. But, they lack a local forum or platform for participating in the governance of the sector, together with their municipal and for-profit counterparts. However, before new channels of participation can be developed alongside the existing representat-ive ones politicians must be willing to engage in serious debate about the role of the third sector in providing and governing welfare services. Thus, the attitude of the state appears to determine whether citizens will also be encouraged to particip-ate in the governance of a sector or welfare service.

Increased user influence has some critics who maintain that it poses a threat to liberal representative democracy. Hirst's (1994) proposal for associative democracy sees it as a necessary supplement to liberal democracy, rather than a replacement. Here citizens become the co-producers of the welfare services they demand and pay for by taxes and user fees. Here third sector organizations and non-governmental organizations can become the co-managers of welfare services provided to their members and other social groups, but financed by the state, and TSOs and NGOs can also become the co-governors of welfare provision and welfare policy, alongside the state and perhaps the market, in new governance networks (ibid.). Thus, it is on the output side of the political system that we must focus our attention and devote our efforts to develop and revitalize democratic theory and provide welfare state theory with a clear service provision focus.

The attitude of the central government will be decisive in determining whether Sweden will continue on a highly polarized ideological black/white path of public vs. private that excludes a greater role for citizens and the third sector in the production and governance of social services. The attitude, pronouncements and actions of the central government are crucial, since it has a quasi monopoly of power in a unitary system like Sweden. Will it promote the continued polarization of opinion, simplistic black/white alternatives or will it promote a more nuanced view of the complexities of welfare service production that go beyond simple questions of ownership.

The new non-socialist coalition's attitude to greater citizen participation and the third sector provision of welfare services remains an open question. Will it promote a third way – one where citizens and the third sector can play an active role in the provision of welfare services? How will the social democrats and their allies react during four, eight or more years of opposition? Will they perhaps embrace co-production, greater citizen participation in the provision and governance of welfare services as a way to promote the renewal of the welfare state and the regeneration of democracy? That too remains to be seen.

Note

1 The TSFEPS Project, Changing Family Structures and Social Policy: Childcare Services as Sources of Social Cohesion, took place in eight European countries between 2002–2004. See www.emes.net for details and reports. The eight countries participating in it were: Belgium, Bulgaria, England, France, Germany, Italy, Spain and Sweden.

References

Alford, John, 2002; Why do Public Sector Clients Co-Produce? Towards a Contingency Theory; *Administration & Society*, vol. 34/1: 32–56.

Aronsson, Peter, 2001; *Lokalt folkstyre – kulturarv som utmanar*/Popular Local Governance – Cultural Heritage That Poses Challenges; Stockholm: Sv. Kommunförbundet.

Blomqvist, Paula, 2003; The Choice Revolution: Privatization of Swedish Welfare Services in the 1990s; *Social Policy & Administration*; vol. 38/2: 139–155.

Blomqvist, Paula and Bo Rothstein, 2000; *Välfärdsstatens nya ansikte. Demokrati och marknadsreformer inom den offentliga sektorn*; Stockholm: Agora.

Dahlberg, Magnus and Evert Vedung, 2001; *Demokrati och brukarvärdering*/Democracy and Consumer Evaluations; Lund: Studentlitteratur.

Easton, David, 1965; *A Systems Analysis of Political Life*; New York: J. Wiley & Sons.

Esping-Andersen, Gösta (ed.), 1996; *Welfare States in Transition: National Adaptations in Global Economics*; London, Thousand Oaks and New Delhi: Sage Publications.

Evers, Adalbert, 2006; Complementary and Conflicting: The Different Meaning of "User Involvement" in Social Services, Ch. 7 in *Nordic Civic Society Organizations and the Future of Welfare Services. A Model for Europe?*; Matthies, Aila-Leena (ed.); Copenhagen: Nordic Council of Ministers, TemaNord 2006: 517 (pp. 255–276).

Häggroth, Sören, 2005; *Staten och kommunerna*/The State and Municipalities; Stockholm: SOU: Ansvarskommittén.

Herlitz, Ulla, 1999; Bygdens organisering/The Organization of Villages; *Civilsamhället*; Stockholm: Demokratiutredningens forskarvol. VII, SOU 1999: 84.

Hirst, Paul, 1994; *Associative Democracy. New Forms of Economic and Social Governance*; Cambridge: Polity Press.

Hirst, Paul, 2002; Democracy and Governance, in *Debating Governance, Authority, Steering and Democracy*; Pierre, Jon (ed.); Oxford: Oxford University Press.

Ingelstam, Lars, 2007; *Ekonomi på plats*; Linköping: Linköpings universitet tryckeri.

Jarl, Maria, 2001; *Ökad brukarinflytande* (?)/Increased User Influence (?); Stockholm: Justitiedept. Ds 2001: 34.

Klasson, Torgny, 2000; Medborgardeltagande, brukarinflytande och konsumentanpassning. Tre idealmodeller av medborgerligt deltagande i och inflytande över kommunal serviceproduktion; Kap. 2 i Klasson, Torgny and Lena Agevall (eds), *Demokrati i praktik*; Lund: Studentlitteratur.

Montin, Stig, 2000; Between Fragmentation and Co-ordination – The Changing Role of Local Government in Sweden; *Public Management*; vol. 2/1: 1–23.

Montin, Stig, 2006; Demokrati på entreprenad. En fallstudie av demokratiutveckling i Västerås kommun; *Kommunal ekonomi och politik*; vol. 10/4: 39–74.

Montin, Stig and Ingemar Elander, 1995; Citizenship, Commercialism and Local Government in Sweden; *Scan. Pol. Studies*; vol. 18/1: 29–51.

Nyhlén, Jon, 2007; Vägar till friskolor. – En studie av lokala beslutsprocessor; Umeå: Ph.D. course paper.

Osborne, Stephen and Kate McLaughlin, 2004; The Cross-cutting Review of the Voluntary Sector. Where Next for Local Government – Voluntary Sector Relationships?; *Regional Studies*; vol. 38/5.

Ostrom, Elinor (ed.), 1975; *The Delivery of Urban Services: Outcomes of Change*; Beverly Hills: Sage.

Ostrom, Elinor, 1999; Crossing the Great Divide: Coproduction, Synergy, and Development, Ch. 15 in *Polycentric Governance and Development. Readings from the Workshop in Political Theory and Policy Analysis*, McGinnis, Michael D. (ed.); Ann Arbor: University of Michigan Press.

Parks, Roger B., *et al.*, 1981 and 1999; Consumers as Co-Producers of Public Services: Some Economic and Institutional Considerations; *Policy Studies Journal*; vol. 9: 1001–1011 and Ch. 17 in *Local Public Economies. Readings from the Workshop in Political Theory and Policy Analysis*, McGinnis, Michael D. (ed.); Ann Arbor: University of Michigan Press.

Pestoff, Victor, 1984; *Konsumentinflytande och konsumentorganisering, den svenska modellen*; Stockholm: Finansdepartementet, Ds Fi 1984: 15.

Pestoff, Victor, 1989; Organisationers medverkan och förhandlingar i svensk konsumert-politik; *Förhandlingsökonomi i Norden*; Copenhagen: DJÖF & Oslo: Tano.

Pestoff, Victor, 1994; Beyond Exit & Voice in Social Services – Citizens as Co-Producers, in *Delivering Welfare – Repositioning Non-profit and Co-operative Action in Western European Welfare States*; Vidal, P. and I. (eds); Barcelona: CIES.

Pestoff, Victor, 1998; *Beyond the Market and State. Civil Democracy & Social Enterprises in a Welfare Society*; Aldershot, Brookfield: Ashgate.

Pestoff, Victor, 2003; *Making Citizenship Meaningful*; Östersund: Research Report.

Pestoff, Victor, 2006a; *A New Architecture for the Welfare State. Promoting Civil Democracy through Citizen Participation, the Third Sector and Co-production*; Östersund: Mid-Sweden University.

Pestoff, Victor, 2006b; Citizens as Co-Producers of Welfare Services: Childcare in eight European countries, *Public Management Review*; vol. 8/4: 503–520.

Pestoff, Victor, 2006c; Co-Production, the Third Sector & Functional Representation in Sweden; Budapest: ESF Exploratory Workshop on Civil Society.

Pestoff, Victor, Peter Strandbrink and Johan Vamstad, 2004; Childcare in Sweden – A Summary Report; Brussels: European Commission, final report.

Prentice, Susan, 2006; Childcare, Co-Production and the Third Sector in Canada; *Public Management Review*; vol. 8/4: 521–536.

Public Management Review, 2006; Special Issue on Co-production: the Third Sector and the Delivery of Public Services, vol. 8/4.

Sörensen, Eva, 1998; New Forms of Democratic Empowerment. Introducing User Influence in the Primary School System in Denmark; *Statsvetenskapliga tidskrift*; vol. 10/2: 129–143.

Sörensen, Eva, 1999; Democratic Governance and the Changing Role of Users of Public Services; Research Paper No. 3/99; Roskilde: RUC, Denmark.

Tsukamoto, Ichiro and Mariko Nishimura, 2006; The Emergence of Local Non-Profit – Government Partnerships – the Role of Intermediate Organizations in Japan; *Public Management Review*; vol. 8/4: 567–582.

Vamstad, Johan, 2004a; Local Government and the Non-public Providers of Preschool – a Characterisation of their Relation in the Swedish Welfare State; Enschede: Euroloc Annual Summer School of Local Government.

Vamstad, Johan, 2004b; (Not) Dealing with Diversity – How Change is Managed in the Swedish Welfare State; Östersund: course paper.

Vamstad, Johan, 2007; Governing Welfare. The Third Sector and the Challenges to the Swedish Welfare State; Östersund: Ph.D. manuscript.

van Kersbergen, Kees and Frans van Waarden, 2004; "Governance" as a Bridge Between Disciplines: Cross-disciplinary Inspiration Regarding Shifts in Governance and Problems of Governability, Accountability and Legitimacy; *European Journal of Political Research*; vol. 43/2: 143–171.

Wiklund, Hans, 2004; Bristande affinitet som demokratiproblem; Sundsvall: C-uppsats.

11 Co-governance and co-production

From the social enterprise towards the public–private co-enterprise[1]

Francesco Manfredi[2] *and Mirella Maffei*[3]

Introduction

After years of analysis and debate, today the issue of co-governance and co-production in the sector of public personal services[4] requires the definition of new organizational and managerial models concerning not only relations between existing organizations, but also the characteristics of new types of enterprises.

At a moment when the definition and the components of the "social enterprise concept" are still under investigation, we have to address the issue as to whether this form of entrepreneurship is always the best answer to the requirements of co-governance and co-production of the system as a whole and/or its most important parts.

The need to broaden and articulate the debate regarding these exchange processes and the actors operating in the sector, is also the result of new practices which have developed in Europe as a result of the evolution of public-private partnerships from contracting-out models towards new forms of integrated entrepreneurship.

At the same time, thanks to the emphasis on the local dimension and on the dynamics of the community, the boundaries of the analysis overcome the mere practise of "zero-sum games", where stable conditions of balance are achieved.

It can actually be said that there is the need:

- to increase the level of transparency and the quality of interaction among actors;
- to increase the level of involvement and participation of organizations and individuals;
- the qualitative and quantitative level of responses to the needs of the community should be increased where the available resources are the same, and where there is a lesser amount of resources available the level of such responses should remain constant;
- to increase the propensity to long-term strategic planning of public actors;
- to acknowledge and codify the governance role of the sector and the non-profit actors;

- to improve the individuals' predisposition and their ability to work in an integrated environment towards long-term relationships;
- to activate all communitarian resources in order to support shared goals.

As a consequence of the above, the characteristics of mixed enterprises can be briefly defined as follows:

1   the mixed enterprise is an integral part of the social and economic "system" of the community;
2   it can play the role of a coordination mechanism in order to overcome the inefficiencies of the sector and ensure the efficiency of the answers provided, making relations more fluid and improving the processes of exchange;
3   it can act as a mechanism of managerial experimentation;
4   it is characterized by a strategic alliance meant to reduce uncertainty and facilitate the access to resources;
5   it is characterized by a strategic alliance that allows partners to pursue new organizational models and new managerial strategies;
6   it is an organization with governance and control mechanisms defined on the basis of:

- statutory agreements (level of participation, nomination of board members and directors, etc.);
- organizational processes (reporting, planning and controlling process, quality certification, social balance, analysis of stakeholders' satisfaction, etc.);
- strategic management of human resources (mechanisms of recruiting, training, informing, rewarding; balance of competences, etc.);
- Informal mechanisms (social control);

7   it provides citizen-consumers with a warrant mechanism.

This chapter therefore aims at assessing the characteristics of (and the opportunities offered by) an entrepreneurial model that overcomes the intrinsic limits of collaborative relationships based either on lobbying relations or on the usual exchange between client and supplier.

Public–private relations in terms of co-governance and co-production: towards a definition of the partnership concept

The recognition of the important role of non-profit actors in the creation of public personal services is leading to the legitimation of their public function.

However, their development has gone through different stages which have been associated to the different forms used to structure the relations between public administrations and the non-profit sector.

These forms shall be analysed, in order to understand their evolution and, above all, in order to explore new types of organizations that could be adopted in the production of personal services.

The concept of "co-governance": from a systemic perspective to a partnership one

The diffusion of the New Public Management paradigm[5] in Europe, has introduced a series of market-based mechanisms in the management of local public services, which, while not representing a clear sign towards the construction of authentic partnerships[6] has however managed to delineate a series of contractual instruments that could govern relations between local governments and their non-profit partners.

This model, however, has been criticized on the basis of the fact that its collaborative approach allows governments to maintain control over the "policy making process", relegating the third sector to the role of a mere "service agent".[7]

Yet, even within these limits, it must be acknowledged that this paradigm has stimulated the debate (which would later develop considerably), concerning the concept of "public governance".

Here the concept of *governance* is to be understood as opposed to the concept of *government*, which is identified as a form of direct and incisive top-down action over the forces of the system and which appears to be based on a rigid exercise of formal power.[8]

Thanks to the concept of governance, the emphasis moves to the government's ability to deal with the needs of the community, through an adequate governance of the system and the economic parts involved,[9] focussing on the importance of public–non-profit forms of cooperation.

Thus, further value is given to the concepts of *pluralistic governance* and (particularly inter-sector) *partnership*:

> this paradigm pushes for a lean, efficient government whose main role is to support private and voluntary action with a minimum of regulation and interference. Thus the dominant, controlling State gives way to the facilitator, partner State.[10]

The participative dimension of the concept of governance is also strong in the Anglo-Saxon meaning of "community governance",[11] which gives emphasis to the role the non-profit sector should play during the phase of "policy formulation and service management".

Suggesting, once again, that "governance" should indicate the use of *organized forms* of public-private interaction, at different levels, J. Kooiman identifies cooperation and collaboration as the basic mechanisms of exchange amongst the players involved in the implementation of public policies.[12]

More precisely, he introduces the meaning of "co-governance", emphasizing the aspect of "co-participation".

Among the various forms that could be suitable to exercise this "co-participation", he distinguishes the "public–private partnerships", a notion on which it is worth focusing on for a moment.

The fundamental characteristics of these partnerships identified by J. Kooiman are: trust and reciprocal adaptation; the pursuit of common goals; the clear definition of inputs, risks and compensation mechanisms, together with the sharing of authority and responsibilities.

All this is intended as a dynamic process on the basis of which the possible balance in terms of power structures and determination of rules can be defined.

Moreover, it should be considered that both parties have the possibility to determine conditions and possible changes within the relation.

It appears clear that whereas at the beginning the more generic notion of governance is understood at a systemic level, it progressively identifies a more restricted level, a level which could be defined, strictly speaking, in terms of partnership.

From this perspective, the interactions and the symmetry of decisional power, among the actors who interact in the governance process at the level of the system, can be similarly traced by the mechanisms used to define the roles and relative influences within the partnerships' field.

The conceptual variant of "co-governance", defined by W. Kickert and J. Koppenjan as a "negotiating governance" according to which the negotiating procedures that link the parts involved are emphasized,[13] appears likewise interesting.

In this sense, the idea of co-governance is very close to that of corporate governance, understood here in its "broad perspective".[14]

Indeed, in this sense "governance" comprises, on the one side, the "institutional order" on the basis of which the organization is governed; and, on the other, those mechanisms and conditions that regulate the relationship among various actors, in order to realize the company's goals.

The players considered in this perspective are not only managers and shareholders, but also the stakeholders.

Consequently, this connotation seems extremely appropriate to the analysis of the relations between actors such as public and non-profit ones, whose institutional aims involve different typologies of stakeholders.[15]

Thus if, in a way "corporate governance means public governance",[16] so that "the same underlying principles you find in corporate governance also apply in their standards for good public governance", it becomes possible to claim that the concepts of co-governance and corporate governance are mutually dependent.

In fact, the underlying principles of both concepts are indeed those of transparency, participation and accountability.

The analysis of the functionality of co-governance in a specific partnership, at both systemic and corporate levels, will also imply the examination of the tools used to balance a series of elements.

In particular, we are referring to the roles assigned to each stakeholder and his/her relative importance; the amount of resources provided by each one; the extent to which culture, norms and controls are shared; the mechanisms of reward and compensation.

Considering all of the above, it is now possible to provide a succinct definition of co-governance, in particular within the context of personal services.

In order to determine "co-governance", "*the involvement and participation of the collaborating parts in the governance of the accord; the balance of decisional power in the phases of planning, other than delivery, of services; as well as the sharing of the mechanisms of reward and control*" shall therefore be adopted.

The concept of "co-production": from "citizen participation" to public–non-profit joint production

The idea of co-production first appeared in the 1970s in response to the growing financial crisis of the public institutions in charge of social services, in an attempt to find possible solutions to this problem.

There are several perspectives from which we this phenomenon can be analysed, ranging from the economic to the social and the organizational ones.

According to the economic approach, L.L. Kiser and S.L. Percy consider the overlapping between "consumption" and "production" as the very origin of the concept, stating that "co-production involves a mixing of the productive efforts of regular and consumer producer", so that "consumers can increase the amount and/or quality of the service they consume by directly contributing to their production".[17]

Similarly, J. Brudney and R. England define co-production as a "direct citizen involvement in the design and delivery of services with professional and service agents", in the attempt to produce *more services at less cost*.[18]

G. Whitaker[19] and E.B. Sharp[20] keep the meaning of participation of citizen-consumers in the production of services, mainly in the phase of "execution".

According to them, the interaction between those who benefit directly from the service and the authority that officially delivers it, should be able to *improve its efficacy*.

The service is therefore understood as a "*joint product*" of the activities of the state and the citizens[21] and, as it is emphasized, citizens have the possibility to influence the formulation and the implementation of those public policies of which they are the beneficiaries.

By referring also to the advantages in terms of cost reduction, C.H. Levin highlights the social aspect of co-production, presenting it as a *mechanism which could generate social capital*, therefore reinforcing the relationship between citizens and Public Administration.[22]

Although different aspects of the phenomenon are emphasized, it is clear that the general meaning of the concept is basically the direct involvement of citizen-consumers in the production of services.

Nevertheless, while initially literature was characterized by a political or sociological tone, recently the debate about co-production has found new directions of analysis.

While fundamentally maintaining the "consumer-co-producer" idea, the attention has been shifted to the organizational, as well as inter-organizational, logics lying behind this concept.

In more recent works definitions can be found that seem to be more appropriate to seize the heterogeneity of a phenomenon that is actually witnessing a proliferation of collaborative forms in the production of services, also thanks to the involvement of not only citizens but also of different parties.

E. Ostrom, for instance, defined co-production as "the process through which inputs used to provide a good or service are contributed by individuals who are not in the same organization".[23]

This definition was criticized because it was considered too generic, and because it depicts inter-organizational cooperation as an exception rather than the common practice it actually is.[24]

In spite of the fact that Ostrom himself actually would consider citizens or groups of citizens as co-producers, this basic notion could be useful to adequately encapsulate the distinctive elements of new public–non-profit collaborative forms.

The idea of *collective action* and *joint contribution of input* to the production, on the part of *distinct organizations*, appears fairly close to the concept of partnership that was discussed above.

An even broader characterization of co-production is provided by T.L. Cooper and P.C. Kathi, who identify it as a "deliberative democracy, where there is an emphasis on eliciting broad public participation in a process".[25]

In this sense, the *participation* of *different kinds* of parties is highlighted as a key aspect, and through the concept of deliberative democracy, the creation of a context of institutional practices that promotes collaborative plans is encouraged.

The organizational perspective is further emphasized by the concept of "institutionalized co-production" elaborated on by J. Johsi and M. Moore and defined as a "provision of public services through regular, long-term relationships between state agencies and organized groups of citizens, where both make substantial resource contribution".[26]

It is clear, then, that the tendency is towards *long-term collaboration* with *significant resource contributions* from participants.

Apparently, the *leit motiv* of the literature on co-production is the fact that the latter is perceived as a process able to improve both effectiveness and efficiency of the service delivery, while creating more opportunities for citizens to take part in the "public action" in a democratic way.

International research on several cases, in different areas of production involved in the public and social services, confirms the positive effects of co-production, as discussed above.[27] Nonetheless, the concept of co-production seems somehow incomplete.

Indeed, although the positive effects of this phenomenon which were previously pointed out, have now been accepted, it has not been demonstrated that these effects are to be exclusively related to the fact that the co-producers coincide with the citizens who are also the direct consumers of the services.

In other words, the more generic definitions of co-production, that emphasize the importance of common contributions and collaborative long-term relations seem better suited to account for the factors determining the potential of improvement of the service themselves.

What determines the development of the supply of services seems actually to be the *sharing of goals and resources*. And this "sharing" can exist between government and citizens, but not in an exclusive relationship.

Without doubt, the literature mentions that more complex organizational forms exist, collective or group-based, participating in the production of services.[28]

However, in this case no formal mechanism of coordination is presumed, neither among citizens, nor between citizens and the government.

Existing literature refers to the existence of voluntary associations, cooperative forms and, more generally, social enterprises, that is, organizations acting as "vehicles" to help the relation of co-production between the state and citizens.

Also in this case, then, the value conferred to the third sector is mainly instrumental and as it concerns proper entrepreneurial organizations, even though they might still be non-profit, the concept of co-production must be differentiated from the notions of "parallel" and "ancillary" production,[29] (which can be amalgamated to the notion of supply), or, on the contrary, to concurrent relations between the state and the third sector.[30]

Somehow, we still seem influenced by a rigid separation between public and private organizations, but the time has come to overcome these anachronistic Weberian influences.

Indeed, if the involvement of social enterprises is discussed, no relation has yet been conceived which might assume an actual sharing of goals and resources between the government and the Third sector, something that, on the contrary, seems to happen only at an elementary level.

Their participation in the production of the same services they benefit from, also raises problems that have not been thoroughly investigated so far: for instance, co-producer-citizens and other consumers of the same service (or indeed co-producer-citizens and the community in general) might have different interests.

This is particularly true if we consider the potential utilitarianism and the limited rationality that characterize individuals' behaviour; and even when human conduct is inspired by solidarity and altruism, the limits of the "hedonistic egoism" that often leads human moral action has to be taken into consideration.

Thus, the single citizen that becomes co-producer, irrespective of the fact that s/he could be inspired by "self interest", "altruism or other social values",[31] might assume a sort of "altruistic utilitarianism"[32] as the goal of his/her actions, thereby mistaking the individual good with the common good.

Furthermore, there are also reservations about the professional competences and the experience that citizen-co-producers should have.

It is equally important that, in the sector of public personal services, consumers alone do not have the possibility to correctly judge the quality of the service received.

As a consequence, it is necessary to have a multidimensional evaluation of quality, which involves the different actors engaged in the service.[33]

For these reasons, the focus should be on the definition of co-production forms capable of generating the same effects described above, but which act according to the economical orders of institutions that might go beyond the mere inclusion of citizens in the production.

Furthermore, in terms of co-producers, those organizations that have the necessary competencies and that are able to represent a broader spectrum of stakeholders should be considered.

Therefore a shift from a "customer oriented" perspective to a "stakeholder oriented" perspective should be made, in the pursuit of a truly "public" interest.[34]

This representation should act through organizational and managerial structures and mechanisms, which, for example, go beyond the simple participation of parents in the activities of the nursery school attended by their child.

The managerial repercussions implied by the administration of such relations and their outcomes actually become fundamental.

We are therefore faced with a new concept of "co-production", understood here as the *"involvement of different organizations in the production of services, with significant contribution and concrete sharing of inputs, in a long-term collaborative perspective and with a democratic participation in the formulation and implementation of the policies and strategies related to the services"*.

The aim of all this is of course the pursuit of the same benefits initially outlined by the former concept, through forms which, however, are now more similar to that of partnership.

S.P. Osborne and K. McLaughlin had already assumed a similar position in relation to the concept of co-production, anticipating for the non-profit actor, rather than for citizens themselves, the role of co-producer.[35]

However, according to their definition, the production is carried out in parallel or coordinated forms, so that inputs are not shared and co-transformed.

The connotation given to the term of "co-production" – actually intended by Osborne as productive coordination – is therefore different.

In addition, this connotation is residual, in the sense that the perspective of coordination still regards the third sector as a mere supplier of services.

To sum up, in comparison to the previous definitions, this new concept tries to keep the economic dimension (optimization of resources, higher level of efficiency) as well as the social one (greater interaction among stakeholders, better understanding of customer needs, creation of social capital).

What is now different, is the managerial and organizational perspective, which is now more complex and which recognizes in the inter-organizational partnership as the basis for an effective co-production.

The relational forms: from coordination to partnership

As previously discussed, in comparison to what happened in the past, empirical evidence and the interests of non-profit actors are progressively moving towards forms that involve the third sector in a more effective and determinate way.

In the normally used forms of "support", "promotion" and "agreement", there is no joint action and no reciprocal obligation, neither in the use of resources that could be dedicated to the activities nor in the results to be achieved.

The form of "concession" and "accreditation" are however different, since they can allow a greater sharing of resources in terms of inputs.

In spite of this, the role of the third sector in a collaborative relationship clearly remains subjugated to the preferences of the public administration and the available resources.

Indeed, it is the mixed enterprise that seems more easily comparable to a partnership.

The use of a mixed form of enterprise might represent a significant improvement of the process of legitimating of the role of non-profit sectors, from mere suppliers to "partners" of the public administration. This seems particularly true in the field of the management of personal services.

In order to outline a classification of the different relational forms adopted, by referring back to the dimensions of co-governance and co-production, it is clear that the mixed enterprise seems to be the form that leans more towards these concepts than others do.

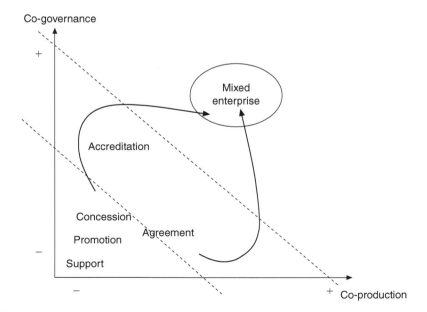

Figure 11.1 Classification of the public-non-profit relational forms in Italy.

Table 11.1 Co-governance determinants in public-non-profit relationships

Co-governance	Participation of the parts in the governance of the relationship	Balance of decisional power in the planning phase	Sharing of control mechanisms
Support	Absent: public financial support	Absent: the NPO does not undertake any obligation	Absent: no negotiated target to achieve
Promotion	Low: procedural agreement	Very low: duties assumed by NPO are limited to the entity of promotional benefits	Absent: discretional control of PA
Agreement	Moderate: contract in relation to the economic-financial content of the relationship	Moderate: exercise of public functions on the part of the NPO	Very low: right of "exit" for the NPO
Concession	Very low: unilateral action of PA	Very low: clear supremacy of PA	Absent: PA's exclusive control and right to revoke. These are effective at anytime and without restrictions
Accreditation	Very low: limits determined by the contract	Moderate: participation in the formulation of general plans	Moderate: PA's *ex ante* control
Mixed enterprise	Significant: formal contract, expression of the negotiating and organizational autonomy of the parts	Significant: direct participation in the governance' process	Significant: rights of "voice" and "exit" for both partners

In actual fact, the paradigms inspiring both co-governance and co-production appear evident in this form (Tables 11.1 and 11.2).

This can be easily demonstrated by comparing the contents in the different relational forms that are typical of these concepts.

For the sake of simplicity, only those forms that have already been mentioned shall be compared, as these are normally adopted when contracting-out.

It is clear that, only the mixed enterprise presents features that can be properly defined as typical of a "collaborative" relationship.

Indeed, with "collaboration", the parts explicitly want to determine formal relations, with clearly defined roles (or roles which can be defined *in itinere* under common agreement), and the transparent features of the participants.

Thus, it is only at a collaborative stage that it becomes possible to establish a proper partnership which, as underlined before, presupposes a level of mutuality between parts, a mutuality that only a formal relationship can actually grant.[36]

Table 11.2 Co-production determinants in public-non-profit relationships

Co-production	Significant contribution and sharing of inputs	Democratic participation in the implementation of the policies of service delivery	Long-term perspective
Support	Absent: mere transfer of subsides from PA	Absent: no integration of activities	Absent: PA's *una tantum* action
Promotion	Absent: PA's dispensation of benefits	Very low: PA only promotes initiatives related to the social purposes of the NPO	Absent: short-term agreement
Agreement	Very low: potential sharing of assets and resources distinctively owned by PA	Moderate: agreement on the process of service delivery and the conditions of accessibility	Very low: short-term contract
Concession	Absent: the NPO operates with its own means and withholds every related income	Very low: NPO manages the service autonomously	Very low: no guarantee of continuity is offered to the NPO
Accreditation	Very low: PA subsidizes or finances those services that are delivered by the NPO with its own means	Very low: NPO delivers the service autonomously	Very low: no formal obligation on PA's part and precarious conditions for the NPO
Mixed enterprise	Significant: contribution of capital and specific resources	Significant: representation of both parties in the Board and in other executive bodies	Significant: intrinsic to this enterprise

The shift, from one form to another, is clearly a gradual and incremental process, resulting from the development over time, of different characteristics of both public and non-profit organizations.

This change determines and is determined by the growth of various problems related to the environment, among which reference can be made to the "vagueness about the role, the competences and the boundaries between public and private sectors",[37] that require the formulation of new strategies.

Strategies capable of defining roles, tasks and respective missions, of increasing stakeholders' involvement in the processes of strategic planning, of reducing decision time, of creating consent about policies and a common agenda of actions.[38]

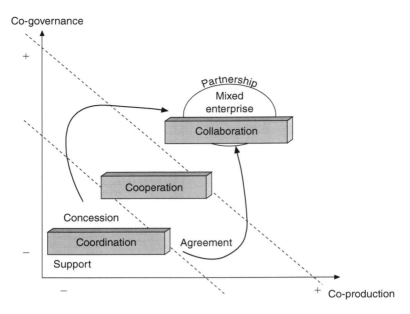

Figure 11.2 Evolutional stages of public-non-profit relationships.

Thus, it becomes necessary to have at our disposal more complex and structured tools than before.

This is why mixed enterprises represent the most appropriate solution.

A model of co-enterprise: the case of Parmainfanzia SpA

Pro.Ges is a social cooperative with its headquarters in Parma, operating in the
field of public personal services.

It has operated for more than ten years in the field of children's educational
services and it was born, like other cooperatives in the Emilia Romagna area, in
order to provide "personnel's substitution" within public services.

However, in conjunction with the development of similar social realities, a
series of problems in the environmental context began to intensify.

The imposition of a roof to the expenses of local agencies, the ties imposed
by the economic and financial parameters set by the Pact of Stability, together
with the continuous increase of the demand for services, made local agencies
unable to guarantee the fulfilment of the population's needs.

The major concern within childcare services related to nursery schools, where
up to 60 per cent of applications remained unanswered.

It is in this context that, during the 1990s, the out-sourcing of services began.

Soon after it was created, Pro.Ges began to tender for the services contracted
out by the municipality of Parma.

The most common forms of negotiation used were "concessions" and "agreements".

Concurrently, during this phase Pro.Ges improved the production and management of its own services.

It thus invested more in the property's assets and broadened the scope of its activities from a geographical point of view.

It is clear that Pro.Ges progressively distinguished itself as a "social enterprise".

The portfolio of services was enriched, as new typologies were added to the services traditionally delivered.

It is clear that in this phase Pro.Ges went through the "collaborative strategy" stages, during which the cooperative reaches a higher awareness of its own work; different stakeholders agree on common goals and visions; and new connections are created.

All of this was in order to improve the capability of responding to environmental stimuli and promote innovation.

Even if the relationship was much more formalized than before, it remained however precarious, particularly from Pro.Ges' point of view.

Being determined *a priori*, the relationship did not allow the non-profit part to make investments supported by a strategic and operational long-term perspective.

The basis for negotiation with the municipality was predominately related to the price; hence Pro.Ges' experience and innovative ability were not valued by parameters of evaluation of tenders that were exclusively defined on cost basis.

Evidently, a fast developing reality such as Pro.Ges could not be satisfied with such a situation.

By being constantly measured and controlled only in terms of cost, the cooperative's work was demeaned.

On the contrary, the cooperative was putting lots of effort into the reorganization of its internal processes, which would have allowed a better monitoring of clients' requests, both internally and externally, in favour of a constant redefinition of the service supplied and a better understanding of the needs of all potential consumers.

Furthermore, there were problems with the public services that the municipality was no longer able to solve by itself.

There were also other issues regarding the costs for spaces and structures.

In order to guarantee better safety within the buildings and to re-qualify the existing spaces, from 2000 to 2003 the municipality progressively increased its investments for kindergarten and nursery schools, planning other investments for the period from 2003 to 2005.

For this reason, the municipality felt the need to search for new managerial forms, capable of overcoming these problems and the mixed enterprise seemed to be the most appropriate managerial formula.

The constitution of the mixed enterprise "Parmainfanzia"

At that moment, Pro.Ges was already managing a number of kindergartens, some of which were its own and managed under agreements, and others totally contracted-out by the municipality of Parma.

Such managerial forms did not satisfy Pro.Ges, which with the formula of short-term contracting-out (maximum two-three years), had no incentives to invest.

It was felt that there was a need to initiate long-term projects that would permit the engagement of funds in new structures and the development of human resources.

In reality, the selection of the partner for the constitution of the company was not meant to find just someone who could manage the structures.

Rather, what was hoped for was a partner who could also take the responsibilities related to the design of services, the building of new structures and the organization of new activities, even subsidiary to the delivery of the main service.

Indeed, the municipality had the following strategic goals:

1   increase the places available (for both kindergartens and nursery schools);
2   plan and realize formative activities;
3   create a study and research centre on infancy;
4   enhance the external visibility of the pedagogical-educational model of municipal services;
5   construct and develop a "quality system" of services based on the ISO model;
6   sell advisory services to other agencies.

It is clear that, in order to pursue the objectives mentioned above, it was necessary to achieve an effective territorial integration of the private and public organizations dealing with educational services.

Such integration was very well suited to the characteristics of Pro.Ges's "entrepreneurial formula".

Indeed, Pro.Ges seemed to act as a local organization closely integrated within its territory of action, and as such it could produce a significant impact on the referring community, mainly in terms of "trust building".

Obviously, among the resistances that the municipality would have to face by adopting this new formula, there were the "psychological" and cultural barriers on the basis of which it was common to associate the public aspect of the service with the juridical nature of the delivering organization.

As to the service itself, the search for a partner with qualified planning capabilities was intended to lead to the offer of constant incremental and radical innovations, in both the service and its organization.

Additionally, from this perspective, over the years Pro.Ges demonstrated its ability to diversify, differentiate and propose innovative services that are actually being implemented in Parmainfanzia.

However, the main added value of Pro.Ges relates to the provision of contributions of an organizational, managerial and, particularly relevant here, financial nature.

Mechanisms of "co-governance" in Parmainfanzia

According to the concept of co-governance previously delineated, its criteria of analysis should be: the parts' degree of participation in the governance of the agreement; the level of fairness of decisional powers in the planning phase of the policies related to the services; the sharing of the control mechanisms.

Beginning with the first dimension, it is interesting to analyse the contributions carried out by both partners.

Pro.Ges contributed to the social capital with a majority stake of the 51 per cent of the total capital.

The municipality underwrote the remaining 49 per cent.

However, for the first time in Italy in such circumstances, the private partner was given the opportunity to hold a majority stake in the shareholders' body, notwithstanding a series of essential guarantees for the protection of the interests of the general public.

In any case, this is something that should not be underestimated, in terms of trust accorded to the partner, and the risk of social acceptance consequently run by the municipality.

For the remainder, the characteristics of the contract were delineated with deliberation of the Municipal Assembly, which approved the "outlines" of the Memorandum of Association, the Statute of the Company and the "Contract of Service".

After the selection of the private partner, these documents were defined in more detail with the agreement of both parties, still in compliance with the indications given by the municipality, and the limits set by law to the parties' contractual autonomy in such particular companies.

The actual legislation on joint-stock companies with public minority stock provides for the compliance with a series of conditions to preserve the common good, among which:

1 the local authority's prerogative to nominate at least one member of the Board of Directors, possibly the Executive Committee and the Supervisory Board;
2 the exclusion, until the fifth year after the constitution of the society, of any deed of transfer of shares, their different entitlements and any other action that could determine the private partner's loss of its position as a majority shareholder;
3 the public partner's right to express its (motivated) approval of the above-mentioned actions if they are initiated by the private partner.

On the basis of all this, in the Statute of the Company a clause of approval was inserted in favour of the municipality, a clause that is applicable in case of transfer of shares from the private partner to other third parties.

This approval still has to be justified with unbiased motivations. Moreover, any disposal of shares has been prohibited until 2008.

This, in order to avoid a change in the proportion of shares as was initially established, and to prevent the economic and financial damages that could follow.

The entry of partners that, because they were not evaluated on the basis of public evidence criteria, as Pro.Ges was, could risk altering the quality and the continuity of the service delivered, is thus prevented.

Obviously, if Pro.Ges did no longer consider the participation in the company convenient and wanted to sell its stock quickly, such limitations may limit its right of "exit clearance".

It is therefore possible to state that, *in summa*, the government of the agreement has been fairly administered, notwithstanding the compulsory cautions in favour of the common good.

Simultaneously, those limitations related to the structure of the stock capital should not be so onerous for a partner such as Pro.Ges, whose main wish is to engage, in a reliable and continuative way, in a long-term relation.

As far as the balance in terms of the power for deciding on the policies of the services' management is concerned, it becomes necessary to identify the mechanisms that regulate the decisional processes in the relevant bodies.

The decisional body par excellence is obviously the Board of Directors, where the strategies relating to the management of the service are established.

Here, the assessment of the different interests appears particularly difficult.

On the one hand, as a majority shareholder, Pro.Ges should have a certain influence within this body, which should lead to a consistent representation.

On the other hand, however, a company that manages public services cannot avoid bearing a strong influence on the public agency, even if this holds a minority stock.

Indeed, it has the institutional responsibility and the competence to exercise the functions of direction and control.

This is why the Statute provides the municipality with the right to nominate two directors out of five, one of which is the President.

Considering that the decisions of the Board of Directors are made by absolute majority, such distribution of agencies is surely relevant in terms of the protection of the interest of the majority stakeholder.

Actually, it is clear that the majority stock of Pro.Ges does not correspond to an equivalent power within the Board of Directors.

If this is so, it is because even with three representing directors, Pro.Ges lacks the necessary vote to make strategic decisions.

This is justified by the municipality as a "political guarantee".

With common consensus, "para-company pacts" were also stipulated.

According to these, the parties agree on the sanctions applicable in case of breach of either the contract or its clauses; the cases in which the entrustment of the service can be revoked; the modalities of resolution of potential disagreements.

Also in this case, the common intent to reduce as much as possible the potentiality of conflicts appears clear.

The issue as to the actual kind of power of governance Pro.Ges was enjoying, within the mixed enterprise, as a majority shareholder, also came to the fore.

At first glance, in fact, it would seem that the series of legal and discretional restrictions that the municipality imposed on the partner, could spoil the real value of its decisional power.

Nonetheless, the fact that a voice was however given to the prerogatives of the private part in such an important body, is certainly important, especially if we consider, as discussed above, that this right is almost always absent in other relational forms.

With two directors out of five, the municipality basically maintains a sort of "right of veto", as it should be, for those who must safeguard the interests of the general public.

Now Pro.Ges has the opportunity to make its proposals in the phase of planning, an opportunity that was previously completely absent, since Pro.Ges used to proceed only in response to the requests determined *a priori* by the municipality, with its call for tenders to contract-out services.

In addition, the discretional power of Pro.Ges is absolutely fundamental in the operational sphere, since it owns the right to nominate the General Manager, whose role should bridge the gap between planned and implemented strategy.

Actually, it is in this sphere that Pro.Ges is able to bring real added value to the partnership.

Its organizational and managerial distinctive competencies help to handle the operational part of the service better, especially in comparison to what the municipality operating alone could do.

What seems to be clear in the institutional order so defined, is that a clear definition of roles was chosen and agreed upon, so that each partner was aware, from the very beginning, of the extent of its power and responsibilities, and of the limits of its agency.

These roles, however, were defined on the basis of the respective functionalities and competencies.

Furthermore, each partner exercises a certain control on both strategic and operative decisional processes; within each of these, however, whoever holds compelling prerogatives in either sphere is more influential.

It is however important that, during the formulation of the strategies, Pro.Ges has a substantial right to be heard in order to co-govern and contribute to the policies that underlie the services.

Furthermore, in Parmainfanzia there is another body where the interests and the visions of the two partners can be compared, so that the managerial activities can have a consistent "imprint".

This is in reference to a body of coordination, defined in the contract as "joint technical committee", whose task is to elaborate and define pedagogical issues ensuring some homogeneity in the management of the municipal educational services.

This committee is composed by the person who is responsible for the nursery schools and the kindergartens of the municipality of Parma, the Managing Director of Parmainfanzia and other coordinators belonging to Pro.Ges.

The control is mainly exercised by the public agency on the work of Parmainfanzia, and in the case of the mixed enterprise, the control is both formal and substantial.

From a formal point of view, in fact, the typologies of control provided for by the law are:

1   verifications and assessments, which could be carried out also by accessing directly the structures entrusted with the management of the services;
2   direct acquisition of documents, information and other elements that could be useful if action of resolution for non-fulfilment of the contract should be taken;
3   notification of possible irregularities to the Board of Directors.

The place for substantial control, on the contrary, is mainly within the Board of Directors, where the municipality can supervise the effective conduct of the service.

Here "control" goes from the management of the economic resources to the contents of the various actions to be undertaken for the delivery.

An additional form of control, one that concerns the characteristics of the service delivered, can take place inside the joint committee, where Pro.Ges holds wider discretional spaces.

Due to this, besides other reasons, the formula of the mixed enterprise differs from the forms of contracting-out previously used by the municipality.

With the mixed enterprise one is accredited and controlled on the basis of shared standards.

These are actually agreed on by the partner, both ex ante (with the underwriting of the "Contract of Service"), and *in itinere*, during all the activities of the company.

Furthermore, in order to make the governance control more objective and effective, the decision was made to resort to external advisory companies that periodically write up reports containing both economic and qualitative evaluations, thereby monitoring the state of achievement of the goals settled as standards.

In addition to these reports, clearly there are the normal financial reports provided for by law for joint-stock companies.

According to the analysis that has been performed, it is now possible to make some considerations about the mechanisms of co-governance at work in Parmainfanzia.

As the company's institutional order makes clear, among the critical concerns, there is the strong control exercised by the public partner.

The latter, while remaining the official holder of the service, and also because of its institutional competences, exercises a role of control certainly stronger than that which a normal minority shareholder would have.

This role is however balanced by the discretion granted to Pro.Ges within the operational sphere, where it assumes greater responsibilities.

This, in its turn, determines Pro.Ges's greater influence on the public policies related to the service.

The operations that follow shape, whether directly or indirectly, the direction assumed by the policies related to the services.

In addition to such mechanisms of a "more indirect" nature, however, the municipality also wanted to entrust the private partner with the responsibility of planning and building the necessary structures to improve the service.

According to the partners, however, even though the intentions were clear, the ability of the private part to make incisive proposals, in terms of plans and projects, has developed over time.

Simultaneously, its level of involvement in the governance has grown, with the subsequent assignment of more responsibilities on the municipality's part that were fairly proportioned to the level of risk assumed by Pro.Ges in entrepreneurial terms.

Mechanisms of "co-production" in Parmainfanzia

The first characteristic of an effective co-production should be the contribution and the sharing of inputs between partners.

As discussed above, besides the contribution of capital, proportional to the shares underwritten, there were further contributions.

On Pro.Ges's part, there was a significant endowment of intangible resources, in terms of technical know-how and trust on the local community's part, which seemed to be particularly useful to legitimate the ambitious initiative of the municipality towards citizens.

Pro.Ges's crucial contribution was related to human resources, as it introduced in the kindergartens and the nursery schools managed by Parmainfanzia, personnel who had been already accredited and who already had experience in the sector.

On the contrary, the infrastructures were initially bought by the municipality, with the relative pertinences, accessories, equipment and pieces of furniture.

While remaining the property of the municipality, Parmainfanzia could use them in exchange of a rent, whose amount can be considered quite favourable if compared to current market prices.

Having thus defined the estate of the company, it is interesting to analyse the set up cost of the structures.

First, it is necessary to bear in mind that among the municipality's priorities, when Parmainfanzia was created, there was the intention to supply services in compliance with the qualitative standards of the municipal services, at a lesser cost than the service directly produced.

In more economic terms the cost of the contracted-out services does not include a series of indirect costs, which derive from the delivery of other supplementary services that are still carried out by the municipality but which could instead be handled directly from the mixed enterprise.

Particular reference is made to activities such as:

1   "sector direction", with functions of planning, coordination and control for all the educational services and the operating structures of kindergartens and nursery schools;
2   "direction of the kindergartens and nursery schools services", that dealt with the coordination and control of the specific activities carried out in the schools;
3   "pedagogical coordination", with functions of pedagogical-educational planning, survey of formative needs, arrangement of annual plans, coordination of structures, relation with families;
4   "administration office", capable of handling lists, administrative activities, collections, payments, relationships with suppliers, internal control management;
5   "consumers' counter", which should cover the function of reception of enrolment requests, as well as acting as a source of information in relation to the accessibility to the services.

Within Parmainfanzia, the directional activities (no. 1, 2) are instead managed respectively by the Board of Directors and the General Management.

The pedagogical coordination (no. 3) operates within the joint committee constituted by Pro.Ges and the municipality.

The administrative activities (no. 4) are performed by the staff of Parmainfanzia, which, as determined by the "Contract of Service", deals with the consumers, the relationships with suppliers, the ordinary maintenance of structures and the internal control, etc.

The "consumers' counter" (and therefore, the enrolments and relative lists) is the only element that remains of municipal competence.

Since it is the official responsible for the public service, the municipality has to control such functions in compliance with the principle of fair accessibility.

The municipality can therefore make remarkable savings on indirect costs.

Furthermore, the scale economies that originate from the mixed enterprise allow all the structures that were previously managed indirectly to concentrate on a unique subject, thereby creating critical mass and the dilution of structures costs.

It is clear that what influences the cost of the service is mainly related to the personnel, which for the nursery schools reaches peaks of 84 per cent.

With Parmainfanzia, this cost is considerably reduced thanks to the adoption of a flexible and straightforward organizational structure.

This way, the "techno-structure" becomes more ductile and reactive to environmental changes.

The rest of the management of the personnel (from selection to recruiting, training and development), is directly entrusted to Pro.Ges.

Parmainfanzia, in fact, does not hire educators and pedagogues; it prefers to use those of the private partner.

Hence, everything that relates to human resources and the organizational activity of the service, is managed through Pro.Ges, its structures and its offices.

This, thanks to the stipulation of a contract between Parmainfanzia and Pro.Ges, according to which the latter is assigned a major part in the operations, from personnel management, to all the activities related to suppliers (of didactic or consumption materials, sanitary facilities etc.), or related to the commercial and financial aspects.

This is what also happens in relation to goods and services of an instrumental nature (e.g. cleaning facilities), that represent the second factor that influences the direct cost of the service.

It is clear that the main determinants of the cost are contractually assigned to the private partner that, being more market-oriented, is able to guarantee lower costs than the public ones.

Fixed costs for Parmainfanzia are, therefore, almost insignificant.

The choice of such a straightforward organizational structure enables extremely bearable service costs to be kept.

This allows Parmainfanzia to practice tariffs that are lower (by 22 per cent for nursery schools and 27 per cent for kindergartens) than the full cost the municipality would have to sustain with the in-house production.

On the contrary, the tariffs applied to users are determined by the municipality, according to the "Contract of Service", in order to grant citizens a fair access to the services.

This way, any risk of monopolization of the service is avoided, in so far as access, just like it used to be, is actually regulated by the municipality.

Parmainfanzia is just entitled to submit a modification of the tariffs to the Municipal Assembly, namely the competent body that can evaluate these proposals and decide consequently.

The typology of services supplied is *in primis* the same that was traditionally supplied by the municipality.

Furthermore, other strategic services have been developed, adding actual value to the previous municipal management of the service and this has been possible thanks to the high professional competencies (both specialist and managerial), of Pro.Ges.

These additional services recently created are "company kindergartens", "domiciliary and familiar educators" and "advisory services".

All of these are projects of common interest, which Pro.Ges was already

Table 11.3 Cost comparison between in-house provided and Parmainfanzia services

Full cost for child*	In-house municipal production	Parmainfanzia
Kindergartens	€801	€622
Nursery schools	€548	€402

Notes
* Costs calculated when Parmainfanzia was first established.

experimenting, and that the municipality would not have been able to start alone.

The municipality has the possibility to involve the company interested in the service, in the subvention and the management of the service, simultaneously creating further places for children in its relative territory, at less cost.

Indeed, Pro.Ges allows a better and more varied provision of services, supporting initiatives of different entities.

Different forms of organizational innovation have been implemented:

1 supply of existent services to new targets that, because of the restrictions previously affecting the municipality, were not able to have access to the service;
2 qualitative improvement of existent services, for example by extending the opening time of the structures;
3 new services to existent targets, as with the domiciliary educators;
4 completely new services to new targets, as the advisory services offered to other public and private operators of the sector, or the recently founded Research Centre.

Moreover, the autonomy of the new company permits the "de-bureaucratization" of certain administrative procedures still pertaining to the municipality, so that with Parmainfanzia the ability of the authority responsible for the services to answer quickly to the changes of a fast developing market is improved.

The fact that through Parmainfanzia the municipality is taking part in calls for tenders and other activities that it would have not been allowed to do alone (as these activities are not provided for in its Statute), stands as an example.

This is also what is enhancing the visibility of the municipal educational model outside the city, one of the goals of the mixed enterprise.

The latter actually aimed at the creation of a "pedagogical brand" that could value the experience of the municipality, through the private partner, also beyond the city boundaries.

In short, a sort of "co-branding" activity, where the municipality exploits the visibility, in organizational and managerial terms, of a leader of the sector such as Pro.Ges.

In reality, this model of co-enterprise did not produce positive, manifest effects immediately.

The advantages have been maturing over time and follow the positive outcomes of the common operation.

Within the respective organizations of the partners, there were of course initial resistances and inertias.

Indeed, within the municipality, the staff dedicated to the educational services perceived Parmainfanzia as a competitor.

The members of Pro.Ges, on the contrary, were afraid they would lose autonomy in the management of their services, with negative consequences for the work dynamics within the cooperative.

These concerns have been overcome thanks to the conscious adoption, within the new enterprise, of a managerial and leadership style that, in terms of communication and collaborative attitude, might be considered to be as transparent and open as possible.

At the same time, inside the single organizations, there was an effort to emphasize the positive approach managers and directors had to the new project, in order to create and increase trust amongst the staff.

The dialogue between managers and collaborators dedicated to the implementation of plans has been stimulated; the personnel have been challenged, consensus has been created.

As a consequence, spaces of uncertainty, which could in fact encourage conflicts, are almost entirely absent, mainly because of the choice to define the respective functions precisely, without leaving anything vague.

Thus, some duties have to be undertaken by the public and the private partner together, others have to be managed separately.

This clearly reinforces the conviction that there is a mutual need for each other.

Hence, even potential tensions or misunderstandings (often of a political nature), are overcome thanks to the fact that the parties agree and understand the each other's goals; goals that converge within the company and the choices taken within the relevant bodies.

It can therefore concluded that there is a democratic participation in the implementation of the policies of service delivery, with a clear definition of the different duties of the two parties, coherently with the distinctive competences provided by each one.

Notes

1 This term is used both by French scholars such as M. Bedard, E. Poltier, M. Tereraho (co-enterprise), and English ones, such as S. Brooks, L.D. Musolf, D.L. Spencer, A.R. Vining (in terms of mixed-enterprise), in order to refer to the economic agent with public–private ownership and governance.
2 Associate Professor of Public and Non-profit Management at Lum Jean Monnet and at Bocconi University, par. 1, 2, 3.
3 Assistant Professor of Public and Non-profit Management at Lum Jean Monnet, par. 4.
4 "Public personal services" are here understood as social services (care for the elderly, care for the disabled, individual and family care), healthcare services, educational services, cultural, sport and leisure services.
5 Hood C. (1991) "A Public Management for all seasons?", *Public Administration*, vol. 69, n.1.
6 Mackintosh M. (2000) "Economic cultures and implicit contracts in social care", *Journal of Social Policy*, vol. 29, n.1.
7 Gutch R. (1990) "Partners or Agents?", NCVO.
8 Zuffada E. (2000) *"Amministrazioni pubbliche e aziende private"*, EGEA.
9 Meneguzzo M. (1995) "Dal New Public Management alla Public Governance: il pendolo della ricerca sulla amministrazione pubblica", *Azienda Pubblica*, n. 3.
10 Brinkerhoff J.M., Brinkerhoff D.W. (2002) "Government-nonprofit relations in com-

parative perspective: evolution, themes and new directions", *Public Administration and Development*, n. 22.
11 Clarke M., Stewart J. (1998) "Community governance, community leadership and the New Labour government", London: YPS.
12 Kooiman J. (2003) *Governing as Governance*, Milan: Sage.
13 Kickert W., Koppenjan J. (1997) "Public management and network management: an overview", in Kickert W., Klijn E., Koppenjan J. (eds) *Managing Complex Networks-Strategies for the Public Sector*, Washington DC: Sage.
14 Zattoni A., (2000) *"Economia e governo dei gruppi aziendali"*, EGEA.
15 Manfredi F. (2003) *"Le strategie collaborative delle aziende non profit. Economicità, etica, conoscenza"*, EGEA, paper presented at the Annual Meeting of the American Society of Public Administration.
16 Euromoney, Maggio 2006.
17 Kiser L.L., Percy S.L. (1980) "The concept of coproduction and its implications for public service delivery", Annual Meeting of the American Society for Public Administration.
18 Brudney J., England R. (1983) "Toward a definition of the co-production concept", *Public Administration Review*, vol. 43.
19 Whitaker G. (1980) "Coproduction: citizen participation in service delivery", *Public Administration Review*, vol. 40, n.3.
20 Sharp E.B. (1980) "Toward a new understanding of urban services and citizen participation: the coproduction concept", *Midwest Review of Public Administration*, vol. 14.
21 Sharp E.B. (1980) "Toward a new understanding of urban services and citizen participation: the coproduction concept", *Midwest Review of Public Administration*, vol. 14.
22 Levine C.H. (1984) "Citizenship and service delivery – the promise of co-production", *Public Administration Review*, vol. 44.
23 Ostrom E. (1996) "Crossing the great divide: co-production, synergy and development", *National Civic* Review. vol. 24, n.6.
24 Johsi A., Moore M. (2004) "Institutionalized co-production: unorthodox public service delivery in challenging environments", *The Journal of Development Studies*, vol. 40, n.4.
25 Cooper T.L., Kathi P.C. (2005) "Neighborhood councils and city agencies: a model of collaborative coproduction", *National Civic Review*, Spring.
26 Johsi A., Moore M. (2004) "Institutionalized co-production: unorthodox public service delivery in challenging environments", *The Journal of Development Studies*, vol. 40, n.4.
27 Pestoff V. (2004) "Co-production and personal services in eight European countries", Ljubljana EGPA Conference, Third Sector Group.
28 Brudney J., England R. (1983) "Toward a definition of the co-production concept", *Public Administration Review*, vol. 43.
29 Pestoff V. (2004) "Co-production and personal services in eight European countries", Ljubljana EGPA Conference, Third Sector Group.
30 Young D.R. (2000) "Alternative models of government-nonprofit relations: theoretical and international perspectives", *Nonprofit and Voluntary Sector Quarterly*, vol. 29, n.1.
31 Pestoff V. (2005) "Hurdles to the third sector and the democratisation of the welfare state", Berna EGPA Conference, Third Sector Group.
32 "Second Treatise of Government" by J. Locke, 1690 (free of copyright).
33 Manfredi F. (2003) "Le strategie collaborative delle aziende non profit. Economicità, etica, conoscenza", EGEA.
34 Manfredi F. (2003) "Moderne strategie di marketing per il settore non profit", "Terzo Settore", Il Sole 24 Ore n.4.
35 Osborne S.P., McLaughlin K. (2004) "The cross-cutting review of the volountary sector: where next for local government-voluntary sector relationships?", *Regional Studies*, vol. 38, n.5.

36 Brinkerhoff J.M. (2002) "Government-nonprofit partnership: a defining framework", *Public Administration and Development*, vol. 22, n.1.
37 Manfredi F. (1998) "Il paradigma della competizione collaborativa come modello per la gestione dei rapporti tra soggetti pubblici.e. privati", in *Azienda Pubblica*, n.5.
38 Manfredi F. (2000) "Dal paradigma della competizione collaborativa alla definizione di nuovi ambiti relazionali per lo sviluppo delle aziende non profit", *Non profit*, n.1.

Bibliography

Bédard M.G., Tereraho M.N., Bernier L. (1998) "La configuration stratégique de l'entreprise mixte: pour la distinction public vs privé au plan organisationnel", *Annals of Public and Cooperative Economics*, vol. 69, n.1.

Brinkerhoff J.M. (2002) "Government-nonprofit partnership: a defining framework", *Public Administration and Development*, vol. 22, n.1.

Brinkerhoff J.M., Brinkerhoff D.W. (2002) "Government-nonprofit relations in comparative perspective: evolution, themes and new directions", *Public Administration and development*, n.22.

Brooks S.R. (1985) "The mixed ownership corporation as an instrument of public policy", miméo.

Brudney J., England R. (1983) "Toward a definition of the co-production concept", *Public Administration Review*, vol. 43.

Eckel C.C., Vining A.R. (1985) "Elements of a theory of mixed enterprise", *Scottish Journal of Political Economy*, vol. 32, n.1.

Emmert M., Crow M.M. (1987) "Public-private cooperation and hybrid organizations", *Journal of Management*, vol. 13, n.1.

Gittel R., Vidal A. (1998) *Community organizing. Building Social Capital as a Development Strategy*, London: Sage.

Healey P. (1997) *Collaborative Planning: Shaping Places in Fragmented Societies*, Houndsmill and London: Macmillan.

Johnson C., Osborne S.P. (2003) "Local strategic partnerships, neighbourhood renewal and the limits to co-governance", *Public Money and Management*, July.

Johsi A., Moore M. (2004) "Institutionalized co-production: unorthodox public service delivery in challenging environments", *The Journal of Development Studies*, vol. 40, n.4.

Kickert W., Koppenjan J. (1997) "Public management and network management: an overview", in Kickert W., Klijn E., Koppenjan J. (eds) *Managing Complex Networks-Strategies for the Public Sector*, London: Sage.

Kingsley G.T., McNeelj J.B., Gibson J.O. (1997) *Community Building: Coming of Age*, Washington DC: The Urban Institute.

Kiser L.L., Percy S.L. (1980) "The concept of coproduction and its implications for public service delivery", Annual Meeting of the American Society for Public Administration.

Levine C.H. (1984) "Citizenship and service delivery – the promise of co-production", *Public Administration Review*, vol. 44.

Linden R.M. (2002) *Working across Boundaries: Making Collaboration Work in Government and Nonprofit Organizations*, Hoboken, NJ: Jossey-Bass.

Longoria T. (1999) "The distribution of public–private partnerships: targeting of voluntary efforts to improve urban education", *Nonprofit and Voluntary Sector Quarterly*, vol. 28, n.3.

Manfredi F. (1998) "Il paradigma della competizione collaborativa come modello per la gestione dei rapporti tra soggetti pubblici.e. privati", *Azienda Pubblica*, n.5.

Manfredi F. (2000) "Dal paradigma della competizione collaborativa alla definizione di nuovi ambiti relazionali per lo sviluppo delle aziende non profit", Milan: *Non profit*, n.1.

Manfredi F. (2003) *Le strategie collaborative delle aziende non profit. Economicità, etica, conoscenza*, EGEA.

Menard C. (2004) "The economics of hybrid organizations", *Journal of Institutional and Theoretical Economics*, n. 160.

Osborne S.P. (1996) "Voluntary and non-profit organizations and innovations in local services: the case of the personal services", *Local Government Policy Making*, vol. 23, n. 5.

Osborne S.P. (1997) "Managing the coordination of social services in the mixed economy of welfare: competition, cooperation or common cause?", *British Journal of Management*, vol. 8.

Osborne S.P., Flynn N. (1997) "Managing the innovative capacity of voluntary and non-profit organizations in the provision of public services", *Public Money & Management*, Oct–Nov.

Osborne S.P., McLaughlin K. (2003) "Modelling government-voluntary sector relationships: emerging trends and issues", *European Business Organization Law Review*, n.4.

Osborne S.P., McLaughlin K. (2004) "The cross-cutting review of the volountary sector: where next for local government-voluntary sector relationships?", *Regional Studies*, vol. 38.5.

Ostrom E. (1996) "Crossing the great divide: co-production, synergy and development", *World Development*, vol. 24, n.6.

Pestoff V. (2004) "Co-production and personal services in eight European countries", Ljubljana EGPA Conference, Third Sector Group.

Pestoff V. (2005) "Hurdles to the third sector and the democratisation of the welfare state", Berna EGPA Conference, Third Sector Group.

Sharp E.B. (1980) "Toward a new understanding of urban services and citizen participation: the coproduction concept", *Midwest Review of Public Administration*, vol. 14.

Weil M. (1996) "Community building: building community practice", *Social Work*, vol. 41, n.5.

Whitaker G. (1980) "Coproduction: citizen participation in service delivery", *Public Administration Review*, vol. 40, n.3.

Part VI
Third sector–governmental relationships

12 The evolving state–third sector relations in Turkey

From subservience to partner status?

Korel Göymen[1]

Introduction

The third sector (TS) is made up of all those entities that are not for profit and not part of government, together with volunteer activities which sustain them. These entities, nowadays, are major players/partners in different sectors and areas of service provision, such as health, education, culture, housing, rural services, sports and recreation. It should be emphasized from the start that there is no agreed upon single term or definition to refer to these entities. Among others, the terms civil society and non-profit sector are frequently used interchangeably. In this study, though acknowledging the extensive discussions on the subject and recognizing the important nuances/differences in the content and coverage of the various terms, nevertheless, for sake of convenience, the terms third sector, non-governmental organizations (NGOs) and civil society will be used interchangeably. The main justification for this approach is that the interaction of all these entities with the state can be handled within the same conceptual framework and generalizations.

Two things are certain concerning the third sector. One, it is gaining further recognition in most countries and its centrality to the well-being of society, economy and polity is now widely accepted. Two, its relationship with the state is most ambiguous and generates most concern and debate. The type of interaction of the third sector with the state has varied historically in different societies, and still does. This does not mean that the topic does not yield itself to certain generalizations and commonalities. For instance, many claim that, historically, free associations have been integral to the conceptualization of citizenship, social solidarity and collective action in Western European societies (Harris, 1990; Lewis, 1995, 2004). Lewis (2004: 170–171), further suggests that the interdependence of the third sector and state is crucial for the understanding of European welfare regimes now. She adds that "in the more recent period of welfare state structuring, TS organizations have once more come to the fore in many countries as potential employees, and providers of welfare to the state" (Lewis, 2004: 171).

The same type of development is also observed in Turkey, although she comes from a different state tradition and cultural context. It is the aim of this chapter to study the evolving state–third sector relations in Turkey, both to determine where Turkish civil society stands on the subservience–autonomy scale and interrelate these observations/evaluations to trends else where.

Theoretical discussions on state–third sector interaction

While one can easily talk about the recent resurgence of the TS, it is still generally portrayed as being subservient to the state, delivering services at the behest of, and often under contract, to the state (Lewis, 2004: 171). Some, like Şimşek (2004: 46) even believe that concepts such as civil society and the notion of non-governmental organizations (NGOs) have been overused, causing ambiguities, misunderstandings, stereotypical judgments and oversimplifications. Another view is that:

> oversimplification has often described the state and civil society as belonging to completely opposite spheres. This implies that the state is a gigantic and pervasive power the normal functioning of which is at least authoritarian, if not totalitarian. In modern societies, especially in non-western settings ... such a stark binary opposition is neither necessarily correct or helpful.
>
> (Beller-Hann and Hann, 2001: 32, quoted in Şimşek, 2004: 46–47)

Şimşek (2004: 47), further, warns us that civil society is not homogeneous and consists of different types which may have variegated interests; and that they often have internal contradictions and may exhibit authoritarian tendencies. This warning is in order because neither the state (the various institutions representing it over different issues, often exercising "bureaucratic politics") nor civil society are monolithic structures and should not be treated as such.

Şimşek underlines two basic approaches within the wealth of diverse literature on civil society, namely "the liberal paradigm", and "the critical paradigm" (p. 50). According to Larry Diamond, a proponent of the "liberal paradigm" (1994: 5), which Şimşek quotes (p. 50), civil society "is the realm of organized social life that is voluntary, self-generating (largely) self-supporting, autonomous from the state, and bound by a legal order and a set of shared values". This definition of civil society only partly fits the Turkish scene. Some third sector organizations in Turkey, such as chambers of trade, handicraft, industry and professional bodies of medical doctors, pharmacists, lawyers, engineers, etc. have compulsory membership. Furthermore, some restrictive rules of civil service (particularly the punitive ones) also apply to them. These so-called "para-statal professional bodies" are good examples of "hybridity". Also, most Turkish third sector organizations are not even "largely" self-supporting, but are dependent either on the state, international organizations, and/or northern NGOs for funding (Skip Report, 2006a: 15,19).

A proponent of "critical paradigm", Bjorn Beckman (1997: 3), again quoted in Şimşek (2004: 50), argues that "the concept of civil society needs to be disengaged from its incorporation into a liberal theory of state-society relations, where state and society are juxtaposed as separate and conflicting spheres and suggests that it should be possible to talk about "patriarchal, Islamic, communist and fascist civil societies" (Beckman, 1997: 2). It is only a step away to hypothesize, based on these views, that different organizations of civil society, or the same organizations at different times may be supportive of different regimes, including non-democratic ones. Recent Turkish history and history of the third sector in Turkey is supportive of this hypothesis. During the two military interventions, between 1960–1980, almost all of the third sector in Turkey, at least in discourse, sided with the state, as then, represented by the military. Many "secular" NGOs applauded when the military forced out of office the Islamist government of Necmettin Erbakan in 1998.

Keyman and İçduygu (2003) also stress that "it would be a mistake to attribute an ipso facto manner 'positivity' to civil society, insofar as it involves not only democratic discourses, but also essentialist identity claims, voiced by religious and ethnic fundamentalism, and arguing for reconstructing the state-society/individual relations on a communitarian basis".

Hampson (2003: 8) draws our attention to yet another sore point in state–third sector relations and suggests that "state regulation of institutions of civil society is problematic everywhere" and adds that "areas of activity most susceptible to illegitimate interference by the state are the media, human rights organizations, religious groups and organizations based on a common nationality/ethnicity".

Akarcalı (2003: 11) on the other hand, maintains that "activities of NGOs should not be perceived as a threat to the state because their activities are not against the state but complementary to it".

Carothers (2000: 4), after refuting the idea that NGOs will one day replace the state, advocates that "civil society groups can be much more effective in shaping state policy if the state has coherent powers for setting and enforcing policy. Good non-governmental work will actually tend to strengthen, not weaken state capacity". But, Akarcalı (2003: 11), in resigned manner, believes that the Turkish state is not yet ready to involve civil society in policy and decision-making, and pinpoints the problem as lack of transparent administration and difficulties in accessing information.

The general milieu of state–third sector interaction

The gist of that argument is that there is a marked statist orientation (*étatism*) in Turkey, which stresses community over its members, uniformity rather than diversity, and an understanding of law that emphasizes collective reason instead of the will of membership (Heper, 1985: 8, quoted in Kalaycıoğlu, 2002a: 67). Such a statist orientation tended to view politics as leadership and education of the "uncivilized" masses through the intervention of state or bureaucratic elites. The "State" is suspicious of social groupings, associations and organizations of all kinds that are not under its close surveillance. Hence, the reservoir of goodwill for freedom of association has been shallow. An interventionist and distrustful "state" often leaves little room for any kind of vigorous social activity and associability to flourish (Kalaycıoğlu, 2002a: 68).

Nevertheless, it is possible to refer to "*the legitimacy crisis of the strong-state tradition*" in Turkey since the 1980s. Turkish modernization, since the beginning of the Republic, has been characterized by and has given rise to the "strong-state tradition". This tradition means, first, that the state has assumed the capacity of acting almost completely independent from civil society; second, that the state, rather than the government, has constituted "the primary context of politics"; and third, that the state has been involved in the process of the production and reproduction of cultural life. However, since the 1980s, the emergence of new actors, new mentalities and the new language of modernization, as well as democracy as a global point of reference in politics, has made culture and cultural factors an important variable in understanding political activities. Thus, the call for democratization as the main basis for the regulation of the state–society has become the global/local context for Turkish politics. This means that new actors acting at the global/local levels and calling for democratization have confronted the privileged role of state at the national level (Keyman and İçduygu, 2003: 223).

In spite of this confrontation, due to the remnants of the state tradition, Turkey still does not nurture a fertile environment for civil society. Under the circumstances, one does not necessarily expect to find much evidence of associability and civic activism. However, the ideal typical representations of state–civil society relations often do not match the complexity of the socio-political reality. What is meant by this is that although traditions matter, political structures and behaviour tend to change over time (Kalaycıoğlu, 2002a: 68). This is what is happening in Turkey now.

Kalaycıoğlu (2006: 251), claims that although there is a strong state tradition in Turkey, the actual strength of the state is at best dubious. A better way of defining the state according to him, is as coercive (*ceberrut*), and even arbitrary, rather than strong. It seems as if it is not the strength, but the relative weakness, of the Turkish state that constitutes an impediment to the development of civil society. This weakness leads to a lack of regulation, extraction and distribution capabilities of the state, which renders the state elite (centre) somewhat vulnerable and fearful of the dissatisfaction of the masses (periphery).

The image of the state in Turkey is ambivalent, both punishing and rewarding. It is small wonder that the Turkish state has come popularly to be referred to as the "Papa State". When challenged, it turns into a nasty and cruel (*ceberrut*) mechanism of suppression; but when socio-political forces cooperate with it, there is much to be gained from its benevolence (Heper, 1985: 103, quoted in Kalaycıoğlu, 2006: 250).

Sunar enriches the discussion by stating that Turkey seems to demonstrate the outlook of a "passive-exclusive state", defined as a state that "resists the entry of disadvantaged groups in the official domain of the state regime but neither combats nor promotes civil society". He further argues that the passive-exclusive state does not have the same attitude towards all groups in civil society. For instance, the Turkish state allows organization of economic groups, or associations based on gender; but it is watchful of religious associations and actively resists associability on the basis of cultural ethnicity. The passive-exclusive nature of the state reinforces its relative weakness. A weak state extends its resources and boosts its capacity by ignoring large swathes of civil society, which it is not, in any case, able to regulate and control. Accordingly, only those associations that are perceived as bent on sedition and radical conspiracy, and hence deemed to be security risks, are seriously monitored, prosecuted or suppressed. The rest are either simply left alone or cooperatively engaged (Sunar, 1998: 370).

Evidently, a problem emerges for ethnic and religious non-conformists who would like to have recognition, respect and representation within the political system. The problem is that they want these on their own terms, without adapting to the rules of the political game. The Kurdish nationalists, for example, demand a political voice and recognition in the fullest sense. Religious radicals demand representation and respect in all institutions of the political system, however much they contest and condemn the rules and regulations of the institutions they operate under. The state, on the other hand, demands that the "non-conformists" first accept and fully internalize the principles of the Republican system, the constitution and the laws, and the related rules of the political game. So there ensues a crisis in the political participation to which a compromise solution is nowhere in sight (Kalaycıoğlu, 2002b: 262).

Kalaycıoğlu, like Sunar, also stresses the differential treat of the state. The dramatic experiences with the earthquake of 1999 clearly indicated that various civil initiatives, and especially the self-help associations, enjoy widespread popular support in Turkey. There is scant evidence that self-help organizations are considered with suspicion either by the authorities, or by the people at large. Solidarity associations (such as the beautification organizations (güzelleştirme dernekleri), regional solidarity associations (hemşehri dernekleri), mosque-building societies (cami Yaptirma cemiyetleri) and the like are hardly at risk. Although advocacy groups seem to receive rough treatment from the law enforcement authorities as they challenge their authority, or suggest ways to limit them, such treatment seems to give the impression of being sporadic rather than systematic. Even among the advocacy groups, those that seem not to be perceived by the law enforcement authorities as challengers of the raison d'être of the republican regime and/or the indivisibility of the state, do not seem to be necessarily harassed. In essence civic initiative and activism seem to be gaining acceptance, rather than being brushed aside by the state institutions or by the populace at large as Turkey nears the European Union (Kalaycıoğlu, 2002a: 60).

The tragic and devastating events of 1999 have also led us to think of civil society organizations seriously. The Marmara Earthquake on 17 August, 1999, destroyed a large portion of the most developed industrial region of Turkey, causing almost 20,000 deaths and thereby creating one of the most tragic events of the century, and then there was the Düzce Earthquake on 12 November. These two disasters made it very clear to Turkish people the strong state is in fact very weak in responding and coping with serious problems. This failure of the Turkish state to respond quickly to crisis situations have given rise to a common belief among people that civil society organizations and a more participatory political culture are necessary for the efficient and effective solution of various problems confronting Turkish society (Keyman and İçduygu, 2003: 227).

There are also a number of problems associated with the culture, values and self-image of civil society entities. Although, in discourse they seem to have a universal outlook, "paradoxically, most of the civil society organizations in Turkey, in fact, see globalization as 'a process to be resisted in the long run' or as 'a problem to be seriously dealt with in order to make its impacts positive for Turkish society'. In other words, the general intellectual discourse of civil society, which sees globalization as one of the contributory factors for the development of civil society organizations in Turkey, does not correspond to the way in which civil society organizations themselves speak about the utility of globalization. In other words,

> civil society organizations appear to be "quite skeptical" in the way in which they approach the question of the long-term impacts of cultural globalization. This skepticism sometimes operate in a strong fashion, to the extent that globalization is seen as nothing but a new form of imperialism creating undemocratic power relations in the world on behalf of rich countries. Sometimes, it takes the form of seeing globalization as an objective reality that produces both positive an negative impacts; positive in the sense of confronting the power of the strong state and creating a platform for the protection of civil rights, and negative in the sense of supporting the liberal hegemonic vision of the world, based on free market ideology.
>
> (Keyman and İçduygu, 2003: 228)

Keyman and İçduygu claim (2003: 228), this is a "boundary problem"; that is, to what extent civil society organizations in Turkey are in fact operating as a "civil society organization" in terms of the scope and the content of their activities, their relation to the state, and their normative and ideological formations. The general definitional discourse on civil society in Turkey finds the institutional distinction between the state and society as a "sufficient condition" for thinking of organizations taking place outside the boundaries of the state as civil society organizations. However, this definition does not involve two important criteria, used in the literature to define civil society organizations, namely, that they are issue-specific organizations, and that they are not interested in creating or supporting ideological societal visions. In fact, most of the democratic civil society organizations in Turkey (as they are popularly referred to by the "left" of the political spectrum), have an ideological platform and are active in the political sphere.

When we approach civil society organizations in Turkey on the basis of these two definitional criteria, we see that most of them act to the contrary, that is, their activities are not issue-based in scope and content; instead they are embedded in big societal visions. First of all, there are civil society organizations whose activities are framed, to a large extent, by big societal visions, such as, Kemalism, a modern Turkey, the protection of contemporary civilized life, the secular-democratic Turkey or Islamic order, Islamic life, a socialist Turkey, and Kemalist Women, to name a few. Second we see that while civil society organizations institutionally are situated outside the state, they can have strong normative and ideological ties with state power.

(Keyman and İçduygu, 2003: 228)

We had mentioned that traits of culture and individual/institutional values are of great importance. Cooperation and solidarity among members of civil society organizations emerges only if they can trust each other, and show civic tolerance towards one another. A minimum of interpersonal trust is needed for total strangers to become partners in an economic corporation, a philanthropic organization, a self-help group, or a neighbourhood watch group. Interpersonal trust is the cement that holds a gathering of individuals together in a voluntary association. Social tolerance for dissenting opinions, views, ideas and even lifestyles is required for different groups and gatherings to differ yet co-exist in a competitive or even a conflict-ridden milieu, which is the case in most societies. Therefore, it is essential that, members tolerate other associations and groups of which they disapprove, dislike, or oppose (Kalaycıoğlu, 2002a: 63).

When we examine the level of interpersonal trust it seems as if nine out of ten people in Turkey do not trust their fellow human beings. It is probably no coincidence that, since the rapid development or capitalism in the 1950s most of the successful corporations in Turkey have been "family firms". Under these circumstances primordial ties (lineage, regional bonds, marriages etc.) emerge as the only bases on which partnership can be established. Consequently, civic associations come to be marred by the cultural impediment of lack of interpersonal trust in Turkey (Kalaycıoğlu, 2002a: 64).

Associational life in Turkey, therefore, is still influenced by blood ties (*akrabağlik*), marital religions (*hısımlik*), and local or regional solidarity (*hemşehrilik*) bonds created among men in military service (*askerlik*) and through religious orders (*tarikat*). Successful partnerships appear mostly to stem from such primordial or traditional ties. Moreover, effective linkages to institutions of political power are still activated through ties of this kind. Urbanization and social mobilization have eroded some of those primordial/traditional ties, yet their presence is still widely noticeable (Kalaycıoğlu, 2002b: 269).

Turkish culture also appears to be characterized by lack of social tolerance for dissent. Values surveys indicate that most respondents do not express tolerance of neighbours who seem to have a lifestyle that deviates from their own. Such shallow social tolerance induces voluntary associations to function with few members, who "look and act alike". A plenitude of voluntary associations emerges with low participation and a proclivity for viewing the rest of society as untrustworthy, and intolerable. Nor do voluntary associations evince an eagerness to engage with other voluntary associations, deliberate issues with them or cooperate and coordinate their activities to promote joint goals (Esmer, 1999: 87–90).

On the other hand, values surveys indicate that feelings of political efficacy are rather strong and widely distributed in Turkey. Some effective associations, like the Turkish Businessmen and Industrialists Association (TÜSIAD), the Confederation of Turkish Trade Unions (Türk-Is), and the Turkish Union of Chambers and Stock Exchanges (TOBB) often benefit from their cooperation with the state, rather than cooperation with other voluntary associations to pressure the state. What Turkey is experiencing is not only a fragmented civil society, but one consisting of voluntary associations that are better at rivalry than mutual cooperation. As a rule, voluntary associations do not seem to consider the state as an adversary, but rather an ally to be mobilized against their competitors. So, voluntary associations tend to campaign for state attention, subsidies, and assistance, while seeking to eliminate or eclipse their closest rivals (Kalaycıoğlu, 2002a: 61–63).

Only a few associations however, have such capacities, or access to sizeable political resources like votes, wealth or information. The vast majority are too small and under-resourced to matter to most political parties and elites. Their principle opportunity to exert influence depends on the willingness to form enduring coalitions with other voluntary associations, and thereby enhance their access to political resources (from finance to public participation in civic initiatives and elections). However, this brings us to another debilitating hurdle: civil society seems to be made up of fragmented and fractionalized voluntary associations involved in constant rivalry among themselves. This allows the state to have a passive-exclusive attitude towards the associations (Kalaycıoğlu, 2002b: 269).

Impediments to state–third sector partnership

Other than obstacles in the path of state–third sector collaboration, emanating from the political/administrative culture and legacy, there are also structural, institutional, management impediments which also have to be overcome. Therefore, there is a lot to be done, on the part of Turkish third sector entities and state institutions to prepare them for meaningful and effective collaboration. A recently conducted survey (Skip, 2006a, 2006b), attests to this need. Major findings of this comprehensive survey has been summarized below.

Present state of Civil Society Organizations (CSO)

- The situation generally reflects a low level of communication and cooperation between CSOs both within Turkey and with other international counterparts and networks. In terms of connectedness, 90 per cent of CSOs report limited connections with outside Turkey, and limited connections with other Turkish CSOs. Existing connections are largely based on personal relations between the leaders of CSOs.

- While an increase in the number of networks of CSOs is observed, for example, among disabled persons' groups, women's groups, environmental groups, and most recently, human rights groups, there are very few registered CSO "umbrella" organizations. Only trade unions and chambers and professional associations are fully organized under umbrella organizations, and they are quite active.
- CSO networks advocating policies regarding freedom of thought and expression are perceived to be the most active and successful.
- Alternatives to umbrella organizations are flexible alliances or platforms. Such platforms exist e.g. environmental platforms, women's groups platform, the "Democracy Platform", youth platforms and various union federations/confederations representing common interest.
- CSOs fulfilling some social charity functions such as education campaigns, disaster-related search and rescue activities, health scans, childcare/fertility studies etc., are better supported by the authorities, media and the people.
- The third sector of Turkey generally seems to be rather dispersed and disorganized. There are some exceptions like the platforms on social dialogue, human rights, disabled persons' rights, ethnic culture, environmental and women rights, and some mostly charitable foundations.

Observations related to legal developments and state practices

- The Law on Associations and ensuing regulations were modernized and a similar modernization of the Law on Foundations has just been concluded. As a result, convergence has taken place, reducing the difference between an association and a foundation, in legal status.
- In terms of representativeness, there remains a perceived difference, with government officials lending a higher degree of representation to a Chamber or Foundation, not, least due to the social and historical status. The establishment process of foundations is also seen as making this organization form less prone to political influence.
- In relation to the legal framework for decentralization, the Laws on Municipalities, Metropolitan Municipalities as well as Provincial Special Administrative Units now contain provisions for collaboration between municipalities and CSOs. However, overall, it is a fair assessment that the government is basically still functioning through the central control of the ministries and the Prime Ministry. Government representation through their extensive regional and local structures (at district and sub-district level) is still by far the most dominating element in local health, education, labour, social care, and economic development.
- There is a lack of single governmental strategic focal point regarding civil society development in Turkey. The absence of a programmatically based

strategic approach largely leaves the extent and practice of civil society inclusion up to the individuals in the responsible directorates and ministries, without a set of rules as to terms of collaboration.

- In terms of relations with civil society, pivotal are the State Governors at the provincial level. Not only do the governors play a role in policy execution, for example, registering trade unions, chairing the Foundations for Social Assistance and Solidarity, but in several instances the governor is instrumental in even convening regional civil society platforms.
- The relative weakness of national CSO structures has led to a dilemma concerning civil society autonomy. It seems that some CSOs and key foundations seem to exist to justify government policy. On the other hand, human rights organizations pull the other way, maintaining a critical attitude regarding governmental policies. The risk emanating from both attitudes is of course, that mutual trust can not be established and civil dialogue cannot be maintained, in this atmosphere.

CSO perceptions of the new milieu

- Many CSOs are cautiously optimistic about the emerging legal environment for civil society. A majority of respondents to the survey claim that the registration process of CSOs is generally fair, inexpensive, fast, easy and according to law.
- CSOs are less satisfied with the level of government interference with their activities. A majority report that government continues to meddle into CSO affairs and activities (36 per cent report these are somewhat common, 33 per cent report that they are quite frequent). Among the most common complaints was the point that CSOs, particularly trade unions, are often prevented from organizing protests and/or boycotts, and strikes.
- In addition, laws and regulations continue to include vague language, increasing the discretionary powers of government authorities. Although CSOs continue to highlight positive political will, they are sceptical about implementation. Many complained that state officials do not treat CSOs equally. It is frequently noted that oppositional CSOs, which are not in parallel with state policies and ideology, are ignored or marginalized whereas those sympathetic benefit from positive discrimination. Therefore, most CSOs do not find the state reliable and accordingly healthy communication cannot be developed.
- On the other hand, it should be noted that CSOs generally find collaboration with local government easier. Organizations active in fields such as environment have better relations with the general and local public authorities.

Limited policy impact of CSOs

According to recent case studies deficiencies in impacting public policy can be ascribed to:

- Few CSOs have this aim; narrow and short term policies supplant strategic planning engendering lack of citizen respect and trust of CSOs.
- CSOs lack skills and capacity to launch and pursue successful campaigns to influence and inform public opinion.
- CSOs are ineffective in organizing coalitions for joint advocacy initiatives, which weakens their ability to be effective, and they lack mechanisms to disseminate information.
- The State has rarely provided CSOs with the space or the opportunity to influence policy and as such, even successful attempts and campaigns have rarely had any impact on joint policy-formulation.

Constraints for cooperation between the state and third sector

Major findings of the Training Needs Assessment Skip Report (2006a: 6–7) are as follows:

- First, there is a big gap in the willingness for cooperation expressed by public sector managers in public speeches and the actual levels of cooperation in reality. This means that there is a difference between policy and practice.
- Second, although there is plenty of evidence of informal arrangements for cooperation, there are only a few examples of formalized cooperation. It would appear that the driving attitude of the public sector is to encourage and support informal cooperation, but to avoid entering into any legally binding forms of partnership or arrangements that may lead to the authorities being held publicly accountable.
- None of the NGOs contacted for this study had any experience of being directly involved in policy development or the prioritization of local development planning. Their main preoccupation is with service delivery, rather than one of advocacy.
- In the instances where the informants remarked on evidence of organized civil society participation in setting local development plans, they also reported that the mechanisms for such cooperation are purely advisory and are lacking in any authority. Thus, local development committees tend not to be taken very seriously as their decisions are usually not binding.
- The public sector tends to sign up to partnership projects with CSOs working at mostly national level and only with well-known reputable ones.
- Public sector officials are often suspicious of the "real motives" of CSOs, attesting to the general problem of the lack of trust in Turkish society.
- There is a mutual problem of unfamiliarity, on the part of CSO representatives with state practice and conversely about "CSO culture" of government officials.

Recommendations for better cooperation

- At the local level, to establish a single contact person or focal point to assist in the coordination of inter-sector partnership. This person/unit would help to build relationships between NGOs and the public sector, as well as providing a database of partnership opportunities.
- The concept of NGO should be clearly defined to those in decision-making positions within the public sector. Similarly, NGOs themselves should make a concerted effort to both explain their missions and actions to the public sector and to encourage the public sector to get involved in any communication networks that they set up.
- NGOs with different, but related objectives should try to come together in a larger coalition.
- Organizing workshops where different NGOs and public sector (both in local and central level) can come together for sharing experiences related to project assessment, project design and preparation, joint proposal writing and resources mobilization, and implementation.
- Activities should be undertaken to ensure a better understanding amongst grassroots organizations of the local frameworks of NGOs and the laws effecting cooperation.

The following select cases of state–third sector collaboration in Turkey have been realized within this milieu.

Select cases of state–third sector collaboration

Case 1: community centres for social care and child protection

Community centres under the Directorate of Social Services and Child Protection Agency (SHÇEK) are designed to address social problems of selected localities. Rapidly modernizing urban areas are the focal points. Participation of municipalities and CSOs in the establishment and the planning and execution of the activities of the community centres is governed by regulations, requiring that they carry out their activities in collaboration with local governments, public authorities, universities and CSOs.

Typically, community centres deal with a large number of care and social integration problems. Sensitivity creation and training is an important activity of the centres. Courses on pre-natal and post-natal care, home economics, literacy, gender rights are central activities as well as counseling of different groups at risk. The centres typically also have special programmes for children and youth, they also organize, self-help and solidarity networks in the local communities for the promotion of social integration.

Community centres are usually formed through a protocol between at least three parties. For example, for the Ankara Şafaktepe Community Center, a three-party protocol between SHÇEK, the Mamak Municipality and Union of Turkish

Women has been signed. The same formula is used for the Antalya Şafak Community Center between SHÇEK, the Antalya Rotary Club and Kepez Municipality. In this arrangement, SHÇEK, representing central government, and municipalities, representing local government provide legal legitimacy and funding; whereas the CSO provides local insight, volunteer personnel and sometimes, also funding.

Case 2: urban housing – the Batikent Project

The very rapid rate of urbanization in the aftermath of the Second World War (averaging around 7 per cent per annum), besides creating severe inadequacies of infrastructure and services in cities, also led to the emergence of unplanned, irregular and illegal squatter-type of housing (called *gecekondu* in Turkish, literally meaning built overnight). This emergency situation necessitated quick and practical solutions in the form of planned mass housing. One pioneering project was the Batıkent Project (meaning the city in the west) in Ankara. This gigantic project (targeting construction of 55,000 units), had three main components/partners; the municipality responsible for acquisition of the land and its planning; housing cooperatives to mobilize and organize the demand; and private enterprise responsible for actual construction. In this cooperative scheme, the municipality provided legality and legitimacy; the cooperatives mobilized the savings of their members (which naturally proved to be inadequate since the project targeted low-income residents, so "bridge-credits" were obtained from the European Resettlement Fund); and private enterprise, which provided technology and know-how. The project was successfully concluded three administrations later (approximately 15 years, between 1978–1993), creating an integrated urban region with a population of 300,000. The union of cooperatives (Kent Koop), developed into a national structure, initiating several similar mass housing projects in different parts of Turkey. Most of the participating private companies, based on the prestige and experience that came with Batıkent grew into the most prominent developers in the country. The role of private enterprise (construction companies), and civil society (housing cooperatives formed with the active participation of labour unions, associations, professional bodies) included participation in the decision-making processes of the project. Decisions pertaining to density, type of housing, services on site, credit conditions and management of the site, were taken jointly. Another novel aspect of the project was that housing cooperatives were transformed into management units of neighborhoods once their members were settled in their new homes. Thus, Batıkent became a successful example of public/private enterprise/civil society collaboration, which has been frequently replicated since (Göymen, 1981).

Case 3: Dikmen Valley Urban Regeneration Project

A good example of deliberative democracy and public-private collaboration has been provided by the Dikmen Valley Urban Regeneration Project, implemented in the capital city of Ankara, in the 1990s. In certain parts of Ankara, a type of dualism manifested itself with irregular, unplanned, lower quality dwellings (*gecekondu*) encroaching prestigious sections of the city. This situation not only meant lower living standards for "*gecekondu*" people, but serious shortages of infrastructure (no land available for new schools, hospitals, parks, childcare centres etc.) and degraded environmental standards for all. So, the metropolitan municipality initiated a participatory planning/implementation project under the concept of "project democracy". The then mayor, Mr. Karayalçın described "project democracy" as the "involvement of all those to be affected by a particular project" in all aspects and stages of the project, not only in a requesting/demanding position but actually as a decision-maker (Karayalçın, 1990). The main instrument utilized to facilitate such participation was a "joint decision-making committee", bringing together planners, municipal officials, neighborhood muhtars (elected headmen), representatives of housing cooperatives and other civil society organizations in the area and private construction companies (Bademli, 1990; Karayalçın, 1990; Kuntasal, 1993). The stakeholders in this case (around 10,000 inhabitants living in the *gecekondus*, in rather primitive conditions) were represented by housing cooperatives formed for this purpose. The main idea of the project was that gecekondu dwellers would consent to the tearing down of their single-storey houses to be replaced by new modern semi high-rise, larger apartments. Until the new buildings were completed, they would move away (with support from the municipality, in cash or in kind) and agree not to seek expropriation compensation. The new buildings, as well as some social and physical infrastructure, would be built by private enterprise, which would recover the cost by selling on the market the additional apartments allocated to them after all former residents of the area were settled. The project was completed in the early 2000s; former residents are settled in their new homes; private enterprise has sold most of their allocated apartments; green areas have been extended considerably, creating a "green corridor" in the heart of Ankara; service standards and social infrastructure have vastly improved, eradicating the social/physical duality in this part of the city. During this process, true to the spirit of deliberative democracy, all stakeholders fully participated in different phases of the project, preparing the agenda, initiating debate, contributing to both plans, construction, landscaping and managing conflicts. The success of the project led to initiation of similar projects and reinforced faith in public–private–CSO collaboration (Göymen, 2002).

Case 4: role of Turkish NGOs in Turkey's integration with the European Union

Civil society organizations have started playing important roles also in international relations. One such case is their contribution to EU–Turkey relations.

In candidate countries, civil society organizations act in two different ways. On the one hand, they transmit the major economic, political and social dynamics of the EU to their countries and create the necessary environment for the transformation of the state and society in line with the values of European integration. On the other hand, they try to influence EU decision-making mechanisms and lobby for the acceleration of the process from the EU side. However, it is important to note that these functions are not valid for the Euro-sceptic and anti-EU civil society organizations (Seyrek, 2005: 198).

Relations between Turkish civil society and the EU actually have two dimensions. On the one hand, the EU has been supporting the development of civil society organizations in Turkey as an important element of a working democracy. On the other hand, since many Turkish civil society organizations see EU membership as a catalyst for a more democratic and modern country, they have been supporting the integration process of Turkey to the EU. In this sense, there is a reciprocal collaboration in the nature of this relationship (Seyrek, 2005: 199).

The integration process and the EU itself have played a significant role in the development of Turkish civil society. Changes in the legal framework, social structure and mentality throughout the integration process have created the necessary environment for such a development. Taking into consideration the recent enlargement process, such a development has become more visible in the case of Turkey (Seyrek, 2005: 200).

Civil society organizations have influenced the integration process in two different ways. First, while working in their own specific area, such as human rights, they also use European standards, namely the Copenhagen Political Criteria, as a base for their efforts. Within this context, reforms in Turkey were strongly supported by civil society organizations campaigning for progress not just for the EU integration process itself but also for socio-political development of Turkey. Second, various civil society organizations have started to play a role in putting pressure on the government, in monitoring the integration process in a comprehensive way and in giving technical assistance in some instances.

Turkish civil society has a significant role as independent sources of information on the socio-political situation of the country, implementation of the reforms in compliance with the Copenhagen Political Criteria and other problems dealing with the integration process. The European Commission finds it easier to evaluate a situation and implement relevant policies if it has access to several different perspectives. Consultations can thus be said to contribute to the efficiency of the system and civil society organizations are thus important tools. Sometimes, critical views expressed by these organizations during such consultations create conflicts with the government, accompanied by accusations of "betrayal of national cause". Nevertheless, there are more cases of collaboration between the state and third sector related to EU issues than conflict.

Conclusion

The main conclusion which comes out of this study is that although the Turkish third sector has made considerable progress on the subservience–autonomy scale in its relations with the state, partnership status, quantitatively and qualitatively has not been reached. It is also an open question for other countries whether full autonomy vis-à-vis the state has been achieved, is possible and, for that matter, desirable. On the other hand, there is no denial that, countries which come from a more liberal political/administrative tradition, have succeeded in establishing a variety of mutually beneficial partnerships with the state. There are a number of inhibiting factors and impediments for Turkish third sector in achieving an autonomous position and dealing with the state, on equal footing. The main obstacle is the political/administrative culture, which does not seem to nurture a fertile environment for civil society. The centralist, etatist tradition stresses community over free citizens; favours uniformity rather then diversity; exalts the almost "holy" state and expects conformity and subservience (Heper, 1985; Kalaycıoğlu, 2002a).

This state is suspicious of social groupings, associations and organizations of all kinds that are not under its close surveillance. Admittedly, state dealings with and response to various CSOs are differentiated, depending on their "trustworthiness" and proven loyalty. In the debate, whether the state in Turkey is strong or in reality weak but suppressive and arbitrary because it is weak, the latter position seems to be more valid (Kalaycıoğlu, 2006). But, whichever the case, a "passive-exclusive" state resists the entry of certain "suspicious" groups in the official domain of the state regime, but neither combats nor promotes the rest (Sunar, 1998). To make matters worse, various surveys show that, a major ingredient of healthy civil society, interpersonal and inter-institutional trust, is low in Turkey, constituting a major obstacle to associability, except among those with primordial or traditional ties (Kalaycıoğlu, 2002a). Turkish culture also appears to be characterized by lack of social tolerance for dissent and deviation from standard lifestyles and behaviour. This results in CSOs with limited "look and act alike" type of membership; with a tendency to view the state and the "other" with suspicion; not exhibiting an eagerness to cooperate with the state or other CSOs, only on the basis of common goals (Esmer, 1999). Thus, it is possible to claim that some basic conditions for the healthy development of the third sector do not fully exist in Turkey. Furthermore, one can add that some societal values and aspects of political culture, as mentioned above, are not fully supportive. On the other hand, there is no denial that considerable progress has been made since the Second World War. The transition to a multi-party system and pluralization of polity and society; the emergence of a dynamic local government system, partially counter-balancing the etatist "centre"; speedy economic development and creation of a middle class and an entrepreneurial culture; budding of CSOs; and last but not least, conferral of candidate status of the European Union, thus making Turkey open to this potent impact, have all contributed to the dawning of a more conducive atmosphere for the third sector. Recently, there has been a proliferation of new legislation, generally affecting the third sector positively. Thus, some of the technical hurdles seem to have been eradicated on paper. But, these positive changes in legislation are not fully reflected in practice. There is considerable opposition and "foot dragging" on the part of the bureaucracy, responsible for implementation. Once again, this shows that institutional culture is slow to change.

The new, relatively "open" and liberal atmosphere in Turkey has given rise to a type of "legitimacy crisis" of the state. Formerly, there was one type of "modernity", as expressed and represented by the state, but now in the new "discursive space", as Keyman and İçduygu (2003) label it, there are alternatives. Turkish third sector organizations feature prominently in this "discursive space", and propagate their own versions of "modernity". They frequently challenge the "statist" tradition in the process and voice their own democratic/religious/etnonationalist/essentialist identity claims. The point to underline here is the sometimes anti-democratic nature of these claims, expressed by some of these circles, in denial of the basic constitutional tenets, not accepting the "basic rules of the game".

On the third sector scene, there are more problems to be solved, and to facilitate better collaboration between state and third sector organizations more hurdles "to jump over". First of all, there seems to be a lack of clarity in the mission, purpose, and priorities of many CSOs. Several of them do not exhibit all the features usually associated with CSOs; and are para-statal or hybrid at best. Most of them, have a weak financial base and can mostly survive thanks to various forms of state, international organizations, EU, and/or Northern NGO support. This is hardly an atmosphere conducive to "autonomy". Furthermore, there seems to be more rivalry than cooperation among third sector organizations; therefore, networking is limited. These characteristics do not make Turkish third sector organizations ideal potential partners of the state. On the state side, there is a general reluctance to collaborate with the TS, unless it is absolutely necessary. This is largely due to the institutional culture which has been discussed, but also due to lack of knowledge of opportunities, possibilities, and the synergy that can be created. Another contributing factor is lack of clarity which regards respective responsibilities and accountabilities. All these seem to have been partially surmounted at the local level, as most of the cases presented illustrate. There is now added incentive to form partnerships, through EU funding, which envisages collaboration of various stakeholders, toward common goals.

This study is an attempt to "photograph" the present-day scene in Turkey, regarding state–third sector interaction. Needless to say, this is a "moving" picture, set in a dynamic, ever-changing milieu. It is difficult to prophesize in which direction, on the subservience–autonomy scale things will develop, although, for the time being, there is reason for optimism. The future orientation of the third sector in Turkey will much depend on the inculcation of new societal and institutional values supportive of it, through socialization, the educational system, and extensive training.

Note

1 Dr. Göymen is professor of political science and public administration at Sabancy University in Istanbul (goymen@sabanciuniv.edu).

References

Akarcalı, Bülent (2003), "The Function of Non-Governmental Organizations", *Role of NGOs in Development, International Conference*, Istanbul.

Bademli, Raci (1990), "Urban Projects" (in Turkish), *Ankara Bülteni*, Vol. 9, pp. 4–5.

Beckman, Björn (1997), "Explaining Democratization: Notes on the Concept of Civil Society", in Elizabeth Özdalga and Sune Persson (eds), *Democracy, Civil Society and the Muslim World*, Istanbul: The Swedish Research Institute, pp. 1–15.

Beller-Hann and Hann, Chris (2001), *Turkish Region: State, Market and Social Identities on the East Black Sea Coast*, Oxford: School of American Research Press.

Carothers, Thomas (2000), "Civil Society", *Foreign Policy*, Winter 1999–2000, Issue 117, pp. 12–18.

Civicus Report (2005), *Civil Society in Turkey: An Era of Transition*, Istanbul.

Diamond, Larry (1994), "Rethinking Civil Society: Toward Democratic Consolidation", *Journal of Democracy*, Vol. 5, No. 3.

Esmer, Yılmaz (1999), *Devrim, Evrim ve Statüko*, Istanbul: Kanaat Matbaasi.

Göymen, Korel (1981), "Batıkent Housing Project as a Case of Local-Level Public Policy Implementation" (in Turkish), *Proceeding of Turkish Urbanism Congress*, Ankara, Middle East Technical University Press.

Göymen, Korel (2002), "Participation Dimension of Metropolitan Governance: Project Democracy in Ankara", *IASIA International Conference*, Istanbul.

Hampson, Françoise (2003), "Civil Society, the State and NGOs", *Role of NGOs in Development, International Conference*, Istanbul.

Harris J. (1990), "Society and State in the Twentieth Century", in F.M. Thompson (ed.), *The Cambridge Social History of Britain 1750–1950*, Vol. 3, Cambridge: Cambridge University Press.

Heper, Metin (1985), *The State Tradition in Turkey*, Beverly: Eothen Press.

Kalaycıoğlu, Ersin (2002a), "Civil Society in Turkey, Continuity or Change?", in Brian Beeley (ed.), *Turkish Transformation*, Beverly: The Eothen Press.

Kalaycıoğlu, Ersin (2002b), "State and Civil Society in Turkey: Democracy, Development and Protest", in Amyn B. Sayoo (ed.), *Civil Society in the Muslim World*, London: I.B. Tauris, pp. 250–269.

Kalaycıoğlu, Ersin (2006), "Chapter on Turkey", in Kesselman, M., Krieger, J., Joseph, W. A. (eds) *Introduction to Comparative Politics*, Boston: Hugtin Muflin.

Karayalçın, Murat (1990), "Ankara of the 21st Century" (in Turkish), *Ankara Dergisi*, Vol. 1, pp. 5–15.

Keyman, Fuat and İçduygu, Ahmet (2003), "Globalization, Civil Society and Citizenship in Turkey: Actors, Boundaries and Discourses", *Citizenship Studies*, Vol. 7, No. 2, pp. 219–234.

Kuntasal, Kunt (1993), "Dikmen Valley Project" (in Turkish), *Ankara Söyleşileri*, Ankara: Mimarlar Odası, Ankara Şubesi.

Lewis, J. (1995), *The Voluntary Sector, The State, and Social Work in Britain*, Aldershot, Avebury.

Lewis, Jane (2004), "The State and the Third Sector in Modern Welfare States: Independence, Instrumentality, Partnership", in Adalbert Evers and Jean-Louis Laville (eds), *The Third Sector in Europe*, Cheltenham: Edward Elgar Publishing Inc.

Seyrek, Demir Murat (2005), "The Role of Turkish NGOs in the Intergration of Turkey into the EU", *Turkish Policy Quarterly*, Vol. 3, No. 3.

Şimşek, Sefa (2004), "The Transformation of Civil Society in Turkey: From Quantity to

Quality", *Turkish Studies*, Vol. 5 No. 3 (Autumn), Cheltenham: Edward Elgar Publishing Inc., pp. 46–74.

Skip Report (2006a), *A Cluster Analysis for Improving Co-operation between the NGOs and the Public Sector in Turkey*, Ankara, p. 54.

Skip Report (2006b), *Training Needs and Attitudes Assessment Study*, Ankara, p. 24.

Sunar İlkay (1998) "Politics of Citizenship in the Middle East", in Suna Kili'ya Armağan, İstanbul: Güven Matbaasi.

13 The uneasy partnership of the state and the third sector in the Czech Republic

Pavol Frič

Introduction: third sector internal heterogeneity

As far as we can speak about cooperation between state and third sector, first of all we should realize that the third sector is not a unified or fully concerted collective actor. The quality of the collaboration on a large scale therefore depends on the variability of NGOs and their collective representatives. Insofar we can speak about the partnership between state and third sector, we should know what the basic features of the Czech third sector internal heterogeneity are. To answer this question we should go back to the communist era of the sector "development". Under the communist regime the overwhelming majority of independent NGOs were either closed down or centralized and fully under the control of the communist party and the state. These state-owned organizations were those, where the communist government, in line with its ideology, felt the need to guarantee – by law – that the "working people" would be provided with some services (above all, social or healthcare ones), or, wanted to use them for its own political benefit (mostly in the area of schools). The state maintained "non-profit organizations" – so-called budgetary and contributory organizations (ROPO) – still exist and compete with NGOs in their activities. In the welfare areas, where they are most active, they represent the dominant form of providing services and managing problems of citizens. Another key factor of the communist-era heritage is the split of the Czech third sector into the so-called old and new NGOs. The old organizations are those with roots in the communist period, while the "new" NGOs have emerged since 1989. From a quantitative perspective, the new NGOs are clearly much more numerous while the old NGOs can boast a considerably larger number of members (Frič, 1998). The old organizations are concentrated in professional advocacy, sports, recreation and leisure, while the "new" NGOs dominate in areas such as human rights, environment, and health or social services.

Literature dealing with the third sector generally distinguishes between two basic types of NGOs: *service and advocacy*. The first type focuses its attention primarily on providing services of various kinds; they cooperate or compete with commercial or state organizations providing similar services and try to hold their own by means of the efficiency and quality of the services offered. The second type concentrates chiefly on defending the rights and interests of various

Table 13.1 Typology of NGOs in Czech Republic

Type of activity	Type of interest pursued	
	Mutually beneficial	*Public beneficial*
Service	1. service mutually beneficial NGOs sport, recreation, community development, interest associations	2. service public benefit NGOs social and health care, education, humanitarian assistance, charity
Advocacy	3. advocacy mutually beneficial NGOs trade unions, employees' associations, unions, professional organisations	4. advocacy public benefit NGOs environmental protection, human and civil rights, consumers' rights

groups of people (or public interests); it seeks to influence the decisions of public administration and it mobilizes the general public in support of its demands. In these activities they interact both with representatives of the public administration and with political parties and various interest groups.

The following figure is an attempt to illustrate the internal heterogeneity of the Czech third sector by means of typology using the two basic dimensions of the activities of NGOs in society: type of activity and type of interest pursued. By combining them we obtain four types of NGOs, which have, as we will see later, markedly different relations with the state. The first type is represented by "service mutually beneficial organizations", the second by "service public benefit organizations", the third by "advocacy mutually beneficial organizations", and fourth by the "advocacy public benefit organizations".

Vehicles of the first and third type are largely old NGOs. Vehicles of the second and third type are largely new NGOs.

Basic theoretical approaches

Is a partnership between the state and the third sector possible? Why should the state and the third sector cooperate? To answer these questions we can use several theories. Insofar as it is possible to speak of partnership between NGOs and the state, it is in two areas:

1 provision of services;
2 framing the political agenda.

The provision of services and the framing of the public policy agenda are at the centre of several theoretical approaches. However, the present chapter will seek to analyze the issue of partnership between the state and the third sector chiefly from the standpoint of:

1   economic theories that concentrate more on the sphere of the service provision;

2   sociological and politological theories that have more in common with the framing of the political agenda;

3   public policy theories are focused on both spheres but rather than why try to give answer on the question how state and NGOs cooperate.

Economic theories

The approach that stresses the service function of NGOs is based on economic theories in which the dominant role is played by the theories of *market failure* and *state failure*. Both theories are based on the "rational choice" principle and focus their attention on the question of the provision of public goods. The market failure theory postulates that the free market of itself is not capable, to the requisite extent, of securing for citizens public goods, i.e. goods and services universally available to all citizens. In certain cases the market subjects need not find the production of public goods a sufficiently profitable activity. This results in a shortage of them and provides scope for the creation and functioning of NGOs.

Moreover, the market need not fail only insofar as it is incapable of saturating all the various needs of the population. In certain cases it is not capable of creating a sufficiently credible environment for the conduct of commercial transactions. So-called "contractual failure" often occurs when the consumers lack adequate information in order to assess the quality of the goods and services they are paying for. Since the producers of the goods and services are in possession of that information there it results in an "informational asymmetry", which, from the consumer's standpoint, can only be overcome by the producer's trustworthiness. That is why consumers eventually prefer to choose NGOs, which do not operate on the market solely in pursuit of maximum profit (Hansman, 1987).

The market's failure to supply public goods is regarded by classic economics as the raison d'etre of the state. However, the eminent economist Burton Weisbrod has pointed out that in a democracy the state is only able to fulfil satisfactorily the role of supplier of public goods if the majority of voters are ready to support the production of a particular public good (Weisbrod, 1977). Where there exist major differences of opinion about which public goods the state should provide and which it should not, it will also be very difficult for the government to obtain majority support for its public policies and so there will continue to exist many unsaturated needs and demands for public goods. Clearly such "state failures" will occur more frequently in heterogeneous societies comprising many and varied social, religious, ethnic and other groups, than in more homogeneous societies. According to Weisbrod, this situation leads people to create NGOs in order to ensure a supply of services and goods that neither the market nor the state is able to provide them.

By making the creation of NGOs conditional on the failure of the market or the state, the above-mentioned theories tend to offer a picture of conflictual relations between the state and the third sector. Nevertheless, the following theory, which emerges from the two previous ones, seeks to disprove that impression.

This is the *interdependence theory*, which rejects the assumption of inevitable conflict between the state and NGOs. On the contrary, it identifies on both sides elements that preordain cooperation between the state and NGOs. Put simply, one might say that they mutually assist each other to compensate for their shortcomings and so each side is dependent on the other.

> nonprofit organizations are often active in a field before government can be mobilized to respond. They often develop expertise, structures, and experience that governments can draw on in their own activities. Beyond that, nonprofit organizations often mobilize the political support needed to stimulate government involvement, and this support can often be used to ensure a role for the nonprofit providers in the fields that government is persuaded to enter. Finally, for all their advantages, nonprofit organizations have their own significant limitations that constrain their ability to respond to public problems.
>
> (Salamon and Anheier, 1996, p. 17)

The state's shortcoming is its inflexible reaction to newly emerging needs and the costly bureaucratization of the solutions supplied. However, both non-profit and profit-making organizations are able to display flexibility and economic efficiency. Except that, in the view of Salamon and Anheier, the state will tend to prioritize cooperation with the civil section, because it realizes where the market fails and also knows that it can demand from NGOs what profit-making organizations would refuse to supply. On the other hand the lack of resources for solving more extensive social problems is the main limiting factor that forces NGOs to turn to the state. So according to the interdependence theory, in addition to market and state failure there is also a question of the *failure of NGOs*.

Politological theories

Whereas economic theories perceive NGOs as an economic actor, politological theory tends to view them as a political actor. The underlying framework of these theories is a conflictualist attitude that pictures society as a set of many larger or smaller groups competing with each other for scarce resources. The role of the state is to regulate this competition to avoid any undesirable escalation of conflicts between various groups. The reasons why the state should be interested in cooperation with NGOs in the sphere of framing the political agenda are explained chiefly by politological theories. These include the *interest group theory* or *interest representation theory*, which regard the state as a guarantor of freedom of association and NGOs as one of the subjects that play a part in the articulation, aggregation and, in certain cases, representation of interests in society. For instance, there are currently hopes that the NGOs will overcome the so-called "democratic deficit" that is such a widespread phenomenon in modern democracies. According to those theories, it is in the state's interest to cooperate with NGOs, since it would have prevent social conflicts from escalating. *Elite theory* takes a similar view. According to one version of that theory, the "demo-elite theory" (Etzioni-Halevy, 1990), NGOs constantly give rise to the emergence of "counter-elites" that should progressively infiltrate the elites in order to ensure elite circulation in society. Unless such infiltration occurs and the old elites shut themselves away from the rest of society, elite circulation is interrupted and society faces the threat of revolutionary explosion. It is therefore in the interest of the state to cooperate with the NGOs on the basis of the principle of "tolerant dissent". *Civic culture theory*, for its part, regards NGOs as schools of political participation, which raise citizens' political competence, participation and competence being very important for a well-functioning political system (Almond and Verba, 1989). The state should support NGOs because it is in its interest to maintain the political system in good shape.

Sociological theories

NGOs' interest in cooperating with the state in framing the political agenda is explained by sociological theories of social movements. The first of them is *resource mobilization theory* (McCarty and Zald, 1973). This maintains that the success of social movement organizations (the absolute majority of which are NGOs) depends on the capacity of their leaderships adequately to allocate and mobilize resources (money, experience, information, grassroots membership, voluntary work, contacts with influential individuals, top experts, etc.). If the leaders of those organizations are to achieve maximum effectiveness in the contest for resources, they and their organizations must achieve maximum institutionalization and professionalization. However, the trend towards professionalization also engenders a reduction in conflict strategies vis-à-vis the state authorities and more frequent use of moderate and cooperative strategies such as lobbying. So resource mobilization theory maintains that successful organizations with plentiful resources are motivated to cooperate with the state.

Similar thinking about the motives of NGOs to cooperate with state is expressed by *political opportunity theory* (Tilly, 1978). According to this theory the success of social movements (in their endeavour to penetrate the political system the influence public-policy decision-making) depends:

1   on the degree of a political system's openness or otherwise;
2   the character of the authorities' reaction;
3   the existence and status of allies in the political power configuration.

Political opportunity theory postulates that social movements and their organizations will be more likely to cooperate with state institutions if a political system is more open, the reaction of the official authorities is more amenable and their allies are more powerful. If the opposite is the case they are more likely to opt for conflict strategies.

According to *collective identity theory* (Melucci, 1988) the exercise of the advocacy function of NGOs is dependent on their collective identity. This theory is based on the discovery that so-called "new social movements" tend to be expressive rather than instrumental by nature, i.e., their supporters are more interested in sharing some kind of meaningful collective identity and helping to form it, then in acquiring positions of power. On the other hand, the collective identity theory recognizes that the more explicit and shared is the identity of the movement's members the greater the capacity of the social actor (the third sector) to mobilize its supporters and assert its interests (Touraine, 1988), i.e., to induce (pressurize) the government to govern responsibly and effectively (Putnam, 1993), which also includes cooperation with NGOs when framing the public policy agenda.

All in all one may observe that none of the above-mentioned economic failure theories excludes cooperation or partnership between the state and the third sector and that each of the above-mentioned welfare regimes allow for the possibility of cooperation between these subjects, although obviously the scope for partnership is more or limited in all cases. Likewise, politological and sociological theories to do with NGOs accept that cooperation between state and the third sector is possible and do not exclude the possibility that it might assume the nature of a partnership. Basically speaking, what emerges from the theories mentioned is that the stronger the third sector the greater its motivation to cooperate with the state. So, paradoxically as it may seem, victory in a conflict leads to greater cooperation.

Public policy theories

Another theoretical concept that could provide an interesting insight into the relationships between the state and the third sector in respect of service provision is Esping-Andersen's concept of three regime-types of welfare state (Esping-Andersen, 1990). The first of these is the *liberal regime*, which is typified by resistance to greater state involvement in social services, preferring instead solutions based on private and voluntary initiative. In this regime NGOs are regarded as an integral part of the market. Cooperation with the state is strictly formalized and based on commercial principles. The state confers on greater privileges on NGOs than on profit-making ones. Its typical features are a high level of professionalization and the efficient marketing of its activities.

The second type is the *social-democratic regime*, which favours state provision of services and accords NGOs very little scope to operate in this area. The provision of social, health and educational services is virtually a state monopoly. In the course of time, however, this model is transformed and under the influence of Giddens's "third way" concept (Giddens, 1994) and Beck *et al.*'s concept of "reflexive modernization" (Beck *et al.*, 1994) NGOs gain wider opportunities to operate in the sphere of service provision, particularly in combating unemployment and social exclusion.

A characteristic feature of the third type, the so-called *conservative welfare regime* is the subordination of NGOs to the authority of the state. The state administration cooperates with a limited number of NGOs, which it selects itself and accords specific privileges (in the form of financial support, access to information and the opportunity to take part in the decision-making process). NGOs become clients of the state and tend towards bureaucratization and cartelization, which enable them to protect their privileged positions. One consequence is a limitation of conflictual advocacy activities and concentration on lobbying and service provision. The privileges isolate the NGOs from the market and bureaucratization gradually isolates them from the citizenry.

Public policy analytical framework comprises also other several theoretical insights on the state–NGOs relations. First of all, one should take into account an organizational actor-oriented approach based on the observation that state organizations and NGOs as the specific units of our analysis are organized as collective, interconnected and interdependent policy actors. From this perspective one can see the sub-national public policy situation as the plurality of policy actors who cooperate towards or compete over control of the policy process in different fields. The advantage of this perspective is its ability to take into account the internal third sector heterogeneity. It allows us to have a more comprehensive view of the multiple policy stakeholders and of policy-making as a collective effort. This approach relies mainly on policy network theory (Carlsson, 2000; Peterson, 1995; Rhodes, 1990; Rhodes and Marsh, 1992) and the advocacy coalition framework (Sabatier and Jenkins-Smith, 1993, 1999' Sabatier, 1998). For example, according to Sabatier policy actors "can be aggregated into a number of advocacy coalitions composed of people from various governmental and private organizations who share a set of normative and causal beliefs and who often act in concert" (Sabatier, 1993, p. 18). The advocacy coalition framework helps to explain changes in public policy (sub-systems) by analysis of activities of different policy coalitions embedded in a set of relatively stable parameters and influenced by external events.

A difficult partnership in the conditions of the Czech Republic

The view from the economic standpoint

There is certainly no need for any complicated proof that there are plenty of shortcomings on the part of the state and the third sector in the Czech Republic, which could mutually compensate each other. On the other hand, it should be stressed that in terms of "economic strength", the Czech third sector is much worse off than its Western European counterparts. It is many times smaller than the average in Western Europe. Moreover the state contribution to the overall budget of the third sector in the Czech Republic is considerably smaller than in the case of the Western European countries. This means that compared to Western Europe, the Czech state does not do enough to compensate for the inadequacies of its third sector. Nevertheless it must be added that the Czech Republic is definitely better off in this respect than most of the post-communist countries of Central Europe.[1]

Table 13.2 The share of the third sector in the total number of workers in the national economy (excluding agriculture)

(Data for 1995, in %)	*Salaried workers*	*Workers and volunteers*
Western Europe (average)	7.0	10.3
Central Europe (average)	1.1	1.7
Czech Republic	1.8	2.9

Source: Salomon, Anheier *et al.* Global Civil Society, 1999.

Table 13.3 Share of three basic resources in the financing of the third sector

(Data for 1995, in %)	*Income from donations*	*Income from the state*	*Income from activity of NGOs*
Western Europe (average)	7	50	43
Central Europe (average)	20	28	52
Czech Republic	14	39	47

Source: Salomon, Anheier *et al.* Global Civil Society, 1999.

Economic theories indicate that partnership (cooperation) between the state and the third sector in the Czech Republic is possible and practical examples shows that the partnership really works! Why is the partnership so uneasy, then?

The view from the political perspective

Cartelization of the political environment

The politological approach considers the relationship between NGOs and the political parties as the key factor of cooperation between the state and the third sector, and in the Czech Republic this has not been optimal for a long time. The situation of the new political parties created after 1989 was not easy. Not only did they have to aggressively seek and find their own identity in competition with many rivals, they also faced many problems with funding their very existence. The fact that parties were not rooted in specific social strata meant that (apart from the Communist Party), they did not have an extensive membership or stable (loyal) electorate. Moreover, the situation was such that only a spectacular election campaign, with all the high costs it involved, could ensure their continued survival in parliament. In that respect they shared in the general crisis of the mass political parties of Western Europe for which they were not prepared. The growing cost of party activity, insufficient funds from membership subscriptions and difficulties with seeking support from private sponsors forced them (in common with their Western models) to be increasingly involved with the state, which provided them with a source of income for their activities in the form of state contributions based on election scores. The outcome of that form of consolidation of political parties' social situation was a profound alienation of party interests from the interests of civil society and even looser ties with the unconsolidated third sector. Cooperation with weak NGOs promised neither increased votes nor increased funds into party coffers. On the contrary, according to Katz and Mair the process of coalescence between political parties and the state means that political parties do not have to compete to survive any more in the same sense as before (when competing as regards the definition of public policies) and made the right conditions for forming a cartel, where all parties share the same sources and survive (Katz and Mair, 1996). Controlled by the political parties, the state becomes not just the source of their survival, but also a barrier to the entry of new actors (emerging from the third sector) into the political arena.[2]

Centralism and technocratic pragmatism

Maybe an even greater danger for the day-to-day life of the NGOs than the cartelization of the political environment was the obsessive tendency towards centralism of parties in government, whereby they sought to tackle their difficulties in implementing their own notions of social transformation. Paradoxically this assertion also applies to parties that proudly made of show of their neo-liberal policies. In a strong (and paternalist) state, ruling political parties found an optimal instrument for implementing their own visions of economic reform, irrespective of their own ideological orientation. In pursuit of party interests technocratic pragmatism prevailed over ideological orthodoxy. The influence of this style of government was also reflected in the gradual blurring of ideological differences between parties and in the expectation that each party can cooperate and govern with any other party (with the exception of extremist parties, of course). In the course of the reform it became increasingly clear that it made no difference which party was in power; it would anyway do what its (seemingly) ideological opponent would have done (e.g., privatization was pursued by both right-wing and left-wing governments). This has produced a technocratization of political elites, for whom the most important thing is the technology of power, when "the goals of political activity are regarded as familiar and their designation is not regarded as the major issue" (Strmiska, 1993, p. 110). The "new" style of government, typified by centralism and technocratic pragmatism, was in marked contrast with the expectations of the NGOs as regards their cooperation in framing public policy concepts and involvement in decision-making processes. Its implementation virtually pushed the activities of NGOs to the margins of the social transformations then taking place.

Strictly representative democracy

What was particularly incompatible with the technocratic concept of government was the notion of "robust democracy" (Salamon, 1999), or the "broader concept of democracy" (Strmiska, 1993, p. 108), which are part of the ideology of civil society. This idea does not accept the restriction of democracy to the political sphere and the concentration of democracy on representative democracy. Its main pillars are:

1   permanent communication between voters and their representatives;
2   the widest possible public participation in decision-making, and;
3   explaining the exercise of power to the citizenry, i.e., consistent implementation of the subsidiarity principle.

Technocratically-minded political elites are, on the contrary, natural supporters of a narrower concept of democracy, in which the dominant role is played by political parties and the function of citizens is restricted to electing their representatives. The technocratic elites consider that the broader concept of democracy represents a threat of irrational and incoherent decision-making, deforming the logic of the system of representative democracy (Strmiska, 1993, p. 109).

The controversy about the character of democracy – participative versus representative – was most clearly formulated in the debates between Václav Havel (as President of the Czech Republic) and Václav Klaus (as Czech Prime Minister) in the mid-1990s (Pithart, 1996). That controversy continues and it is clear that on the political stage the narrow model of representative democracy – which better suits the technocratically-minded elites – tends to prevail. The ideology of "proper representative democracy" enables them to effectively counter the demands of the NGOs to exercise their advocacy (political) functions in society. A sure result of technocratic pragmatism is that NGOs are perceived by political elites as illegitimate rivals in a power struggle and not as allies in the framing of the public policy agenda.

The view from the sociological standpoint

The ability to mobilize resources

One of the most recent attempts to produce a comprehensive assessment of the state of the third sector or civil society (Vajdová, 2005) regards the issue of NGOs' funding as generally among their weakest points. According to this analysis, "human resources" constituted the third sector's only strong point. "The organisations of civil society can rely on the large number of people who are willing to commit themselves, are flexible, full of enthusiasm, educated and equipped with expertise for the area they work in (paid employees and volunteers)" (Vajdová, 2005, p. 67). Among the weak points, the analysis straight away includes a whole list of items such as "lack of professionalism" – "organisations lack sufficient professionals capable of strategic planning, fundraising, management, and communication with the public" (Vajdová, 2005, p. 68) – "poor standards of management and decision-making", "limited financial resources", "inability to communicate" and "inability to mobilise".

It is clear from the analyses mentioned that the Czech third sector suffers above all from a lack of inner resources, and that does not apply solely to individual NGOs but to the sector as a whole. The ability of the third sector to behave as a social actor and partner of the state depends chiefly on its inner qualities as a whole, i.e., on the character and density of internal network of mutually linked individual NGOs. The infrastructure of the internal networks (i.e., conceptual, coordinational, facilitational, advocational, evaluational, informational, educational and self-regulational networks) is notably failing in the case of the Czech Republic (Frič (ed.), 2000). The best proof of this assertion is the inability of the sector to mobilize long-term protests by a large number of NGOs from various spheres and fields of activity.

Opportunity for involvement in decision-making

Such opportunities include involvement in committees of experts, in working groups attached to elected local-government bodies, in consultative groups (committees, councils, etc.), in executives, in coordinating bodies, in administrative procedures, in the comments process, etc. These are opportunities that enable NGOs to fulfil one of their fundamental roles, i.e., acting as a "watchdog of democracy". Even though the openness of these opportunities on the part of NGOs frequently criticized (Frič, 2000) overall the system of opportunities to participate in public policy decision-making can be rated relatively open, although it also depends on the specific area of public policy concerned. This is also confirmed by the complex assessment of the state of the third sector referred to earlier (Vajdová, 2005), which points out that the "nature protection" and social services spheres are best off in this respect. In both cases, three-quarters of the non-profit organization members questioned rated the influence of NGOs on public policy as successful (Vajdová, 2005, p. 58).

Collective identity

The collective identity of NGOs falls into two parts. The first part consists of old, or traditional NGOs that survived the era of socialism. The second part consists of new organizations created at the close of the socialist era, but chiefly after 1989. The inclusion of most of the traditional NGOs (various sports clubs, gardening and breeders' associations, voluntary firefighters, hunter's associations, or professional associations) in the third sector is viewed with misgivings by the representatives of the new organizations. They often talk about the third sector as if the traditional organizations did not exist in it at all. The new NGOs regard most of the traditional organizations with a certain sense of superiority, derived from the fact that they were not "embroiled" with the old socialist regime. The new organizations overtly draw their inspiration from the dissident roots of the Czech third sector, avow the ideology of modern civil society and are intensely involved in the inner life of the third sector. Traditional NGOs are conservative and tend to be isolated from the new organizations. They do not assert their old identity from the communist era, but nor do they try to represent the third sector in the eyes of the public. They tend to concentrate on lobbying the state administration, government and parliament. In individual areas their actions are fairly well-integrated vertically as well, and their umbrella organizations (unions) frequently have a mass membership. However, they do not create coalitions between different sectors. They largely build their new collective identity on traditional values, which existed here before the socialist era, while not particularly regarding the ideals of modern civil society, i.e., the idea of a third sector, as an inseparable, stabilizing factor of democracy.

The problem of the collective identity of the NGOs also has an adverse effect by mutually fostering harmful rivalries and hampering their ability to work together to the benefit of common interests (Frič (ed.), 2000). The legitimacy of umbrella organizations is constantly called into question both by representatives of state institutions (who feel the lack of a dependable partner representing the relevant part of the third sector), and also by NGOs themselves (Vajdová, 2005). In the final analysis, the negative influence of the fragmented collective identity of NGOs undermines the process of forming a community of the third sector and its ability to behave as a social actor.

The view from the public policy perspective

The public policy agenda

The rebirth and consolidation of the third sector in the Czech Republic after 1989 would have been impossible without massive state assistance. The effective operation of NGOs as social institutions depended on the decisions and legislative activity of its representatives. It was certainly not easy to make the right and opportune decisions, since the decisions of particular governments and parliaments were always influenced by many different and often contradictory tendencies. This also explains why several not entirely compatible decisions were taken in respect of individual items of the decision-making agenda. Although there was clearly a very broad agenda for deciding on the fate of the NGOs, it could be summarized in three main points, or dilemmas:

1   The choice between tendencies to construct an adequate legal framework for the operation of various different types of NGOs aimed at maximum facilitation of their development, on the one hand, and tendencies to keep the NGOs in a state of financial precariousness and at a comfortable distance from decision-making processes, on the other.
2   The choice between an ambitious restructuralization of the system of public financing of NGOs, on the one hand, and maintenance of the present system, which prefers the old conformist NGOs over the problematical new NGOs, on the other.
3   The choice between maintaining "easily" manageable budgetary and state-subsidized organizations[2a] on the one hand, and creating greater scope for

competition in the provision of services in such areas as education, the health service and social care, on the other.

None of the above-mentioned dilemmas was solved solely in favour of one or other of the conflicting tendencies. In the first case a fairly robust legislative framework was created enabling the operation of the entire range of NGOs. Nevertheless its creation was not entirely straightforward and involved major delays and grave inconsistencies that have led to serious problems for the activities of specific types of NGOs. The that the creation of the legislative framework lagged behind developments in the third sector was one of the main reasons, for instance, why a negative image of NGOs was disseminated among the public during the first half of the 1990s. This was most glaring in the case of foundations, whose legal regulation was very lax at the beginning and allowed them to be misused.[3] Cases of abuse were publicized in the media and used to discredit the role of NGOs in the eyes of the general public (Stein, 1994, pp. 25–26). The situation eased when the legislative framework was altered and the reputation of NGOs improved. Nevertheless the legal environment within which NGOs operate has long been considered the worst out of all the post-communist countries of central Europe.

Regarding the second case, it must be pointed out that although the state has considerably increased its funding of the third sector over the last decade, the system of funding NGOs has not changed very much since the period of government by the Communist Party. Its lack of transparency fosters clientelism and preserves several anomalies in the structure of the third sector inherited from that time (Frič (ed.), 2000). For instance, areas supported under the communist regime, such as sport, recreation and advocacy organizations for various occupations, represent a much great proportion of the sector than in the West.

The state's relatively low support for the third sector in the Czech Republic is related to the solution of the third dilemma. Although the state opened the door slightly for private enterprise in areas such as education, health and social care, the advantages bestowed on the state-founded budgetary and subsidized organizations operating in these areas, virtually preserves their almost monopoly

Table 13.4 Assessment of the legal environment of NGOs*

	2000	2001	2002	2003	2004
Czech Republic	2,0	2,0	3,0	3,0	3,0
Hungary	1,0	1,7	1,4	1,3	1,3
Poland	2,0	2,0	2,1	2,1	2,3
Slovakia	2,5	2,5	2,6	2,5	2,3

Source: USAID, NGO Sustainability Index, 2000–2004; www.usaid.gov/locations/europe_eurasia/dem_gov/ngoindex/2004/.

Note
* Assessed by groups of experts in individual countries on a scale from one to seven, where one is the best and seven the worst.

status.[4] In other words, the solution to the dilemma has tended to promote the idea of a strong state and centralist tendencies.[5] So in the areas mentioned (which in the West are the core of the third sector) the state has tended to concentrate its funding on support for its own "state NGOs" rather than on genuine NGOs. Up to the present no government of the Czech Republic, irrespective of its ideological coloration (and not even after lengthy discussions, project preparation and timid practical trials), has come up with a credible solution to the problem of the "de-etatization" of public services. That is why the third sector in the Czech Republic is relatively small and NGOs has so far been unable to achieve the status they have in the West.

Inconsistency of public policy

The ambiguous solutions of the above-mentioned dilemmas indicate that the state's policies towards the third sector have not entirely crystallized. A more detailed and lengthy review of the development of relations between the government and NGOs have revealed that in none of the countries monitored was the financing and legislative protection of the activities of NGOs consistent. However, the inconsistency of public policy vis-à-vis the NGOs is not so much the outcome of changing ideological stance of governments (representing various social sectors), as unprofessionalism and ad hoc pragmatic solutions taken by politicians under pressure from various interest groups. Public policy vis-à-vis the third sector is not governed by clear and firm principles characterizing the political representation's concept of that sector's role in society, how it is to be consolidated and how to build civil society. It is clear that not a single government has so far produced an integrated concept of the development of the third sector, with which it would identify. So far none has even tried to obtain in a systematic way relevant information about the question of its development (consolidation).

The ignorance of the authorities represents a very great danger for the third sector. It allows strange myths to be disseminated about it and downgrade its status in society. This chiefly concerns two so-called "residual myths" linked with the two main ideological currents that have established themselves on the Czech political scene. The first of them, which emerged from neo-liberal circles, regards the third sector solely as a voluntary sphere with total economic independence from the state; hence state funding of NGOs is regarded as a relic of the communist era. The other myth, which was nurtured on social-democratic ideology, maintains that the welfare state is a universal instrument for solving social problems and that NGOs are simply a relic of efforts by backward traditional societies to tackle their own problems. They are therefore regarded more as an archaic approach to solving social problems, which in a modern society can at most serve to supplement the services of welfare-state institutions.

In a situation in which the requisite data are unavailable and there is not even any interest in them, in which various rumours circulated about the abuse of NGOs and their standing in society, and in which there exists no clear concept, one cannot expect public policy vis-à-vis the NGOs to withstand pressures from contradictory tendencies or to have a consistent form. But why is this so? What is the source of this lack of interest on the part of political-party representatives or public policy institutions? The answer to these two questions was indicated in the preceding analysis of how styles of government take shape. An approach that is verbally encouraging but in practice reserved or even hostile is a logical upshot of awareness of specific party interests and the technocratic style of government adopted. The inconsistency of public policy vis-à-vis the third sector is therefore actually the result of the very consistent approach of the political elites, which might be termed "party pragmatism", i.e., an endeavour to behave as economically as possible within a given term of office.

Shifting coalitional formations[6]

Why is the third sector agenda not at the mainstream of political discourse in the Czech Republic? Why is the sector horizontal policy still focused on its consolidation? Why is the third sector community under-institutionalized and is only emerging for 15 years? To answer these questions we can use the Paul Sabatier's Advocacy Coalition Framework.

CONTINUITY OF "OLD STRUCTURE" COALITIONS

Shortly after the "Velvet Revolution" in 1989 and the passage of a first law on the right of association, there was a huge growth in the numbers of newly registered NGOs. The new (and relatively small) organizations only slowly developed their influence and found it hard to get funds for their activities because they were in competition with the old NGOs. Though the funds of the former "National Front" were transferred to new umbrella organizations (i.e. The Czechoslovak Council for Humanitarian Cooperation and The Foundation of Jiří z Poděbrad), the management of these organizations was still full of people from the old NGOs. In addition, lobbying on behalf of NGOs in Parliament continued to be in hands of a number of old service and advocacy organizations. These had "their people" in ministries, government advisory bodies and parliament, were invited to the meetings of parliament committees and in time acquired information vital for their activity. Old NGOs (including such sundry actors as big umbrella associations of sporting clubs, hunting associations, professional associations, bee keepers, and voluntary firemen) simply maintained their contacts and connections with civil servants[7] and some politicians from the era of National Front. As a result the members of these informal networks (officials and NGOs representatives) were given the pejorative label "old structures". These networks served as a basis for a plurality of long-term "sub-industry" coalitions[8] at all levels of public government and they are still important. Such informal contacts and coalitions allowed old NGOs to be successful in reaching their two general goals: to preserve their access to state budgets (mainly at a central level) and to keep the system of state subsidies distributed according to the number of members in an organization.[9] On the other hand the old NGOs never jeopardized the monopoly of state non-profit organizations (contributory organizations) in the domain of social welfare and accepted the principle of state centralization. Clearly, both these principles served to sustain the power of civil servants. It could be said that up to now, the lobbying of old NGOs in ministries has been much more effective than the lobbying of new NGOs.

It should be also said that all the intermediary bodies discussed earlier in this chapter are for new, not old NGOs. In the "old part" of the Czech third sector we can see only minimal effort to participate in the forms of third sector horizontal activities discussed, and we find only very limited horizontal organizational networks. The most important among them is TRIPARTITA (the Council of Economic and Social Agreement), which has grown in political prominence in recent years. The aim is to keep "social peace" through "social dialogue" or bargaining among three stakeholder types: government, trade unions and employers' associations. It does not represent any other interests, which means that no (other) NGOs participate on its activities. Thus, if one considers the latter two stakeholders to be part of the third sector its activities are in scope; otherwise it is viewed as separate to the third sector community. In fact, the representatives of the third sector community (intermediary bodies) themselves, discussed earlier, are not used to thinking of TRIPARTITA as a possible platform for third sector policy agenda setting or implementation. The new service NGOs have made no serious attempts to become members of TRIPARTITA.

The TRIPARTITA platform was originally established in October 1990 and is still the only voluntary association of stakeholders. Its status has not yet been established by an Act – and has changed over time depending on the attitude of the government in power.[10] The bodies making up TRIPARTITA are: plenary session, presidium, task teams and secretariat. The delegation present in plenary sessions consists of: seven representatives of the government, seven representatives of trade unions and seven representatives of employer unions. To be able to take part in TRIPARTITA the representatives of trade unions and of employers must meet the criterion of representativeness. Every trade organization applying for participation in TRIPARTITA must have a minimum of 150,000 members, and every employer organization 200,000 members.

A PLURALITY OF NEW AD HOC INDUSTRY COALITIONS

Looking back to the short existence of the third sector in the Czech Republic the most successful period – in terms of the sector's ability to affect public policy – seems to be the first post-revolution years (1990–1992), which have been described in the area of public policy as "the time of concepts" (Kalous, 1994). During this period various newly founded NGOs enjoyed influence not only over particular decisions of the state administration but also the general philosophy for resolving problems in society. This was the time when the old (communist) institutions of public policy were destroyed and new democratic ones established. We could see new concepts being developed in the school sector, healthcare sector, in the army, and in the field of ecology (Potůček, 1996, pp. 167–168). The government supported the influx of new professionals coming into the state administration, many of whom had been active in NGOs before. Thanks to the continuing revolutionary social atmosphere, confusion in the forces of "old structures" (among civil servants) as well as personal contacts with the new representatives of the government and ministries, the new NGOs quickly managed to build several spontaneous ad hoc coalitions with politicians and civil servants within different industry fields on the central level. Thereafter, professionals and experts from new NGOs had good opportunities for intervening in the process of developing public policy.[11]

A FIRST CROSS-INDUSTRY COALITION: NIF AND THE EARLY ALLIANCES

At the first free elections after the Velvet Revolution (in June 1990) the government had been formed by a group of new politicians dominated by those who had developed a political profile through active dissent and involvement in the Civic Forum (that organized the movement and can thus be said to be the leader of the Velvet Revolution). Their attitude to civil initiatives and organizations supporting or creating an umbrella for the activities of citizens was almost "naturally" positive as they themselves arose from the third sector. During its term in office, under Petr Pithart, the government started to prepare laws regulating the activity of particular organizations of the third sector, initiated funding for NGOs project grants, and began the process of setting up the Foundation Investment Fund (NIF) in order to support civil society development.[12] In its final year, it was the Pithart government which established a Council for Foundations. This council closely collaborated with influential Prague foundations (NROS – Foundation for Civil Society Development, OSF – Open Society Fund, Olga Havlová Foundation) and some third sector infrastructural bodies (such as ICN – Foundations Information Centre) and started to prepare a plan to distribute the NIF financial returns among newly established foundations that exclusively focused on developing the new service NGOs. This meant that from its beginning the central government advisory body (Council for Foundations) was in coalition with representatives of foundations and new service NGOs from different industries (predominantly social and healthcare).

The agenda of the Council was eventually enlarged to cover the whole third sector and as mentioned earlier was renamed as the Government Council for Non-State NGOs (RNNO). The high points in shared activities that were to follow involved negotiations with parliament in relation to foundations' legislation in 1997; eventually there was also to be the distribution of NIF financial resources in 1999; and the finalization of the document "Strategy for Development of the Non-Profit Sector" in 2000. A key player in these processes was the Donors' Forum which established a special ad hoc group for parliamentary lobbying. The group then went on to transform itself into "SPIRALIS", an independent advocacy NGO, (focused solely on professional lobbying to promote NGOs). These activities led to the strengthening of a third sector horizontal community and of its influence on public policy.

PROBLEMS OF LEGITIMACY AND THE "SELF LIMITATION" RESPONSE

How did the cross-industry coalition proceed, and what constraints did it face? Despite the successes it apparently catalysed, the initial configuration was not to last, as external and internal pressures came together to force major change. During its early successes, a crucial condition for the smooth functioning of the alliance had been its legitimacy in the eyes of third sector members. However, this was not nurtured, setting in train a process of disintegration. From the outside, its functioning was questioned by several politicians and civil servants. The strong Prague foundations and some other intermediary bodies tried, in response, to use their position in the SKK (Permanent Commission of the Conference, i.e., coordinating body of the NGOs National Conferences) to underpin their legitimacy as representatives of the whole third sector. This response initially seemed plausible, because the mission of SKK was, among others, to improve the conditions for the functioning of NGOs and to support the development of the whole third sector.

Yet, the strategy proved to be untenable: there were also constraints on these efforts from within the NGOs policy community. Significant numbers of regional representatives of NGOs viewed the coalition actors as implicated in an undesirable "non-profit oligarchy", which had too much power. There was also more general "grassroots" hostility. Therefore, the SKK had to permanently fight against the erosion of its legitimacy from below, as well as outside. In 1997, it was to fail definitively. At the Fifth National Conference of NGOs the SKK lost its mandate because it was accused of having "spent its energies on representative activities and politics". To avoid the perceived danger of a self perpetuating "non-profit oligarchy" in future, from this moment onwards a "self-limiting" strategy was adopted with alternative parameters. This was to be based on "field and regional integration" for the third sector. A new NGOs coordinating body, the Council of NGOs (RANO), was set up purely as a discussion platform for NGOs. Under the new settlement, the role of this Council would not include negotiating as a representative of the third sector with the administration or with parliament. A new nationwide NGOs umbrella organization, ANNO, was established, but this also ruled out acting as a "representative" for the third sector, and its membership is not significant enough to play an important role in the cross-sectoral collaboration at the central level.

A SECOND CROSS-INDUSTRY COALITION

The erosion of the first third sector coalition's legitimacy described above generated a crisis. The coalition was not able to transform its goals and to revitalize its common activities in the new situation. During 2001, the management of RNNO (Government Council for Non-State NGOs) hesitated about whether to close it down, or to start to look for new allies (which would bring with them much-needed "representative legitimacy"). All of this was offered by the nationwide regional and field NGOs' network, OKAMRK. The origin of this network lay primarily not in initiative by individual grassroots NGOs, but more in the regional coalitions of NGOs, i.e., centres for community work (CpKP).[13] It was essentially a response to the weaknesses of RANO in terms of intervention for the benefit of NGOs. It was also perceived to have failed, through incompetence, to involve the third sector in early efforts to access the European Structural Funds. The motivation of NGOs to enter into the processes of NDP preparation at this time was clear: to boost their chances to get finance from the EU SF.

How did the third sector policy actors evolve from this point? The OKAMRK network set up its own working group for regional development in 1998, which also became its executive body. The group members organized annual conferences and made an effort to keep NGOs informed and up-to-date about the progress of work on the National Development Plan. The coalition between RNNO and OKAMRK was formally set up in the working conference at the end of 2001. Their cooperation very quickly led to a situation when RNNO to a considerable extent took over the agenda of the working group OKAMRK. This was clearly evident in the new internal structure of RNNO, which comprises three committees, two of which are involved in regional development, and/or, integration into the EU. Members of the OKAMRK working group became members of the RNNO committees. Thus RNNO became a kind of hybrid (half state-owned, half civil) institution, which on the one hand continuously absorbed impulses and initiatives from NGOs, transforming them into bureaucratic language, and, on the other hand, has made these contributions legitimate as proposals submitted by a central state administration body. However it should be said that most of the problems of third sector consolidation mentioned above were not central to the focus of the second coalition, because RNNO was interested only in problems which the government wanted to be solved. The process was, however, far from monolithic. The willingness of particular ministries and regional governments to cooperate with NGOs on the creation of the National Development Plan[14] was very different. Those civil servants who already had experience with new service NGOs were more positive about the wider participation of NGOs (expressed in the time they spent giving out information, documents for discussions, and willingness to accept comments and propositions). The approach of those civil servants who had most experience with old, advocacy NGOs, was more selective and more discriminating when it concerned new NGOs. They tried not to expand the circle of the old NGOs participating, especially not by new advocacy organizations (e.g. by the organizations of the Green Movement). In the first case civil servants wanted – through the participation of NGOs – to give their documents credibility; while in the other case, they essentially experienced them as a "necessary evil" to make the cause succeed. These civil servants were still looking at the participation of NGOs as "democratic folklore" accepted under the pressure of EU. Generally, those more open and friendly to NGOs happened to be at the regional (and also local) levels rather than at the central level, and some of these cases even resulted in the establishment of several regional cross-industry coalitions, among regional politicians, civil servants and representatives of regional umbrella NGOs (GAC, 2003).

The second coalition has, so far, been *relatively* successful in practice. It is visible mainly in the process of appointing representatives of NGOs to monitoring committees in government and later to ECOSOC (Harvey, 2004). In reality, many of the individuals appointed to these bodies were just the NGOs candidates proposed by the regional and industry networks of NGOs. RNNO managed to play the role of a "policy broker", and has continued to mediate the latent but permanent conflict between civil servants and NGOs representatives. It has become evident that the second cross-industry coalition represents essentially a win-win strategy for the vast majority of the players involved. The new service NGOs have gained a powerful ally and legitimacy in the eyes of state officials. The regional advocacy networks have strengthened their influence and RNNO found its raison d'etre. State officials and representatives of the regional governments acquired legitimate partners (whose mandate was confirmed by the first vice premier of the Czech government, who is also the chairman of RNNO) – prescribed for them by the EU. The powerful, central NGOs partly keep their membership in RNNO, are still in the coalition game, and reasserted their advantageous position for drawing money from the European Structural Funds. As RNNO from its beginnings adopted the new NGOs' views on the role and place of the old NGOs in the Czech third sector, the only losers were the old, advocacy NGOs. It is significant that there is not one old advocacy NGO among the members of RNNO.[15]

Conclusions: applied partnership model

Three models of partnership between the state and the third sector in practice

According to Salamon and Anheier, basically three models of partnership operate in practice, which correspond to Esping-Andersen's three welfare state regimes referred to earlier. The first (which is implemented within the conservative welfare regime) they have called the "German *corporative* model", wherein several associations of NGOs formed a formal cooperative body, with which the government has a duty to consult on matters related to the main social sectors. The second model (operating within the liberal welfare regime) is the "American *interest groups* model", which uses lobbying to provide individual NGOs major scope to influence the outcome of the legislative process, but only in an ad hoc, formally uncodified fashion. The third model (that came out of the new social-democratic regime) could be termed the "*programmed cooperation* model" and it is employed in the UK (Salamon and Anheier, 1994, p. 104).

Of course, each of the above- mentioned models of partnership between the state and the third sector has its advantages and disadvantages. Although the corporative model ensures that representatives of the third sector are consulted about basic public policy issues, the circle of partners from the third sector side is chiefly restricted to historically well-established subjects. In other words, the corporative model tends to conserve the structure of the third sector, in terms both of programme and organization, and leads to greater bureaucratization. The interest groups model is far more open and employs the so-called "contract" of relations between the state and NGOs. On the other hand, it lacks the ability to generate and implement a coherent strategy for developing the third sector or its part of it, both from the point of view of the state and of the third sector. It encourages NGOs to market their activities (Salamon and Anheier, 1994, p. 106) Through compromise the programmed cooperation model seeks to resolve the dilemmas of the previous two models. However, it requires the creation of a respected umbrella organization of the third sector to negotiate the programme aims and procedures with the state on behalf of the decisive majority of NGOs. However, it is very hard to fulfil this condition in view of the great variety of NGOs.

A clash of paradigms

Representatives of Czech NGOs have not yet been capable of articulating clearly what model of partnership with public administration institutions would be most advantageous for them and what they would like to strive for in future. As a result of spontaneous development, in the sphere where old NGOs mostly operate the corporative model is maintained, although it is disputed by the new NGOs. However, the latter have not managed to agree on whether it is prefer-able to opt for building an interest group model or for a compromise middle way of creating a central umbrella organization for the entire not-for-profit sector. In the Czech Republic there is a clash of several paradigms as regards the relation-ship between the state and the third sector (Rymsza and Zimmer, 2004). This clash has made it more difficult to create a single dominant model that would allow a smooth routinization of their partnership.

As Table 13.5 shows, the old NGOs come closest to achieving an ideal model of partnership with the state, particularly those whose activity is chiefly advo-cacy. These organizations with an essentially advocacy role (trade unions, pro-fessional associations, etc.) enjoy the greatest privileges in their relationship with the state, such as favoured communication status[16] and programmatic coop-eration (see TRIPARTITA). The corporativist model also suits old service organizations whose have the privilege of state subsidy based on size of mem-bership, without the need for grant application. Worst off are the new NGOs, the service ones of which have to compete with the ROPO that are favoured by the state, and the advocacy organizations that must overcome the strong aversion of political parties towards the political function of NGOs in society. The advant-age of the new NGOs is that they are strongly represented in the central advisory body of the public administration, i.e. the Government Council for Non-State NGOs (RNNO), in which the identity of the "new third sector" definitely pre-vails. Nevertheless, it is true for old and new organizations alike that it is

Table 13.5 Preferred models of cooperation between the state and the third sector in their four main sub-sectors

Type of activity	Type of interest pursued	
	Mutual benefit	*Public benefit*
Service	1. SMB NGOs **corporativist model** financial privileges	2. SPB NGOs **programme model** competition ROPO advantage: RNNO
Advocacy	3. AMB NGOs **interests groups model** conflictual political function of NGOs	4. APB NGOs **corporativist model** privileged position TRIPARTITA

extremely hard to promote a genuine partnership, in spite of pressures from the EU. Above all, the acute absence of programmatic partnership means that cooperation between NGOs and the state depends on the goodwill or current mood of officials and offers wide scope for clientelism (Frič, 2000). When officials are replaced cooperation has to start virtually from scratch once more. It therefore seems that the most prevalent "model of cooperative relations" between the state and the third sector in the Czech Republic is the asymmetrical model of informal relations.

One may conclude from the above-mentioned analyses of relations between the state and NGOs in the Czech Republic that in many cases these relationships are not partnerial but asymmetrical, with the NGOs being the weaker pole. We may with some justice advance the hypothesis that, in its relationship to the state the third sector is squeezed into the role of a sort of service appendix, intended to supplement, in a "suitable" manner, the services of state NGOs (i.e. ROPO) in line with the notions of officials and politicians. NGOs are supposed to operate where the state organizations do not, or prefer not to. Such notions reduce the role of the NGOs to an extension of the state, intended to ease the pressure on state organizations and to stand in for them in emergency situations.

Developments since the end of the 1990s give grounds for a certain degree of hope. Officials and representatives of NGOs are unusually agreed that since then relations between the state and the third sector have been slowly but surely improving. Although the asymmetrical model still prevails, cooperation is increasing in breadth and intensity.

Notes

1 The following post-communist countries of central Europe were included in the second wave of the JHU comparative project: Czech Republic, Hungary, Romania and Slovakia.
2 This is why Katz and Mair call political parties linked with the state and cut off from civil society "cartel parties" (Katz and Mair, 1996). Similarly Attila Ágh refers to political parties in the post-communist countries as "elite parties" (Ágh, 1992, p. 19).
2a During the communist era the state built a relatively extensive network of

state-owned organizations in the social welfare domain, which may be referred to as "state nonprofit organizations". Emphasis here should be put on the first term: the relevant organizations were owned by the state and functioned as essentially "budgetary and contributory" organizations, directly reporting to the line ministries. State ownership and control in this domain was to stay remarkably constant, despite the change of regime in 1989. These "state nonprofits" still exist and complete with the meaningfully autonomous NGOs. In the social welfare domain they continue to represent the dominant form for providing services and managing citizens.

3 Eva Leś states that "fraudulent activities of so called 'fake foundations' have created suspicion, and cast doubt on the reputation of all foundations in the region" (Leś, 1994, p. 49).

4 In 1999 the social services were funded chiefly by the state (48 percent) and the towns and local communities (36 percent). Just under one-fifth of funding came from churches (10 percent) and other non-profit organizations (7 percent) (Vajdová, 2005).

5 The way this dilemma is tackled is described by Eva Leś as "neo-etatization" prevailing over the subsidiarity principle (Leś, 1999, p. 2).

6 For inspiration and empirical knowledge to writing this part of the text I am grateful to the "Third Sector European Policy" (TSEP) project held in nine European countries under the leadership of Jeremy Kendall (2005). The Czech empirical evidence is based mostly on more than 30 face-to-face interviews with public servants and NGOs representatives (Frič, 2005).

7 Here we have in mind especially those senior civil servants who were in favor of the old communist regime but remained in their positions because of their skills.

8 For example there is still a strong coalition of hunting associations with politicians (across the left–right spectrum) and public servants because many are members of these associations on the local level. Hunting is a particularly significant constituency: in the Czech Republic there are more than 1,000 hunting associations with total membership of 3 percent of the adult population (Frič *et al.*, 2003).

9 Therefore they (often only formally) report a huge number of members.

10 E.g. in 1992 the first government of Václav Klaus took out of the TRIPARTITA agenda the issues of economic and structural policy, narrowed its status to a "consulting platform of the trade unions and employers", renamed it "Council for Dialogue of Social Partners" and as such relegated it to the role of a mere observer. In 1997 the second government of Václav Klaus included the issues of economic policy in the agenda of TRIPARTITA once again, and accepted its new name: "Council of Economic and Social Agreement". In 2000 the government of Miloš Zeman had further strengthened the status of TRIPARTITA by extending its scope to include human resources development (Şlehofer, 2001; Mansfeldová *et al.*, 1998).

11 "The time closely after the political change in 1989 like any other revolutionary time, did not make life complicated by procedural restrictions: it was the time when professionals did not ask anybody anything but just got into the politics" (Potůček, 1996, p. 187).

12 In mid-1992 this Government initiated taking out of the second wave of the voucher privatization 1 percent of all shares to be subsequently deposited to the NIF. The nominal value of thus created assets came close to three billion Czech Crowns (about €90 million).

13 Several of these regional centres had been established during the mid-1990s with the help of the National Democratic Institute.

14 National Development Plan is a key strategic document enabling the Czech Republic to participate in EU Structural Funds and Cohesion Fund programmes.

15 There are only two representatives of the old service NGOs and 14 representatives of new ones – seven Prague-located intermediary bodies and seven regional umbrella advocacy or local service NGOs.

16 "Media monitoring indicates that when the state enters into dialogue with civil society

(and it is covered by the media) in about 70 percent of cases it concerns trade unions or professional associations" (Vajdová, 2005, p. 45).

References

Ágh, A. (1992) The Emerging Party System in East Central Europe. Budapest, Papers on Democratic Transition, No. 13, Hungarian Centre for Democracy Studies Foundation, University of Economics, Budapest.

Almond, G.A. and Verba, S. (1989) *The Civil Culture: Political Attitudes and Democracy in Five Nations*. London: Sage Publications.

Beck, U., Giddens, A. and Lash, S. (1994) *Reflexive Modernization. Politics, Tradition and Aesthetics in the Modern Social Order*. Cambridge: Polity Press.

Carlsson, L. (2000) Policy Networks as Collective Action. *Policy Studies Journal*, 28/3, pp. 502–520.

Esping-Andersen, G. (1990) *The Three Worlds of Welfare Capitalism*. Princeton: Princeton University Press.

Etzioni-Halevy, E. (1990) Democratic-elite Theory: Stabilization versus Breakdown of Democracy. *Arch. europ. Sociál.*, XXXI, pp. 317–350.

Frič, P. (1998) Activities and Needs of Nonprofit Organizations in the Czech Republic: The Results of Quantitative Sociological Research, Agnes and ICN, Prague.

Frič, P. (ed.) (2000) *Strategy of Development of the Non-Profit Sector*. Prague: Czech Donors Forum.

Frič, P. (2000) *Neziskové organizace a ovlivňování veřejné politiky: Rozhovory o neziskovém sektoru II*. Praha: AGNES.

Frič, P. (ed.) (2003) *Èeši na cestě za svojí budoucností: Budoucnost a modernizace vpostojích a očekáváních obyvatelstva. (Czechs on the Road for their Future: Future and Modernization in Attitudes and Expectations of Inhabitants)*. Praha: GplusG.

Frič, P. (2005) The Third Sector and the Policy Process in the Czech Republic. Third Sector European Policy Working Paper No6. LSE-CCS, London and Prague, June 2005, p. 55.

GAC (2003) *Analýza spolupráce nestátních neziskových organizací a veřejné správy na tvorbě krajských rozvojových dokumentů případně dalších dokumentů relevantních pro EU*. Praha: Gabal, Analysis & Consulting.

Giddens, A. (1994) *Beyond Left and Right. The Future of Radical Politics*. London: Stanford University Press.

Hansman, H. (1987) Economic Theories of Nonprofit Organizations, in Powell, W.W. (ed.) *The Nonprofit Sector: A Research Handbook*. New Haven: Yale University Press.

Harvey, B. (2004) The Illusion of Inclusion: Access by NGOs to the Structural Funds in the New Member States of Eastern and Central Europe. Report for the European Citizens Action Service, Brussels: ECAS.

Kalous, J. (1994) Hlavní problémy vzdělávací politiky Èeské republiky v transformačním období (Major Problems of the Educational Policy of the Czech Republic in the Transformation Period), in Potůček, Martin, Purkrábek, Miroslav and Háva, Petr. *Analýza událostí veřejné politiky v Èeské republice I. (The Analysis of Public Events in the Czech Republic I.)* Institut sociologických studií, FSV UK, Praha.

Katz, R.S. and Mair, P. (1996) Changing Models of Party Organization and Party Democracy. *Party Politics*, Vol. 1, No. 1.

Kean, John (1998) *Civil Society: Old Images, New Visions*. Stanford, California: Stanford University Press.

Kendall, J. (2005) Third Sector Policy: Organisations Between Market and State, the

Policy Process and the EU. Third Sector European Policy Working Paper No. 1. LSE-CCS, London and Prague, June 2005, p. 27.

Leś, E. (1994) *The Voluntary Sector in Post-Communist East Central Europe*. Washington: Civicus.

Leś, E. (1999) Is the Principle of Subsidiarity Suitable for Central Europe? Paper prepared for PragueVoluntas Conference "Ten Years After".

McCarty, J.D. and Zald, M.N. (1973) *The Trends of Social Movements in America*. Moristown: General Learning Press.

Mansfeldová, Z., Èambáliková, M. and Brokl, L. (1998) Sociální partnerství jako forma institucionální reprezentace zájmů české a slovenské společnosti, Final Research Report, Praha: Open Society Institute.

Melucci, A. (1988) Getting Involved: Identity and Mobilization in Social Movements. *International Social Movement Research*, Vol. 1, pp. 329–348.

Peterson, J. (1995) Policy Networks and European Union Policy Making: A Reply to Kassim. *West European Politics*, 18/2, pp. 389–407.

Pithart, P. (1996) Rival Visions. *Journal of Democracy*, Vol. 7, No. 1, January.

Potůček, M. (1996) Jak se formovala veřejná politika v Ceské republice po roce 1989. (How was the Public Policy Formed in the Czech Republic after 1989), in Potůček, M., Purkrábek, M. and Háva, P. *Analýza událostí veřejné politiky v Ceské republice II. (The Analysis of Public Events in the Czech Republic II.)* Institut sociologických studií, FSV UK, Praha.

Putnam, R. (1993) *Making Democracy Work: Civic Traditions in Modern Italy*. Princeton: Princeton University Press.

Rhodes, R.A.W. (1990) Policy Networks: A British Perspective. *Journal of Theoretical Politics*, 2/3, pp. 292–316.

Rhodes, R.A.W. and Marsh, D. (1992) New Directions in the Study of Policy Networks. *European Journal of Political Research*, 21/1, pp. 181–205.

Rymsza, M. and Zimmer, A. (2004) Embeddedness of Nonprofit Organizations: Government – Nonprofit Relationship, in Zimmer, A. and Priller, E., *Future of Civil Society: Making Central European Nonprofit-Organizations Work*. Berlin: VS Werlag.

Sabatier, P.A. (1993) Policy Change over a Decade, in Sabatier, P.A. and Jenkins-Smith, H.C., *Policy Change and Learning: An Advocacy Coalition Approach*. Oxford: Westview Press, pp. 13–39.

Sabatier, P.A. (1998) The Advocacy Coalition Framework: Revisions and Relevance for Europe. *Journal of European Public Policy*, 5/1, pp. 98–130.

Sabatier, P.A. and Jenkins-Smith, H.C. (1993) *Policy Change and Learning: An Advocacy Coalition Framework*. San Francisco and Oxford: Westview Press.

Sabatier, P.A. and Jenkins-Smith, H.C. (1999) The Advocacy Coalition Framework, in Sabatier, P.A. (ed.) *Theories of the Policy Process*. Colorado: Westview Press, pp. 117–166.

Salamon, L.M. (1999) The Nonprofit Sector at a Crossroads: The Case of America. *VOLUNTAS*, Vol. 10, No. 1.

Salamon, L.M. and Anheier, H.K. (1994) The Emerging Sector: The Nonprofit Sector in Comparative Perspective – An Overview. The Johns Hopkins Comparative Nonprofit Sector Project, Institute for Policy Studies, JHU, Baltimore.

Salamon, L.M., Anheier, H.K. *et al.* (eds) (1999) *Global Civil Society: Dimensions of the Nonprofit Sector*. Baltimore: The Johns Hopkins Center for Civil Society Studies.

Salamon, L.M., Anheier, H.K. and Associates, (1996) Social Origins of Civil Society:

Explaining the Nonprofit Sector Cross-Nationally. The Johns Hopkins Comparative Non-profit Sector Project, Institute for Policy Studies, JHU, Baltimore, Working Paper No. 22.

Şlehofer, K. (2001) Tripartita – Institution for Co-operation between the State and Non-governmental Organizations, in Kabele, Jiří and Mlčoch, Lubomír, *Institucionalizace (ne)odpovědnosti: globální svět, evropská integrace a české zájmy (Institucionalization of (Ir)responsibility, Global World, European Integration and Czech interests)*. Praha: Karolinum, pp. 484–492.

Stein, R. (1994) *The Not-for-Profit Sector in The Czech Republic*. Prague: The Information Center for Foundations and Other Not-for-Profit Organizations.

Strmiska, Z. (1993) Socio-politické kultury a postoje v podmínkách ekonomické přeměny ve střední a východní Evropě, in Politická a ekonomická transformace v zemích střední a východní Evropy. Praha, CEFRES, No. 3.

Tilly, C. (1978) *From Mobilization to Revolution*. Reading: Addison-Wesley Publishing Company.

Touraine, A. (1988) *Return of the Actor: Social Tudory in Postindustrial Society*. Minneapolis: University of Minnesota Press.

Vajdová, T. (2005) *Èeská občanská společnost 2004: po patnácti letech rozvoje*. Brno: CERM.

Weisbrod, B. (1977) *The Voluntary Nonprofit Sector*. Lexington: Lexington Books.

14 Institutionalising relationships between government and the third sector

The case of the Estonian "Compact"

Tiina Randma-Liiv, Daimar Liiv and Ülle Lepp

Introduction

Relations between government and the third sector have been a focus of interest for researchers since the 1980s. Most of the previous studies in the field have addressed the relationship between government and the third sector either in the context of service provision (e.g. Anheier and Seibel, 1998; Gidron *et al.*, 1992; Kramer *et al.*, 1993; Salamon, 1987, 1995; Taylor and Lewis, 1997; Taylor and Bassi, 1998; Young, 2000) or with an emphasis on the involvement of NGOs in political decision-making processes (e.g. Bullain and Toftisova, 2005; Casey, 1998, 2004; Craig *et al.*, 2004; Kramer, 1981; Taylor *et al.*, 2002; Taylor and Warburton, 2003).

An important landmark in the institutionalisation of NGO-government cooperation has been the signing of cooperation agreements between governments and the third sector, the so-called "compacts". The adoption of this type of agreements started with the signing of a compact in England and the rest of the UK in 1998, and has continued with the introduction of similar agreements in Canada and in Europe (Croatia, Denmark, Estonia, France, Hungary).

Analyses of the preparation and implementation of compacts in Anglo-American countries are well represented in scientific literature (e.g. Brock, 2000, 2004; Craig *et al.*, 2002; Elson, 2006; Morison, 2000; Osborne and McLaughlin, 2002; Phillips, 2001, Phillips and Levasseur, 2004; Plowden, 2003). However, a limited number of studies have addressed the relations between government and the third sector in the post-communist countries of Central and Eastern Europe (Anheier and Seibel, 1998; Jenei and Kuti, 2003; Jenei and Vari, 2000; Kuti, 1992, 1996, 1997, 2001; Osborne and Kaposvari, 1998; Regulska, 2001; Svetlik, 1992). With one exception (Toftisova, 2005), compacts adopted in the Central and Eastern European countries have not been analysed yet. This chapter attempts to contribute to filling this gap by taking a close look at the preparation and implementation of the Civil Society Development Concept in Estonia.

The primary focus of the authors is on the "process" (rather than the specific content) of reaching and implementing the Estonian compact.[1] The authors of the paper have been involved in various capacities in the preparation and implementation of the compact for Estonia, which has provided them with excellent opportunity for participant observation. The results of these observations have been complemented by in-depth interviews with civil servants and NGO leaders, and a study of the minutes of the parliament's deliberations in the matter. The present paper will highlight a number of problems related to the compact process in both the public and the non-profit sectors, and offer a number of general recommendations which could be useful for other (post-communist) countries aiming to institutionalise the relationships between their governments and the third sector. Although the authors are aware of the problems related to the terms used in connection with the third sector (e.g. "third sector", "non-profit sector", "voluntary sector" and "NGOs"), these will be used interchangeably in the chapter.

Development of the relationship between government and the third sector in Estonia

The history of the development of the third sector in Estonia dates back to the nineteenth century, when in the 1860s the predecessors of modern non-profit organisations sprung up at the dawn of the era of national awakening. The establishment of an independent Estonian Republic in 1918 was an important catalyst for the growth of the third sector. Ruutsoo (2002: 63) describes this as follows: "for the first time in the Baltic nations' history, essential processes related to nation-building – community building, civil society building, and state-building – could develop simultaneously and contribute to each other's progress". During the early 1930s, a total of 12,000 voluntary associations were registered in Estonia (Reiman, 1933: 189). The Soviet occupation of 1940 dissolved all associations based on civic initiative. Independent civic activism was almost "invisible" during these times, and civil society in its classical form destroyed (Ruutsoo, 2002: 393).

However, several authors (e.g. Lauristin and Vihalemm, 1997; Götz and Hackmann, 2003) have pointed out that the tradition of voluntary action in Estonia survived even after five decades of Soviet occupation. Civic movements contributed remarkably not only to the reconstruction of democratic governance but also to the independence movement itself. As Lauristin and Vihalemm (1997: 75) argue: "the energy of cultural resistance accumulated during the years of Soviet power was released in mass liberation movements". Some politically active associations such as the Estonian Heritage Society, the Forum of Estonian Artists' Unions, the Estonian Popular Front, and the Estonian Citizens' Movement were founded in the late 1980s. Alongside environmentalists these associations became the forerunners of the national independence movement. Ruutsoo (2002: 181) refers to the 1986–7 period as "the mobilisation of civil courage", and to 1988–90 as the "movement society" years, which were followed by gradual institutionalisation of civic initiatives after Estonia declared independence from the Soviet Union in August 1991. In 1995, the Estonian Parliament (*Riigikogu*) passed the Foundations Act, and in 1996 the Non-Profit

Table 14.1 Registered non-profit associations and foundations 1993–2006

Year	Non-profit associations	Foundations	Total
1993	4,635	n/a	4,635
1994	6,003	n/a	6,003
1995	9,114	n/a	9,114
1996	10,994	8	11,002
1997	12,078	85	12,163
1998	14,835	218	15,053
1999	11,610*	306	11,916*
2000	13,668	373	14,041
2001	15,904	436	16,340
2002	17,775	502	18,277
2003	19,382	571	19,953
2004	21,294	638	21,932
2005	22,721	689	23,410
2006	23,892	710	24,602

Source: Register of Companies and Register of Non-profit Associations and Foundations.

Note
* by 1 March 1999, non-profit associations and their unions had to apply to be transferred from the Company Register to the Non-profit Associations and Foundations Register. The organisations which failed to comply were subject to compulsory winding-up proceedings.

Associations Act. These laws created a firm, stable and modern legal environment for the establishment and functioning of NGOs and brought forth a large variety of non-profit associations (see Table 14.1).

It is possible to distinguish between three periods in the development of relationships between government and the third sector in Estonia from 1991 to 2007.

1991–6: government busy with state-building efforts, ad hoc development of the third sector, declining civic engagement

When analysing the development of the relations between government and the third sector, account has to be taken of the fact that the revolutionary events of the early 1990s simultaneously swept through all levels of the Estonian society. Together with the restitution of Estonia's statehood, the newly created (restructured) government organisations had to guarantee the normal functioning of society and the carrying out of radical reforms in numerous areas of life (monetary reform, property reform, land reform, privatisation, return of unlawfully expropriated property to legal owners, drafting of new legislation). Hence, within a very short period of time, a huge number of extraordinarily complicated and time-consuming tasks had to be implemented.

Rapid and radical changes of the early 1990s often required fast decision-making and robust action, sometimes at the price of ignoring voices that could have been heard. Thus, during the transition many reforms were carried out in a top-down manner. Since the entire society was undergoing major changes, it was relatively easy for politicians, public institutions and eventually all social groups to accept new initiatives without any public debate. This, however, also meant no incentive for cooperation between public institutions and NGOs. Instead, a decision-making culture developed which embodied careless and sometimes even arrogant attitudes towards external recommendations and critique.

Despite the growth in the number of non-profit associations, civil engagement was very limited, with the exception of a select few NGOs with some political roles, whose independence was based on foreign funding. Ruutsoo (1996: 112) claims that the early 1990s were characterised by a dramatic decline in the most active forms of participation typical of "movement society" (demonstrations, marches, pickets), which could not be compensated by the increased formal participation. A survey conducted in 1996 revealed that 81 per cent of ethnic Estonians and 92 per cent of the non-Estonian population had not participated in any political activities based on civic initiative (Ruutsoo, 2002: 360). The same tendency emerges from the results of the World Values Survey of 1990–1 and of 1995–7 (Howard, 2003: 71–72), which show a decline in organisational membership in all post-communist countries. This decline is partly explained by the economic difficulties experienced by those countries in the early 1990s. As Howard (2003: 74) states: "it takes a certain level of economic well-being for the people to be able to devote time and energy to organisational activities and countries with greater economic means should have higher levels of organisational membership". However, in addition to economic reasons the decline of civic engagement in Estonia has been influenced by the stark absence of involvement culture in the Soviet period, the use of the enormous but short-lived engagement during the independence movement in 1990–1 as the basis for comparison, the entrance of NGO leaders to party politics, and by the urgency of fundamental reforms that had to be carried out by the new democratic government.

1997–2001: gradual strengthening of the third sector, random recognition of individual NGOs by public institutions, limiting the role of NGOs to that of service providers

By the late 1990s, a few NGOs had been able to develop into opinion leaders and centres of specific expertise and information. However, as elsewhere in Central and Eastern Europe (Lomax, 1997), the interest of the state in the development of civil society in Estonia was limited. The political forces that dominated in the *Riigikogu* in the 1990s were not interested in the development of independent civic activism or of civil society (Ruutsoo, 2002: 366). The Estonian Human Development Report (1999: 39) concludes that:

the lack of openness in state administration and in the political decision-making processes, the unwillingness of the political and business elite to take seriously opinions different from their own, and the loyalty of the groups close to power primarily to associations related to their own background had an obstructive influence on the development of the civil society into a serious partner.

Third sector organisations were rarely consulted in the political decision-making process, the consultations themselves were random and involved only a limited number of umbrella organisations, employers' associations and trade unions. There was practically no understanding of the need to conduct any consultations with the representatives of civil society.

Instead, politicians and civil servants tended to take a rather pragmatic view of NGOs by seeing them more in the role of (public) service providers and less as participants in the decision-making process. This is reflected in Taylor and Lewis (1997: 44–45) who find that:

> partnership with the voluntary sector requires a recognition from central government that statutory and voluntary sectors have complementary not parallel strengths and that neither can substitute for the other. Otherwise, from playing a complementary role, voluntary organisations could find themselves becoming not even a true alternative to statutory provison but an agent, a pale imitation.

The instances of non-profit organisations being placed in the position of an alternative rather than a complementary service provider have been common in Estonia. Especially after the economic crisis in 1997, a few political and administrative leaders publicly declared that one of the primary tasks in the involvement of NGOs in public service provision was to attract additional financial resources, often available for non-profit organisations only. The all-out privatisation process also contributed to the development of the image of NGOs as (public) service providers (the privatisation of clinics, theatres, social services, etc.).

A few Estonian examples also support the following position taken by Young (2000: 149): "a dynamic economy creates social dislocations that stimulate non-profit sector initiatives to address social needs in a supplementary mode, in the context of a relatively passive or unresponsive government". As various forms of foreign aid were available for NGOs in the mid-1990s, state institutions were only too happy to leave quite a few important policy fields, e.g. HIV/AIDS prevention and violent crime victim support wholly in the purview of the third sector (after 2004 these have been partially "re-nationalised" in Estonia – which appears to corroborate the "cycle theory" of Young (2000)).

From 2002 to 2007: institutionalisation of relations between government and the third sector, recognition of both economic and political roles of NGOs, serious problems with funding available to voluntary organisations

Until the beginning of the twenty-first century, relationships between the government and the third sector in Estonia developed on the basis of short-term one-off contracts and were often dependent on individual public officials who happened to support cross-sectoral cooperation. A considerable degree of political and administrative instability also influenced the hectic and random practice of cross-sectoral relations. Twelve different Cabinets were in office during the period of 1991–2007. The coalition governments have usually included at least three parties, which has tended to result in rather unstable power relations. Anyone who has experienced the "prisoner's dilemma" type of relationships knows that building trust requires a certain level of stability. Since trust can only arise as a result of repeated interaction between the same partners, a constant change of partners creates a context that effectively counteracts any partnership and network building (Peters, 1998; Milward and Provan, 2000). Additional difficulties emerge from the fact that the decentralised Estonian public sector is characterised by a wide diversity of working methods and development levels (Randma-Liiv, 2005). Although several public organisations have involved various interest groups and NGOs in their decision-making process, these one-off arrangements should still be viewed as "pocket developments" which do not have a considerable effect on the cross-sectoral relations.

In this situation, the biggest Estonian NGO umbrella organisations perceived the need for a more systematic and organised way of cooperation with the state. As it appeared useless to develop relationships with individual politicians and top civil servants, whose office terms usually tended to be rather short, the aims were set at a greater institutionalisation of the relations between government and the third sector. The main reason for the preparation of the Estonian Civil Society Development Concept (EKAK) was the need to create a shared basis of understanding for the cooperation between the public and the non-profit sectors and to consolidate basic recognition for the non-profit sector as a whole. The issue of third sector finances was of great importance, especially taking into account the absence of transparency in schemes governing the funding of non-profit organisations from public budgets, and the increasing sense of financial crisis among Estonian NGOs following the departure of important foreign donors.

Meanwhile the political and administrative elites had gradually started to recognise the challenge of moving from the practices of early transition years, during which new policies and programmes had to be adopted immediately, to more careful preparation and evaluation of new policy initiatives that required cross-sectoral partnership. The policy-making process had thus become more transparent, creating new and easier-to-understand channels for NGOs wishing to become involved in decision-making. The accession to the European Union in

2004 has also had a positive effect on cross-sectoral consultations since several EU instruments (e.g. the White Paper on European Governance of 2001, the Mandelkern Report of 2001) require the policy-making processes to include a consultation of stakeholders.

Preparation of the Estonian Civil Society Development Concept

The initial idea of the Estonian Civil Society Development Concept was developed within the framework of the cooperation project of the UNDP and the Estonian government titled "Strengthening Estonian NGOs' Sustainability" (1998–2000). The project was coordinated by the widest-recognised umbrella organisation of Estonian NGOs, the Network of Estonian Non-Profit Organisations (NENO). In the course of legal and accountancy consultations provided to a large number of NGOs, consultants started discussing the idea of preparing a strategic document for cooperation between NGOs and the government. The main reasons behind this idea included the need expressed by the NGOs consulted for a clear framework and standards of cooperation with the government and an access to decision-making over public budgets.

After several meetings among NENO, the non-profit leaders, social scientists and civil servants, the initial plan emerged to use the format of a national strategy passed by the Estonian parliament *Riigikogu*. The project team presented the idea to the members of the *Riigikogu* in June 1999. These presentations succeeded in securing the acceptance and support of a number of leading MPs as a result of which initial talks were launched for the preparation of a cooperation memorandum between the largest Estonian non-profit umbrella organisations and all interested political parties. It should be mentioned at this point that the parliamentary elections of March 1999 had brought to power a coalition of progressive political parties (and their energetic democratically oriented leaders). Explicit support of the leaders of these political parties was crucial for the initiation of the preparation of the EKAK.

As a result of the introduction of the British Compact during the visit of the representatives of the British National Council for Voluntary Organisations to Estonia, the British Compact was found to constitute a suitable format for Estonia. The NENO team then successfully applied to amend the joint project between UNDP and the Estonian government. As a result, the goals and actions of the project were refocussed from providing consultations to individual NGOs to the drafting of the EKAK. Under the amendment, the remaining funds of the project (approximately US$90,000) were allocated almost entirely to the drafting process.

Since the drafting of the EKAK was supported by Estonian political leaders, there were no restrictions to its rapid progress. As a result, in December 1999 ten biggest NGO umbrella organisations and all of the ten political parties represented in the *Riigikogu* of the time signed a Cooperation Memorandum that expressed the commitment of its signatories to the elaboration of the EKAK and the formation of a Cooperation Chamber bringing together Estonia's political parties and third sector umbrella organisations. The provision of the closing article of the memorandum was a landmark sign of changing perceptions of the relationship between the public and the non-profit sectors: "The dialogue between political parties and non-profit associations is aimed at developing a new understanding of the relationship between the public and the non-profit sectors in today's democratic society and at achieving a substantive growth of civic initiative".

The preparation process of the EKAK can be divided into two main periods. The first dates from the elaboration of the first draft until its rejection by the *Riigikogu* in spring 2000. The second includes the preparation of a new draft by a small expert group, followed by public debate, the acceptance of the draft by the National NGO Roundtable, and its ultimate adoption in the *Riigikogu* in 2002.

During the first period, a coordinating body was formed by the leaders of NGO umbrella organisations, chaired by a project coordinator appointed by the NENO. Eight loosely connected working groups were established and assigned the task of preparing the different thematic parts of the EKAK. However, serious substantive conflicts arose between two different schools of thought within the non-profit sector. The first supported a broad and more Anglo-American based approach to NGOs as the basic framework of the EKAK. The other tried to lean the draft towards a more limited view of the third sector, with special attention given to cooperative associations (mainly agricultural). The cooperative movement has its historical roots in the First Republic of Estonia (especially in the 1930s) when cooperatives were rather widespread and received lavish support from the government. Despite the fundamental disagreements outlined above, both groups basically agreed on the need to cooperate with public authorities.

However, conflicts not only between these different approaches to the third sector but primarily between various NGO leaders soon poisoned the collaborative atmosphere in and between the working groups and the project coordinator. As a result, the initial draft of the EKAK lacked clear vision and backbone. Because of contradictions over the basic push of the document as well as insufficient coordination skills and a lack of substantive expertise in drafting it, the first draft presented to the Culture Committee of the *Riigikogu* in April 2000 was rejected by the MPs as inadequate. The Committee's criticism of the document was devastating (minutes of the Committee of Cultural Affairs sitting of 18 April 2000):

MARJU LAURISTIN: … My criticism starts from the fact that everything is turned on its head in this draft … One cannot say that it is a task of the state to create civil society. This would run against the very concept of civil society …

PEETER KREITZBERG: Such concepts should be formulated with the utmost care. To begin with, it ought to be elementary to correct simple misprints.

The Culture Committee suggested that another draft version of the EKAK be prepared, this time with the help of academic experts.

This fiasco caused a crisis in project management and by September 2000 had resulted in the replacement of the project leader and of the Executive Director of the NENO. The new leadership of the NENO and the new project coordinator decided to prepare a new draft from the scratch and to reorganise the entire drafting process. Instead of the previous system of working groups consisting of voluntary members whose output would not be subjected to revisions by a competent editorial body, a small drafting group of independent and internationally recognised experts was formed. After a month of intensive work the new draft was published in the nationwide daily *Eesti Päevaleht*. It was also sent to 3,000 NGOs by email. In order to introduce the ideas of the Concept and to discuss these with different NGOs and public officials, 15 regional roundtables with a total of approximately 400 participants were organised all over Estonia (Liiv, 2001). The ideas proposed in these meetings as revised by the expert group became the basis for amendments to the draft. In addition, a number of experts were asked to conduct a study on cross-sectoral expectations and views in Estonia (Ruutsoo *et al.*, 2004), the outcomes of which were introduced to the *Riigikogu* (the Constitutional Law Committee, the Cultural Affairs Committee and the Social Affairs Committee) together with the new draft in December 2000. As a result, the new draft was accepted by the MPs as a suitable basis for opening the debate.

Meanwhile the former project coordinator and the former Executive Director of NENO distanced themselves from the project and together with a few umbrella organisations made an attempt to amend the rejected draft and to regain control of the process. To clarify such power struggles, the NENO organised the first National Roundtable of Estonian NGOs which became a major public forum for Estonian non-profit organisations. The draft of the EKAK was approved by the representatives of more than 220 non-profit organisations of the Roundtable in February 2001. The support of the National Roundtable gave final legitimacy to the new draft and, after the necessary editing, it was officially entered on the parliament's agenda in April 2001. According to the resolution of the Speaker of the *Riigikogu*, it was then assigned as a matter of national importance to the Committees of Cultural Affairs, of Constitutional Law and of Social Affairs for preparing the debate of the full House. In October 2001 the above-mentioned committees arranged a public hearing of the EKAK and formed a small editorial committee consisting of two representatives of NGOs and two MPs from each committee in order to prepare the final text of the document.

The substance of the EKAK did not change much in the *Riigikogu* since the MPs involved supported the preservation of the partnership approach and backed the majority of ideas proposed by the third sector. At the same time three significant amendments were introduced. First, the structure of the text was changed by replacing the sections setting out the different characteristics of both sectors by a single section focussing on their common ground. By that, reference to most of the features exclusively characteristic of the non-profit sector were eliminated from the document. Second, MPs tried to avoid specific implementation promises. MP Paul-Eerik Rummo, chief rapporteur of the matter in the final reading in the *Riigikogu* gave the following reasons for this position: "Giving a highly detailed list of specific steps is not an appropriate style in strategic documents. Hence, in order to make the implementation of the Concept more flexible we have edited out all such specific references throughout the document" (minutes of the *Riigikogu* plenary sitting of 12 December 2002). As a result, in regard to matters of representation of the non-profit sector in the main implementing body of the EKAK, the document was worded in the most general terms; all references to specific implementation activities were deleted and replaced by general guidelines. Third, the wording of the EKAK was changed by deleting the purportedly leftist concepts (such as "social capital" and "social cohesion") and emphasising a more liberal and individualistic approach towards civil society. References to state support for NGOs were effectively eliminated and replaced by an emphasis on voluntary action by citizens. These amendments resulted from the prevalently liberal political orientation of the majority of MPs working with the text of the EKAK. Despite the amendments, the document preserved its initial values of partnership and participatory democracy. The EKAK was debated and adopted by the *Riigikogu* on 12 December 2002.

The EKAK brought into public debate the issues of effective cooperation between public bodies and NGOs, and relations between the state and civil society. Lagerspetz (2003) describes the drafting process of the EKAK one in which the Estonian NGOs defined themselves, their relations with the public sector, their relations with each other and their overall role in society for the first time in Estonian history. It is therefore difficult to underestimate the role of the EKAK in developing and systematising the roles of various actors in the new Estonian democracy.

It is interesting to note that the Executive did not have any role in the preparation process of the EKAK. The possibility of a systematic involvement of the Executive was discussed in the initial phase of the preparation of the EKAK but finally rejected due to several reasons. As the events immediate preceding the drafting of the EKAK in Estonia had proved, coalition governments were only able to stay in power for a short time and there was always the danger that a new one would take a different view of the project. The parliament, on the other hand, was seen as capable of giving an enduring guarantee to the stability of the approach eventually decided. It was also expected that discussions in the *Riigikogu* would secure the EKAK and the non-profit sector the public attention that both needed. All necessary resources for the preparation of the EKAK had to be secured by the non-profit sector itself. Most of these were found through the cooperation project with the UNDP as well as through the Baltic–American Partnership Program. Consequently, the EKAK was initiated, prepared and accepted not because of the Executive but despite it.

Implementation of the EKAK

Since compacts are not legally binding documents, implementation is of key importance in any compact process. The authority of a compact is derived from its endorsement by the government and, through the consultation process involved, by the voluntary sector itself (Plowden, 2003: 423). The successful implementation of compacts is likely to depend on the bodies and institutions designated to carry out specific implementation tasks and on the readiness and commitment of their members to proactively tackle potential problems. Also, the resources allocated for the implementation process are likely to be a major determinant of the success of the compact.

The adoption of the EKAK was considered the starting point of a long-term process of developing partnership between the government and the third sector. However, the absence of the Estonian Executive in the preparation of the EKAK caused problems of awareness, ownership and commitment on the part of the Executive. After the general elections of March 2003, the new coalition decided to authorise the Minister for Regional Affairs to deal with matters concerning civil society (including the implementation of the EKAK). The first step taken by the Minister was to convene the Joint Committee of representatives of the public and the third sectors. Initially, the Joint Committee formed three working groups: one to deal with legislative matters, one with finances and statistics, and one with civic education. The working group of finances and statistics was later renamed the sustainability working group. The work of the Joint Committee was to be supported and coordinated by the Department of Local Government and Regional Administration of the Ministry of Interior.

The nomination of non-profit sector representatives to the Joint Committee became a rather sensitive issue. The draft EKAK submitted to the *Riigikogu* had proposed that the National Roundtable of Estonian NGOs should nominate the representatives of the sector. However, because of the novelty of the Roundtable, this article was deleted without introducing any specific provisions governing membership of the Joint Commitee in its place. It allowed the Executive to draw up its own list of possible NGO representatives by asking ministries to name organisations they would like to see represented in the Committee. Consequently, the initial list consisted mainly of the representatives of NGO umbrella organisations closely cooperating with the ministries on specific issues. Naturally, no "trouble-maker" NGOs were included. Similarly, no NGOs dealing with the general issues of the non-profit sector appeared on the initial list because they had no "partner Minister" to propose them. As a result, the NGOs which had played a leading role in the preparation of the EKAK opposed this arrangement and eventually achieved a few seats on the Committee as a compromise solution. Personal appointments of representatives were left to the discretion of the selected NGOs.

The issue of representation is often complicated in the non-profit sector. Even in old democracies with strong and widely recognised third sector organisations, this problem has been difficult to solve (Phillips, 2003). In transitional societies with a number of new and ambitious NGOs, and with no widely recognised and proven umbrella organisations, the representation is even more complicated (see also Toftisova, 2005: 14). Such a top-down nomination of NGO representatives created a situation where the Estonian third sector was represented in a crucial decision-making body mainly by government-friendly individuals, some of whom lacked both the interest as well as the knowledge and skills to influence decisions. As one NGO leader put it: "Some of the non-profit members (of the Committee) have never contributed to the discussion or said anything sensible. A few of them do not even participate in the meetings or working groups of the Committee" (interview with an NGO leader, 30 July 2006). A civil servant sitting on the Joint Committee claimed that:

> until 2006 there were no rules in the Committee by-laws on how to replace a member in case he or she does not participate. In practice we are in dire need of such a mechanism because some of the NGO representatives do not participate or are not capable of participating in the work of the Committee. In case of civil servants it is easy to ask the respective Ministers to make replacements.
>
> (interview with a public official, 4 April 2006)

The main concern with the Government membership in the Joint Committee was twofold. First, quite a few public institutions failed to nominate their representatives, most likely due to a lack of interest and motivation. Second, the ministerial nominees to the Joint Committee tended to be low-rank civil servants with no actual decision-making power. Moreover, some of them were: "definitely not overly excited about being nominated to the Committee and took to their membership of this Committee as a ballet dancer would take to milking a cow", as one of the NGO leaders put it (interview with an NGO leader, 30 July 2006). As a result, there was considerable turnover among the members of the Joint Committee during the first two years of its sessions.

The situation with representatives of the Executive in the Joint Committee changed radically in the first half of 2006. Finally, all ministries were able to nominate their representatives, and the civil service rank of these increased substantially. As expressed by a member of the Joint Committee, "in most cases new government representatives have had already some experience of working with NGOs and at least hold some sway in the issues" (interview with a public official, 4 April 2006). In addition, as one NGO representative remarked:

> some of the initial government representatives have already made rather impressive careers and are approaching top-rank positions in their ministries with considerable power and influence. And because of the EU rules requiring extensive consultations in the decision-making process, these officials, despite their limited knowledge of the matter, have suddenly become the most informed persons in their ministries on cooperation issues, approached by everybody else for advice.
>
> (interview with a public official, 4 April 2006)

It has been observed that the gap between formal acts and procedures on the one hand and their actual implementation on the other represents a far-reaching problem in most post-communist countries (Verheijen, 1998). Indeed, already in the first meeting of the Joint Committee, one of the leading principles of the EKAK – partnership between the two sectors – was called into question. The proposal to introduce a co-chairmanship of the Committee was rejected by officials and the Minister for Regional Affairs was appointed single Chair. In order to counterbalance this scheme, parity co-chairmanships of individual working groups were created.

During the first two years, the actual work of the Committee was dominated by a few widely recognised NGO leaders who actively participated in the preparation process of the EKAK and became co-chairmen of working groups. They set up an initial agenda and secured the preparation and implementation of the first Action Plan for 2004–2006. In an interview given to the authors of this paper, one of the active NGO leaders confided that:

> there was nothing to be expected from the civil servants since the vast majority of them did not have any inkling of and understanding for the issues. After the first meeting it was clear that we had to assume responsibility and start tackling the issues … Fortunately, the civil servants trusted us. Some of them were quick learners and soon became genuine supporters of the EKAK ideas.
>
> (interview with an NGO leader, 24 July 2006)

It is difficult to assess the first results of the EKAK since the first Action Plan has not run its course yet. The focus of the first years of implementating the EKAK has been on carrying out an analysis of the general situation of NGOs, and on specifying the tasks for the following years. Consequently, a number of surveys and studies have been conducted on third sector statistics, on the indicators for measuring the implementation of the EKAK, the finances of the third sector, on voluntary work, non-registrable informal associations, umbrella organisations and participation in the decision-making process. However, perhaps the most important outcome of the implementation process, one that can be observed already at the time of writing this paper is the fact that the government has gradually started to recognise the need for cooperation with the non-profit sector. Additionally, organised events have been launched to honour voluntary work and volunteers. A document titled "Best Practices in Community Involvement" has been drawn up in collaboration with the State Chancellery. This project is important because it is among the few that cover all ministries and is supported by the Prime Minister personally. The least developed field has been that of the promotion of civic education where very little progress has been achieved so far.

Two structural problems have come to the fore during the implementation process. Gradually, members of the Joint Committee have lost their initial enthusiasm for:

making beautiful plans for activities for which no funds were allocated and no plans for future allocations existed ... The money allocated for the work of the Joint Committee covers only the cost of our correspondence and of tea for Committee meetings. The funding fails even to buy sugar for the tea.

(interview with an NGO leader, 18 September 2006)

The work in the Joint Committee has proceeded on a voluntary basis which has made it very difficult to get the best and the brightest to join in. In 2006, less than €45,000 was allocated from the national budget for the implementation of the EKAK. This sum is even less than that granted annually for the EKAK by the non-governmental Baltic–American Partnership Program. Another structural problem concerns coordination within the non-profit sector since the NGO representatives on the Joint Committee have distanced themselves from the Representative Council of the National Roundtable of NGOs because of excessive workload. By that an important link between the Roundtable and the Joint Committee has been severed, and the importance of the Rountable as a representative body of non-profit sector in the framework of the EKAK implementation process reduced considerably.

A major change in the implementation of the EKAK took place in the first half of 2006 when the Executive rolled out an initiative of its own, announcing the preparation of the Agenda for Supporting Civic Initiative in 2007–10. On the one hand, the Agenda can be seen as a success of the EKAK process – for first time the Executive itself has recognised that cooperation with the non-profit sector is an important political topic and should be accorded corresponding attention. On the other hand, the Agenda is rather limited in its scope. It merely lists the existing functional tasks of government departments, chiefly in matters of regional development, which have very little to do with civic initiative and the political roles of NGOs. It is in effect a step backwards because it tries again to limit the role of NGOs to service provision. The Agenda is taking the necessary attention (and funding) away from the EKAK, and NGOs do not see much they can do to influence it. The new situation was reflected by a very low number of amendments proposed by the NGOs to the Agenda, a vast majority of which were not accepted either. Thus, on the one hand, the leaders of NGOs feel that the situation is changing and now is an important moment to shape future developments but on the other they often express views such as:

I just do not have the energy and will to fight this inadequate Agenda. We do not even understand what the Agenda means in the context of the work of the Joint Committee. Let's hope that the new Government will change the Agenda after the 2007 general elections.

(interview with an NGO leader, 18 September 2006)

The authors can here only agree with Eva Kuti, who writes that:

in most Eastern European countries there are several explicit and implicit government policies influencing non-profit organisations, and they often lack consistency. The explicit, publicly expressed policy can be supportive. But at the same time, the practical measures and implicit policies developed at different policy levels may be harmful for the non-profit community.

(Kuti, 2001: 194)

Lessons learned

The institutionalisation of relationships between the Estonian public and the non-profit sectors has not only contributed to the cross-sectoral partnership but also helped the government and the society to build an understanding of the nature of the third sector. Consequently, in addition to the specific objectives of the EKAK, a few broader goals have been achieved as well. In this respect, the entire process of preparing and implementing of the EKAK holds various lessons which might be useful for other, especially post-communist countries who are planning to institutionalise the partnerships between their public sectors and non-profit organisations.

- Many politicians and senior civil servants in post-communist societies are not ready to discuss true partnership between the non-profit and the public sectors because of their insufficient civic education and poor understanding of the basic principles of governance. Therefore, it is crucial to find individual supporters in the top ranks of decision-makers. Trust and relational capital (Capello and Faggian, 2005: 77) seem to be of key importance in developing and institutionalising cross-sectoral partnership. As evidenced by the Estonian case, the genuine supporters of partnership among politicians and senior civil servants tend to have intellectual or academic backgrounds or a personal link to NGOs.
- The internal diversity within the non-profit sector, the lack of sector-wide cooperation as well as the problems of authority to represent the entire sector may complicate negotiations with the public sector. Power struggles within the non-profit sector, when rendered public, may considerably undermine the legitimacy of that sector and cast a shadow of doubt on the whole process of reaching an agreement. On the other hand, the institutionalisation process forces individual NGOs as well as their umbrella organisations to look for common ground and to clarify their values, roles and identity. The preparation and implementation of a compact can be seen as a litmus test telling the progressive and constructive NGO opinion leaders from specific lobbies, and is likely to contribute to the rise of new NGO leaders.
- As also indicated by Morison (2000: 125), the institutionalisation of relations between government and the third sector serves as a learning opportunity for both parties by allowing them to take a closer look at the values, interests, strategies, people, financing, internal problems as well as the "language" of each other. Thus, it is not only the ultimate goal of signing a compact that is important, but also the very process of elaborating one and implementing it. Hence, for the purposes of learning, but also for

the consistency of implementation, the creation of a widely perceived sense of "ownership" should be strived for. This can be attained by gradually involving as many politicians, civil servants and NGO leaders as possible in the process of preparing the compact.

- Partnership with NGOs is not likely to be among the top priorities of politicians. Consequently, an important challenge for NGO leaders is to learn to play effectively on the short-term interests of politicians and to push the institutionalisation process towards yielding tangible results by consistently covering the issue in the mass media and systematically applying pressure to politicans to advance it. An important tool for introducing the non-profit sector to politicians is the use of reliable data on NGOs. As the statistics on NGOs are poor in most post-communist countries with the exception of Hungary (Kuti, 2001: 194–195), it is essential to improve these and to create a comprehensive register of non-profit organisations. This would provide policy-makers and NGOs themselves with information about the size, scope, structure of and developments in the third sector.
- The transparency of third sector finances is one of the most burning issues for both sectors (Kuti, 2001: 194; Regulska, 2001: 189). It may become the main stimulus for dialogue on and the institutionalisation of cross-sectoral relationships. The withdrawal of foreign aid for NGOs in post-communist countries (Kuti, 2001: 198) substantially affects the funds available for the non-profit sectors which, in turn, makes them more dependent on the state.
- The implementation of a compact requires both human and financial resources, especially during the first years (Elson, 2006: 41) of the process. Ample amounts of both types of resources will be needed to carry out the necessary training, prepare specific guidelines for cross-sectoral cooperation, develop sub-documents of the "compact" (e.g. Best Practices in Outsourcing Public Services, Best Practices in Community Involvement, Principles of Funding Civic Associations from the National Budget, Strategic Plans for Voluntary Action), introduction of best practices, carrying out pilot projects, and monitoring the entire implementation process. A central, knowledgeable and influential implementation body is an important prerequisite for successful implementation of a compact (Elson, 2006: 40).
- Finally, the EU accession has considerably contributed to civil servants' understanding of the involvement of NGOs in the policy-making process. Consultative decision-making policies of the EU have made civil servants more motivated in institutionalising government–third sector relationships.

Summary

This chapter analyses the relationships between the public and the non-profit sectors in post-communist societies using the example of Estonia. Estonia is among the few countries which have institutionalised the relationship between the public and the non-profit sectors by elaborating the Estonian Civil Society Development Concept in 2002. The authors investigated the preparation and implementation of the EKAK with a focus on the "process" of institutionalisation rather than its substantive issues. The preparation of the EKAK was explored by analysing the motives and the very start of the drafting process, the interests and differences of opinion in the government and the third sector itself. The analysis of the implementation of the EKAK was carried out for the period from 2002 to 2006. Issues related to the organisation of the central cooperation body and the representation of the Executive and the third sector, the formulation of the working agenda as well as the financing of the cooperation were discussed. The paper concludes by highlighting several problems affecting cross-sectoral partnership in both the public and the non-profit sector, and by providing relevant advice which could be useful for other (post-communist) countries which aim to institutionalise the relationship between their governments and the third sector.

Note

1 The full text of the Civil Society Development Concept is available on the website: www.ngo.ee/7337.

References

Anheier, H.K. and Seibel, W. (1998) The Nonprofit Sector and the Transformation of Societies: A Comparative Analysis of East Germany, Poland, and Hungary in W. Powell and E. Clemens (eds) *Private Action and the Public Good*, New Haven & London: Yale University Press, 177–189.

Brock, K.L. (2000) The Devil's in the Detail: The Chrétien Legacy for the Third Sector. *Review of Constitutional Studies*, 9:(1&2), 263–282.

Brock, K.L. (2001) State, Society and the Third Sector: Changing to Meet New Challenges. *Journal of Canadian Studies*, 35:4, 203–220.

Bullain, N. and Toftisova, R. (2005) A Comparative Analysis of European Policies and Practices of NGO-Government Cooperation. *International Journal of Not-For-Profit Law*, 7:4, 64–112.

Capello, R. and Faggian, A. (2005) Collective Learning and Relational Capital in Local Innovation Processes. *Regional Studies*, 39:1, 75–87.

Casey, J. (2004) Third Sector Participation in the Policy Process: A Framework for Comparative Analysis. *Policy and Politics*, 32:2, 241–257.

Casey, J.P. (1998) Non-Government Organizations as Policy Actors: Immigration Policies in Spain. Unpublished PhD thesis, Universitat Autònoma, Spain. Available at: http://blues.uab.es/mgp/papers/casey2.html.

Commission of the European Communities (2001) European Governance. White Paper. Brussels, 25.7.2001. COM (2001) 428 final.

Craig, G., Taylor, M. and Parkes, T. (2004) Protest or Partnership? The Voluntary and Community Sectors in the Policy Process. *Social Policy & Administration*, 38:3, 221–239.

Craig, G., Taylor, M. and Wilkinson, M. (2002) Co-option or Empowerment? The changing Relationship between the State and the Voluntary and Community Sectors. *Local Governance*, 28:1, 1–11.

Elson, P.R. (2006) Tracking the Implementation of Voluntary Sector-Government Policy Agreements: Is the Voluntary and Community Sector in the Frame? *International Journal of Not-For-Profit Law*, 8:4, 34–49.

Gidron, B., Kramer, R.M. and Salamon, L.M. (1992) *Government and the Third Sector: Emerging Relationships in Welfare States*. San Francisco: Jossey-Bass Publishers.

Götz, N. and Hackmann, J. (2003) Civil Society in the Baltic Sea Region: Towards a Hybrid Theory in N. Götz and J. Hackmann (eds) *Civil Society in the Baltic Sea Region*. Aldershot, Burlington: Ashgate, 3–16.

Howard, M.M. (2003) *The Weakness of Civil Society in Post-Communist Europe*. Cambridge: Cambridge University Press.

Human Development Report (1999) *Civil Society Resources in the Modernization of Estonia*, 36–40.

Jenei, G. and Kuti, E. (2003) Duality in the Third Sector. The Hungarian Case. *The Asian Journal of Public Administration*, 25:1, 133–157.

Jenei, G. and Vari, A. (2000) Partnership between Local Government and the Local Community in the Area of Social Policy: an Hungarian Experience. *Public Management*, 2:2, 239–249.

Kramer, R. (1981) *Voluntary Agencies in the Welfare State*. Berkeley: University of California Press.

Kramer, R., Lorentzen, H., Melief, W. and Pasquinelli, S. (1993) *Privatization in Four European Countries: Comparative Studies in Government-Third Sector Relationships*. Armonk: M.E. Sharpe.

Kuti, È. (1992) Scylla and Charybdis in the Hungarian Nonprofit Sector in S. Kuhnle and P. Selle (eds) *Government and Voluntary Organizations: A Relational Perspective*. Aldershot: Avebury, 185–197.

Kuti, È. (1996) *The Nonprofit Sector in Hungary*. Manchester and New York: Manchester University Press.

Kuti, È. (1997) Hungary in L. Salamon and H. Anheier (eds) *Defining the Nonprofit Sector: a Cross-National Analysis*. Manchester and New York: Manchester University Press, 469–492.

Kuti, È. (2001) Different Eastern European Countries at Different Crossroads in H. Anheier and J. Kendall (eds) *Third Sector Policy at the Crossroads*. London and New York: Routledge, 193–202.

Lagerspetz, M. (2003) From NGOs to Civil Society: A Learning Process. *University and College Level Third Sector Studies in Countries of Central and Eastern Europe*. Budapest, The Third Sector Studies in Central and Eastern Europe International Academic Network, 81–91.

Lauristin, M. and Vihalemm, P. (1997) Recent Historical Developments in Estonia: Three Stages of Transition (1987–1997) in M. Lauristin, P. Vihalemm, K. E. Rosengren and L. Weibul (eds) *Return to the Western World: Cultural and Political Perspectives on the Estonian Post-Communist Transition.* Tartu: Tartu University Press, 73–126.

Liiv, D. (2001) Koostöökokkulepped Suurbritannias ja mida meil on neist õppida [Compacts between the Government and the Third Sector in the UK and what we can Learn from them]. *Riigikogu Toimetised*, 3, 261–266.

Lomax, B. (1997) The Strange Death of "Civil Society" in Post-Communist Hungary. *Journal of Communist Studies and Transition Politic*, 3:1, 41–63.

Mandelkern Group on Better Regulation. Final Report. 13 November 2001. www.better-regulation.ie/attached_files/upload/static/1145.pdf.

Memorandum of Co-operation between Estonian Political Parties and Third Sector Umbrella Organisations (2000). *Riigikogu Toimetised*, 1, 258.

Milward, H.B. and Provan, K.G. (2000) Governing the Hollow State. *Journal of Public Administration Research and Theory*, 10:2, 359–379.

Morison, J. (2000) The Government-Voluntary Sector Compacts: Governance, Governmentality, and Civil Society. *Journal of Law and Society*, 27:1, 98–132.

Osborne, S.P. and Kapośvari, A. (1998) Nongovernmental Organizations, Local Government and the Development of Social Services: Managing Social Needs in Postcommunist Hungary. *Discussion Papers* No. 4. Budapest: CEU/OSI.

Osborne, S.P. and McLaughlin, K. (2002) Trends and Issues in the Implementation of Local "Voluntary Sector Compacts" in England. *Public Money & Management*, 22:1, 55–63.

Peters, G.B. (1998) Managing Horizontal Government: The Politics of Co-ordination. *Public Administration*, 76, Summer, 295–311.

Phillips, S. (2003) In Accordance: Canada's Voluntary Sector Accord from Idea to Implementation in K. L. Brock (ed.) *Delicate Dances: Public Policy and the Nonprofit Sector.* Montreal and Kingston: McGill – Queen's University Press.

Phillips, S. and Levasseur, K. (2004) The Snakes and Ladders of Accountability: Contradictions between Contracting and Collaboration for Canada's Voluntary Sector. *Canadian Public Administration*, 47:4, 451–474.

Phillips, S.D. (2001) More than Stakeholders: Reforming State-Voluntary Sector Relations. *Journal of Canadian Studies*, 35:4, 182–202.

Phillips, S.D. (2003) Voluntary Sector-Government Relations in Transition: Learning from International Experience for the Canadian Context in K.L. Brock (ed.) *Delicate Dances: Public Policy and the Nonprofit Sector.* Montreal and Kingston: McGill – Queen's University Press, 17–70.

Plowden, W. (2003) The Compact: Attempts to Regulate Relationships Between Government and the Voluntary Sector in England. *Nonprofit and Voluntary Sector Quarterly*, 32:3, 415–438.

Randma-Liiv, T. (2005) Performance Management in Transitional Administration: Introduction of Pay-for-Performance in the Estonian Civil Service. *Journal of Comparative Policy Analysis*, 7:1, 95–115.

Regulska, J. (2001) NGOs and their Vulnerabilities during the Time of Transition: the Case of Poland in H. Anheier and J. Kendall (eds) *Third Sector Policy at the Crossroads*. London and New York: Routledge, 183–192.

Reiman, H. (1933) Ühingud vaimse kultuuri alal [Cultural Associations]. *Eesti Statistika*, No. 2, 189–198.

Ruutsoo, R. (1996) The Emergence of Civil Society in Estonia 1987–1994 in R. Blom, H. Melin and J. Nikula (eds) *Between Plan and Market Social Change in the Baltic States and Russia*. Berlin and New York: de Gruyter, 97–121.

Ruutsoo, R. (2002) *Civil Society and Nation Building in Estonia and the Baltic States: Impact of Traditions on Mobilization and Transition 1986–2000 – Historical and Sociological Study*. Rovaniemi: Lapin Yliopisto.

Ruutsoo, R., Rikmann, E. and Lagerspetz, M. (2004) A Broadening Debate: Is the Estonian Society Ready for Civic Initiative? in M. Lagerspetz, A. Trummal, R. Ruutsoo and E. Rikmann *Non-Profit Sector and the Consolidation of Democracy: Studies on the Development of Civil Society in Estonia*. Tallinn, Avatud Eesti Fond: Greif OÜ, 48–85.

Salamon, Lester M. (1987) Partners in Public Service: The Scope and Theory of Nonprofit Relations in W.W. Powell (ed.) *The Nonprofit Sector – A Research Handbook*. New Haven and London: Yale University Press, 99–117.

Salamon, Lester M. (1995*) Partners in Public Service: Government-Nonprofit Relations in the Modern Welfare State*. Baltimore: The Johns Hopkins University Press.

Svetlik, I. (1992) The Voluntary Sector in a Post-communist Country: the Case of Slovenia in S. Kuhnle and P. Selle (eds) *Government and Voluntary Organizations: A Relational Perspective*. Aldershot: Avebury, 198–210.

Taylor, M. and Bassi, A. (1998) Unpacking the State: The Implications for the Third Sector of Changing Relationships Between National and Local Government. *Voluntas*; 9:2, 113–136.

Taylor, M. and Lewis, J. (1997) Contracting: What does it do to Voluntary and Nonprofit Organisations in P.6 and J. Kendall (eds) *The Contract Culture in Public Services: Studies from Britain, Europe and the USA*. Aldershot: Arena, Avebury.

Taylor, M. and Warburton, D. (2003) Legitimacy and the Role of UK Third Sector Organizations in the Policy Process. *Voluntas*, 14:3, 321–338.

Taylor, M., Craig, G. and Wilkinson, M. (2002) Co-option or Empowerment? The Changing Relationship between the State and the Voluntary and Community Sectors. *Local Governance*, 28:1, 1–11.

Toftisova, R. (2005) Implementation of NGO-Government Cooperation Policy Documents: Lessons Learned. *International Journal of Not-For-Profit Law*, 8:1, 11–41.

Verheijen, T. (1998) Public Management in Central and Eastern Europe: the Nature of the Problem in T. Verheijen and D. Coombes (eds) *Innovations in Public Management: Perspectives from East and West Europe*. Cheltenham: Edward Elgar, 207–219.

Young, D.R. (2000) Alternative Models of Government-Nonprofit Sector Relations: Theoretical and International Perspectives. *Nonprofit and Voluntary Sector Quarterly*, 29:1, 149–172.

The study for this chapter was supported by the Estonian Target Financing grant no. SF0140094s08 and by the Estonia Science Foundation grant no. 7441.

Part VII

The rise of hybrid organizations

15 Hybrid organisations

Background, concept, challenges

Adalbert Evers

Introduction

The word "hybrid" means that elements which usually do not go together or belong to different spheres get intertwined within one organisational being. In recent years the author of this contribution together with (see Evers and Laville 2004) or parallel to other colleagues (see Brandsen *et al.* 2005) has taken up this notion in order to describe organisations that in a way tie together characteristics, that get usually separated in state, market and third sector organisations. This contribution will in its first part sketch the background concepts and the special notion of the third sector as an intermediary sphere that is behind my concept of what hybrid organisation means. The second part of the contribution will once again summarise what I see as constitutive for hybrid organisations and clarify what difference it makes to those concepts, that draw clear demarcation lines between state, market and third sector organisations. In a third and final part open and controversial questions and challenges for further research will be sketched. Altogether this may allow for an overview on a topic I have hitherto dealt with in several publications.

Background: the third sector as an intermediary sphere

Whether it is the prefix "voluntary", "non-profit" or "independent" – there have been various theoretical and political concepts that are united in the attempt to describe their object of studies as a clear cut sector. I myself use the word "third sector" just as a working tool, indicating with this neutral label, that by using it no special theoretical link to one of the existing concepts is included.

Since the early 1990s there have been attempts to conceptualise this third sector differently (see Evers and Laville 2004a); for my contributions to this developments the word "intermediary" has been central (Evers 1995). The idea was to capture society as a whole as constituted by the interaction of basic spheres, each of them linked with some key principles: the state, the market economy and community. For some analysts, e.g. in the social policy debate, this is already all there is, for example G. Esping Anderson (2002: 11) who argues that the state, the market economy and the family – a community archetype – are the three basic "welfare pillars" of society. In contrast to that, third sector research builds on the assumption that a third sector is next to market, state and community/family as another basic cornerstone.

However, the idea behind understanding this third sector rather as an *intermediary sphere* was first of all, that in contrast to the other sectors, that are linked with ever dominating key principles, this "sector" is (at least in modern democratic market societies) more a kind of plural public space, where different values coexist. The special element that is formed in this space, deliberate association and social solidarity, is coexisting with others, like e.g. possessive individualism and rivalry. Different to that:

- the modern republican state is marked by such basic values and principles like unification and hierarchical decision-making;
- for the market economy, besides the guiding instrumental orientation, competition and the search for profit are key principles;
- for community special bonds of obligation, but as well of care and affection, are basic (see the similar parallel concept of these three basic institutions as developed by Offe 2003).

The idea behind the third sector as an intermediary sphere is, that beneath its principles of associating freely, there is always the presence and impact of the other spheres just mentioned: associations get guaranteed and regulated by *state* law; as soon as they offer goods and services, their "social economy" is exposed to the *market* economy principles and finally some associations and their organisations are after all not so voluntary at all – being enshrined in religious traditions, ethnicity and the respective *communities*. This all makes up, as it has been argued, for a special degree of plurality and diversity to be found in this public space; the social field of the intermediary sphere beyond the core areas of state, market and community is marked by all kind of intertwining and balances between solidaristic and associational values, quests for unity and diversity, efficiency and expression, by attempts to cultivate communities and to break up with them.

Up until today there is – except in economics – little theory of a "third sector". Due to this and the nearness of the third sector to what is debated as the "civil society" one has been tempted to merger or nearly identify third sector and civil society (for the notion of a "civil society sector" see Salamon and Anheier 1997b). In this chapter I will not go into the problems of such an attempt. It should instead of that once again be enumerated what makes the concept of the third sector as an intermediary public sphere different from other concepts and viewpoints:

- It is suggested, to see the third sector in contrast to the other poles or sectors as being not to the same degree marked by a central principle; it is rather the enormous plurality and diversity of orientations and organisational forms and principles that springs to the eye.

- The impulses that come from the poles of the state, the market and the world of communities are highlighted, attention is given to their very presence in the third sector; however, vice versa from the public space and the third sector as well impulses can go to the other sectors, e.g. softening and liberalising formerly "strong" communities, establishing a more participatory state-structure or affecting those parts of markets, that are more socially and locally embedded as most of the others.
- The diverse third sector organisations in a field under opposed influences are often unstable and/or changing; sometimes their history is marked by trajectories where they, for example spring off a local community and end up near to a ministry or the marketplace.
- Finally, rather than speaking of a sector with clear demarcation lines one should be aware of the grey zones, where it is unclear, where public principles end and the privacy of community begins and where the outskirts of state–public institutions are to be found nearby third sector organisations, with each side operating in firm partnership; therefore sphere is more accurate than sector.

It should be remembered that such an analytical perspective is at some points at odds with the most widespread concept of the third sector, the one that has been developed in the context of the Johns Hopkins research and its impressive international measurements of third sectors (Salamon and Anheier 1997a). The Johns Hopkins concept is, by the way, not a theoretical but a classificatory approach, that tries to demarcate the third sector by a number of characteristics of the organisations that make it up. When compared with the analytical perspective sketched above, three issues are controversial, each of them having to do with the intermingling between the third and the other "sectors"

The most widespread controversy has been about the demarcation line towards the (market) economy. The "non-distribution constraint", used by the Johns Hopkins approach, basically says that no surplus is to be distributed among members (in order to prevent a for-profit-orientation). From the perspective sketched above the core issue is a different one. What counts here is the degree, the influence from other sides can restrict and counterbalance for-profit logics; the real issue would then be the political and social embeddedness, or, in a more limited view, the type of governance of a third sector economy (Borzaga and Mittone 1997). As long as its embeddedness and governance guarantees that it is not-for-profit in the first place, it may well make profits.

A less perceived controversy is about state–third sector interrelationships; it pictures in different ideas of the third sector as part of civil society. While in a sectorial perspective third sector organisations are an essential feature of a "civil society sector", the perspective sketched above would rather argue that a civil society is the outcome of proper interrelations and positive interactions between the foundational democratic impulses that can come from the state on the one hand (e.g. guaranteeing associations by law, assuring them status and resources) and from society (association building and volunteering) and finally community (e.g.: loyality) and even the market (e. g. entrepreneurship) on the other hand. A civil (or: a more civic) society at large is not to be identified with the special realm of civil society or a (third) sector.

Finally after mentioning issues that are concerned with the interactions of the third sector with the state and the market economy, one should not forget to look at community as well. The idea, to count into the third sector only voluntarily founded associations with democratic internal rules (as the Johns Hopkins criteria catalogue is stating) is questionable (see as well Walzer 2004 on "involuntary constraints"). Many organisations are "more or less" voluntary, like the ones near to religious organisations, ethnic groups and as well those founded on communities of class and ideology; even the more "freely chosen" ones are by their internal structure not always democratic and civil societies do allow for different types of internal organisation (see those under church law). A restrictive concept of "voluntary" organisations, as used in the Johns Hopkins classification, leaves out much of what exists outside states and markets and it has little to contribute to the present debates on multiculturalism and the role of ethnic communities in civil societies. These debates however mirror the fact that "community" and its non-voluntary and meagre democratic features have seen a "ack" in the last decades and that they can not altogether be simply cut off from a civil society and a third sector. (for example, muslim-linked educational services acting as acknowledged partners of state–public policies within the third sector). One can however argue as well on a more abstract level. From the very moment on when a community principle like "care", that is about personal interrelations, is not anymore a private but a public issue, it is an element that integrates communities at least partly into civil society.

As a final remark it should be added here, that a theoretical concept, which is more about the intermingling of spheres and principles than about the borders of sectors, has been sketched once more, because it is a first step that paves the way for a better understanding the topic of hybridisation and hybrid organisations.

Concept: hybrid organisations

One can say that the concept of hybrid organisations is a logical step, once one conceives the third sector not as a special apart phenomenon but as an intermediary field under influence, with a sometimes light, sometimes deep impact of principles, that are essential in state organisations, in the marketplace or in community life. A good point for demonstrating this by an initial example is the concept of active citizenship (see, for definitions and debate, Kymlicka 2002). By volunteering citizens the demarcation line between "third" and "state sector" is already blurred. Volunteering as active social and economic cooperation as well as by participating in public debates cross-cut institutions that belong to the state and the municipalities and to third sector organisations; they are to be found in associations but as well in schools, in municipal-owned museums as well as those that lean on a foundation. There is the principle of volunteering. But is there a voluntary sector?

Instead of summing up immediately what constitutes the analytical notion of a hybrid organisation, it might be useful to point at some practical examples that – even though taken from research in the German context (Evers *et al.* 2002) – can be found as well in other European societies. The examples demonstrate that the demarcation lines between various sectors and the principles usually tied to them are not so clear – as it has just been shown for the principle of active citizens volunteering.

- A public school offers its rooms to groups and associations in the community, makes contracts with enterprises, cultural and sport associations that take over part of the lectures; by a reform, the school can be managed like an enterprise, having its own budget, an additional management director and the right to hire and fire; given that background, the school is expected to compete with others, developing own areas of excellence etc.
- A museum, that is part of the spectre of local state-public services builds a museum shop and café, run professionally and with a clear commercial target; but a large part of the personnel are volunteers and the whole operation serves the aim to get additional resources for its global cultural mission as a public service.
- A theatre simultaneously modernises its management, upgrades the role of the support association that accompanies it by tradition, intensifies public relation work, the search for sponsorships and transforms its legal status from a municipal-owned organisation to a company with limited liability for purposes of the public good (GemGmbH); yet it stays a public and does not transform into a private for-profit organisation.
- A municipal swimming hall that would, due to financial difficulties of the municipality, otherwise have been closed, changes its legal status; it is now carried by a multi-stakeholder association; the municipality as one of the stakeholders underwrites its commitment to a fixed financial contribution; the key factor for the possibility to uphold and develop such a construction is the ability of the association to undertake entrepreneurial activities for bettering management and services, to address new user groups etc., once again market and civil society elements match with the purpose of a public social service.
- In a municipality with a high number of unemployed, a voluntary organisation, linked to the church, establishes a work integration enterprise; the very aim is a social one (keeping people near to their social environment and the labour market); yet it is important to sell the products (various second-hand items) and the whole initiative would hardly exist without funding from a public programme that offers financial support for work for the public good as well as training and educational measures in that context.

The unifying aspect of these examples is that in each and every case there is, within the respective organisations as a constitutive element, the presence of state, third sector, community and market elements. The gravitation centre for such hybrids is for sure mostly somewhere between "state" and "third sector"; but community markets are addressed and concerned as well.

Switching now to an analytical perspective, four different dimensions of hybridisation have been distinguished (see also Evers *et al.* 2002; Evers and Laville 2004b; Evers 2005).

The first dimension of hybridisation concerns *resources*. Taking up again the school example, not much has to be said about the central role of state-public financing. It is however remarkable, to what degree market components can take shape by a differentiation within state-financing – that is, when additional financing can be acquired in the course of competing for a public subscription or funds of a time-limited state-programme that may allow to take part in a model project. Where there was firm public funding one finds now an internal market. Another type of resources is constituted by the various supportive elements from the society and various communities: this may be support associations that collect money; advisory boards that care for publicity; a multi-stakeholder constituency that guarantees support from various sides in the local society and its communities; various kinds of (public-private) partnerships; furthermore volunteering can play a role, sponsorships and support from foundations. Obviously all these forms of "social support" presuppose a society and communities that are not simply indifferent or only in it for their own sake – a society that is to some degrees "civic" after all, committed to the well being of others, the public good and the community at large.

I have therefore assembled all these various forms of social support under the label of "social capital" (Evers 2001; Evers *et al.* 2002). In such a perspective it becomes as well apparent, that injecting public services a dose of civil society support (like the ones sketched above) does not only mean to use and exploit but as well to challenge and cultivate a spirit of concern and trust of the respective citizens and community members. This is the logic of social capital that can only be upheld and grow to the degree it gets used and invested. There is as well a clear link with the concept of "welfare mixes" (Evers 1995; Johnson 1998) that conceives welfare as a co-product of what markets, welfare states, families and other communities and third sector organisations contribute. The examples refer to organisations with a mixed resource structure, offering in the respective policy sector products and services, that may be worshiped differently, depending what the respective users and policy-makers think is most important. With an eye on a public school that has much autonomy and is community-rooted, some may like that it upholds the notion of a public service; others may worship the fact that it deals with its autonomy in an entrepreneurial way; once again others are most inclined to the value the respective school gives to community bonds and civic mindedness.

Two other dimensions that are constitutive for a hybrid character of an organisation are *goals* and forms of *governance*. In the school system for example, governance takes place by market mechanisms, as far as parents can choose between different public schools that compete for pupils; there is a hierarchical steering mechanism at work simultaneously in the setting of curricula and

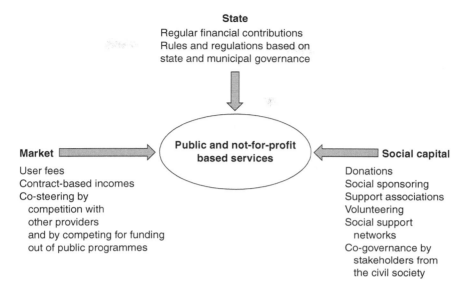

Figure 15.1 Public and not-for-profit services as hybrid organisations.

quality standards; finally the local civil society and its communities have a say, such as through the school board, or the influence exerted by a parent support association. For the users involved this can mean both "voice" and "choice" at a time and, furthermore, by their active commitment they are co-producers of the quality of the school service. Within the governance debate all this has meanwhile been raised under such titles as systems of "co-governance" or under the notion of "mixed governance" (Kooiman 2000; Newman 2001: 11f.). The steering mechanisms that operate simultaneously in such a form of governance have to be seen in conjunction with organisational goals and status. Different to commercial organisations, neither state-public nor third sector service providers are directed by the one overarching goal of being "for profit". Their broader and less clearcut defined concepts of success constitute at the same time a chance and challenge. The chance is to negotiate and develop a complex agenda made up by various goals competing goals. This is reflected in the often met new language of self appraisal many new initiatives and service suppliers use today – advertising themselves as effective and committed, rooted in the local community but likewise being aware of what is up on the international stage. The challenge results from the complicated tasks of balancing the diversity of goals and to keep them compatible in a "balanced scorecard". Taking once again the example of a school, one can see that state-based universal quality criteria should be fulfilled, while at the same time trying to develop a unique profile by special offers and services that help in the market rivalry with other local schools. Finally the linkages with partners in the neighbourhood may influence the agenda as well.

The processes of hybridisation with regard to resources, goals and governance can thirdly and finally lead to a search for a new complex *corporate identity* that reflects the multiple roles and purposes of an organisation. For example, in the field of cultural institutions, like museums and theatres, there is a constant debate to what degree they should commercialise, see their public just as customers to satisfy, to what degree they should follow what is called in Germany the "public mandate to education" or rather be guided by the preferences of their various stakeholders. Maybe they should try to outbalance the various components in a way that turns multi-dependency into a source of limited autonomy. A good example of such dilemmas are the big social security associations in Germany in the field of health. On the one hand, state regulation obliges them to offer all clients the same degree of coverage, something that blocks a competitive relationship; politicians like to treat these officially independent public bodies often like their servants, something that denies their role as autonomous public bodies. On the other hand, reforms in the last years have established a notion of them as being competitors on a market, where customers look for the best insurance offer; this all collides after all with the fact that many of them come from a tradition of organised solidarity alongside professional communities ("technicians' insurance") where the ethos was not about switching between insurers to the one with the best offer at the moment. This may illustrate the unfinished and perhaps to a degree open process of search for an identity – beyond the traditional ones of being a clear cut public service, a private enterprise or a third sector organisation.

Having offered a sketch of the analytical concept of hybrid organisations and pointing to the links of this purpose with practical policy developments on the ground, it should finally be mentioned that there is a possible link with a policy suggestion to be made. The concept of hybridisation can be conceived as a point of departure and reference for the strengthening and survival of such aims like revitalising active citizenship, open communities and social solidarity, linking them with market virtues, like a sense for opportunities and entrepreneurship. It is in such a perspective that the notion of hybrids as *social enterprises*, intertwining social aims, some degree of state-public support, entrepreneurial spirit and community roots, is used as a label with normative undertones (see for the field of occupational and social integration the various attempts in, Nyssens 2006). The notion of social enterprise is oscillating between being an analytical and classificatory (Defourny and Nyssens 2006) concept and a concept with normative undertones, claiming that an amalgam of market economic, social and political principles may make up for an additional tool in strategies that search for new balanced concepts of coping with the present pressures of change.

Summing up and looking back on both notions, the one of intermediary sphere and the one of hybrids, one can say that both items propose the same difference in perspective. It is a perspective on loosening sectorial bonds and loosening links between sectors and their guiding principles. Market-based principles are by no means confined to the market sector, as the complaints about an overall economism but as well the appraisal of "social entrepreneurship" show; vice versa, volunteering is not an exclusive principle of third sector organisations – it can as well play a role in the public sector; and citizenship virtues are claimed by market organisations that strive for an image as "corporate citizens". It is not sector that matters in the first line, but the relative impact of certain values and orientations throughout sectors. Therefore, often "nonprofitness makes no difference" (Dekker 2001) – when it is just based on a formal status of sector adherence and not on a cluster of values. There may be as many third sector organisations behaving like public service providers, as there are public services that adopt a third sector style of organisation and operation – including volunteers, looking for community roots and adapting to the needs of their special constituency.

Challenges: open questions and tasks for research

In this last section topics for clarification will be taken up that may show as well avenues for further theoretical and empirical work.

An often raised issue is concerning the *potential reach of the concept of hybrids*.

Does it mean to understand all third sector organisations as such? This is certainly not the case. In that part of the third sector, where organisations are not concerned with services but basically with advocacy, like NGOs, elements besides associationism and independent socio-political action will play a marginal role, especially when their mission is to protest against, e.g. the ecological consequences of some plans of big business and big bureaucracies. Those organisations are no hybrids, because they do not rely on special public funding and support (besides the general guarantee for all citizens and organisations to associate and express freely). What about service-providing organisations? Obviously in each and every "sector" there are core areas, where the respective sector-specific foundational principles and values are by large uncontested. This holds true for, a fully professional and state-funded public hospital service as well as for a commercial medical service chain with international shareholders.

Then there are organisations *on the way towards hybridisation* but with one element (still) clearly dominating all others; in the public sector this may be a school that does a bit of using community support but is by large still under public authority control. It may as well be those enterprises that are all too easily called "social enterprises", just by the fact that they have, for example, signed a special code of conduct towards their employees, offering them possibilities for volunteering or by the fact that their statements on corporate identity entail some purposes concerning their obligations as corporate citizens in the respective municipality. Nevertheless, one can say that some parts of public and marketed services are more "civic" than others and this has to do with a degree of hybridisation, especially the impact of social capital. After all, it goes without saying that in large parts of the third sector for organisations that deliver services "hybridity" is, as Brandsen *et al.* (2005) underline, a "permanent and inevitable characteristic".

It should be added as a footnote, that there are a form of hybrids, which are much more important than the "four component" organisations we deal with here; all those "two component" hybrids, in between of state and market, that are far from any commitment to local community or civil society organisations: public banks, enterprises that offer services like energy, water, etc., large parts of the traditional "social economy" of cooperatives, "Sparkassen", special saving banks etc. Their legitimacy is in these days not only challenged by an EU-administration that is busy to have a clearly delineated EU-wide market sector without selective state-interference. These organisations are as well rightly criticised in public debates, when it is argued that they represent more a joint venture of state and market elites instead of a public control and democratic governance of market powers, that should entail as well some saying of active civil society organisations like consumer groups. Hence, the question should not be "state or market" but "politics against markets", with a concept of politics however, that brings civil society, its public sphere and consumer organisations back in.

Furthermore it should be underlined that hybrid organisations are not a phenomenon that is exclusively linked with the third sector, even though "mixed" constitutive elements are mostly to be found in that sphere. Processes of hybridisation should be differentiated from hybrids. The respective impact of an element that belongs to the principles and logics of another sector, like a public service being "community based" or a work integration enterprise being contracted in by the labour market administration, must reach a certain level of significance in order to give a full meaning to all the chances and problems that are associated with hybrids – in practice and theory. What shows as well is the tight link of issues of organisational research on hybrids with debates on governance and regulation, especially such phenomena like "co-governance" and "mixed governance". Because principles such as governance by a set of stakeholders from public and private sectors can be discussed both under a societal and an organisational perspective.

The second question to be raised here is concerning the fact that *a limitation of the notion of "hybrid" is its one-sidedness, addressing foremost its vital potentials rather than its destructive sides*. The examples of hybrid organisations and hybridisation that have been pointed out were deliberately selective in order to give an idea about opportunities. Obviously the same attention should be given to tensions and destructive effects that accompany the "invasion" of new and additional principles or a change of their balance. Obviously hybridisation can be seen as a process of "deconstruction" and institutional isomorphism that is in its major part negative, destroying inherited identities. This may happen when the strategic aim is one of assimilating third sector organisations with a strong civic and associative flavour to commercialism and/or etatism, making them similar to all those organisations that fill the space between market and state. It is this aspect and negative process of hybridisation that is often raised as a point of concern in the debates about the contract culture between state and third sector organisations. The question "can hybridisation be sustainable?" (Bode *et al.* 2006) is not only a matter of power and dominance, with one rationale being so much stronger than the others. The problems have as well to do with the fact that the respective logics and their proponents, predominantly located in different spheres, have difficulties respecting each other and searching for good links and balances. This does not only concern the well-known conflict between managerialism and logics of "care" or "social work" in social services; problems can as well show up by needs for multi-goal orientations and multiple loyalties, issues that have already been raised in this paper when discussing the quest for a new corporate identity of organisations going hybrid. Finally on the level of the European Union there seems a certain clash between:

- the social and policy trends towards hybridisation on the ground to be found throughout Europe, and;
- the aim of the Commission in many areas (except perhaps agriculture) to make the delineations between states and markets as clear and strict as possible.

The European Commissions' aim not to allow any "dedifferentiation" between state and market logics, no status besides that of a state public service and service providers that compete on markets, would finally mean to restrict the impact of civil society and third sector organisations to the political sphere only, for example, to consumer advocacy and pressures for better market regulation. It would be difficult then to legitimise any special status for old and new "social enterprises" in social service provision.

The third issue is about *the impact of a focus on the single organisations compared to a focus on networks of organisations* that span across sectors. In many policy areas one can observe these days all kind of cross-sectional public-private partnerships, or networks of actors and organisations, where the role of the single unit is heavily dependent on the balance between the two partners or the multitude of networked organisations. To what degree are organisations in such partnerships going hybrid and to what degree on the reverse forced to sharpen their respective profiles? Public–private partnerships seem to live exactly from the difference between the two partners – e.g. the solidness of the public institution and the alert flexibility of a small agency operating on a not-for-profit basis. A good example for this may be urban renewal. Here at once big investors, building industries, politicians and administrators but as well initiatives for community building have to cooperate, new spaces for public deliberation take shape and simultaneously new public–private partnerships. The issues of a right balance of goals and principles and of the right mix of resources as the have been raised before with respect to hybrid *organisations* are here much more important on the *inter-organisational* level. To what degree can in the respective project for urban revitalisation democratic principles of community building, public deliberation and participation outbalance hierarchical decision-making and the forces of for profit competition as different principles of governance? (see for this issue, as well as the debate on principles of co-production,

Public Management Review 8 (4) 2006). How much economic stimulation is needed in such a renewal area and to what degree should policies invest in community building? These are questions about the balance of competing interests and logics and building principles for a loose trans-sectional alliance, entailing both businessmen and community leaders as stakeholders.

Summing up on a more abstract level, one can say that there is the possibility to analyse "mixes" both on the level of a single organisation and on the level of the "mix" of influences and logics on the level of organisational networks. For the nature of a single organisation and for policy-effects, network-impacts on single-member organisations might matter more than the formal status of an individual organisation.

This leads to a fourth and final point. It is a more general methodological consideration on *the limits of a structural socio-political analysis and the need for a more historical approach* when it comes to discuss the embeddedness of an organisation in an economic, socio-cultural and political environment.

While it makes some sense analytically to link state with "hierarchical steering" and "being obliged to universal principles and the public good", real states in history vary enormously on this point and with democracy a difference comes into the game that makes abstract reasoning about "state" questionable. The same can be said when it comes to the degree a society is civic, to the nature of communities and to market economies, which are to different degrees footloose and globalised or still embedded in the social and political life of a nation. The difference between ideal-types and real historical presentations of the sectors shows that it is a long way from an abstract analytical statement on hybridity towards understanding hybridisation in a historical context. Furthermore, in a historical view, i.e. in reality, the meaning and impact of what is labelled by an analytical view as state-, community- societal or market-principles is not separated but all these elements get their place alongside with others in discourses. Neo-liberal, social-democratic or third-way discourses will give then a different place to these elements. What is dominant in one will have a subordinated role in another concept. Such discourses usually entail complex ideas of the nature and (ought to be) place of social services and the third sector. With respect to this, discourse analysis, by its difference from the abstract structural and not context-bound analytical reasoning has a special potential.

Therefore further analyses of processes of hybridisation should – unlike in this chapter – take real examples not only as an illustration for very general theory building, but as a part of studies of concrete trends, discourses and practices, in a country or a policy field, etc. The clear cut gap between this quest for a more historical and "at place" orientation and the rather general and structural-analytical view taken in this chapter on hybrid organisations says something about scientific challenges not yet met.

References

Bode, I., Evers, A. and Schulz, A. 2006: Work integration social enterprises in Europe: can hybridization be sustainable, in: Nyssens, M. (ed.): *Social enterprise. At the crossroads of market, public policies and civil society.* Routledge, London and New York.

Borzaga, C. and Mittone, L. 1997: The multistakeholder versus the non-profit organization, Università degli Studi di Trento, draft paper No. 7.

Brandsen, T., van de Donk, W. and Putters, K. 2005: Griffins or chameleons? Hybridity as a permanent and inevitable characteristic of the third sector, in: *International Journal of Public Administration*, vol. 28 (9/10) 2005: pp. 749–766.

Dekker, P. 2001: What crises, what challenges? When nonprofitness makes no difference, in: Anheier, H.K. and Kendall, J. (eds): *Third sector policy at the crossroads. An international nonprofit analysis.* Routledge, London and New York.

Defourny, J. and Nyssens, M. 2006: Defining social enterprise, in: Nyssens, M. (ed.): *Social enterprise. At the crossroads of market, public policies and civil society.* Routledge, London and New York.

Esping-Andersen, G. 2002: *Why we need a new welfare state.* Oxford University Press, Oxford.

Evers, A. 1995: Part of the welfare mix: the third sector as an intermediate area, in: *Voluntas*, 6 (2): pp. 119–139.

Evers, A. 2001: The significance of social capital in the multiple goal and resource structure of social enterprises, in: Borzaga, C. and Defourny, J. (eds): *The emergence of social enterprise.* Routledge, London, pp. 298–311.

Evers, A. 2005: Mixed welfare systems and hybrid organizations: changes in the governance and provision of social services, in: *International Journal of Public Administration*, vol. 28 (9/10) 2005: pp. 737–748.

Evers, A. and Laville, J.L. 2004a: Defining the third sector in Europe, in: Evers, A. and Laville, J.L. (eds): *The third sector in Europe.* Edward Elgar, Cheltenham and Northampton, pp. 11–44.

Evers, A. and Laville, J.L. 2004b: Social services by social enterprises; on the possible contributions of hybrid organisations and a civil society, in: Evers, A. and Laville, J.L. (eds): *The third sector in Europe.* Edward Elgar, Cheltenham and Northampton, pp. 237–256.

Evers, A., Rauch, U. and Stitz, U. 2002: Von öffentlichen Einrichtungen zu sozialen Unternehmen. Hybride Organisationsformen im Bereich sozialer Dienstleistungen. Berlin.

Giddens, Anthony 2003: Neoprogressivism – A new agenda for social democracy, in: Giddens, Anthony: *The Progressive Manifesto.* Polity Press, Oxford, pp. 1–34.

Johnson, N. 1998: *Mixed economies of welfare. A comparative perspective.* Prentice Hall Europe, London.

Kooiman, J. 2000: Societal governance: levels, models and orders of social-political interaction, in: Pierre, J. (ed.): *Debating governance: authority, steering and democracy.* Oxford: Oxford University Press.

Kymlicka, W. 2002: Citizenship theory, in: Kymlicka, W.: *Contemporary political philosophy – an introduction.* Oxford University Press, Oxford, pp. 284–326.

Newman, J. 2001: *Modernising governance. New Labour, policy and society.* The Policy Press, Bristol.

Nyssens, M. (ed.) 2006: *Social Enterprise.* Routledge, London and New York.

Offe, C. 2003: Civil society and social order. Demarcating and combining market, state and community, in: Offe, C. (ed.): *Herausforderungen der Demokratie*, Campus Verlag Frankfurt a. M, pp. 274–296.

Salamon, L.M. and Anheier, H.K. 1997: The civil society sector, in: *Social Science and Modern Society*, Vol. 34, No. 2, January/February, S. 60–65.

Salamon, L.M. and Anheier, H.K. 1997a: *Defining the nonprofit sector: a cross-national analysis*, Manchester University Press, Manchester.

Walzer, M. 2004: Involuntary association, in: Walzer, M.: *Politics and passion. Toward a more egalitarian liberalism*. Yale University Press, New Haven & London, pp. 1–20.

16 Teachers and middle managers in a hybrid educational sector

Marlies Honingh

In this chapter we report on a study into the organisational behaviour of teachers and middle managers in the Dutch vocational education and training (VET) sector. The fact that in 1996 publicly and privately funded schools for vocational education and training were brought together in one legal framework created a historic new situation in the Netherlands. Since that time schools with different institutional histories, goals and orientations providing vocational education and training have been embedded in a complex and hybrid environment. When comparing the organisational behaviour of teachers and middle managers in publicly and privately funded schools differences were found. The performed multilevel analysis and analysis of variance (ANOVA) show there are differences among teachers as well as among middle managers. The analyses furthermore reveal that teachers' and middle managers' attitudes to education seem to be affected by different factors.

A hybrid[1] vocational education and training sector

As in many European countries, the provision of vocational education has never been a purely public or private activity in the Netherlands. Vocational education has its origins in the guilds systems, which combined *work*, entrepreneurship, vocational education, a quality assurance system and the stimulation of financial equality (Goudswaard, 1981). After the abolition of the guilds in 1798, the responsibility for providing vocational education was taken up by local initiatives, foundations and employers. In 1919 the first national vocational education act came in force, from then on, former ad hoc regulations gained a permanent states and financial regulations were harmonised.

In the 1920s and 1930s aspects of vocational education were slowly incorporated into the Dutch school system, and after the Second World War this process speeded up as policy-makers realised that vocational education could play a substantial role in the revitalisation of the economy. The growing government interest in vocational and adult education at that time was based on the expectation that education could contribute to reducing unemployment rates and stimulating the integration of immigrants. Although these schools became more and more dependent on the government and its legislation for the execution of tasks,

Dutch schools for vocational education never became purely public institutions, as a consequence of the need to orientate on the labour market and the practical character of vocational education.

In the early 1980s the focus on alignment with the labour market became stronger, this ushered in a period of major educational reforms. The impact of the reforms in the Dutch VET (vocational education and training) sector that followed New Public Management (NPM) ideas, can be seen in four types of changes: changes in ownership; changes in funding and financial management; changes in accountability; and up-scaling (Honingh and Karsten, 2007). As a consequence, schools had to operate in a more market-oriented environment and were forced to merge into large Regional Training Centres (ROCs). The number of schools for vocational education fell dramatically from about 300 in 1986 to 40 in 2005. All of the new regulations were introduced in the new Adult and Vocational Education Act that came into force in 1996.

A second smaller category of schools providing vocational education in the Netherlands has always operated on a for-profit basis. The history of these schools goes back to the end of the nineteenth century, when teachers started to provide distance learning as the government failed to provide sufficient vocational education (Backx, 1994). This kind of education was institutionalised and commercialised after the First World War, as the number of courses provided by these schools grew and they expanded their operations over a wider range of occupational sectors. To assure quality and to protect participants from disasters, government discussed whether inspecting the private schools would be necessary (Backx, 1994). However, as the government decided against this, the schools developed their own quality assurance systems.

Consequently, the two types of education were regarded as separate worlds until the new Adult and Vocational Education Act came into force in 1996. This law brought the two worlds together and incorporated the publicly and privately funded schools into the same legal framework. Private providers of vocational education have since then been allowed – and can be licensed – to offer the same curricula as the publicly funded schools (ROCs). The privately funded schools now have to comply with the rules on registration of courses, quality assurance, educational organisation and consumer protection in the same way as publicly funded schools. The Central Register of Vocational Courses counted 120 schools[2] providing privately funded courses in 2004–2005 (CREBO register). The privately funded schools are smaller than publicly funded schools and often provide courses in only one or two disciplines.

Reflecting on the history of the VET sector, it becomes clear that the position of publicly funded schools has shifted between the market and stronger dependence on government over time. It is important to bear in mind that these movements basically resulted from economic growth or decline. As the position of the publicly funded schools changed, the curricula, educational purposes and the functions ascribed to education altered as well. The history of privately funded schools is less marked by such changes as these schools always focused on labour market demands, the market and customers' wishes to ensure their survival.

Given the history of the VET sector, the combination of privately and publicly funded schools in the same legal framework, and the combination of government regulation with the logic of the market, publicly and privately funded schools now have to operate in a complex hybrid environment.

The study

The history of the Dutch VET sector and the recent educational reforms both show that the organisation of schools and the provision of education have often been determined by strategic considerations based on economic developments and political aspirations. Since the introduction of NPM in the Dutch VET sector, schools have been encouraged to learn from business and to focus on operational details as part of the process of becoming ever more efficient organisations. Consequently, discussions about the core function of schools, the characteristics of providing education and their consequences for the school organisation have been pushed into the background. Brandsen *et al.* (2005) referred to characteristics of products and services third sector organisations[3] bring about as an object of study, with a view to gaining a better understanding of the third sector and investigating whether there is such a thing as third sector rationality. They argued that focusing on these products and services seems to be of interest, as many of the services that third sector organisations provide contain a 'caring' or a 'relational' component.[4] Whatever 'caring' means, Isenbarger and Zembylas (2006) concluded that caring is an important aspect of education. As a consequence of the 'caring' component in the provision of a service, a large share of the products or services these organisations provide can be labelled as *co-products*. Both clients and service providers play a role in the 'production process' and influence the outcomes and final product. Nevertheless, in the management and implementation of change and reform agendas by governments, teachers' ideas about the purposes and principles of care and commitment to pupils' learning and achievement are seldom acknowledged or valued (Day *et al.*, 2005).

Schooling performs many essential functions in a sophisticated democratic society (Chitty, 2002). In analysing these functions two key attitudes can be distinguished, the first is the curriculum-centred attitude and the second is the pupil-centred attitude. Denessen (1999) described this dichotomy as the most common division of views about the purpose of education. Underlying these two different purposes lies the classic debate about the *vocational function* of education versus education aimed at *fostering independence and responsibility* (Kley and Van der Felling, 1989). The vocational approach is functional and fits into the more economic approach to education, whereas the pupil-centred approach emphasises the personal development of individual pupils or students and preparing them to participate in society. In reflecting on the history of the Dutch VET sector, it becomes clear that these two perspectives on education in turn dominated education policy.

Attitudes to education matter in education policy since they involve expectations about schools, teacher behaviour, managerial behaviour, educational programmes and the organisation and financing of schools. As a consequence of the market-oriented reforms in education, teachers' and managers' expectations have moved in the direction of market thinking. Denessen (1999) described how achievement-oriented thinking in education was associated with the introduction of more free-market operations in schools. When the emphasis of education policy is on the economic function of education, managers and teachers notice that they increasingly have to reckon with the demands of industry and pupils, funding based on qualifications, management protocols and the market.

Honingh and Hooge (2004) analysed the structure of the goal-means relation in a recent policy document for the VET sector and reported that *contributing to the knowledge economy* and *being responsible for the socialisation of pupils to encourage them to become active and participative citizens* are the two central goals schools should achieve nowadays. The combination of these two goals, that may sometimes conflict, is a new departure since both perspectives have taken their turn at dominating education policy in the VET sector. Van Veen (2001) argued that congruence between policy reforms and teachers' attitudes to education reduces the risk of tensions within the organisations and increases the chance of a successful adaptation to education reforms. The recent reforms in the VET sector and in particular the requirement to contribute to the knowledge economy as well as to the socialisation of pupils implies that a further investigation of teachers' and middle managers' attitudes to education is needed.

Teachers and middle managers in publicly and privately funded schools

Many studies assume that there are differences in the organisational behaviour of public and private sector organisations (Bozeman and Bretschneider, 1994; Le Grand, 2003; Boyne and Walker, 2004). Jacobs (1992) explained the divergent behaviour patterns as being caused by divergent values and morals in the public and private sectors, which are visible in the aims, orientations and values prevailing in public and private organisations. Since publicly and privately funded schools were used to operating in 'different worlds', as Backx (1994) asserted, their environments and missions differed. Privately funded schools were generally not used to focusing on the socialisation of pupils but on competition and the continued existence of the school, so we expect the teachers and middle managers in privately funded schools to have a more output-oriented attitude to education. Since publicly and privately funded schools have now been brought together in the same legal framework and have to combine public arrangements with the logic of the market, we felt that it would be interesting to investigate attitudes to education of teachers and middle managers in publicly and privately funded schools. Specifically we focused on differences within these two groups with regard to their attitudes. In addition we investigated which factors affected teachers' and middle managers' attitudes to education.

Teachers' attitudes to education in publicly and privately funded schools

In a recent study Honingh and Oort (2008) investigated teachers' attitudes to education in three disciplinary branches: catering and tourism, health and social care and economics and administration,[5] in publicly and privately funded schools in the Dutch VET sector. The items in the questionnaire were based on Denessen's (1999) questionnaire measuring secondary school teachers' attitudes to education.[6] Honingh and Oort (2008) labelled the pupil-centred attitude *socialisation* and the curriculum-centred attitude *goal-oriented*. The socialisation scale consisted of five sub-scales and the goal-orientation scale consisted of three sub-scales. On the basis of a multilevel analysis,[7] Honingh and Oort (2008) found that there was little difference between teachers in publicly and privately funded schools in terms of their belief in the importance of socialising students. The concept of socialisation revolves around the students' functioning and developing their talents, and it seems to be closely tied in with what teachers see as the essence of their role. Prior research in publicly funded schools revealed that teachers perceive focusing on the socialisation of pupils and the guidance of pupils as important aspects of their job (e.g. Isenbarger and Zembylas, 2006; Van Veen, 2005; Day *et al.*, 2005). Honingh and Oort's study (2008) found that this was also the case for teachers working in privately funded schools. The minimal differences[8] between teachers in publicly funded and privately funded schools indicate that the image that the teachers themselves had about their professional duties was so stable that it was not affected by the context in which they were working. See Table 16.1 for a summary of the results.

Differences among teachers

Female teachers, moreover, attached significantly more value to socialising the students than male teachers. This applied to teachers in all three sectors: health and social care, catering and tourism, and economics and administration. Since all of the variables that did have an effect on the importance teachers ascribe to socialisation are teacher characteristics, we have to conclude that the context hardly influences teachers' attitudes to the socialisation of pupils. This seems to be in line with Day's (2005) conclusion that, whilst teachers may well mobilise 'occasional identities' in response to new challenges and changing circumstances, nestled within this flexibility they have a set of core value-based identities which relate to strongly held purposes and principles of care and commitment to pupils' learning and achievement, and which transcend transitory agendas of imposed change.

In analysing the extent to which teachers have a goal-oriented attitude, Honingh and Oort (2008) found a significant difference between teachers in privately and publicly funded schools. Teachers working in privately funded schools had a stronger goal-oriented attitude. This means that these teachers placed more emphasis on achievements, planning and completion of the course

Table 16.1 Effects of state funding, teacher characteristics, organisational characteristics and appointment characteristics on teachers' attitudes to education

	Socialisation			Goal-oriented		
	B	S.E.	P	B	S.E.	P
Fixed effects						
State funding	-0.201	0.247	0.416	-0.631	0.283	0.022
Disciplinary sector:						
horeca (vs) administration)	0.342	0.105	0.002	–	–	–
care (vs) administration	0.687	0.094	0.000	-0.267	0.080	0.000
Years in service	–	–	–	–	–	–
Female versus male	0.373	0.083	0.000	–	–	–
Age	–	–	–	0.096	0.036	0.008
Full-time equivalent	0.116	0.048	0.016	0.106	0.046	0.022
Freelance contract	–	–	–	–	–	–
Teaching time	–	–	–	–	–	–
Teaching at lower level	–	–	–	–	–	–
Teaching at higher level	–	–	–	–	–	–
Hrs worked at home/week	0.113	0.035	0.002	–	–	–
Time spent on gen. duties	0.123	0.043	0.004	–	–	–
Time spent on another job	–	–	–	–	–	–
Random effects	S^2			S^2		
Public school units $\sigma^2 \mu_0$	0.015	0.019	0.422	0.000	0.000	0.000
Public school teacher $\sigma^2 e_0$	0.918	0.052	0.000	1.010	0.054	0.000
Private school teacher $\sigma^2 e_0$	1.332	0.377	0.000	1.860	0.523	0.004

Notes

N = 730

B = Regression coefficient

S^2 = variance components

S.E. = standard error

P = significance level at 0.05.

Continuous scores have been standardised with an average score of 0. Nominal variables have binary codes.

than their colleagues in publicly funded schools. Teachers working in privately funded schools seemed to regard themselves as having a contract with the students. They saw themselves as having made an agreement to educate the students and to guide them along a marked-out path towards a qualification. This is a different way of working from the approach followed by teachers in publicly funded schools, so the context in which teachers work seemed to be related to their attitudes on this point.

These findings also show that it is possible to combine two attitudes to education. This is in line with Denessen's conclusion (1999) that both attitudes could co-exist and should not be seen as contradictory concepts, though it is important to acknowledge that the two attitudes do sometimes conflict.

Based on the analyses carried out, it is not possible to show why teachers in publicly funded schools had a less goal-oriented attitude and whether they experienced tensions as a result of combining the two attitudes to education. Further research is needed to investigate why teachers in publicly funded schools have a less goal-oriented attitude to education than their colleagues in privately funded schools. Gleeson and Husbands (2003) observed tensions in publicly funded schools between what teachers believe in, and what their tasks include as a consequence of increased pressure resulting from management protocols, a stronger focus on performance measurement, accountability, and the publication of school performance data.

In addition, the disciplinary branch in which the teachers worked also had an effect on the extent to which teachers had a goal-oriented attitude to education. Teachers working in the health and social care sector had a less goal-oriented approach to education than those teaching economics and administration. The disciplinary branches seemed to have a strong effect on teachers' attitudes, although it is questionable whether it was the school or the disciplinary branches having a strong influence on teachers, or whether personal characteristics determined in which school or disciplinary field someone started teaching.

The other two predictors that had a significant effect on the extent to which teachers have a goal-oriented attitude were age and the number of hours they work. Older teachers and those appointed to work a higher FTE percentage were significantly more goal-oriented.

Middle managers' attitudes to education

Middle managers have a pivotal role in filtering market reforms and in mediating change in the education workplace, as they are located in-between senior management and the teachers. Logically, middle managers have to translate strategic policy into practice in a way that is acceptable to both groups. Gleeson and Shain (1999) concluded that the professional mandate of middle managers is bound up with reducing potential conflicts of interests and minimising possible signs of a 'them and us' scenario. In this respect they concluded that middle managers filter change in both directions between senior management and lecturers, buffering potential conflicts. As a consequence of the up-scaling in the publicly funded schools in the Dutch VET sector, the middle management tier has increased since 1996. To get an idea of differences and similarities in the organisational behaviour of publicly and privately funded schools, it would therefore be interesting to find out whether and to what extent the attitudes of middle managers in publicly and privately funded schools differ.

In the schools in which Honingh and Oort (2008) investigated teachers' attitudes, the middle managers working in the same disciplinary branches were also requested to fill in a questionnaire. Since we were interested in the organisational behaviour of middle managers that are responsible for the provision of education in the fields of economics and administration, catering and tourism, and health and social care in senior secondary schools, we contacted all 151 middle managers in the Dutch VET sector that are responsible for education in these three fields. 119 of them promised to fill in our questionnaire. Between April and June 2005 we received 83 completed questionnaires (after correction 79 were usable) which is 69 per cent.

The items and scales in this questionnaire were based on existing and validated measurement instruments. As the scales developed by Denessen (1999) were designed to measure teachers' attitudes in secondary education, it was necessary to translate the items and make them applicable to middle managers in the VET sector. The developed questionnaire consisted of 15 sub-scales with Cronbach's alpha between 0.71 and 0.86 (in total 66 items). The middle managers were asked to reflect on their attitudes to education and the schools' educational mission. The allocation of the seven sub-scales measuring middle managers' attitudes to education to the two scales focusing on the *socialisation tasks of the school* and attitudes that stress *pupils' performance* was based on substantive theoretical considerations and on a principal components analysis. The principal components analysis of sub-scale scores confirmed the existence of the two main dimensions (explaining 65 per cent of the variance), and the pattern of factor loadings (after promax rotation) corresponded with the classification described above. The *socialisation tasks of the school* component comprised the following sub-scales: accessibility of the school, fostering citizenship behaviour and taking the private circumstances of pupils into account. The attitude stressing pupils' *performance* included the following sub-scales: focus on pupils' performance, exam pass rates as a quality indicator, focus on pupils' career opportunities and monitoring of pupils' careers. Items were presented to the respondents in the form of propositions and the respondents were asked to indicate to what extent the attitude described corresponded to their own attitude.

Differences among middle managers

The attitudes to education among middle managers were compared on three dimensions. First of all we compared the middle managers in the three disciplinary branches on base of an analysis of variance (oneway ANOVA). In contrast with the teachers, the middle managers working in diverse disciplinary branches did not differ significantly in the extent to which they focused on the socialisation tasks of the school. Nor did they differ in the extent to which they stressed the pupils' performance levels. As middle managers have often worked as teachers, it is relevant to find out whether those who did not have a teaching job before have different attitudes to education. With an independent sample T-test both groups of middle managers were compared. The middle managers in this study that had worked as teachers (N=65) did not differ significantly in their attitudes to education from the those who had not worked as teachers (N=14), which is a remarkable result. In addition, the T-test showed that female (N=24) and male (N=55) middle managers did not differ significantly in their attitudes to education (see Table 16.2 for a summary of the results). The results of the analyses that had been performed raise the question as to what predictors affect middle management attitudes to education.

Middle managers in publicly and privately funded schools

Comparing the attitudes to education of middle managers (N=68) in publicly funded schools with those of middle managers in privately funded schools (N= 11), the T-test revealed significant differences. As the privately funded schools are generally much smaller than publicly funded schools, the resulting samples of middle managers from the two groups were unequal in size: 68 middle managers from 35 publicly funded schools and 11 middle managers from eight privately funded schools. The comparison of the middle managers in publicly and privately funded schools showed a significant difference in the extent to which the middle managers in the two sectors focused on the social tasks of the school. Middle managers in privately funded schools placed less emphasis on the social tasks of the school, so access and encouraging citizenship behaviour were less of an issue for them than for their colleagues in publicly funded schools.

The extent to which middle managers in publicly and privately funded schools paid attention to pupils' performance did not differ significantly. Examining the sub-scales of this component, we found that middle managers in privately funded schools placed significantly more emphasis on exam pass rates than middle managers in publicly funded schools. This finding seems to be logical as middle managers in privately funded schools are used to focusing more strongly on the school's continued existence, competition and image.

Differences between teachers and middle managers

This section brings together the attitudes to education of teachers and middle managers in publicly and privately funded schools, enabling comparisons to be drawn between the organisational behaviour of teachers and middle managers in the two sectors. Since not all of the items and sub-scales in the teacher and middle management questionnaires were formulated identically, it was impossible to combine all the data into one figure. Nevertheless, we will attempt to sketch some differences in the 'patterns of attitudes' between publicly and privately funded schools that are based on the relative differences found between

Table 16.2 Comparisons among middle managers. Attitudes of middle managers compared in publicly and privately funded schools in three disciplinary branches

| Managers | Attitudes to education | | | | | | Socialisation tasks | | |
| | Pupils' performances | | | | | | | | |
	Mean	SD	Prob*				Mean	SD	Prob*
In privately funded schools (*n* = 11) (13.9%)	−0.022	1.151	0.937				−0.746	1.383	0.007
In publicly funded schools (*n* = 68) (86.1%)	0.004	0.983	–				0.120	0.878	–
Horeca (*n* = 18) (22.8%)	−1.791	0.960	0.588				−0.388	0.783	0.172
Administration (*n* = 30) (38.0%)	−0.022	0.916	–				0.096	0.992	–
Care (*n* = 31) (39.2%)	0.126	1.108	–				0.132	1.088	–
Female (*n* = 24) (30.4%)	0.089	1.010	0.605				−0.139	0.847	0.377
Male (*n* = 55) (60.9%)	−0.039	1.002	–				0.607	1.061	–
Has worked as a teacher (*n* = 65) (82.3%)	0.274	0.975	0.603				0.022	1.033	0.683
Has not worked as a teacher (*n* = 14) (17.7%)	−0.127	1.139	–				−0.099	0.854	–

Notes

N = 79, * = Probability in oneway ANOVA, analysis of variance used to test for differences among two or more independent groups. Scores have been standardised with an average score of 0 and a standard deviation of 1.

teachers in publicly and privately funded schools and between middle managers in publicly and privately funded schools.

1   Since teachers in publicly and privately funded schools did not differ in the extent to which they focused on the socialisation of pupils, whereas managers in privately funded schools focused significantly less on socialisation, we expected differences in their attitudes on this point to be greater in privately funded schools than in publicly funded schools.[9] It remains a question whether this is an issue in privately funded schools and whether differences between attitudes of middle managers and teachers might cause tensions within the organisation.

2   Middle managers in privately funded schools did not differ significantly from middle managers in publicly funded school in the extent to which they focused on pupils' performance. The only sub-scale in which significant differences were found was the one measuring the extent to which middle managers stress exam pass rates as a quality indicator. Since teachers in privately funded schools placed more emphasis on performance than their colleagues in publicly funded schools, I expected the attitudes of teachers and middle managers in publicly funded schools to differ more than in privately funded schools. It is important to note that the introduction of stronger managerial control by focusing on output rates and quality reports as well as on the development of tailor-made learning pathways causes tensions in the publicly funded schools (e.g. Van Veen, 2005; Gleeson and Husbands, 2003).

The above summary of the results indicates the following: a dissimilarity in the position both attitudes to education have within schools a difference between publicly and privately funded schools, or a combination of both clarifications. Based on this rough outline, we conclude that the pattern of attitudes teachers and middle managers have to education differs between publicly and privately funded schools. These differences are in line with the differences in the institutional histories of the schools. Consequently we expected both types of schools to also cope differently with differences between the attitudes of middle managers and teachers.

Furthermore, some of the predictors that had an effect on the teachers, disciplinary branches for example, did not seem to make any difference to the attitudes of middle managers. Why do teachers in distinct disciplinary branches have different attitudes to education whereas middle managers working in different disciplinary branches do not? This finding raises questions such as: what are middle managers attitudes based on and which predictors affect their attitudes?

Conclusions

This chapter examined the organisational behaviour of teachers and middle managers in the Dutch VET sector. Given the characteristics of providing education and the complex environment in which publicly and privately funded schools in the Dutch VET sector operate, teachers' and middle managers' attitudes to education were investigated. The comparisons among teachers and among middle managers in publicly and privately funded schools revealed a mixed picture of differences and similarities.

The results indicate that providing education and the social development of pupils are inseparable in the eyes of the teachers. As the presence or absence of public funding did not affect the teachers' attitudes in this respect, we have to conclude that providing education has its own unique dynamic. The same can be said about the entire teaching profession, which seems to be stable since teachers in both public and privately funded schools agreed on the extent to which they focused on the socialisation of pupils.

Although teachers shared some attitudes, they differed in the extent to which they had a goal-oriented attitude. Overall, teachers in privately funded schools showed stronger goal-oriented attitudes and their approach to guiding pupils was based on their feeling that they had made an agreement to educate them. The extent to which teachers had a goal-oriented attitude seemed to be affected by the environment in which they worked.

Middle managers in publicly funded schools attached more importance to the social aspects and purposes of schooling than middle managers in privately funded schools. In the extent to which they focused on pupils' performance levels, the differences were not significant, with the exception that middle managers in privately funded schools had significantly higher scores on the sub-scale measuring exam pass rates as an indicator of school quality.

These comparisons allow us to conclude that there are indeed differences between teachers and middle managers in publicly and privately funded schools. Whether these differences lead to tensions and how teachers and managers deal with these differences is not clear and needs further investigation. This is especially the case in privately funded schools as little is known about the relations between teachers and middle managers in these schools. In publicly funded schools, tensions between teachers and middle managers seem to have increased as a result of a stronger focus on output rates and quality reports as well as on the development of tailor-made learning pathways.

Teachers and middle managers appear to arrive at their views on education in a different way; the middle managers' outlooks seems to be less stable and more changeable than those of the teachers. At times of change or when the school has to respond flexibly to change, this could lead to tension and partial adaptation by the organisation.

Furthermore, middle managers buffer between the strategic decisions of senior management and the teachers, so they have to compromise and sometimes lose sight of grassroots practice in the classroom. It would be interesting to investigate further how the attitudes and views of middle managers come about. This is certainly an important issue in the debate about the professional development of managers in education and new managerialism.

Most of all it is important that policy-makers realise the distinctive logic and purposes of providing human services like education. Debating educational purposes needs to be of continuous concern in educational policy.

Notes

1 Organisations, arrangements or structures in which a mixture of pure and incongruous origins, (ideal) types, 'cultures', 'coordination mechanisms', 'rationalities', or 'action logics', can be found, are often referred to as hybrids (Brandsen *et al.*, 2005).
2 The number of schools that actively provide privately funded education is smaller since some of the schools are entitled to hand out diplomas although they do not provide courses.
3 The third sector is a sphere of ideas, values, institutions, organisations, networks and individuals located in between the family, the state and the market (Anheier *et al.*, 2001).
4 In this article the focus is on education in which there is a direct relation between service provider and client. There are also third sector organisations that focus on indirect caring, like environmental organisations.
5 Of the respondents, 21.5 per cent taught catering and tourism, 42.3 per cent worked in the field of health and social care, and 36.2 per cent taught economics and administration.
6 Denessen developed a questionnaire for secondary school teachers to determine the extent to which they had a curriculum-centred attitude or a pupil-centred attitude.
7 The effects of state funding and other predictor variables on organisational behaviour were investigated using multilevel regression analysis. In this way, by distinguishing between residual variance at the individual level and residual variance at the level of the disciplinary unit, it was possible to account for dependencies in data that came from teachers working in the same disciplinary units of public schools. In private schools, either the teachers did not operate in disciplinary units, or the disciplinary units were much smaller, so it was not possible to distinguish residual variance at the level of the disciplinary sector for teachers from privately funded schools. We therefore applied a multilevel model with a random intercept with three types of variance: public school disciplinary sector variance, public school teacher variance, and private school teacher variance (cf. Roberts and Roberts, 2005).
8 Looking at the average scores of the teachers in the publicly funded and privately funded schools, we found that teachers in publicly funded schools attached slightly greater value to citizenship education, students' progress and their private circumstances than did teachers in privately funded schools.
9 Since the average score of teachers was higher than the middle managers' average score (both measured with a five-point scale) we can assume that the difference between teachers and middle managers in their attitudes to socialisation was greater.

References

Anheier, H.K., Glasius, M. and Kaldor, M. (2001) Introducing Global Civil Society in Anheier, H.K., Glasius, M. And Kaldor, M. (eds) *Global Civil Society.* Oxford: Oxford University Press.

Backx, H.A.M. (1994) *Het particuliere onderwijs; een onderzoek naar de rol en de taak van de wetgever inzake het niet door de overheid bekostigde onderwijs.* Tilburg: Academisch proefschrift.

Boyne, G.A. and Walker, R.M. (2004) Strategy Content and Public Service Organizations. *Journal of Public Administration Research and Theory*, 14: 2 pp. 231–252.

Bozeman, B. and Bretschneider, S. (1994) The 'Publicness Puzzle' in Organization Theory: A Test of Alternative Explanations of Differences between Public and Private Organizations. *Journal of Public Administration Research and Theory*, 4: 2 pp. 197–223.

Brandsen, T., Van de Donk, W. and Putters, K. (2005) Griffins or Chameleons? Hybridity as a Permanent and Inevitable Characteristic of the Third Sector. *International Journal of Public Administration*, 28: 9&10 pp. 749–765.

Butt, G. and Lance, A. (2005) Secondary Teacher Workload and Job Satisfaction. *Educational Management Administration and Leadership*, 33: 4 pp. 401–422.

Chitty, C. (2002) *Understanding Schools and Schooling*. London: Routledge.

Day, C., Eliott, B. and Kington, A. (2005) Reform, Standards and Teacher Identity: Challenges of Sustaining Commitment. *Teaching and Teacher Education*, 21: 5 pp. 563–577.

Denessen, E. (1999) *Opvattingen over onderwijs; leerstof- en leerlinggerichtheid in Nederland*. Apeldoorn: Garant Uitgevers NV.

Gleeson, D. and Husbands, C. (2003) Modernizing Schooling through Performance Management: A Critical Appraisal. *Journal of Education Policy*, 18: 5 pp. 499–511.

Gleeson, D. and Shain, F. (1999) Managing Ambiguity: Between Markets and Managerialism – a Case Study of 'Middle Managers in Further Education. *The Sociological Review*, 47: 3 pp. 461–490.

Goudswaard, N.B. (1981). *Vijfenzestig jaren nijverheidsonderwijs*. Assen: Van Gorcum.

Honingh, M.E. and Hooge, E.H. (2004) Koers II ontbeert heldere lijn. *Profiel*, 6 pp. 19–21.

Honingh, M.E. and Karsten, S. (2007) Marketization in the Dutch Vocational Education and Training Sector: Hybrids and their Behaviour. *Public Management Review*, 9: 1 pp. 135–143.

Honingh, M.E. and Oort, F.J. (2008) Teachers' organisational behaviour in public and private funded schools *(submitted for Publication)*.

Isenbarger, L. and Zembylas, M. (2006) The Emotional Labour of Caring in Teaching. *Teaching and Teacher Education*, 22: 1 pp. 120–134.

Jacobs, J. (1992) *Systems of Survival: a Dialogue on the Moral Foundations of Commerce and Politics*. New York: Vintage.

Kley, P. and Van der Felling, A.J.A. (1989) Onderwijs en subculturele oriëntaties in Vogel, P. (ed.) *De school keuzen en kansen*, pp. 39–59. Muiderberg: Coutinho bv.

LeGrand, J. (2003). *Motivation, Agency, and Public Policy*. Oxford: Oxford University Press.

Roberts, C. and Roberts, S.A. (2005) Design and Analysis of Clinical Trials with Clustering Effects due to Treatment. *Clinical Trials*, 2: 2, pp. 152–162.

Van Veen, K. (2005) Lesgeven, een vak apart in Van den Brink, G., Jansen, T. and Pessers, D. (eds) *Beroepszeer waarom Nederland niet goed werkt*, pp. 196–206 Amsterdam: Uitgeverij Boom.

Van Veen, K., Sleegers, P., Bergen, T. and Klaassen, C. (2001) Professional Orientations of Secondary School Teachers towards their Work. *Teaching and Teacher Education*, 17: 2 pp. 175–194.

Part VIII
Social enterprise

17 The role of social enterprises in Europe

A core element or a distraction in the provision of public services?[1]

Isabel Vidal[2]

Introduction

One of the objectives of the European Science Foundation's exploratory workshop, "The Third Sector in a Changing Europe: Key Trends and Challenges", was to move forward in our understanding of the concept of social enterprise". Osborne (2006) formulated the following question: what role(s) do/should third sector organisations play in the provision of public services – and is social enterprise a core element of this role or a distraction? Nyssen (2006b) citing Defourny (2001) responded: "Social enterprise does not represent a conceptual break with institutions of the third sector but rather a new dynamic within it – encompassing both newly-created organisations and older ones which have undergone an evolution". In the course of the last ten years the term "social enterprise" has come to be used more and more frequently but with diverse meanings. Kerlin (2006) did a comparative analysis of the different meanings that the term takes in the US and in Europe. In this chapter the meaning adopted by the EMES Network will be used.[3]

Objective

This chapter has two primary objectives. The first is to continue reflecting on the concept of social enterprise. Our interest is not in knowing the types of activities being carried out by social enterprises, nor which legal models are being applied, or how the profits obtained from economic activity are being distributed. Our interest is focused on moving forward in our understanding of how an organisation, understood as the formal expression of coordination among different stakeholders, is governed and consequently, managed. The characteristic of being a multi-stakeholder enterprise determines the form of governance of the organisation as well as the distribution of profits: understood as benefits obtained by different stakeholders working in partnership.

The second objective is to evaluate whether the investigation carried out by the EMES Network between 2001 and 2004 helps to understand what conditions facilitate the creation of trust among different stakeholders, how this asset is produced and built-up, and finally what its impact is in terms of economic sustainability as well as in terms of social well-being and cohesion.

Theoretical approach

The theoretical approach used is that of the institutional school that defines the enterprise as a mechanism of coordination for different stakeholders who have decided to act in partnership, or at least in formal and structured dialogue in order to increase their benefits beyond what each of them could obtain acting alone.

Analytical basis

In order to provide this reflection, we use the knowledge gained during the past years from two research projects. The first is related to the provision of collective childcare services and the second is found in the domain of social inclusion. These projects are the following:

*   Changing Family Structures and Social Policy concerns the provision of services for young children, the transformation of family, structures and functions, and development in social policy (TSFEPS) in eight European countries.[4]
*   The Socio-Economic Performance of Social Enterprises in the field of integration work (PERSE). The project focused on studying the importance of social enterprises in the promotion of public policies supporting people with difficult employability in 11 European member states.[5]

Structure

This chapter is structured as follows: the next section recognises the historical tradition of enterprises in Europe throughout the last two centuries that have not been driven by profit maximisation. This is recalled by looking at the importance of the rise of cooperatives in the middle of the nineteenth century and subsequently the rise of mutuals, with the objective of defending the interests of their members.

In the third section we look at the strategic reorganisation carried out by nonprofit organisations starting in the 1970s as they progressively took on the role of economic actors. This section concludes by pointing out the opportunities that are currently opening up for social enterprise due to the growing demand for public services in our countries.

In the fourth section we look at how in Europe today, conditions exist to facilitate the convergence of a business tradition that does not maximise profits and organisations that produce and provide services to third parties. The convergence of these two traditions leads to the concept of social enterprise. A detailed reflection on the definition of social enterprise found in Borzaga and Defourny

(2001) is developed. This definition places emphasis on social enterprise as a multi-stakeholder organisation. This strongly determines the governance and management of the organisation as well as the distribution of profits – understood not only as cash benefits, but also fundamentally as surpluses that facilitate the attainment of objectives that the stakeholders in an organisation cannot attain individually, or might be able to attain, but with a greater use of resources; in other words, with a less efficient use of resources.

The fifth section explores capital of trust, understood as an approach to social capital in the area of organisations. This approach is what makes it possible to understand the potential development of social enterprises and especially their economic sustainability over time. However, capital of trust is an asset that has to be cultivated. To do this, the social enterprise must develop a clear and formalised strategy of transparency in which the process of rendering accounts or accountability become key instruments in the enterprise's ability to maintain and increase the stakeholders' trust in its day to day internal work.

The sixth section explains some of the main results related to the usefulness of the concept social enterprise in the sectors that produce and provide collective childcare services and to those that produce and provide services to facilitate the integration of people systematically excluded from the workforce. This section also reflects on the social enterprise's lack of appeal for some economists, especially related to its relative lack of importance in relation to other operators – such as governments, conventional businesses, or all the organisations that form part of the larger group known as the third sector – and related to its lack of visibility at least at present. In conclusion, the seventh section attempts to respond to the question raised in the title of this chapter.

The tradition in Europe of businesses not driven by profit maximisation

In Europe at least since the Industrial Revolution, there has been a tradition of enterprises that have not been driven by profit maximisation. In the middle of the nineteenth century the market was not very developed and there was no welfare state. As a result, some collectives were voluntarily organised, and they created enterprises to serve their interests. The most frequent legal models were cooperatives and mutuals. In the middle of the 1840s the workers in the textile factories in the town of Rochdale near Manchester created one of the first experiences in the modern consumer cooperative movement. This experience was rapidly repeated in other European towns that were going through their own industrialisation process. There are reports of the creation of cooperatives in Belgium, Spain and France as well. These first textile workers organised themselves and created businesses to produce the goods their "shopping baskets" required at cheaper prices and/or with better quality than what was offered by the retail distribution industry at that time. These original consumer cooperatives were then followed by agricultural, worker, and housing cooperatives, and also by mutuals to provide social and healthcare services.

The cooperatives and mutuals were born in Europe in the nineteenth century in order to carry out entrepreneurial activity related to the social objective for which they had been established: to cover those needs that were not being provided for by the conventional private market or the state. From the beginning, consumer cooperatives operated as purchase centres, buying at wholesale prices and selling at the wholesale price on the retail level. This made it possible for cooperative members to maintain their purchasing power during economic periods in which the rate of inflation was superior to salary increases. The entrepreneurial activity carried out by the different branches of cooperatives has never had the objective of maximising profits, but rather, it has always been a vehicle to obtain the social objectives for which the organisation was set up.

The governance of cooperatives and mutuals is as important as their entrepreneurial activity. A valid way to understand how these organisations are governed is to look at their formal definition, which is association of persons. This means that the political power of each of the members is based on the principle of "one person one vote" and not on the financial capital contributed by each of the members. These organisations were born with the objective to increase the well-being of all their members. The mission of cooperatives and mutuals has always been to produce goods and services so that members – through the purchase and/or use of the goods and services, are able to cover some of their individual needs not being provided for by the conventional private market or the state at the quantitative or qualitative level they require.

From the standpoint of economic analysis, cooperatives and mutuals are organisations that allow their members to satisfy various unsatisfied demands.[6] These organisations are also known as "mutual aid" organisations. Their primary objective is to provide aid to their members by carrying out entrepreneurial activity. However, it is important to remember that at least until the mid-twentieth century these organisations did not limit themselves solely and exclusively to carrying out entrepreneurial activity as the only instrument to support their members. In addition, they promoted a wide range of social activities. Cooperative members dedicated their free time to participating in formative activities on cooperative premises or having family celebrations such as weddings or dances on a Sunday afternoon. As a result, the cooperatives born in the mid-nineteenth century and extending throughout Europe in the twentieth century were schools for the promotion of democracy, participation, local identity, and a principal source of social capital.

In economic analysis this mutual aid among members is also related to the concept of necessity.[7] In Spain the worker cooperatives experienced very strong growth between 1975 and 1995, a period characterised by the persistence of high unemployment rates and an unconsolidated welfare state (Vidal, 1987). The concepts of mutual aid and necessity continue to be valid in order to understand the rediscovery of enterprising associations among certain collectives in moments of uncertainty. Currently in Argentina, for example, the unstable economic situation that started in 2002 has facilitated the rediscovery of worker cooperatives by some collectives of unemployed people and those at risk of becoming unemployed for the purpose of creating their own employment.

The sudden appearance of non-profit organisations as economic operators

After the two world wars the path toward strong economic growth began in the countries that made up Western Europe. This permitted the development of mature markets in many sectors and the creation of social welfare state models characterised by their growing capacity to produce and provide public services. The sustainable institutional and economic growth registered for more than two decades permitted Western Europe to cease to be a poor region. In this new institutional setting old necessities disappeared, new ones arose and the organised civil society reshuffled the organisational instruments it had at its service. Associations, operating foundations and other non-profit organisations such as voluntary organisations also appeared on the scene as economic actors.

As governments built their welfare state models, they promoted important contractual relationships with private organisations. In this new scenario non-profit organisations, which had arisen in the first place as advocacy organisations, expanded their capacities, began to combine voluntary resources with contracted resources and progressively moved in the direction of producing and providing public services. Associations developed in France and Belgium and social and solidarity cooperatives in Italy, due to the welfare states in these countries opting for the use of associations and cooperatives in the management of some social services, especially for those requiring direct daily and stable relationships with the users of these public services.[8] The consolidation of the relationship between government and non-profit organisations explains why in countries such as Holland, Ireland and Belgium, a greater percentage of the active population with respect to the total working population is employed in the non-profit sector; as opposed to the United States, which comes in fifth place in the ranking done by Salomon (1995). As Brandsen (2007) has pointed out, Salomon (1995) shows that the growth of the state and the growth of the non-profit sector go hand in hand, which is contrary to the supposed effect of "crowding out", which suggests that the development of a welfare state would reduce the presence of non-profit organisations in the society or on the other hand, that the reduction of the welfare state would strengthen the non-profit sector.

Presently the growth in demand for public services in our countries represents new market opportunities for enterprises dedicated to the personalised and creative provision of services to people. These new markets are permitting the rise of new enterprises which combine the economic rationale of generating wealth and making money with the political rational of promoting cohesion and social well-being.

New necessities, new markets and new organisational responses: social enterprise

Organisations are living organisms that evolve through disappearance, the creation of new ones or the reorganisation of existing ones. At the present time, the cooperative organisations that arose in the Industrial Revolution and the non-profit organisations – reinforced by the first welfare state models – are converging to confront a new service society, based on what Laville (2001) called proximity services. Here the quality of the service is going to be determined by the relationship between producer and consumer, worker and user in the type of organisation providing these services as well as in the institutional environment in which these organisations must carry out their activities. The result of this convergence has been the rise of what the EMES Network has defined as social enterprise.[9] For this group of investigators social enterprise is initiated by a group of people who voluntarily organise and create an enterprise with the explicit purpose of benefiting the community. The social enterprise includes those organisations whose principle mission is to provide mutual aid for their members, as well as those citizen initiatives whose objective is to assist third parties.

One of the main objectives of the EMES Network is to emphasise that social enterprises are organisations combining professional resources and voluntary resources with a market focus, or that are progressively moving into the market, private or public. As a consequence its members are entrepreneurs who assume economic risks. Its characteristics as an enterprise are important to differentiate the social enterprise from other non-profit organisations whose main activities are lobbying and advocacy and also to exclude other non-profits that are properties of a third party. The definition then focuses on the governance of the social enterprise: who has the political power and how is political power exercised in the organisation?[10]

The markets for relational services are characterised by the existence of incomplete contracts that generate transaction costs and, as a consequence, this does not facilitate the most efficient production and distribution of goods and services for all interested parties. In order to reduce inefficiency, the EMES Network has proposed that not only founder members participate in the governing bodies of these organisations but also the users, clients and suppliers; all groups whose interests are affected directly or indirectly by the activity of the organisation should have a voice. This is the concept of the multi-stakeholder enterprise.

The conceptualisation of social enterprise as a multi-stakeholder organisation means thinking about the enterprise not only in its capacity as producer but also as a mechanism of coordination for different stakeholders (Bacchiega and Borzaga, 2001). In order for different stakeholders to coordinate there have to be three different circumstances that are closely linked to the raison d'être of this coordination. The first is that there has to exist uncertainty (incomplete and asymmetric information), and because of this the possibility of loss for the decision-maker. The second is that there has to be strategic interdependence, which means the results for one party depend on what the other party does. The third circumstance is that the possibilities of benefits derived from working in a network must be substantial, since thanks to this costs are reduced or increased considerably. Without the circumstances of uncertainty or interdependence, it would not be necessary to trust. Trust means being convinced of the soundness of someone or something, with no more security than good faith. It is about expectations, suppositions, beliefs in the probability that the future actions of others will be beneficial, favourable or at least not detrimental to the groups' own interests. For Bacchiega and Borzaga (2001), the existence of a multi-stakeholder enterprise is the result of a process of building and accumulating reciprocal trust among the different interest groups in the organisation.

The characteristic of being a multi-stakeholder organisation determines the democratic character of the decision-making. Social enterprises are organisations that are governed by democratic criteria or at least, have circuits of participation not dependent on the contribution of financial capital to the organisation. The criteria of multi-stakeholders also determine the answer to the question, how are profits distributed? In the definition offered by the EMES Network (Borzaga and Defourny, 2001), the social enterprise is not understood to mean only an enterprise that is formally bound to the non-distribution of profits. Such a legal definition of the social enterprise may be considered as an important characteristic but not a necessary one. For Sacconi and Faillo (2005) the multi-stakeholder characteristic demands that there be an equitable distribution of profits among the different stakeholders in the organisation. In this enterprise profile, a substantial part of the cash profits are reinvested in order to build the capacity to produce and provide the most benefits for the different stakeholders in the enterprise. In other words, more important than profits and how they are distributed, are the benefits obtained by each of the stakeholders in the organisation. For governments, being a stakeholder in a social enterprise may be the only efficient way and the most effective way they have to achieve positive results in the struggle against social exclusion.

Social capital, capital of trust and the social enterprise

For economists, capital is a hard asset resulting from a costly investment that depreciates and that has value because it offers benefits of some type. The concept was first applied to commercial capital and machines (physical capital). But over time, the number of elements considered to be capital has grown to include relational capital. Social capital has reappeared with great force in the course of the last fifteen years adding itself to the long list of assets which are recognised to have a potential influence not only on economic results but also on other aspects of social activity. The concept of capital of trust forms part of the wider concept of social capital.

The approach to social capital in the multi-stakeholder enterprise is different from the habitual approach to social capital in macro studies, which usually places non-economic relationships in the foreground in the generation of social capital, and highlights in particular, all the effects of a political nature. In the concept of the multi-stakeholder enterprise these very interesting non-economic dimensions of social capital are not ignored, nor is there the intention to ignore one of the most attractive characteristics of the concept of social capital, which is its multidisciplinary character.

The majority of economists are more interested in the effects of social capital on growth, efficiency and productivity (Alesina and LaFerrara, 2002; Sobel 2002). Nevertheless, other approaches by economists toward social capital consider its development in the area of organisations. Although these papers don't often speak of social capital per se, the nature of the problems analysed is very similar: the generation of relationships of trust and cooperation and their value as an intangible asset (Williamson, 1993). Organisations are created with the purpose of facilitating the coordination of physical, non-material and human resources through formal and informal structures (Salas, 2001).

In the case of the social enterprise, the first question that must be analysed is if economic relationships could be relevant in the generation of social capital. According to the interdisciplinary definition of social capital proposed by the SCIG (2001), social capital is the fruit of social relationships and consists of the expectation of benefits derived from preferential treatment among individuals and groups. In other words, social relationships in certain circumstances produce expectations of favourable behaviour from other stakeholders. These expectations are called social capital because they are an asset that produces various effects.

Situations in which there is imperfect information create an atmosphere of distrust among stakeholders and a high degree of uncertainty. As a result, stakeholders make decisions in the market and inside the organisation based on what others are doing. Because of this, psychological and sociological factors become important and concepts such as cognitive bias, impartiality, reciprocity, group identity, team mate behaviour and social status are relevant (Akerlof, 2002).

Sacconi and Faillo (2005) use this focus to analyse the importance of social capital as an asset that permits social enterprises to increase their comparative advantages in relation to other organisations acting in the same market segments. They analyse social capital as the result of an investment and accumulation process responding to the logic of maximisation of an objective function of each one of the interest groups in the organisation. They think that each stakeholder's desire to form part of and participate actively in the enterprise must be the result of the decisions of a rational optimiser. In this type of approach, stakeholders invest or consume their resources only if this contributes to maximising their objectives. In particular, the accumulation of capital of trust will be the result of an investment that stakeholders make over time because they consider that investment as the best option for the allocation of their resources.

From this perspective, in order to measure the results of this participation it is necessary to identify how the process of collaboration operates and to evaluate the benefits derived from it. Therefore, the social enterprise should develop a process of rendering of accounts or accountability and quality assurance of the process of informing its stakeholders about the results obtained. This accountability process could lend support to the enterprise's strategic and operative management in the following ways:

1   It would help to maintain consistency between the enterprise's systems and activities and its ethical and social values.
2   It would favour understanding of the impact produced by its systems and activities, incorporating the perception of the stakeholders related to this impact.
3   It would serve as part of a general framework for internal control that would permit the organisation to identify, evaluate and better manage the risks to the stakeholders derived from its performance.
4   It would facilitate knowing the stakeholders' legitimate interests for information concerning what the impact of the organisation's activities on the community should be, as well as concerning what the decision-making processes are.

Reporting on the results of a social enterprise consists of explaining and justifying the actions, omissions, risks and subordinations for which someone is responsible, and in relation to the persons that have a legitimate stake. In order to comply with its rendering of accounts, the social enterprise has to offer explanations about its actions, omissions, risks and subordinations. Besides the requirements of transparency, the rendering of accounts involves the wider obligation of receptivity and conformity. Transparency refers to the duty to report to the stakeholders. Receptivity understood as the capacity to provide answers (responsiveness) refers to the responsibility of the organisation with respect to its acts and omissions, including the decision-making process and the results of its decisions. Receptivity involves a commitment to develop processes and objectives in the organisation that will permit a continual improvement in its degree of compliance. Conformity refers to respect for both political and practical norms of reference, and communication of the policies and the results attained (for more detail see Baldin, 2005 and Sacconi and Faillo, 2005).

Results of working with the social enterprise as unit of analysis

After defining the concept of social enterprise the EMES Network carried out two research projects to see if there were entrepreneurial experiences complying with the meaning of social enterprise as laid out in the previous two sections. The two projects were:

•   TSFEPS Project:[11] Changing Family Structures and Social Policy, which concerns the provision of services for young children, the transformation of family, structures and functions, and development in social policy in eight European countries.

• PERSE Project: The Socio-Economic Performance of Social Enterprises in the field of integration work. This project focused on studying the importance of social enterprises in the promotion of public policies supporting people with difficult employability in 11 European member states.

Case study methodology was utilised in the two projects. Project PERSE was focused solely on the analysis of enterprises acting in the area of social integration through work. Project TSFEPS analysed public, conventional private and social enterprises. In this section we will look at some of the main results obtained and also point out some of the benefits and limitations to the use of the social enterprise as the unit of analysis for the study of these two sectors.

Some of the results obtained

The methodology used in carrying out the TSFEPS Project and PERSE Project confirmed that it is not easy to find enterprises that meet the economic and social characteristics of the social enterprise (as defined by the EMES Network) in all the countries and in the two sectors. However, if one considers that this is a theoretical definition and that its objective is to mark a trend toward a specific type of organisation, then it is possible to find organisations that could be called social enterprises in these two sectors.

One element that has an influence on the profile of the social enterprise is territory, understood as a place having a very strongly defined historical identity. As a result, the context is not a blank slate; history, culture, relationships between governments and private conventional and social organisations determine, or better said, select the ways in which the social enterprise can develop. As a result, it is important to pay attention to territory as a place populated by people, institutions and enterprises in relationship; the way all these people, institutions and enterprises live together is key to understanding the characteristics of the social enterprise in that territory. In short, the second important conclusion was that the existence, importance and development of the organisational profile is highly determined by what the French literature would call the territorial matrix; that is, the institutional, economic, social, and historical setting of the territory in which this organisational profile is developed. The study of the social enterprise requires previous knowledge of the territorial, institutional, and social context as the basis of investigation. If it exists, the way it is received and organised is distinct in each of the countries forming part of the two projects. This second conclusion does not preclude the role of supranational structures like, for example, the European Commission which in its member states exercises a very important influence on the other levels of government in order to reach certain objectives like, for example, improving the supply of collective childcare services both quantitatively and qualitatively, or creating new mechanisms for social integration for persons with more difficult employability. However, the instruments used in each one of the territories to reach the same public objectives and the role played by the social enterprise as one of these instruments varies from one country to another, even though the results pursued may be identical. As a result, the two research projects confirm that in the European member states there is a tendency toward convergence in public policy but the way these public policies are managed and especially the relative development of the social enterprise depend on the territorial matrix.

The third conclusion, which is related to the second, is that each sector is its own world:[12] the sector of providing childcare services is different from that of providing services to people trying to find employment. As each sector is its own world, the development of the social enterprise in each varies.

Among the stakeholders playing an important role in the development of social enterprise are those persons responsible for public policy. The two research projects have shown that the ways of connecting and coordinating developed by governments for the production and provision of services are very important in each of the participating countries in order for the social enterprise to develop in a specific sector. The TSFEPS Project demonstrated that the social enterprise in the sector providing childcare services has very little presence in Spain, unlike for example, in Belgium, France, in some parts of Germany, and Sweden where the associations of parents in collaboration with the territorial governments have their own niche in the market in this sector. In Spain the cooperatives, foundations and associations providing collective services to children under three years old are considered by government and perceived by the society in general to be conventional private enterprises.

Comparative analysis of these two projects also leads to the impression that social enterprise is more appreciated by those persons responsible for public policies to promote employment than by those promoting collective childcare services. Independently of the results obtained from these two projects, there are many more examples of government and private enterprises working in partnership in the sector of social integration through work than in the sector of collective services for young children.

At this point in our analysis it is important to evaluate the degree of trust established among different social operators and especially the degree of trust that social enterprise has developed in the fabric of society. After having participated in the PERSE project the impression obtained is that the social and solidarity cooperatives in Italy have been capable of developing levels of trust that are becoming a very important asset for their growth and consolidation as enterprises.

In the PERSE Project, more focused on the study of the applicability of social enterprise, it was ascertained that generally speaking in all the participating countries, producing is an instrument for work integration social enterprises. The aim of the integration enterprise is to transmit a series of skills and behaviours to help people to be able to enter the labour market. The work integration social enterprise is not a project of private interest. It is a project of collective interest. Consequently, the work integration social enterprise cannot be thought of as an enterprise competing in the free market. It has to be thought of as an organisation that belongs to a group of stakeholders (here the importance of the concept multi-stakeholder) citizens that work following norms that have been discussed and approved by different stakeholders and legally regulated by the public authorities. The concept of the multi-stakeholder enterprise means cooperation among different stakeholders. Among these stakeholders there are other enterprises and governments, primarily in the territorial area. In this context, cooperation between social enterprises and conventional enterprises does not imply, as it is understood in the economics literature, competition. Instead it means employing forms of collective action to resolve problems in a reality in which each of the actors working alone would not be capable of solving or would not have sufficient advantages to solve. The work integration social enterprise is a very good example of the necessity of multi-stakeholder action, of cooperation among community groups, conventional enterprises, and government to promote social integration. The concept of multi-stakeholder, of cooperation by working in a network, must not only be sought in the production of goods and services but also in the formation of skills and human capacities. The principal benefits that social enterprise contributes to its stakeholders are the improvements obtained by each of its stakeholders. The function of the work integration social enterprise lies in the organisation of a training project dedicated to guaranteeing over time the transmission of behaviour and work skills. Production is one of the consequences, not vice versa.

From this last analysis, two results can be deduced:

1   Protection, positive discrimination measures and fiscal bonuses that the work integration social enterprise receives in some countries should not be understood as disloyal competition against the interests of conventional enterprises. On the contrary, work integration social enterprise must be understood as an instrument belonging to all the community, which must facilitate cohesion and the social integration of people with difficult employability.

2   The territorial governments make available to work integration social enterprises, resources and support designed to reduce the loss of economic competition that the hiring of persons at a low level of productivity brings.

The benefits of using the social enterprise as unit of analysis

From the point of view of socio-economic research the social enterprise is making it possible to analyse some organisations as formal mechanisms of continuous relationships among different stakeholders who voluntarily act in coordination with each other to obtain better results than they could obtain acting alone. The perspective of studying the enterprise as the result of the coordination of different interests is often absent from economics studies. The perception of the organisation as a formal relationship among different stakeholders with the purpose of facilitating the coordination of physical, non-material and human resources allows one to talk about the existence of social capital inside the organisation – understood as the trust that has accumulated over time among these groups of stakeholders. Working in coordination forming part of an entrepreneurial project makes explicit the need for a more important level of involvement among the different stakeholders than a strategic temporary alliance. It means that the different stakeholders are involved in a project that does not have an expiration date. From this perspective the social enterprise can be conceived of not as a private project but as a collective project at the service of different stakeholders.

The main obstacles for the study of a sector using the social enterprise as unit of analysis

Today the main obstacle for economists who study social enterprise and in a more general way, the organisations making up the third sector or the social economy, is the uncertain or debatable theoretical status of these concepts and concretely of the concept of social enterprise, which is the focus of this chapter. Among economists the approach to the enterprise that dominates is that of an organisation that produces goods and services and whose objective in the market economy is to generate profits. Too frequently organisations are classified as public or private. And in the area of private organisations no distinctions are made. The researchers who focus their attention on the procurement of services by governments make reference to enterprises and give the impression that all enterprises have only one objective; all organisations in the private sector act based on economic rationalism.

A second important obstacle for the study of social enterprise is the lack of legislation in the majority of countries with the occasional exception such as the recently passed social enterprise law in Italy. One of the results of this lack of institutional recognition of social enterprise is its scarce practical importance and its non-existence in the statistical information provided by the different national statistical systems. As a result, the methodological research continues to be the case study. This methodology is valid for the first phase of research and analysis and especially for sensing innovations taking place in the area of organisations. But in the medium and long term this methodology is limited, and finally the researcher who wants to obtain quantitative results must make generalisations without distinguishing among the behaviours of different organisations acting in different sectors.

Another obstacle to the social enterprise awakening more interest in researchers in the social science disciplines is its relatively minor importance in comparison to the importance of other economic actors such as conventional enterprises or governments as producers and suppliers of services in general. In Spain, for example, utilising a broader concept of social enterprise, cooperatives and non-profit organisations account for five out of 100 of the total number of private organisations acting in the area of production for the year 2005 (National Institute of Statistics, 2006 and Vidal, 2007).

Conclusions

Based on the analysis carried out, we are in a better place to respond to the question posed in the title of this chapter: Should social enterprise be a core element in the provision of public services or is it a distraction? We have approached the concept of social enterprise utilising the conceptual framework of multi-stakeholder organisation. We have looked at the development and impact of the cooperative enterprises and mutuals in a reality characterised by a process of technological change, the liberal state and the non-existence of regulated workers' rights. In this concrete historical environment, some collectives organised and created their own structures with the primary definition of "mutual aid" organisations. In the second half of the twentieth century, the construction of the social welfare state in some European countries facilitated the strengthening of mutuals and associations as arms of management for governments. Associations were contracted by mutuals to provide public services. The result was the rise of the non-profit sector to produce and provide services. Starting in the last quarter of the twentieth century, operating foundations began to rise in a more intense way in some countries more than in others because of specific legal incentives, as occurred in Spain. Over time cooperatives, associations and foundations have begun to operate in the sectors related to the production and supply of public services. This convergence, together with the growing demand for relational services in Europe, is allowing the emergence of a new profile of enterprise within the third sector whose primary characteristic is its definition as a multi-stakeholder initiative.

One of the important results of the TSFEPS and PERSE Projects has been that you cannot isolate the development of social enterprises from the decisions of government. It is in the governance of the public authorities wherein resides in an important but not exclusive way, the explicit option of promoting the social enterprise among the different organisational options available. For the past decade the subject of the governance of an organisation has begun to generate a certain amount of literature. In the case of local governments Proeller has pointed out that "governance is proclaimed to be the rising topic, set to become the central model of local government discussions and to receive more attention than public management in future debates" (Proeller, 2006: 9). Andrews *et al.* make reference to mismanagement. They consider that one path that local governments can take to increase their performance is "to work in partnership with the voluntary and especially the private sector when delivering services", even though they recognise that the benefits of working in partnership can be tempered by the additional contracting costs that are generated – especially costs related to transaction, trust and rent seeking (Andrews *et al.*, 2006: 279). We could continue citing more quotations but the objective now is to underline the fact that there is a rich literature focused on government and the important role of governance in the performance of production and provision of public services. In the area of the conventional enterprise, the literature related to corporate governance and the concept of the multi-stakeholder has perhaps generated less literature but it is a subject that is becoming important (Kristensen, 2001; Moon, 2002 and Zadek, 2005). Consequently it is not at all strange that in the area of the third sector, the concepts of the multi-stakeholder enterprise (Borzaga and Defourny, 2001) and of co-governance (Pestoff, 2008) are beginning to be raised.

In the current state of reflection there does not exist just one single concept of governance. Pestoff (2008) writes, "the concept of governance gained extensive attention recently, becoming a buzzword in social science. It is used in a wide array of contexts with a wide divergence in meanings". In this chapter the concept of governance being used is not that of working in network or temporary collaboration, but rather in multi-stakeholder initiatives in which the different stakeholders form part of the governing organs of the organisation and have the right not only to speak but also to vote. The analysis used attempts to respond to questions such as: what happens inside an organisation governed by different stakeholders who might have different interests? The levels of meso and macro analysis have not been used; rather attention has been focused on the micro level of analysis: the organisation.

The results obtained with the PERSE and TSFEPS Projects raise new areas of work. It is necessary to continue studying the impact of multi-stakeholder governance inside the social enterprise, not only as it affects the management of the organisation but also in the way it affects the work of directors and workers. It is also important to study the impact on governments as they get directly involved in the governance of private organisations. It is also necessary to continue working to better detect the conditions needed to facilitate the development of a favourable atmosphere for the social enterprise. Disposing of a battery of material indicators to recognise this atmosphere is going to make it easier to measure the level of trust accumulated by the enterprise among its stakeholders. We must also continue to resolve the problems of interpretation inherent in the process of formation of values such as credibility, reputation and trust with other stakeholders with whom the enterprise works in partnership. Related to accountability, what is the role of regulation, self-regulation and above all transparency? What is the impact of these changes for the other stakeholders, governments, conventional enterprises, families, and the community? For the social enterprise to develop it must first accumulate trust. However, the other stakeholders – governments, enterprises, the community, family – must be able to value the presence of social enterprises. Possibly the definition of the social enterprise laid out by the EMES Network refers more to the standard analysis of what the profile of an enterprise operating in the sector of public services should be than to the positive analysis of how the dominant enterprise operating today in the provision of public services actually is.

Notes

1 This chapter is a revised version of the paper written for the Exploratory Workshop of the European Science Foundation "The Third Sector in a Changing Europe: Key

Trends and Challenges" Corvinus University, Budapest, 6–8 December, 2006. The author also acknowledges the useful and insightful comment of Adalbert Evers, Victor Pestoff and Dennis Young on the first version of this paper. Responsibility for the content, however, lies with the author alone, as always.

2 Member of the EMES Network and professor at the University of Barcelona.

3 The EMES Network is a non-profit association whose members are research centres and academics from different social science disciplines. Ten years ago a particular concept of the social enterprise began to develop. More detailed information about the academic perspective of the EMES Network can be found by going to its website: www.emes.net.

4 Belgium, Bulgaria, France, Germany, Italy, Spain, Sweden, the UK. The national TSFEPS reports are available on the EMES site: www.emes.net. For an overview of the different contributions from the TSFEPS Project see Fraisse (2006) published in the Bulletin of CIES.

5 Belgium, Denmark, Finland, France, Germany, Ireland, Italy, Portugal, Spain, Sweden and the UK. The national PERSE reports are available on the EMES site: www.emes.net. One outcome of this research work is found in Marthe Nyssen (2006a).

6 Consumer co-operatives provide the shopping basket of basic goods for their members; mutuals provide a social plan and health services; associated work cooperatives, the creation and maintenance of employment; the agricultural cooperatives, better marketing of the products obtained from the land, etc.

7 During the 1980s the rediscovery of worker cooperatives was the subject of three doctoral theses which were later published: Demoustier, 1981; Vidal, 1987 and Defourny 1990.

8 We are referring to childcare services, home care services for dependent persons, or services to integrate persons with physical or psychological disabilities into the labour market.

9 A complete and well-reasoned definition of the concept of social enterprise can be found in the book by Borzaga and Defourny (2001). The concept of the social enterprise is advanced in Nyssen (2006a).

10 A mechanism available to researchers in responding to these questions is to use available theories. Being a multidisciplinary network of researchers, there are various theories utilised proceeding from different perspectives of analysis.

11 It should be pointed out that in this same collective work, Pestoff (2008) uses the results obtained by the TSFEPS Project to reflect on the concepts of co-production and co-governing. It confirms that in France and Germany, in contrast to Sweden, there exist experiences of co-governance between governance and families in the service of production and provision of childcare services.

12 A conclusion which may be surprising though it was already known. For the American case see Hammack and Young (1993).

Bibliography

Akerlof, G.A. (2002), Behavioural macroeconomics and macroeconomics behaviour, *American Economic Review*, 92 (3): 411–433.

Alesina, A. and La Ferrara, E. (2002), Who trusts others, *Journal of Public Economics*, 85: 207–234.

Andrews, R., Boyne, G.A. and Enticott, G. (2006), Performance failure in the public sector: misfortune or mismanagement, *Public Management Review*, 8 (2): 273–296.

Bacchiega, A. and Borzaga, C. (2001), Social enterprises as incentive structures. An economic analysis, in C. Borzaga and J. Defourny (eds) (2001), *The emergence of social enterprise*, London and New York: Routledge, pp. 273–295.

Baldin, E. (2005), Sistema di governance e sistema di accountability nel nonprofit, *Impresa Sociale*, 74 (4): 62–81.

Borzaga, C. and Defourny, J. (ed.) (2001), *The emergence of social enterprise*, London and New York: Routledge.

Brandsen, T. (2007), The third sector and public services: an evaluation of different theoretical perspectives, CIES, no. 45. available online: www.grupcies.com.

Defourny, J. (1990), *Démocratie cooperative et efficacité économique. La performance comparée des SCOP françaises*, Bruxelles: De Boeck.

Defourny, J. (2001), From third sector to social enterprise, in C. Borzaga and J. Defourny (eds) (2001), *The emergence of social enterprise*, London and New York: Routledge, pp. 1–28.

Demoustier, D. (1981), Entre l'efficacité et la démocratie:les coopératives de production, Paris: Entente.

Fraisse, L. (2006), The third sector in the local governance of childcare services, en CIES, no. 39, available online: www.grupcies.com.

Hammack, D. and Young, D. (1993), *Nonprofit organizations in a market economy*, San Francisco: Jossey-Bass.

Kerlin, J.A. (2006), Social enterprise in the United Status and Europe: understanding and learning from the differences, *Voluntas*, 17 (3): 247–265.

Kristensenj, J. (2001), Corporate social responsibility and new social partnerships, in C. Kjaergaard and S. Westphalen (eds), *From collective bargaining to social partnership*, Copenhagen: The Copenhagen Centre. Available online: www.copenhagencentre.org.

Laville, J.L. (2001), France: social enterprises developing proximity services, in C. Borzaga and J. Defourny, (eds) (2001), *The emergence of social enterprise*, London: Routledge, pp. 100–120.

Moon, J. (2002), The social responsibility of business and new governance, *Government and Opposition*, 37 (3): 385–408.

National Institute of Statistics (2006), DIRCE: www.ine.es.

Nyssen, M. (ed.) (2006a), *Social enterprise. At the crossroads of market, public policies and civil society*, London and New York: Routledge.

Nyssen, M. (2006b), The third sector and the social inclusion agenda: the role of social enterprises in the field of work integration, paper presented at the Exploratory Workshop of the European Science Foundation "The Third Sector in a Changing Europe: Key Trends and Challenges", Corvinus University, Budapest, 6–8 December, 2006.

Osborne, S. (2006), The third sector in a changing Europe: key trends and challenges, paper presented at the Exploratory Workshop of the European Science Foundation "The Third Sector in a Changing Europe: Key Trends and Challenges", Corvinus University, Budapest, 6–8 December, 2006.

Pestoff, V. (2008) Co-production, the third sector and functional representation in Sweden, in Stephen P. Osborne (ed.) (2008) *The Third Sector in Europe. Prospects and challenges*, London: Routledge, pp. 159–182.

Proeller, I. (2006), Trend in local government in Europe, *Public Management Review*, 8 (1): 7–29.

Sacconi, L. And Faillo, M. (2005), Come emerge l'impresa sociale? Uno sguardo d'assieme alla teoria della complementarietà tra ideologia, governance e accountability, *Impresa Sociale*, 74 (4): 82–105.

Salamon, L. (1995), *Partners in Public service: government–nonprofit relations in the modern welfare state*: Baltimore and London: John Hopkins University Press.

Salas, V. (2001), Cultura y Confianza en las organizaciones, paper cited in F. Pérez (dir.)

(2005), *La medición del capital social. Una approximación*, Madrid: Fundación BBVA, p. 20.

SCIG (2001), Social capital: a position paper, Social Capital Interest Group, Michigan State University.

Sobel, J. (2002) Can we trust social capital?, *Journal of Economic Literature*, XL, March: 139–154.

Vidal, I. (1987), *Crisis económica y transformaciones en el mercado de trabajo. El asociacionismo económico en Cataluña*, Barcelona: Diputación de Barcelona.

Vidal, I. (2007), Third sector. images and concepts in Spain, available online: www.emes.net.

Williamson, O. (1993), Calculativeness, trust and economic organization, *Journal of Law and Economics*, 34: 453–502.

Zadek, S. (2005) The logic of collaborative governance, Working Paper no. 3, The Corporate Social Initiative, Kennedy School of Government, Harvard University.

Websites

www.copenhaguencentre.org
www.emes.net
www.grupcies.com

18 Social co-operatives for persons with mental health problems in Greece

A specific form of social enterprise

Dimitris Ziomas

Introduction

Compared to the approaches which are applied in other countries, Greece has created a unique legislative framework for the inclusion of people with mental health problems into employment. This framework provides for the establishment of Social Co-operatives of limited liability, which constitute, thus far in Greece, the only institutionalised form of a "social enterprise" type of organisation.

The Social Co-operative, as provided by the Greek Law No. 2716/1999 (Article 12), is a specific form of a co-operative organisation, which serves both economic and social-therapeutical purposes. It aims, in particular, at the socio-economic re-integration and vocational re-insertion of persons with mental health problems, contributing in this way to their therapy and, to the greatest possible extent, to their economic self-sufficiency. In the pursuit of this overriding objective, Social Co-operatives are considered commercial organisations and can develop and perform any economic activity in an entrepreneurial manner.

As regards its legal basis, its unique feature is that the Social Co-operative constitutes both an "enterprise", basically productive and trade-oriented organisation and, at the same time, a "mental health unit". The challenge therefore is to find the best possible way to manage both functions or objectives in balance and to avoid promoting the one at the cost of the other.

Moreover, another novel feature of the Social Co-operative is that, unlike the other types of co-operatives where membership is composed of only one type of stakeholder, its formation requires a wider partnership relationship consisting of the following three main categories: persons with mental health problems, mental health professionals and other persons and agencies from the local community.

Given the above, a number of issues and questions are raised, which this chapter attempts to address and discuss as thoroughly as possible.

The state of play of the Third Sector in Greece

It is generally accepted that in almost all old member states of the European Union, especially since the mid-1990s, there has been a remarkable growth of the "third sector" or the "social economy sector", whereby these terms refer to all those socio-economic activities that fall neither within the scope of the traditional private business sector nor of the public sector. It should be noted, however, that the legal forms and the historical experiences and traditions of such socio-economic activities vary considerably from country to country.

In Greece, over the last ten years, one observes the emergence of a more local, less visible part of the "third sector", consisting of initiatives, projects and agencies which are taking shape around the less formalised tasks and challenges such as: new social problems, environmental problems, concerns about unemployment and the social exclusion of vulnerable social groups etc. These initiatives, however, run mainly on limited programme funding,[1] supported in their majority by the European Union's Social Fund financing, and not on stable local funds though there are notable exceptions. Nevertheless, it is only the minority of these initiatives that base their strength on local solidarities, including voluntary work and civic commitment, elements which are still underdeveloped in Greece.

Notwithstanding the fact that most of these initiatives have sprung up mainly in response to the availability of European Union funds, their impact has been positive, especially in the provision of social and welfare services including work integration activities. This is obviously due to the fact that the existing forms of state provision in this area have been inadequate to deal with high unemployment and the emerging situations of social exclusion that Greece has been facing during the last decade. Moreover the role of such initiatives has become even more significant over recent years, given the fact that public social policy spending has been under control, while there is uncertainty about the outcomes of public social policy programmes and especially of employment policies and measures.

In short, it appears that many of the initiatives which are considered part of the "third sector" are being gradually accorded certain legitimacy in Greece. At the same time, the need for facilitating new forms of co-operation and partnership through new institutional arrangements that would promote, among other things, the development of the social economy sector, has entered the political discussion in Greece. Undoubtedly, a major stimuli for this has been the EU's guidelines and recommendations on the linking of employment promotion and local development and on exploiting, in particular, the potential of the social economy sector to create jobs.

However, in spite of the above, with the exception of the social co-operatives of limited liability, which this chapter presents, no public policy has been developed as yet in Greece with respect to exploiting the potential of the social economy sector. Thus, differently from many other European Union member states, the "third sector" or the "social economy sector" as a relevant category for employment policy formation has attained, thus far, only a marginal position in Greece. The notion and knowledge regarding "social economy" remains still low in Greece and there is a profound lack of any dedicated institutional or legal arrangements for action.

A short overview of the evolution of the forms of work integration activities for mentally ill people in Greece

Since the early 1990s, largely under the influence of European Community's Regulation 815/84, most psychiatric hospitals in Greece began increasingly to be engaged in the task of preparing mentally ill patients for social rehabilitation, including the provision of employment opportunities, as well as the provision of housing facilities which would allow the mentally ill to lead independent or semi-independent lives in the community. For, it was increasingly becoming self-evident that the establishment of community-based residences and the development of vocational rehabilitation programmes were among the crucial elements of the rehabilitation and de-institutionalisation process which was under way.

Indeed, the 1990s witnessed a growing concern among all those involved in the provision of mental health services in Greece to find the most suitable ways to improve the prospects of mentally ill people re-entering the labour market, which was recognised as one of the basic prerequisites for their social inclusion.

It should be pointed out that this widely felt need, observed in the 1990s, did not apply only to countries like Greece, where psychiatric reform at that time was still relatively young, but even in the more advanced EU member states. Probably this was accounted for by the fact that the de-institutionalisation of the hospitals is underlying the need for alternative services, including work opportunities, which, in turn, increases the needs for independent living and therefore brings about a greater realisation of the necessity of providing job opportunities in this process.

It was in this context that a number of work integration initiatives for the mentally ill living in psychiatric hospitals or in mental health hostels located in the community were established in the first half of the 1990s. These initiatives took mainly the form of either informal "*productive sheltered workshops*" or informal "*Co-operative Therapeutical Units*". Note should be made of the fact that the operation of the latter, namely the "*Co-operative Therapeutical Unit*", though not based on an existing legal framework, it was based on an internal regulation/constitution which provided, among other things, that it would be run by an administrative board composed of hospital personnel and patients employed in the unit.

Moreover, from the mid-1990s onwards, in addition to these initiatives, a number of small-scale productive units for mentally ill people began to emerge, taking the form of either a "*civil society*" organisation or an "*Urban Co-operative*" or "*Agricultural Co-operative*". So, a small number of such initiatives, being characterised by a relative autonomy from the psychiatric hospitals and by an entrepreneurial orientation, employing mentally ill people living outside the hospitals, began to operate during the second half of the 1990s.

Yet, again, even these more developed and formal organisational forms, although providing a better framework for vocational rehabilitation and work experience for the mentally ill, were found to be short of facilitating to the required degree the needs, and especially the therapeutical needs, of the mentally ill people. This was mainly attributed to the fact that the legal framework used by these initiatives was not flexible enough and lacked specific provisions which were required for setting up a "social enterprise" type of organisation, capable of facilitating the re-integration of the mentally ill into employment and of ensuring conditions in which discrimination against them is eliminated. Thus, the need for an appropriate legal and institutional framework was widely recognised.

It was this widely felt need which subsequently led to the adoption of Article 12, which provides for the establishment of *Social Co-operatives of Limited Liability (KoiSPE)*, under Law No. 2716 of 1999 concerning the "Development and Modernisation of Mental Health Services" in Greece. Provisions under Article 12 of this law have been designed in such a way so as to be conducive to the creation of alternative facilities with respect to both vocational rehabilitation and work activities geared to the needs of people with mental health problems. It is important to note that the provisions of Article 12, concerning the establishment of the Social Co-operatives, have taken account of other member states' experiences in this field at that time, and especially that of Italy's where two types of Social Co-operatives were already in operation.

The institution of Social Co-operatives of Limited Liability in Greece

A short profile

The institution of Social Co-operative is a specific form of co-operative which is underpinned by a specific social aim, serving both therapeutic and entrepreneurial purposes. In particular, Social Co-operatives provide the opportunity for their members to regain "unused" skills or to acquire new ones through on-the-job training and work experience and eventually to acquire a permanent job in a somehow "protective" environment or in the regular labour market. At the same time, members of the co-operative learn to work on a collective basis and take some responsibility relating to the performance of the co-operative's activities. It should be pointed out that in these co-operatives, work activities are carried out by both mentally ill people and non-mentally ill people, thus avoiding the creation of a "sheltered" work situation. Furthermore, this initiative has began to paving the way for similar legal arrangements to be made in order to facilitate the establishment of Social Co-operatives by other vulnerable population groups and, in general, the development of the social economy sector in Greece.

The main innovative elements characterising the institution of Social Co-operatives

- It is a new organisational form;
- it ensures compatibility between economic and social objectives;

- it strengthens and promotes partnership relations and arrangements;
- it enhances the mobilisation of the local actors and the local community at large;
- it facilitates and promotes a "bottom-up" approach;
- it constitutes part of the de-institutionalisation process of mentally ill people;
- it is underpinned by an integrated approach;
- it exploits the potentiality of social capital development in a specific territorial context.

The legal basis of Social Co-operatives of Limited Liability

The Greek Law No. 2716 of 1999 concerning "the development and modernisation of mental health services" provides, among other things, for the formation of "Social Co-operatives of Limited Liability", which are legal entities of private law. The Social Co-operatives, as provided by Article 12 of the above-mentioned law, are a specific form of co-operative, given that apart from being basically productive and trade-oriented, organisations are simultaneously considered as mental health units supervised by the Ministry of Health and Social Solidarity.

Note should be made of the fact that there is a restriction with regard to the number of Social Co-operatives that can be established in each mental health sector – "catchment" area, which is usually geographically based: that is, in each mental health sector, usually covering one prefecture, only *one* Social Co-operative can be established.

The Social Co-operatives have autonomy in decision-making through their democratically elected organs. However, the state (and in particular the Ministry of Health and Social Solidarity) has supervisory powers with regard to the legal aspects of its operation, while it monitors the development of Social Co-operatives.

Overall, the legal framework of Social Co-operatives resembles to a certain extent the existing framework provided for the agricultural and urban type of co-operatives established in Greece. For, it provides for the formation of an organisation which possesses the following distinctive features: it requires the joint effort of individuals with a common purpose or problem; it aims at the realisation of a mixture of economic and social objectives; it is not under state control but under collective control and democratic management through democratically elected (one member, one vote) bodies; it can undertake entrepreneurial activities with the emphasis on the production of socially useful products and services; and finally, its operations are funded mainly from the sales of its products and services, while it can receive some donations or state grants.

However, *the new elements* introduced by Article 12 of Law No. 2716/1999 for the establishment of "Social Co-operatives of Limited Liability" renders them different from the abovementioned types of co-operatives. *These elements are the following*:

- it states that the Social Co-operative can serve many purposes and perform any economic activity, in contrast to existing regulations governing urban and agricultural type of co-operatives in Greece;
- it gives the right to mentally ill people to undertake any economic activity;
- it defines the membership shares allocated to each participating group (at least 35 per cent to mentally ill people, not more than 45 per cent to professionals in the provision of services and not more than 20 per cent to unemployed persons, other agencies or organisations with a related purpose, etc.);
- it envisages the participation of two mentally ill people on the administrative board (consisting of seven members) of the Social Co-operative;
- it envisages a salary for mentally ill persons employed by the Social Co-operative, ensuring at the same time their right to continue to receive any disability payments provided by the state.

The objectives of social co-operatives

The basic aim of their establishment is the socio-economic re-integration and vocational rehabilitation of *mentally ill people*, contributing in this way to their therapy and to the greatest possible extent to their economic self-sufficiency. In the pursuit of this overriding objective, Social Co-operatives are considered commercial organisations and can develop and perform any economic activity in an entrepreneurial manner.

Overall, it may be said that the establishment of Social Co-operatives reflect the widely felt need to shift the focus of social and job integration activities from the affliction of the disabled person to his/her potentiality. That is, the need to promote initiatives that take into account both therapeutical aspects and the development of skills and activities of the persons with special needs. In addition, they reflect the widespread tendency to create work situations where the disabled persons are mixed with the non-disabled persons, thereby avoiding the creation of traditional sheltered workshops for the disabled.

Composition of the membership

The potential members of the Social Co-operatives are divided into three distinct categories:

- *The first category involves the mentally ill people, above 15 years of age irrespective of diagnostic category, the stage of illness and their residence without the requirement of them being capable of legal transactions or not. It is obligatory that people in this category represent at least 35 per cent of all members of the Social Co-operative.*

  These members can be employed by the Social Co-operatives of Limited Liability and get paid according to their productivity levels and time of work. In the event of them receiving some form of pension, allowance or other form of benefit, they do not lose these benefits but continue to collect them concurrently and in addition to their Social Co-operatives of Limited Liability salaries. If they are not insured, Social Co-operatives of Limited Liability provides insurance for them in the respective insurance agency.

- *The second category involves the mental health professionals such as psychiatrists, psychologists, nurses, occupational workers, trainers and, in general, those working in the area of mental health. The members of this category cannot exceed the upper limit of 45 per cent of the total number of the Social Co-operative's members.*

  Public servants such as psychiatrists, psychologists, social workers, etc., working at the NHS (National Health System) can also be members of the Social Co-operatives of Limited Liability. These members can be seconded from their Public Service to work (full or part-time) at a Social Co-operative, while they continue to receive their salaries as public servants.

- *The third category involves other individuals as well as legal entities of public or private law. It involves, in particular individuals such as unemployed persons, persons from other vulnerable social groups, etc., as well as agencies and organizations such as local authorities, hospitals, public organizations, etc. Membership of this category cannot go beyond the upper limit of 20 per cent of all members of the Social Co-operative.*

Employment arrangements and regulations in the social co-operatives

Mentally ill people can be employed in the Social Co-operatives and get a salary in accordance with their productivity and the hours worked. This salary is added to any benefit or pension that the mentally ill person is entitled to receive. If the person is lacking social insurance, the Social Co-operative is required by law to provide social insurance coverage.

Co-operative shares

Compulsory co-operative shares: each member receives, upon enrolment, a compulsory co-operative share as defined in the statute of Social Co-operatives of Limited Liability. The co-operative share is the same and of equal value for all members.

Optional co-operative shares: each member has the option of obtaining up to five optional shares. Legal entities of public equity or non-profit legal entities of private equity (public or private sector) have the option of obtaining an unlimited number of optional shares, should there is such a provision in the Social Co-operative's Statute.

Organisational aspects

The managing bodies of the Social Co-operatives are the following:

1   *the General Assembly*, which is the highest decision-making body for all matters concerning the Social Co-operative, composed of all its members;
2   *the Management Board* (or Administrative Council), which is composed of seven members elected by the general assembly and which is responsible for the management and operation of all activities of the Social Co-operative;
3   *the Supervisory Council* which is composed of three elected by the General Assembly and which is responsible for the supervision and monitoring of the activities of the Management Board.

It should also be stressed that all Social-Co-operatives are based on the principle of democratic management, which in turn is based on the clause "one member, one vote".

Social Co-operatives of Limited Liability resources

Social Co-operatives of Limited Liability resources stem from:

*   Funding from the regular state budget or the public investment programme exclusively for co-funding programs from the European Union (EU) or international organisations.
*   Funding from national organisations, the investment program, development programs, EU or international organisations.
*   Legacies, donations and surrender the use of property.
*   Incomes from Social Co-operatives of Limited Liability activities.
*   Incomes from Social Co-operatives of Limited Liability property utilization.

Other aspects of Social Co-operatives

*   *Associating with legal entities of public law. The state, public organisations, local authorities of 'a' and 'b' grade as well as their respective legal entities are supplied with goods and receive services from Social Co-operatives of Limited Liability. In that case, the supply of goods/services offered can take place by contracting with Social Co-operatives of Limited Liability.*

    The above-mentioned state agencies are allowed to give away to Social Co-operatives of Limited Liability, for the purpose of use only, assets (landed property or real estates) and any other form of facilities.
*   *Tax reductions.* Social Co-operatives of Limited Liability are exempted from any kind of taxation, direct or indirect, except VAT.

An overview of the social co-operatives established to date in Greece

The first Social Co-operative was established in November 2002 on Leros island with mentally ill people from the Leros Psychiatric Hospital as well as people from the local community. In total, it employs 41 people of which 27 are mentally ill. Nine more Social Co-operatives have been established recently in Athens (three), Corfu island, Chios island, Crete island (Chania), Thessaloniki, Katerini and Amfissa, which nevertheless are not as yet in full operation of all their forecasted activities. In addition to these ten Social Co-operatives, two more are to be established in the near future (in Athens and on Kefalonia island).

However, it is difficult to make an assessment of their operation and their impact to date on the socio-economic integration of the mentally ill people, given that they are still at an early stage of development.

Problems/difficulties that the Social Co-operatives are facing at the early stage of their operation and development

Problems related to the mobilisation of a wide range of stakeholders

There are serious difficulties in enlarging – opening up the partnership relationship on which Social Co-operatives' establishment is based upon to a wider range of organisations/agencies from the local community (i.e. local authorities agencies, private sector enterprises, social partners' organisations, etc.). For, most of the Social Co-operatives which have been recently established continue to a great extent to rely on the involvement of the psychiatric hospitals as the sole facilitators for the implementation of such initiatives, let alone the fact that hospitals remain an indispensable stakeholder. Besides, the public's attention as well as the political attention to Social Co-operatives continues to be very low.

It is thus of utmost importance that efforts should be concentrated on the promotion of an area-based wider partnership on which Social Co-operatives are established. Exploitation of the social capital and, in particular, of volunteers' involvement should also be given a high priority in this respect.

Issues related to the effective implementation of an ambitious business plan

Although at an early stage of operation and development, it has already proved difficult in practice for the Social Co-operatives to implement an ambitious business plan entailing noteworthy targets as regards the creation of new jobs, especially for the mentally ill people. So, the goods and services Social Co-operatives produce to date are rather of a limited range and it seems that they reproduce to some extent the traditional methods of the "sheltered productive workshops". One of the basic reasons for this is considered to be their limited capital base and their inability to have recourse to resources from the "traditional" financial sources as private enterprises have.

Lack of access to financial resources

The above-mentioned weakness is related to the crucial problem facing Social Co-operatives, namely the fact that they do not have access to financial resources. For, no relevant provisions have been made neither any other institutional arrangements so far with regard to securing some initial financial support for the Social Co-operatives' establishment. Access, in particular, to the bank loans is virtually impossible due to the lack of provisions by public mechanisms to provide collateral to Social Co-operatives as they do to private enterprises.

Lack of exceptional public support

Public and local authorities are still far from entrusting Social Co-operatives with the production of services. Specific arrangements are needed and special provisions should be made for assigning public orders and small contracts to Social Co-operatives.

Lack of managerial skills

Another problem seems to be the lack of competent managerial personnel, capable of taking over the management of the Social Co-operatives. Despite the efforts that have been made, especially under the Community Initiative "EQUAL", to implement a number of vocational training programmes for acquiring appropriate managerial skills for a Social Co-operative, the *"Social Manager"* as an institution is still underplayed and has not been supported adequately by the system of vocational training or the system of higher education. And of course, managerial skills are considered a crucial prerequisite for Social Co-operatives to develop in the light of real market prospects in productive activity and services.

Lack of coordination between the competent public organisations

In most cases, it appears that a number of administrative and bureaucratic problems have delayed, and continue to do so, the actual operation of Social Co-operatives. This is mainly attributed to the lack of coordination between certain public organisations which are involved in areas such the social insurance coverage of the Social Co-operatives' members, the system of benefits to the mentally ill people etc. It seems that the competent public authorities and the public officials are not adequately, and up-to-date, informed as regards the new institution of the Social Co-operative and the specific provisions that the legal framework provides for it.

Concluding remarks

It is of fundamental importance that Social Co-operatives build up and cultivate a sound reputation in the market for their actual skill in improving the occupational capabilities of the mentally ill people and in certifying their level of productivity. And to this end, it is considered necessary to establish a structure of empowerment and ongoing support which will provide the appropriate technical assistance required to increase the number of Social Co-operatives established in Greece and facilitate their proper functioning and further development. The technical assistance structure "Synergeio", which was established under the community initiative programme "EQUAL", constitutes a good example towards this direction. For, the advent of "Synergeio" has facilitated greatly the recent establishment of four Social Co-operatives for mentally ill persons.

The institution of Social Co-operative is certainly incapable of providing alone a solution to the vast problem of the occupational integration of mentally ill people. But, undoubtedly, it provides a tool which lends itself particularly well to coordination with other measures not only with respect to the employment prospects of this vulnerable social group, but also with respect to their social inclusion and, thus, to their full citizenship. In this context, policy-makers must be made fully aware that they have at their disposal a truly innovative measure not only in the field of active employment policies, but also in social policy and other related policies. For, Social Co-operatives can bring about additional benefits. That is, socially worthwhile benefits which are not necessarily directly related to employment development, such as: contribution to local development, promotion of a participatory style, raising community confidence on them and thus enlarging the resource base.

Note

1 Programme funding is frequently only available for a relatively short initial period, after which funding ceases.

Bibliography

Badelt, C. (1997) "Entrepreneurship Theories of the Non-Profit Sector", *Voluntas*, vol. 8, no. 2, pp. 168–178.

Borzaga, C. and Defourny, J. (eds) (2001) *The Emergence of Social Enterprise*, Routledge, London.

Borzaga, C. and Santuari, A. (2000) *The Innovative Trends in the Non-profit Sector in Europe: The Emergence of Social Entrepreneurship*, OECD, conference.

—— (eds) (1998) *Social Enterprises and New Employment in Europe*, Regione Autonoma Trentino-Alto Adige, Trento.

Chrysakis, M. and Ziomas, D. (2002) "Social Economy and Employment: Prospects and Necessary Interventions", *Review of Labour Relations*, vol. 26 (April 2002), pp. 66–77 (available only in Greek).

Chrysakis, M., Ziomas, D., Karamitopoulou, D. and Xatzantonis, D. (2000) *Prospects of*

Employment in the Social Economy Sector, Report, National Institute of Labour, Athens (available only in Greek).

—— (2002) *Prospects of Employment in the Social Economy Sector*, Sakkoulas, Thessaloniki (available only in Greek).

CIRIEC (2000) *The Enterprises and Organizations of the Third System*, International Center of Research and Information on the Public and Cooperative Economy, Liège.

EMES (1999) *The Emergence of Social Enterprises in Europe: A Short Overview*, EMES European Network Bruxelles.

European Commission (1995) *Local Initiatives for Development*, Brussels.

—— (1998b) Pilot Action *Third System and Employment: Directory of Projects*, DGV. A4, Brussels.

European Parliament and European Commission (2000) *Third System Organizations and their Role in Developing Employment*, Brussels.

Evers, A. (1995) "Part of the Welfare Mix: The Third Sector as an Intermediate Area", *Voluntas*, vol. 6, no. 2, pp. 159–182.

Mertens, S. (1999) "Nonprofit Organizations and Social Economy: Two Ways of Understanding the Third Sector", *Annals of Public and Co-operative Economics*, vol. 70, no. 3, pp. 501–520.

Palmer, J. (1999) *Job Creation through the Third Sector: The Role of the Corporate Sector*, a report by the European Policy Centre.

Seyfried, E. and Ziomas, D. (2005) "Pathways to Social Integration for People with Mental Health Problems: The Establishment of Social Co-operatives in Greece", *Peer Review in the Field of Social Inclusion Policies* (www.pr-soc-incl.net).

Ziomas, D., Ketsetzopouloy, M. and Bouzas, N. (1998) "Greece", in Borzaga, C. and Santuari, A. (eds) *Social Enterprises and New Employment in Europe*, Regione Autonoma Trentino-Alto Adige, Trento, pp. 283–310.

—— (2001) "Greece: Social Enterprises Responding to Welfare Needs", in Borzaga, C. and Defourny, J. (eds) *The Emergence of Social Enterprise*, Routledge, London, pp. 136–148.

Part IX
Conclusions

19 The economic analysis of non-profit organisations' management

Marc Jegers

Introduction

The aim of this chapter is to provide a conceptual and intuitive overview of the main insights stemming from a microeconomic, "theory of the firm" like, analysis of non-profit organisation (NPO) management. Apart from more general aspects such as objectives and governance, the main functional domains are discussed: organisational strategy, marketing (volunteers, donations and subsidies, profit activities), accounting (financial accounting, audit, management accounting, accounting manipulations), finance (capital structure, investment analysis, financial vulnerability), and some aspects of human resources management. The literature reviewed proves that the internal functioning of NPOs can be analysed with the same microeconomic instruments and concepts as applied to for-profit organisations or governmental agencies, but also that a large number of topics are still under-researched. Most empirical research has been conducted with US data, though contextual differences might suggest that when the same framework is applied to European organisations, the empirical evidence cannot be expected to be comparable to the US evidence. Furthermore, European researchers are disadvantaged when trying to analyse these topics, due to the lack of standardised data on inputs and outputs of non-profit organisations.

Although there is a long tradition of analysing the for-profit organisation (PO) within a microeconomic framework,[1] a comparable coherent body of knowledge does not exist for the non-profit organisation (NPO). The aim of the present chapter is to collect and present pieces of research on the functioning of NPOs in a structured and non-technical way, hopefully showing their usefulness for both further academic research and daily managerial practice in NPOs. *Theory of the non-profit firm* could be a nice overarching label for these contributions.

Choosing this frame of reference implies ignoring some other important microeconomic achievements in the field of NPOs (besides numerous other valuable approaches), especially the "demand side" question on the existence of NPOs: why are NPOs desirable in society, or at least preferred to other institutional forms (Gui, 1991; Krashinsky, 1986)? Transaction cost theorising (Williamson, 1979, 1991) might suggest some answers to this question, especially when incorporated in widely known reflections on market failure, government failure, public goods, contract failure, client control, or in lesser known theories based on the implications of stochastic demand (Holtmann, 1983) or employee commitment (Francois, 2001).

The focus of the present text is on the internal functioning of NPOs. The most promising microeconomic approach in this respect is the principal-agent theory. Jensen and Meckling (1976) coined the terms involved by stating that a principal-agent relation is "a contract under which one or more persons (the principal(s)) engage another person (the agent) to perform some service on their behalf which involves delegating some decision making authority to the agent" (308). The objectives ("utility arguments" in an economist's vocabulary) of the principal need not be identical to the objectives of the agent, a situation giving rise to "agency costs", which are the sum of the costs the principal has to bear to monitor the agent (*monitoring costs*), the costs the agent incurs in order to convince the principal of his trustworthiness (*bonding costs*), and the eventual welfare loss by the principal as compared to her (theoretical) welfare in a situation with principal and agent having identical objectives. Though stewardship theory assumes this latter situation to be reality or the norm for NPOs, it can at best be considered as an extreme case of a principal-agent relation, in which the difference between objectives is reduced or eliminated (Caers *et al.*, 2006a). Therefore, it is no surprise that most authors accept the principal-agent framework to be relevant when studying the functioning of NPOs (e.g. Brody, 1996; Herman and Heimovics, 1991; Miller-Millesen, 2003; Steinberg, 1990). Both the relation between the board (as the guard of the organisation's objectives) and management, and the relation between management and the other staff[2] can be modelled as principal-agent relations (Caers *et al.*, 2006a), as well as other relations typical for NPOs, such as between donors and the organisation, or, more generally, between multiple stakeholders and the board, or well-known relations in POs, such as between debt-holders and the organisation.

In traditional PO principal-agent research, performance based remuneration schemes for the agents involved are extensively studied as a way to give the agent incentives to act in the principal's interests. The results obtained cannot be easily transposed to the NPO context (Steinberg, 1990),[3] as relevant, objective, and verifiable performance variables are not easily agreed upon (given this would be possible at all). Notwithstanding a few empirical studies revealing small cross-sectional correlations between some selected performance measures and top management remuneration (Baber *et al.*, 2002; Hallock, 2002; O'Connell, 2005), a systematic analysis of performance based remuneration contracts in NPOs is still not available (Brickley and Van Horn, 2002; Preyra and Pink, 2001), if possible at all. This does not imply that other principal-agent insights are irrelevant when studying the functioning of NPOs, as most of the next sections show. They are organised as follows: the concluding section is preceded by sections on strategic management, marketing, accounting, finance, recruitment and selection. Before these, NPO objectives and governance are discussed.

Objectives and governance

It is still true that "there is no consensus among economists regarding the objective function of NPOs" (Schiff and Weisbrod, 1991: 621). This is due to the negative definition of NPOs, as having to respect a non-distribution constraint[4] (Hansman, 1987), implying that there might be no common objectives for all NPOs, and that NPOs might even have conflicting objectives. As far as economic analysis is concerned, this is no real problem, as long as we can assume there are organisational objectives. In the analytical literature, frequently used objectives are, for example, quality and/or quantity of output (Newhouse (1970) is seminal here), recovering costs, cash flow maximisation (Davis, 1972), members' welfare (Canning *et al.*, 2003), "the same goals as the typical client" (Handy and Webb, 2003: 266). Gassler (1997) proposes an overall set of objectives (*utility function*) for NPOs in which the manager is also the founder: own consumption, non-monetary rewards, effort, and output. Furthermore, NPO objectives do not need to be stable, as already pointed out by DiMaggio (1987). They also can be affected by contingencies such as dimension, competition (Brickley and Van Horn, 2002), or type of donors. Somewhat disturbing when considering the board as the guard of the organisation's objectives[5] is the observation that the composition of the board itself, in terms of characteristics such as sex, level of education and professional backgrounds, can affect the revealed objectives of the organisation (Du Bois *et al.*, 2005).[6] This suggests an additional (multiple) principal(s)-agent relation can be analysed for NPOs, with the founders and/or members as principals, and the board members as agents.

Although "the people attracted to managerial positions in the nonprofit sector are those who care relatively little about financial gain and relatively highly about putting their own ideals into practice" (Rose-Ackerman, 1987: 812), we cannot assume they pursue exactly the same objectives as their organisations would like.[7] Therefore, "nonprofit organisations have governance problems that resemble the problems in for-profit firms, but are often far more extreme" (Glaeser, 2003: 39). Unfortunately, this fact did not engender a vast body of empirical work on governance in NPOs (Dyl *et al.*, 1996; Eldenburg *et al.*, 2004), the book edited by Glaeser in 2003 being a rare exception. The papers by Callen *et al.* (2003) and Saidel (1998) deal with important governance related topics (the configuration of the board, advisory commissions and staff), but without looking at overall governance. Therefore, the fundamental insight by Fama and Jensen (1983) still prevails: initiative and implementation should be structurally separated from fiat and control.

Strategic management

As the process of strategic planning in NPOs, as a technique to achieve a set of objectives taking into consideration external and internal factors, does not conceptually differ from strategic planning in POs, one cannot expect to have an NPO-dedicated theory on NPO strategy.[8] There are, of course, numerous guideline-type works on NPO strategic management (Bryson (1991)) is an example), but at the conceptual level they do not really differ from the even more numerous PO strategic management textbooks. Even if we would reduce the idea of strategic management to organisational behaviour, clearly "there is no accepted theory of [NPO] behavior, and little of the empirical work is connected to ... existing theories" (Malani *et al.*, 2003: 181–182).

A few papers explicitly consider strategic differences between POs and NPOs. Examples are Banks *et al.* (1997), who analyse the reactions of profit hospitals and non-profit hospitals to a demand shift in terms of uncompensated care,[9] and Lynk (1995), who studies the adaptation of pricing differences between POs and NPOs with changing market power. As far as differences between governmental bodies and NPOs are concerned, there are even less research insights available, because "theory ... is not strong enough to specify a confident prediction of whether governmental and nonprofit providers will or will not behave differently under each of a variety of conditions" (Kapur and Weisbrod, 2000: 278).

All this does not imply that fruitful cooperation between NPOs, POs and public bodies cannot be possible or profitable. Numerous examples of the opposite exist (Austin, 2000; O'Regan and Oster, 2000).

Marketing

Marketing management

Comparable to the situation of strategic management, the techniques of NPO marketing are not very different from PO marketing, as their aim is to reconcile the organisation's objectives (be it profit or not) with market needs (Shapiro, 1973). Eventual decisions, such as on pricing (Niskanen, 1994) can differ though, but this is due to the fact that objectives differ.

Nevertheless, there are three specific NPO marketing topics: volunteers, eliciting donations/gifts/subsidies, and the interaction between profit activities and non-profit activities by NPOs. They all have clear agency relation features.

Volunteers

As volunteers perform activities on the organisation's behalf, they can be considered agents in a principal-agent terminology. Volunteers are surely not a homogeneous group (Handy *et al.*, 2000): at least a distinction between board members and operational volunteers should be made.

Economically speaking, a person enters in a volunteering relation with a NPO if (monetary and non-monetary) revenues exceed (monetary and non-monetary) costs,[10] or, equivalently, if her utility is expected to increase by being a volunteer.[11] When trying to attract volunteers, this should be taken into consideration, as well as the fact that some of the volunteers' motives to enter the organisation might detract the organisation from its objectives and even generate conflicts within the organisation at large, making a structural and professional management of volunteers a necessity, especially in larger organisations.[12]

When looking at the academic literature on volunteers, it is striking to note that there is almost no comprehensive analysis of the impact of the presence of volunteers on organisational governance.

Donations, gifts, subsidies

In this section we concentrate on donations, gifts and subsidies in cash, ignoring transfers in kind, such as voluntary work for the organisation (Garcia and Marcuello, 2002; Rose-Ackerman, 1996). Donations and gifts are made by individuals and organisations, subsidies are granted by governmental authorities, at whatever level. In most countries, gifts and donations are partly financed by the taxpayer, as they give rise to tax exemptions.[13] Also here, clear principal-agent relations can be observed between the funder-donor (as the principal) and the organisation.

The paper by Duizendstraal and Nentjes (1994) explicitly models a subsidising authority trying to design a way of subsidising[14] to drive NPO management into activities the authority would like to be performed. Without using the wording, they address a typical principal-agent problem.

As far as donations/gifts by individuals are concerned, there is a substantial literature on donors and their donations,[15] as well as on the determination of the optimal level of funding expenses to reach the highest possible level of service, budget, or the maximum of some weighted average of both (Steinberg, 1986). The analysis of agency problems between donors and NPOs is mostly part of the scarce research on corporate governance in NPOs (see p. 343).

Gifts by firms are seldom studied, and if they are, the point of view is mostly the firm's, including agency aspects between the firm's management and its shareholders (Aralumparam and Stoneman, 1995; Useem, 1987). Marx (1999) observes that "companies are increasingly integrating philanthropic management into the formal strategic planning of the firm" (185), which might indicate that corporate philanthropy is driven by profit maximisation considerations, especially when one realises that firms mostly do not assess the effect of their donations on the NPO's outcome (Marx, 1999), making the relation between the firm and the NPO an agency relation without monitoring.

Allying the organisation with a specific firm in the context of the latter's Corporate Social Responsibility (CSR) policy might increase the donations by this firm's clients, as long as they identify themselves one way or another with the firm (Lichtenstein et al., 2004). Clearly, indirect effects on other donors and volunteers should be taken into consideration before deciding to join a CSR scheme.

Finally, it should be borne in the minds of NPO marketing managers that gifts and subsidies are not independent from one another. Internally, obtaining subsidies might reduce the managerial efforts to obtain gifts, which could run counter to the optimal effort as perceived by the board (Brooks, 2005), and externally, obtaining subsidies might either crowd in donations and/or crowd out donations (Brooks, 2003). The crowding in and out effects can only claim some realism if the apparently heroic assumption is made that donors have an idea about the subsidies the NPO they donate to receives (Horne *et al.*, 2005), unless we infer these effects are based on (right or wrong) perceptions.

Profit activities by non-profit organisations

The main argument put forward by NPOs to develop profit activities, is that they generate funds for the pursuit of their non-profit objectives (see Schiff and Weisbrod, 1991, for a model). All kinds of interesting economic problems can be analysed on this topic, such as the potential anti-competitive effects on the profit markets concerned, taxation problems, or the question whether tax exemption of the NPO's profit activities is the most efficient way to promote the NPO's objectives, especially taking into consideration managerial discretion (Bises, 2000). The last point is in fact an agency problem, especially if one assumes that NPO managers also enjoy developing profit activities. Some support for this assumption is found in Du Bois *et al.* (2004), who conclude, based on a sample of 2,103 US NPOs, that organisations where serious agency problems can be expected between board and management initiate more profit activities.

Notwithstanding their direct effect on revenues, indirect effects should also be considered before deciding to invest in profit activities, apart from the fact that the profit activities should be profitable. The commercial flavour of profit activities might negatively affect the commitment of some volunteers (Enjolras, 2002) or the generosity of some donors (Desmet, 1998; Young and Steinberg, 1995).

Accounting

Financial accounting and auditing

Accounting being the registration and disclosure of (transactions affecting) the monetary wealth of an organisation,[16] there is no reason to make a conceptual difference between PO-accounting and NPO-accounting (Anthony, 1980), or, for that matter, between PO-auditing and NPO-auditing. Nevertheless, the roles of accounting and auditing in NPOs can be understood to be different from their roles in POs. Jegers (2002) analyses this in an explicit principal-agent framework, the board being the principal, and management the agent. Apart from their use as a managerial tool, accounting and auditing can be understood as instruments required by an effective board to mitigate agency costs, even in a situation without specific NPO accounting regulations:[17] by having to issue audited statements, they will contain their discretionary behaviour for the benefit of the attainment of the organisational goals, though monitoring by financial statements, even audited, can never be perfect. From the point of view of the board, the cost of accounting[18] and auditing[19] has to be weighed against a possible increase of the organisation's performance.

A typical situation in NPOs, as compared to POs, is, on average, a lower level of expertise in accounting both at the side of board members and the side of staff, especially in smaller organisations (Christensen and Mohr, 1995; Froelich *et al.*, 2000; Miller-Millesen, 2003). This affects the cost of introducing (more sophisticated) accounting systems, and their effect on monitoring quality, and therefore the "best" choices in the fields of accounting and auditing.

A popular theme in accounting theory is the understanding of accounting choices (e.g. between LIFO and FIFO). Most of this research is linked to the presence of performance based remuneration schemes for managers, a typical agency subject, a link less relevant for NPOs. Nevertheless, other arguments have been put forward to understand NPO accounting choices: political cost arguments, based on the idea that high profile NPOs will not be tempted to show profits that are too high (Christensen and Moher, 1995; Robbins *et al.*, 1993), also because this might negatively affect subsidies and donations, and reputation arguments (Leone and Van Horn, 1999), by which managers are assumed to try their utmost to avoid having to disclose losses.

Cost accounting

Cost accounting techniques in NPOs do not need to be different from cost accounting techniques in POs, but here there are specific incentives for rational accounting choices or manipulations. At least two reasons can be distinguished, both of them having a direct agency interpretation. To understand them, we assume three cost categories are established in the organisation's cost accounting system: programme costs (costs of activities, both non-profit and profit), fundraising costs, and other indirect costs.

First, as in most countries profit activities will be taxed, there is an incentive to allocate indirect costs as much as possible to profit programme activities (Weisbrod, 1998; Yetman, 2001).

Second, the general public (containing potential donors) and the authorities (granting subsidies) should be convinced the organisation is an effective one. A way to convey this message is to have programme costs as high as possible (showing high activity levels), and general costs as low as possible (administrative costs as well as fundraising costs). That this mechanism is at work is illustrated by Krishnan *et al.* (2004, 2006).

Finance

Sources of funds

Though the global categories of funds are the same for POs and NPOs (equity or net assets, and debt or liabilities), and the technicalities of managing them are alike, there are also important differences once the further subdivision of equity and debt is considered.

Equity of NPOs can be far more diversified than equity of POs, as different sources can be tapped. Tuckman (1993) distinguishes two categories: internal sources and external sources. The former contain contributions when founding the organisation (in cash or in kind), and profits/losses which have to be retained[20] due to the non-distribution constraint, the latter all kinds of donations, gifts and subsidies. Although all sources are not easily accessible for all sorts of NPOs, too much reliance on one might make the organisation vulnerable (Froelich, 1999).[21] Too much diversification, on the other hand, possibly inflicts mutually exclusive obligations to the organisation. Chang and Tuckman (1994) empirically try to understand equity diversification[22] and find that the non-profit industry which the organisation belongs to affects the organisation's equity diversity, that donative NPOs are more diversified than commercial NPOs, and that NPOs reporting high fundraising costs also have more diversified equity.

Debt of NPOs is more comparable to POs' debt. Apart from the spontaneous forms (such as trade credit or tax accruals), all kinds of financial debts, including bonds, can be observed. A case specific to NPOs is a loan for which the cost is lower than the market cost for a comparable loan (Jegers, 1997).

Cost of capital and capital structure

No doubt equity providers and non-market debt providers do not primarily require the organisation to generate financial surpluses, but expect the organisation's objectives to be aimed at (Ligon, 1997; Wedig, 1994), although they can also hope for a prudent and rational financial management of the organisation's operations. This puts some financial constraints on the organisation's activities, which can be translated by saying the expected (financial) cost of NPO equity is surely lower than the expected cost of non-market debt,[23] and that (by definition) the expected cost of non-market debt is lower than the cost of market debt. This implies that the most efficient capital structure of a NPO would consist only of equity, if potential agency conflicts between donors/subsidisers and management are ignored. One could argue that the ensuing agency costs can be mitigated by having a given amount of debt and debt holders monitoring the organisation's behaviour. Jegers and Verschueren (2006) and Verschueren and Jegers (2004) find empirical support[24] for this argument.

Human resources

Differences between utility functions of principals and agents being central in agency theory, one could expect selection and recruitment to be extensively analysed in profit and non-profit contexts. Nothing is further from the truth. Research on POs mainly concentrated on remuneration schemes, whereas, as already mentioned in the introductory section, agency theory based research on NPOs is scarce.

The idea that selection and recruitment are useful instruments to mitigate agency problems between board and management, and in a board-management-staff chain, is explored in Caers *et al.* (2005a, 2005b, 2006b). In Caers *et al.*

(2005a) an analytical agency model is developed in which a board selects one employee from a pool of applicants with different attitudes towards the organisation's objectives, and with one potential client, who can have different characteristics as to his case (e.g. difficulty level of treatment in a hospital setting). Under some not unrealistic circumstances even employees characterised as being selfish (with respect to their reputation and effort)[25] can be employed. Introducing a manager, more employees and more clients in the model makes the model analytically intractable. Simulations on the combined choice of manager (by the board) and employees (by the manager) results in indications on which kind of manager to select in order to reduce utility loss by the board as much as possible (Caers *et al.*, 2005b, 2006b).

Conclusion

The aim of this chapter was to provide a conceptual and intuitive overview of the main insights stemming from a microeconomic, *theory of the firm* like, analysis of NPO management. In this author's view, it is fair to say that it shows that this kind of analysis can contribute in different ways to our understanding of the functioning of NPOs, even though it is clear that for all NPO-relevant managerial domains there is a wide scope for further research. Given the importance of the third sector in most societies, such an endeavour seems more than warranted.

Seen from a European perspective, one can say that most of the empirical research (even by European researchers) has been conducted with US data, though contextual differences might suggest that when the same theoretical framework would applied to European organisations, the empirical evidence cannot be expected to be automatically comparable to the US evidence. Furthermore, European researchers are disadvantaged when trying to analyse these topics, due to the lack of standardised data in inputs and outputs of non-profit organisations.

Acknowledgements

Comments by Ralf Caers, Rein De Cooman, Sara De Gieter, Cindy Du Bois, R. Scott Gassler, Korel Göymen, Marthe Nyssens and Victor Pestoff on earlier versions of this paper are gratefully acknowledged.

Notes

1 Microeconomics can be defined as the economic analysis of the behaviour of economic agents such as consumers, employees, employers, organisations, and authorities. *Theory of the firm* is the widely accepted term to describe the microeconomics of the PO.
2 On motives (i.e. the arguments in their utility functions) of NPO staff in schools and hospitals, see Schepers *et al.* (2005).
3 On measuring satisfaction with the pay obtained in POs and NPOs, see De Gieter *et al.* (2006).

4 The non-distribution constraint stipulates that NPOs cannot distribute their profits to whatever beneficiaries, such as owners or managers.

5 For an overview of the empirical literature on NPO boards, see Du Bois *et al.* (2007).

6 The results of O'Regan and Oster (2005), though indirect, are compatible with this observation.

7 For an empirical assessment of such differences using discrete choice techniques, see Du Bois *et al.* (2006). These differences are not necessarily an indication of opportunistic behaviour by managers. They can also be the consequence of differences in opinions on objectives or strategies. Miller (2002: 437), after having analysed a rather small sample of 12 US NPOs, suggests that "board members generally do not believe that their chief executives will behave opportunistically".

8 The idea that activity growth as an NPO strategy is constrained by its capital structure, profit and efficiency changes is developed in Jegers (2003).

9 Frank and Salkever (1991) consider the same question, applied to two types of NPOs.

10 Chinman and Wandersman (1999) elaborate on these.

11 For a model of board member volunteers, taking reputational effects into account, see Handy (1995).

12 For an illustration, see Handy and Srinivasan (2004).

13 A welfare analysis of tax exemption rates is provided by Kaplow (1995).

14 They analyse lump sum subsidies, and subsidies based on respectively input, output, and revenues.

15 An overview of the literature up to 1996 is provided by Hewitt and Brown (2000).

16 Some authors such as Trigg and Nabangi (1995) require annual accounts to contain more than financial information, as the NPO's objectives are non-financial. In my view, other ways of reporting are more appropriate to collect and disseminate non-monetary information (Hyndman, 1990; Parsons, 2003), implying that the financial statement is just not the most important document to assess an organisation's performance.

17 Accounting regulations can also be seen as a monitoring instrument between the government, acting as a principal, and the organisation as a whole. The question whether to comply is an economic one: expected advantages and disadvantages have to be compared. For some empirical work on compliance, see Jegers and Houtman (1993) and Krishnan and Schauer (2000). Yetman and Yetman (2004) relate financial statement quality to the presence of debtors or donors, in what we can call an agency relation with the organisation.

18 The cost of introducing accrual accounting (versus cash accounting) and the cost of disclosure can be considered separately (Jegers, 2002).

19 See Beattie *et al.* (2001) for an empirical study on audit fees in the voluntary sector.

20 Chang and Tuckman (1990) discuss some justifications for NPOs to generate surpluses. See also Fisman and Hubbard (2003). Handy and Webb (2003) analyse theoretically possible negative effects on subsidies.

21 Financial vulnerability of NPOs is the topic of Chang and Tuckman (1991), which gave rise to a number of empirical studies on US NPOs (Hager, 2001; Keating *et al.*, 2005; Trussel, 2002).

22 On a US sample of 113,525 NPOs, data for 1986.

23 Or even zero (Sloan *et al.*, 1988). Up to now, no generally accepted theory has been developed to determine the NPO's cost of equity, contrary to the situation for the PO's cost of equity. Notice that for POs, the cost of equity is higher than the cost of debt.

24 Data for 1999 on 22,766 Californian NPOs and 7,295 US cultural organisations respectively.

25 Income is modelled to be fixed.

References

Anthony R.N. (1980) Making sense of nonbusiness accounting. *Harvard Business Review*, 58:3 pp. 83–93.

Aralumpalam W. and Stoneman P. (1995) An investigation into the givings by large corporate donors to UK charities, 1979–86. *Applied Economics*, 27:10 pp. 935–945.

Austin J.E. (2000) Strategic collaboration between nonprofits and businessess. *Nonprofit and Voluntary Sector Quarterly*, 29:1 (supplement) pp. 69–97.

Baber W.R., Daniel P.L. and Roberts A.A. (2002) Compensation to managers of charitable organizations: an empirical study of the role of accounting measures of program activities. *Accounting Review*, 77:3 pp. 679–693.

Banks D.A., Paterson M. and Wendel J. (1997) Uncompensated hospital care: charitable mission or profitable business decision? *Health Economics*, 6:2 pp. 133–143.

Beattie V., Goodacre A., Pratt K. and Stevenson J. (2001) The determinants of audit fees-evidence from the voluntary sector. *Accounting and Business Research*, 31:4 pp. 243–274.

Bises B. (2000) Exemption or taxation for profits of non-profits? An answer from a model incoporating managerial discretion. *Public Choice*, 104:1–2 pp. 19–39.

Brickley J.A. and Van Horn R.L. (2002) Managerial incentives in nonprofit organizations: evidence from hospitals. *Journal of Law and Economics*, 45:1 pp. 227–249.

Brody E. (1996) Agents without principals: the economic convergence of the nonprofit and for-profit organizational forms. *New York Law School Law Review*, 40 pp. 457–536.

Brooks A.C. (2003) Do government subsidies to nonprofits crowd out donations or donors? *Public Finance Review*, 31:2 pp. 166–179.

Brooks A.C. (2005) What do nonprofit organizations seek ? (And why should policymakers care?). *Journal of Policy Analysis and Management*, 24:3 pp. 543–558.

Bryson J.M. (1991) *Strategic planning for public and nonprofit organizations*, San Francisco: Jossey-Bass.

Caers R., Du Bois C., Jegers M., De Gieter S., Schepers C. and Pepermans R. (2005a) Recruiting nonprofit employees: an agency-stewardship theory on motivational differences and selective contracting. European Conference of the ISTR and EMES, Paris.

Caers R., Du Bois C., Jegers M., De Gieter S., De Cooman R. and Pepermans R. (2005b) Selecting the "best" employee for the job: an agency-stewardship view on applicant selection in nonprofit organizations. European Institute for Advanced Studies in Management Workshop on the Challenges of Managing the Third Sector, Belfast.

Caers R., Du Bois C., Jegers M., De Gieter S., Schepers C. and Pepermans R. (2006a) Principal–agent relationships on the stewardship-agency axis. *Nonprofit Management and Leadership*, 16:5 pp. 25–47.

Caers R., Du Bois C., Jegers M., De Gieter S., De Cooman R. and Pepermans R. (2006b) A micro-economic perspective on manager selection in nonprofit organizations. European Academy of Management (EURAM) Conference, Oslo.

Callen J.L., Klein A. and Tinkelman D. (2003) Board composition, committees, and organizational efficiency: the case of nonprofits. *Nonprofit and Voluntary Sector Quarterly*, 32:4 pp. 493–520.

Canning D., Jefferson C.W. and Spencer J.E. (2003) Optimal credit rationing in not-for-profit financial institutions. *International Economic Review*, 44:1 pp. 243–261.

Chang C.F. and Tuckman H.P. (1990) Why do nonprofit managers accumulate surpluses, and how much do they accumulate? *Nonprofit Management and Leadership*, 1:2 pp. 117–135.

Chang C.F. and Tuckman H.P. (1991) Financial vulnerability and attrition as measures of nonprofit performance. *Annals of Public and Corperative Economics*, 62:4 pp. 655–672.

Chang C.F. and Tuckman H.P. (1994) Revenue diversification among non-profits. *Voluntas*, 5:3 pp. 273–290.

Chinman M.J. and Wandersman A. (1999) The benefits and costs of volunteering in community organizations: review and practical implications. *Nonprofit and Voluntary Sector Quarterly*, 28:1 pp. 46–64.

Christensen A.L. and Mohr R.M. (1995) Testing a positive theory model of museum accounting practices. *Financial Accountability and Management*, 11:4 pp. 317–335.

Davis K. (1972) Economic theories of behavior in nonprofit private hospitals. *Economic Business Bulletin*, 24:1 pp. 1–13.

De Gieter S., De Cooman R., Pepermans R., Caers R., Du Bois C. and Jegers M. (2006) Dimensionality of the Pay Satisfaction Questionnaire: a validation study in Belgium. *Psychological Reports*, 98 pp. 640–650.

Desmet P. (1998) The impact of mail order on subsequent donations: an experiment. *Financial Accountability and Management*, 14:3 pp. 203–214.

DiMaggio P. (1987) Nonprofit organizations in the production and distribution of culture, in Powell W.W. (ed.) *The nonprofit sector: a research handbook*, New Haven: Yale University Press.

Du Bois C., Caers R., Jegers M., Schepers C., De Gieter S. and Pepermans R. (2004) Agency problems and unrelated business income: an empirical analysis. *Applied Economics*, 36:20 pp. 2317–2326.

Du Bois C., Caers R., Jegers M., De Cooman R., De Gieter S. and Pepermans R. (2005) The link between composition and preferences of the board: an empirical analysis for non-profit school boards. European Institute for Advanced Studies in Management Workshop on the Challenges of Managing the Third Sector, Belfast.

Du Bois, C., Caers, R., Jegers, M., De Cooman, R., De Gieter, S. and Pepermans, R. (2006) Agency problems between board and manager: a discrete choice experiment in Flemish non-profit schools. European Academy of Management (EURAM) Conference, Oslo.

Du Bois C., Caers R., Jegers M., De Cooman R., De Gieter S. and Pepermans R. (2007) The non-profit board: a concise review of the empirical literature. *Zeitschrift für öffentliche und gemeinwirtschaftliche Unternehmen (Journal for Public and Nonprofit Services)* 30:1 pp. 78–88.

Duizendstraal A. and Nentjes A. (1994) Organizational slack in subsidized nonprofit institutions. *Public Choice*, 81:3–4 pp. 297–321.

Dyl E.A., Frant H.L. and Stephenson C.A. (1996) Governance structure and performance of nonprofit corporations: evidence from medical research charities. University of Arizona, Working Paper.

Eldenburg L., Hermalin B.E., Weisbach M.S. and Woskinska M. (2004) Hospital governance, performance objectives, and organizational form. *Journal of Corporate Finance*, 10:4 pp. 527–548.

Enjolras B. (2002) Does the commercialization of voluntary organizations "crowd out" voluntary work? *Annals of Public and Cooperative Economics*, 73:3 pp. 375–398.

Fama E.F. and Jensen M.C. (1983) Separation of ownership and control. *Journal of Law and Economics*, 26:2 pp. 301–325.

Fisman R. and Hubbard R.G. (2003) The role of nonprofit endowments, in Glaeser E.L. (ed.) *The governance of not-for-profit firms*, Chicago: University of Chicago Press.

Francois P. (2001) Employee care and the role of nonprofit organizations. *Journal of Institutional and Theoretical Economics*, 157:3 pp. 443–464.

Frank R.G. and Salkever D.S. (1991) The supply of charity services by nonprofit hospitals: motives and market structure. *Rand Journal of Economics*, 22:3 pp. 430–445.

Froelich K.A. (1999) Diversification of revenue strategies: evolving resource dependence in nonprofit organizations. *Nonprofit and Voluntary Sector Quarterly*, 28:3 pp. 246–268.

Froelich K.A., Knoepfle T.W. and Pollak T.H. (2000) Financial measures in nonprofit organization research in comparing IRS 990 Return and audited financial statement data. *Nonprofit and Voluntary Sector Quarterly*, 29:2 pp. 232–254.

Garcia I. and Marcuello C. (2002) Family model of contributions to non-profit organizations and labour supply. *Applied Economics*, 34:2 pp. 259–265.

Gassler R.S. (1997) The economics of the nonprofit motive: formulation of objectives and constraints for firms and nonprofit enterprises. *Journal of Interdisciplinary Economics*, 8:4 pp. 265–280.

Glaeser E.L. (2003) Introduction, in Glaeser E.L. (ed.) *The governance of not-for-profit firms*, Chicago: University of Chicago Press.

Gui B. (1991) The economic rationale for the "third sector": nonprofit and other noncapitalist organizations. *Annals of Public and Cooperative Economics*, 62:4 pp. 551–572.

Hager M.A. (2001) Financial vulnerability among arts organizations: a test of the Tuckman-Chang measures. *Nonprofit and Voluntary Sector Quarterly*, 30:2 pp. 376–392.

Hallock K.F. (2002) Managerial pay and governance in American nonprofits. *Industrial Relations*, 41:3 pp. 377–406.

Handy F. (1995) Reputation as collateral: an economic analysis of the role of trustees of nonprofits. *Nonprofit and Voluntary Sector Quarterly*, 24:4 pp. 293–305.

Handy F. and Srinivasan N. (2004) Valuing volunteers: an economic evaluation of the net benefits of hospital volunteers. *Nonprofit and Voluntary Sector Quarterly*, 33:1 pp. 28–54.

Handy F. and Webb N.J. (2003) A theoretical model of the effects of public funding on saving decisions by charitable nonprofit service providers. *Annals of Public and Cooperative Economics*, 74:2 pp. 261–282.

Handy F., Cnaan R.A., Brudney J.L., Ascoli U., Meijs L.C. and Ranade S. (2000) Public perception of "Who is a volunteer": an examination of the net-cost approach from a cross-cultural perspective. *Voluntas*, 11:1 pp. 45–65.

Hansmann H. (1987) Economic theories of nonprofit organization, in Powell W.W. (ed.) *The nonprofit sector: a research handbook*, New Haven: Yale University Press.

Herman R.D. and Heimovics R.D. (1991) *Executive leadership in nonprofit organizations: new strategies for shaping executive-board dynamics*, San Franciso: Jossey-Bass.

Hewitt J.A. and Brown D.K. (2000) Agency costs in environmental not-for-profits. *Public Choice*, 103:1–2 pp. 168–183.

Holtmann A.G. (1983) A theory of non-profit firms. *Economica*, 50:4 pp. 439–449.

Horne C.S., Johnson J.L. and Van Slyke D.M. (2005) Do charitable donors know enough – and care enough – about government subsidies to affect private giving to nonprofit organizations? *Nonprofit and Voluntary Sector Quarterly*, 34:1 pp. 136–149.

Hyndman N. (1990) Charity accounting – an empirical study of the information needs of contributors to UK fund raising charities. *Financial Accountability and Management*, 6:4 pp. 295–307.

Jegers M. (1997) Portfolio theory and nonprofit financial stability: a comment and extension. *Nonprofit and Voluntary Sector Quarterly*, 26:1 pp. 65–72.

Jegers M. (2002) The economics of non profit accounting and auditing: suggestions for a research agenda. *Annals of Public and Cooperative Economics*, 73:3 pp. 419–451.

Jegers M. (2003) The sustainable growth rate of non-profit organizations: the effect of efficiency, profitability and capital structure. *Financial Accountability and Management*, 19:4 pp. 309–313.

Jegers M. and Houtman C. (1993) Accounting theory and compliance to accounting regulations: the case of hospitals. *Financial Accountability and Management*, 9:4 pp. 267–278.

Jegers M. and Verschueren I. (2006) On the capital structure of non-profit organisations: an empirical study for Californian organisations. *Financial Accountability and Management*, 22:4 pp. 309–329.

Jensen M.C. and Meckling W.H. (1976) Theory of the firm: managerial behavior, agency costs and ownership structure. *Journal of Financial Economics*, 3:4 pp. 305–360.

Kaplow L. (1995) A note on subsdizing gifts. *Journal of Public Economics*, 58:3 pp. 469–477.

Kapur K. and Weisbrod B.A. (2000) The roles of government and nonprofit suppliers in mixed industries. *Public Finance Review*, 28:4 pp. 275–308.

Keating E.K., Fischer M., Gordon T.P. and Greenlee J. (2005) Assessing financial vulnerability in the nonprofit sector. Harvard University Working Paper RWP05–02.

Krashinsky M. (1986) Transaction costs and a theory of the nonprofit organization, in Rose-Ackerman S. (ed.) *The economics of nonprofit organizations*, New York: J. Wiley.

Krishnan J. and Schauer P.C. (2000) The differentiation of quality among auditors: evidence from the non-for-profit sector. *Auditing: a Journal of Practice and Theory*, 19:2 pp. 9–25.

Krishnan R., Yetman M.H. and Yetman R.J. (2004) Financial disclosure management by nonprofit organizations. Working Paper.

Krishnan R., Yetman M.H. and Yetman R.J. (2006) Expense misreporting in nonprofit organizations. *Accounting Review*, 84:2 pp. 399–420.

Leone A.J. and Van Horn R.L. (1999) Earnings management in not-for-profit institutions: evidence from hospitals. Rochester, University of Rochester, Working Paper.

Lichtenstein D.R., Drumwright M.E. and Braig B.M. (2004) The effect of Corporate Social Responsibility on customer donations to corporate supported nonprofits. *Journal of Marketing*, 68:4 pp. 16–32.

Ligon J.A. (1997) The capital structure of hospitals and reimbursement policy. *Quarterly Review of Economics and Finance*, 37:1 pp. 59–77.

Lynk W.J. (1995) Nonprofit hospital mergers and the exercise of market power. *Journal of Law and Economics*, 38:2 pp. 437–461.

Malani A., Philipson T. and David G. (2003) Theories of firm behavior in the nonprofit sector: a synthesis and empirical evaluation, in Glaeser E.L. (ed.) *The governance of not-for-profit firms*, Chicago: University of Chicago Press.

Marx J.O. (1999) Corporate philantropy: what is the strategy? *Nonprofit and Voluntary Sector Quarterly*, 28:2 pp. 185–198.

Miller J.L. (2002) The board as a monitor of organizational activity: the applicability of agency theory to nonprofit boards. *Nonprofit Management and Leadership*, 12:4 pp. 429–450.

Miller-Millesen J.L. (2003) Understanding the behavior of nonprofit boards of directors: a theory based approach. *Nonprofit and Voluntary Sector Quarterly*, 32:4 pp. 521–547.

Newhouse J.P. (1970) Toward a theory of nonprofit institutions: an economic model of a hospital. American *Economic Review*, 60:1 pp. 64–74.

Niskanen W.A. (1994) *Bureaucracy and public economics*, Aldershot: Edward Elgar.

O'Connell J.F. (2005) Administrative compensation in private nonprofits: the case of liberal arts colleges. *Quarterly Journal of Business and Economics*, 44:1–2 pp. 3–12.

O'Regan K. and Oster S.M. (2000) Nonprofit and for-profit partnership: rationale and challenges of cross-sector contracting. *Nonprofit and Voluntary Sector Quarterly*, 29:1 (supplement) pp. 120–140.

O'Regan K. and Oster S.M. (2005) Does the structure and composition of the board matter? The case of nonprofit organization. *Journal of Law, Economics and Organization*, 21:1 pp. 205–227.

Parsons L.M. (2003) Is accounting information from nonprofit organizations useful to donors? A review of chariable giving and value-relevance. *Journal of Accounting Literature*, 22 pp. 104–129.

Preyra C. and Pink G. (2001) Balancing incentives in the compensation contracts of nonprofit hospital CEOs. *Journal of Health Economics*, 20:4 pp. 509–525.

Robbins W.A., Turpin R. and Polinski P. (1993) Economic incentives and accounting choice strategy by nonprofit hospitals. *Financial Accountability and Management*, 9:3 pp. 159–175.

Rose-Ackerman S. (1987) Ideals versus dollars: donor, charity managers, and government grants. *Journal of Political Economy*, 95:4 pp. 810–823.

Rose-Ackerman S. (1996) Altruism, nonprofits, and economic theory. *Journal of Economic Literature*, 34:2 pp. 701–728.

Saidel J.R. (1998) Expanding the governance construct: functions and contributions of nonprofit advisory groups. *Nonprofit and Voluntary Sector Quarterly*, 27:4 pp. 421–436.

Schepers C., De Gieter S., Pepermans R., Du Bois C., Caers R. and Jegers M. (2005) How are employees of the non-profit sector motivated ? A research need. *Nonprofit Management and Leadership*, 16:2 pp. 191–208.

Schiff J. and Weisbrod B. (1991) Competition between for-profit and nonprofit organizations in commercial markets. *Annals of Public and Cooperative Economics*, 62:4 pp. 619–639.

Shapiro B.P. (1973) Marketing for nonprofit organizations, *Harvard Business Review*, 5, in Gies D.L., Ott J.S. and Shafritz J.M. (eds) (1990) *The nonprofit organization. Essential readings*, Pacific Grove: Brooks/Cole.

Sloan F.A, Valvona J., Hassan M. and Morrisey M.A. (1988) Cost of capital to the hospital sector. *Journal of Health Economics*, 7:1 pp. 25–45.

Steinberg R. (1986) Should donors care about fundraising? in Rose-Ackerman S. (ed.) *The economics of nonprofit organizations*, New York: J. Wiley.

Steinberg R. (1990) Profits and incentive compensation in nonprofit firms. *Nonprofit Management & Leadership*, 1:2 pp. 137–152.

Trigg R. and Nabangi F.K. (1995) Representation of the financial position of nonprofit organizations: the Habitat for Humanity situation. *Financial Accountability and Management*, 11:3 pp. 259–269.

Trussel J.M. (2002) Revisiting the prediction of financial vulnerability. *Nonprofit Management and Leadership*, 13:1 pp. 17–31.

Tuckman H.P. (1993) How and why nonprofit organizations obtain capital, in Hammack D.C. and Young D.R. (eds) *Nonprofit organizations in a market economy*, San Francisco: Jossey-Bass.

Useem M. (1987) Corporate philantropy, in Powell W.W. (ed.) *The nonprofit sector: a research handbook*, New Haven: Yale University Press.

Verschueren I. and Jegers M. (2004) The capital structure of cultural non-profit organizations: theory and US evidence. EIASM Workshop on Managing Cultural Organizations, Bologna.

Wedig G.J. (1994) Risk, leverage, donations and dividends-in-kind: a theory of nonprofit financial behavior. *International Review of Economics and Finance*, 3:3 pp. 257–278.

Weisbrod B.A. (1998) The nonprofit mission and its financing: growing links between nonprofits and the rest of the economy, in Weisbrod B.A. (ed.) *The nonprofit economy*, Cambridge: Harvard University Press.

Williamson D.E. (1979) Transaction-cost economics: the governance of contractual relations. *Journal of Law and Economics*, 22:2 pp. 233–261.

Williamson O.E. (1991) Comparative economic organzation: the analysis of discrete structural alternatives. *Adminstrative Science Quarterly*, 36: 2 pp. 269–296.

Yetman R.J (2001) Tax-motivated expense allocations by nonprofit organizations. *Accounting Review*, 76:3 pp. 297–311.

Young D.R. and Steinberg R. (1995) *Economics for nonprofit managers*, New York: The Foundation Center.

Yetman M.H. and Yetman R.J. (2004) *The effects of governance on the financial reporting quality of nonprofit organizations*. Conference on not-for-profit firms, Federal Reserve Bank, New York.

20 Conclusions

The state of our knowledge and future challenges

Markku Kiviniemi

From the 1990s the research interests and efforts to study the third sector have increased rapidly. The research has proceeded by approaching the third sector from different perspectives and frameworks related to several scientific disciplines and policy areas. While the societal importance and visibility of third sector organizations has grown quickly, the third sector has become a quite diverse and diffuse field of studies (Anheier *et al.* 2002). The variety of perspectives and themes is well visible also in the contents of this book. This chapter looks at the contents as a whole with a general glance.

First, a general framework is elaborated and represented with the purpose of connecting together different sub-themes of the book. The general framework takes a contextual approach to the third sector by regarding the position of the third sector within society and pointing to types of its relationships to different societal elements: the public sector, the market sector and the civil society. Different sub-themes of the book are then broadly located in this framework. By applying the created contextual perspective, some important views and results of the preceding chapters are raised at the front of conclusions and discussed with the purpose of identifying future challenges for research work particularly in the context of European countries.

A contextual framework for the research of the third sector

Anheier *et al.* (2002) have considered the third sector to be developing at the crossroads of different societal sectors and institutions. Thus, it is reasonable to figure out a broad framework presenting the position of the third sector at these crossroads. Figure 20.1 sketches the main elements of societal relations and suggests that it is fruitful to analyse the third sector in relation to the state, to markets and to the civil society. A general question at the basis of this figure is: what kind of balance is there among the different main elements and how has this balance been changing? This implies a contextual approach to the study of the third sector. In general this approach is close to neo-institutional analyses which emphasize the importance of institutional environments in the development of organizations.

Figure 20.1 can be a starting point to search empirically for different societal

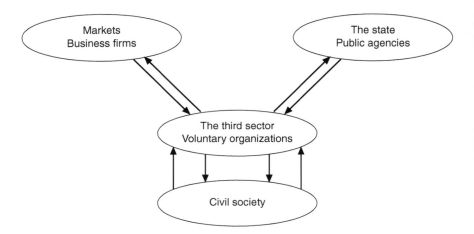

Figure 20.1 Contextual approach in the research of the third sector.

profiles of the third sector organizations (Kiviniemi 2006). What are the 'third sector organizations'? A general conclusion of several studies has evidently been that the formal voluntary associations are the core of the third sector (Salamon and Anheier 1992; Vakil 1997; Lewis 2001).

The voluntary association can be taken as an ideal or pure type in a similar way as there have been ideal types of public agency within the regime of the state and of business firm in the realm of markets. Also other kinds of ideal types can be distinguished as forms of human organizing; there is the clan type and different forms of social networks. However, the public agency, the business firm and the voluntary association seem to be basic types of formal organizations (see Sjöstrand 1997). Five distinctive attributes have been presented as giving a basic description of the third sector organization as association: it is voluntary, self-governing, private, not-for-profit and formally organized (Salamon and Anheier 1992; Vakil 1997; Lewis 2001). Voluntary organizations can create public spaces for civic interaction within civil societies (Kramer 2004: 229; Evers and Laville 2004: 240).

Public agencies do not use voluntary workers and their 'public space' is quite regulated, neither they are self-governing nor private. Business firms are self-governing but they do not have voluntary workers and they act for getting profits. The three pure types of organization – voluntary association, public agency and firm – can however mix with each other so that different kinds of 'hybrid' organizational forms are created. This 'hybridization' can be understood as a sign of particular relationships between different societal elements.

It is important to clarify the nature of the terms in the figure. The state, markets, the third sector and the civil society are conceptual categories which refer to an institutional field including several actors. Thus, they are classifying concepts. Public agencies, business firms and voluntary associations are actors within these institutional fields. In addition, there are many 'hybrid actors' between the institutional fields.

Thus, the societal relations in empirical terms are primarily between the actors, not between the conceptual categories. Actors can break and blur sectoral boundaries and stereotypes (Kramer 2004). The societal relations as concrete phenomena may be regarded as structural (e.g. hierarchies, lateral alliances), functional (e.g. financial and operational cooperation, supply contracts) or socio-cultural (e.g. interactive communication networks). Relations are formed by social exchange, interaction and communication (Knoke 1999). They are also changing, and new forms of relationships and hybrid types are developing for instance because of increasing interdependencies among the main societal elements. There are simultaneously traditional and new emerging profiles of societal relations. It is important to study 'hybridization' in different historical contexts (see Chapter 15). The perspectives of change, tradition and their interplay hold for all groups of actors (Ruostetsaari 2003: 25), and they can be used to analyse the dynamics in the development of societal profiles. Chapter 7 makes a useful start for analysing different theoretical approaches in the studies of the third sector and underlining the promises of transactional and interactive relations between actors.

Relations between the third sector and civil society

The third sector and its voluntary organizations are most often seen as a part of civil society as it is referred in Chapter 2 (also Lewis 2001). Voluntary organizations are thought to be born within the civil society by decisions of its members, citizens. This implies that voluntary organizations have closer relations to the civil society than to the state and markets. However, the position and relations of voluntary organizations to the whole of the civil society may vary. Even if the majority of them have their origins within the civil society, their births may have different backgrounds. Some voluntary associations have a clearly internal background within a given society while some others may be imported or stimulated by external actors. A typical case might be the diffusion of a social movement among different local communities. Also public officials may stimulate the establishment of voluntary associations as a precondition to get some public funding. Even business organizations may establish different associations or clubs for creating stable client circles or a chain of supporting partners. This variety of backgrounds may also imply differences in the relations of associations to the state, markets and civil society.

The density of voluntary associations is often regarded as a sign of the activity level within the civil society. The dimension of density includes two sub-dimensions: the activity in terms of memberships and the activity in terms of participation. Those civil societies which have high level of membership and active participation can be called active civil societies (de Hart and Dekker 1999). Particularly communitarian approaches have seen voluntary associations as an integrating power in local communities. Active local civil society and its empowerment by civic engagement and citizens' associations are seen as the solution when single individuals, states and markets are insufficient for the well-functioning of the society. This integrative approach to voluntary associations has been criticized by arguments that voluntary associations are not representative of the whole civil society. Then, the requirement of equality is not fulfilled in relation to the civil society. Another point of critique is that not all voluntary associations are cooperative in character. The tensions within civil society are reflected into the world of associations.

In terms of democracy, there are at least two different issues concerning the relations between voluntary organizations and civil society. First, the internal democracy of associations may vary in terms of equality of members and openness of decision-making. Second, the external relations of associations to the civil society may vary from 'majority organizations' to 'minority organizations' (Smith and Freeman 1972: 3). The former group includes broad, open, popular and well-known 'flagship organizations', while the latter refers to isolating, closed and possibly oppositional 'islet organizations'. While there are many associations within the civil society, their mutual relations include a variety of social connections. The assessment of the contributions of associations to the civil society should recognize this variety for achieving a reliable score. The degree of inclusiveness can be taken as a general dimension of relations between voluntary associations and the civil society. The degree of social inclusion often has its background in the historical context of societies (see Chapter 2). For instance, the political ideologies and the attitudes of political parties in power may impact strongly on the status and the degrees of freedom in the civil society as seen in Chapters 4, 8, 12 and 14 concerning Romania, Slovakia, Turkey and Estonia, respectively. The strengths and weaknesses within civil society are often resulting from a longer history and development of the political regime and culture.

In addition to the inclusiveness and its historical context, there are other factors causing differences in the relations. There are different types of voluntary associations according to their main mission and primary functions. One of the most evident differences is the division between 'advocacy associations' and 'service associations'. The advocacy associations represent the voice of the civil society towards the decision-making bodies while service associations offer different services either to all citizens or to their own members. Advocacy associations offer public space for *voluntary action*, while service associations offer space for *voluntary work* as stated in Chapter 13.

The degree of support from the civil society manifests the inclusiveness of relations between associations and civil society in cases of both advocacy and service. When an advocacy association gives a voice to a group of citizens it is also a kind of service: offering a channel to make influence. When a service association organizes daily care for children or elderly people it is also promoting something and making influence to something: it is a direct way of influencing the welfare level in a certain civil society. The advocacy operation is an indirect way to influence more broadly at different societal levels, while the service operation is a direct way to make influence usually in a specific situation.

The degree of inclusion is related to the aspect of democracy: the coverage of associations within the civil society in terms of memberships and participation is a possible indicator of a 'democratic culture'. The main type of relations between voluntary associations and the civil society seems to be operational and practical cooperation for the benefit of some community – either local and limited or wide and open. This cooperation may produce social benefits like social empowerment, trust and interactive capacities as by-products of social learning. The broader implications and effects on democracy and welfare are not easy to identify because of their indirect character. The participatory effect is often limited to specific contexts while the development at macro level comes into the picture as an external factor. The confrontation between *the local* and *the global* can perhaps be made more tolerable by local activism. Generally the main part of voluntarism is local and regional in character (Chapter 5).

There are also other kind of third sector organizations than the voluntary associations. The cooperatives are usually seen a special case of the third sector, and particularly they have been seen as a European type of third sector organizations (Evers and Laville 2004). Also cooperatives can be divided into different types, notably a main difference is between producer cooperatives and consumer cooperatives, even if those two types can also be combined. Cooperatives can also vary in being more or less market-oriented and having profit-gaining purposes. Thus cooperatives do not always meet the criteria set by the ideal type of associations. There is still another case of difference within the broad area of the third sector: private foundations. The world of foundations covers a large variety. Some foundations, like 'community foundations', are often quite close to the proper third sector, some others being more hybrid forms (Anheier 2006).

Despite several diversities within the voluntary organizations and their relations, the general trends of recent changes can be broadly identified. The conclusions on that issue by Jenei and Kuti seem to be justified: the growth of the third sector in recent years has implied an increase in the societal weight of voluntary associations and other third sector organizations. This means that there are more channels for citizens to make influence, third sector organizations being of a complementary character in terms of democracy and service capacity. In some cases this increased capacity has implied a real empowerment of the civil society and citizens, while in other cases the change so far has been limited. The general conclusion is the *marche* of pluralism within the civil society supported by the strengthening of organized voluntary activities.

Relations between the third sector and governmental bodies

In the organized societies, the state is the central power-holding institution in the society. The power of the state has both visible-manifest and hidden-latent dimensions, formal and informal aspects. Discussions on clientelism and corporatism have formulated relations between the state and the third sector from the perspective of power. While voluntary organizations are formally self-governing and independent, they can 'voluntarily' search for close relations to the state power. The achieved status of a 'client of the state' or even a 'partner of the state' may imply mutually supporting relations in terms of regular interaction and negotiations, supported projects and social networking. However, the stability of these relations as well as the political economy of the associations may vary as has been the case in Central and Eastern European countries. The formulation on national 'third sector policies' may imply political debates and opposing conceptions on the relations between the state and voluntary associations. Chapter 14 exemplifies very well this aspect and is useful also in illustrating the importance on sharing knowledge and having possibility to learn from each other in the process of decision making at the national level. However, the national third sector policies are not always very consistent as is exemplified in the case of Czech Republic (Chapter 13). Chapter 8 shows how significant differences in the development of relations can arise at sub-national levels among regions and local governments.

More recently the focus of discussions has moved from the issues of clientelism and corporatism more on the production processes of the welfare in terms of public services. The discussion about the 'welfare mix' started at the delineation of the public–private mix concerning mainly the relations between the state and markets. From the 1990s, the relations between the state and the third sector have risen at the centre of 'welfare mix' discussions. It was '(re)discovered' that voluntary associations have had a significant long-term role in the production of welfare services for many decades at least in Western Europe. In the 1990s their potential as an alternative for public services was recognized and also utilized in an expansive way at different levels of government. The strategic importance of voluntary associations for the production of welfare rose quite rapidly in the context of European welfare state reconstructions. New forms and cases of interdependence between the state and the third sector arose. The status of voluntary associations has then tended to change from a complementary one to a recognized alternative provider of services (Lewis 2004). This changed status with increased interdependencies and partnerships has also blurred the nature of relations between the state and the third sector. The new catalyzing and enabling role of the state is not very clear in terms of concrete relationships and interactions. While the discussions concentrate on 'service associations', the existence and position of 'advocacy associations' tend to be forgotten. The majority of voluntary associations, about two-thirds, are really 'service associations' as the statistics presented by Anheier (2006: 82–83) show.

'Welfare mix' can be found both at national and at local level. Concerning the support of the public sector to the associations, the distinction between continuous basic support and temporary project support is evidently important. This distinction can be associated with the categories 'strategic partnerships' and 'operational partnerships'. The former refers to a stable relation between an agency and an association implying possibly that this association is regarded to act for the 'public interest' in an established way. This type of relation may involve corporatist and clientelist tendencies. The latter refers to an agreement for a fixed time to complete a task or project and having often a competitive tendering at the background. This latter type of relation may be characterized as 'programmed cooperation'.

An impact of increased partnerships in service production has been that 'market orientation' has been quite strongly introduced from the public sector to the third sector. This has been leading to more managerial relations between the state and voluntary organizations. Result management has been applied in voluntary organizations on the basis of national public policies. The contracting-out of public services has increased the number of cases working as co-production of public services. For instance, a municipality can organize its social and health services as a combination of public agencies and voluntary organizations. Then, the cooperating voluntary organizations fulfil their role of 'service associations' in terms of co-production. Chapter 10 broadens and deepens the analysis of different levels and forms of cooperative relations between the third sector and the state by using the concepts of co-production, co-management and co-governance and representing empirical examples particularly at the local level. While 'co-production' refers to joint ventures in the delivery of services, 'co-management' refers to shared roles in the management of services (e.g. representation in the managerial bodies) and co-governance refers to planning and developing services together like partners. These three different forms of cooperation are not mutually exclusive but it is fruitful to analyse them also separately.

The contextual approach to the development of voluntary associations leads to regard the relations of associations to governmental bodies, business firms and civil society groups. These relations are often decisive for the changes in associational life and activities. The totality of associations and other third sector organizations can be seen as an intermediary area of societal relations among different actors. Original and traditional location of voluntary associations has been for the most part close to the civil society, and more distant from the state and markets as has been shown in Figure 20.1 above. However, already in this traditional picture the associations have been regarded as 'bottom-up channels' for advocacy or 'local providers' of services and welfare.

In recent decades, the rapid growth of the third sector and associations within it has included also a manifold hybridization of the 'sector'. This development has broadened the intermediate area between the three main societal elements to include more and more different organizational varieties which have brought the 'third sector area' more close to the state and markets simultaneously increasing the heterogeneity within the 'sector'. This development holds particularly for 'service associations' which turn to create new formations: for example foundations which support and back up associations participating in competitive service markets, new partnerships in implementation projects, new cooperatives for producing services and also some associations being reorganized into service enterprises or companies. Instead of debating about the 'basic nature' of the third sector, it could be more fruitful to identify changes in associations, cooperatives and foundations and analyse new forms of organizing citizens' activities. The traditional types of relations, like cooperation and confrontation, complementation

and co-option, have broadened to include co-production, co-management and co-governance in the area of public services.

Relations between 'advocacy associations' and public agencies in general differ from the relations of 'service associations'. 'Advocacy associations' often aim for making influence on the public policies. They represent a bottom-up approach to societal issues, a channel for people as influential citizens. This aim may lead to situations of co-governance, either in a direct or in an indirect way. The direct case of co-governance implies a formal position for the voluntary organization in some decision-making body. The indirect way of co-governance refers to external bodies (committees, councils etc.) or procedures (expert roles, reports, comments etc.) as the place of influence for voluntary associations.

The traditional separation of public and private sectors and powers has been diminishing quite visibly in the late twentieth century and at the start of the twenty-first. This development has implied the densification of relations between voluntary associations and public agencies. The main types of relations have evidently been financial and operational cooperation and market-like contracting. The trends connected with this change are the emergence of new forms of co-governance, co-management and co-production and the related rise of new hybrid forms of organizations. Taken altogether, the relations between the third sector and governmental bodies include often complementary and cooperative relations in the area of service associations as well as confrontational and negotiating relations in the area of advocacy associations.

Intermediary organizational forms between sectors

Increasing functional interdependencies between different societal sectors have been changing their mutual relations in many ways. The rise of a 'contractual state' has given ground for a multiplication of contracting out public services both to private enterprises and to voluntary associations. Networks of cooperation and negotiation have also multiplied both at national and local level. Other consequences of increasing interdependencies are new organizational forms which may include characteristics of different ideal types (public agency, business enterprise and voluntary association).

There are also traditional examples of organizational forms which evidently belong to the intermediary areas between societal sectors. Cooperatives are an old European example of mixing enterprise and association (Evers and Laville 2004: 25). Of course there are different kinds of cooperatives, some of them are more like business enterprises by making profits, some are more like associations by producing services to their members without making profit.

The reforms of the welfare functions of the state during the last decades have produced new governmental policies towards the third sector and voluntary associations. There has been a keen tendency to find out new ways in the production of public services. The result has been a multidimensional mix of public, market and third sector producers of services. The strong rise of public–private partnerships concerned both enterprises and associations. The increase of partnerships led soon to organizational innovations some of which were new businesses in the area of services and some others were newly oriented associations or cooperatives working as service providers (Taylor 2004: 138). On the other hand, many traditional associations turned also to be more controlled by public agencies than before when they took responsibilities for public services. These developments generally implied that a part of associations was losing its original closeness to the civil society while approaching to either markets or governmental bodies or both of them. This development has touched particularly the service associations while the advocacy associations may be more immune to these changes.

The concept of 'social enterprise' has risen to the frontline of discussions trying to interpret the hybridizations among different societal elements. The concept is not very clear since it has different connotations in different countries. The concept can also be overlapping with more traditional social cooperatives. Generally it could be used to refer to established non-profit service providers (Dekker 2004: 159). Then this 'hybrid' is an enterprise but it does not distribute profits as enterprises usually aim to do. Social enterprises may have tax benefits and subsidies – as well as also enterprises quite generally may have. The general trend has been a gradual increase in the area of social enterprises fulfilling functions of some public services. The change may be different in different functional branches and countries. Anyway, it is a primary interest area for research searching for fruitful themes in the study of third sector development. Chapter 6 illustrates this development in the area of labour policy in an interesting and comparative way and also recognizing the contextual national effects in the formation of social enterprises.

When a part of voluntary associations lives through a mutation into a 'social enterprise' or into a 'market-type association' they often lose some of their original features as associations. The share of voluntary work is probably decreasing and the degree of self-governance is reduced. This may imply distancing from the civil society in communication and contacting. Instead, marketing within the service markets and profile-making in relation to public policies take more attention. The hybridization also implies steps towards a more formal professionalism in the area of service production. The impacts of professions are exemplified in Chapters 13 and 16. Chapter 15 suggests a more analytical approach in the study of hybridization. The suggested approach tries to find out the important dimensions of hybridization in terms of resources, goals, ways of governance and corporate identities. The analysis would then focus on changes in these dimensions and taking into consideration also the contextual factors which influence these changes.

The development of the third sector cannot, however, be signed as being one of marketization and contractualization. This trend holds mainly for service associations. The advocacy associations may well remain more close to the original idea of voluntary associations. While advocacy is mainly directed towards public policies, it can make some effects indirectly on the development of public services. 'Advocacy associations' have been regarded to function in a bridging and gap-filling role between civil society and the governmental bodies (Lewis 2001). Thus they create and offer intermediate spaces. Both formal and informal social relations may develop within and through these spaces. Somehow this networking capacity of associations is compensating for the usual closure of public agencies and business firms as formal organizations at least it may lower the thresholds for social interaction. In positive cases, this potential may lead to new multilevel cooperation and alliances as well as to increased synergy and empowerment among actors. Associations can be more successful when they are capable of finding multilevel or cross-sector allies or regular channels of inter-action. Today these multilevel alliances are also created over borders of coun-tries and the importance of international advocacy associations has been remarkable in the last decades. Joint actions of formal institutions and informal networks have been regarded as an important factor for producing innovations, flexibilities and interorganizational synergy (John 2001, 62; Sbragia 2000).

The growth of the third sector has also invoked the issue of 'third sector policy' at the front of national-level discussions. A new trend to develop general frameworks and principles for the collaboration and cooperation among govern-mental bodies and voluntary associations has been launched in the UK during the late 1990s and in France in the early 2000s. The compacts in these countries are evidently aiming to strengthen and consolidate a well-functioning 'partner-ship culture' and simultaneously underlining the trend of 'new governance' (Osborne 2006). It is important that the independent position of voluntary associations is guaranteed in these compacts at least as a principle. The concrete effects of the compacts are still too early to evaluate (Lewis 2004: 181–182). The 'partnership culture' mostly gets its manifestation at the sector level and in the policy and decision-making processes within different public agencies and their partners.

When looking at the whole third sector, it can also be questioned, if the divi-sion into service associations and advocacy association is sharp enough and suf-ficient in this discussion. Functions of advocacy and service can also be combined with each other. There are also other functions for voluntary associ-ations. In the areas of culture and leisure, natural and constructed environment, small-scale infrastructure and local development there is still room for voluntary action. In these different areas the voluntary associations may well serve as ben-eficiary actors for social solidarity and democratic culture.

As a general conclusion, it is not believable to figure out the development of the third sector as becoming increasingly and totally a servant of markets and public policies. Rather, a justified interpretation could be that there are new divi-sions developing within the third sector. The strengthening relations to markets and public policies in the area of service industries may create a new group of social enterprises as a hybrid type. Another part of the third sector may remain close to the traditional ideal type in the areas of culture, environment and soci-etal advocacy.

General trends and challenges

In studying the development of the third sector the importance of societal relations has been highlighted in brief above and in more plural ways in the chapters of this book. The relations of the third sector to the state, markets and civil society can be analysed by means of several dimensions, and the cases of this book tell about the mosaic-like character of the third sector in different societies and epochs. Contextual approaches to the third sector can identify several external factors in the societal environment of the third sector which are making impacts to the relations, their quantity and quality. New public policies, structural and functional changes in the markets and economies as well as cultural and demographic changes within the civil societies, all these major factors together are modifying the societal environment of the third sector. The increased cooperation and partnerships of the third sector organizations with public agencies and enterprises have gradually led to the trend of convergence concerning at least some principles, models and operational techniques within organizations (Lewis 2001: 197). Trends like result-orientation, evaluating efforts and accountability systems are examples of areas in which degrees of similarity in different organizational spheres have been growing.

Voluntary associations as actors are confronting the manifold of changes in different ways. As the field of associations is deeply diversified also the adaptation to changing environments finds many situational forms. Broadly these adaptations can be described as different combinations of 'general organizational doctrines' and unique, situational characteristics. These adaptations also produce innovations which often base on re-evaluations of their opportunities and threats. In some cases a new kind of organizational form is created, in other cases strategic partnerships are searched, and in still other cases the activities of associations are reformed. There are a plenty of scattered observations of these phenomena present in this book.

After all, still more knowledge about the decision processes and managerial operations of the third sector organizations are needed. How has the management of third sector organizations changed during the last decades? What can research tell about changing processes within the third sector? When looking forward the two challenges, the challenge of management and the challenge of analysis of change processes – which are closely related to each other – can be taken at the front of important future issues.

The field of management offers a manifold of sub-themes for research. It seems difficult to accept one definite approach to this area. Both external and internal aspects of management are important for understanding the whole of management challenges in the third sector. Lewis (2001: 140–161) has presented a useful framework for the analysis of managing external relationships of third sector organizations. His framework makes a differentiation between two ladders of relationships: those which are outside the influence and those within the possible influence of third sector organizations. Outside the influence are several macro-level contextual factors: national political structures, macro-economic system, legal frameworks, ecological and broad socio-economic factors. Considering this area, the management may primarily take an adaptive approach. There is also another different group of relationships which are within possible influence: government agencies, other third sector organizations, donors, private enterprises, media and community groups. These actors form the elements for active managerial operations in terms of negotiations, bargaining, lobbying, cooperation and perhaps also co-management and co-governance. Fundraising management is a managerial function which is distinctive for third sector organizations. The analytical framework gives a starting point and room of analysing both for service associations and advocacy associations. The former often make use of cooperative strategies while the latter use typically persuasion and lobbying.

The balance between external relations and internal degrees of freedom in the management of third sector organizations is decisive for their self-governing power. This might well be a main strategic management issue for third sector organizations. The self-governing capacity or autonomy has different aspects, starting from the independence of values and mission and implying both financial and operational autonomy. Because of the increased interdependencies caused by macro-level developments, the managerial processes are often directed towards finding a tolerable compromise between autonomy and dependence. Anyway, the internal functions of management are increasingly influenced by the nature of compromise-finding. The improved capacities and empowerment of concerned people are one possible way to defend human autonomy. The battle about compromise concerns both external monitoring and internal management of budgeting, operative planning and staffing. For the third sector organizations, the management of volunteering is a distinctive feature in comparison to other organizations.

The traditional way of management in voluntary associations has been different from management approaches in public agencies and business firms. The typical manner and its problems in voluntary organizations have been analysed by McGill and Wooton (1975). They identify 'goal ambiguity' and 'conflicting performance standards' as general key problems in the management of voluntary organizations which tend to exercise 'management by doing' as an open process without too much goal-directedness and formal planning. The increased cooperation between the public agencies has implied the import of professional management approaches into the voluntary sector. The New Public Management with its applications has, however, inducted tensions with the more spontaneous and flexible managerial habits of voluntary organizations. After all, the New Public Management has evolved tensions also in a big number of public agencies. Lewis (2001: 164) states that there has also been many strengths in the traditional management of voluntary organizations. Flexibility, flat structure, decentralization and participatory ways of acting can be assessed also as advantages particularly in the search of innovations and creative networking. When voluntary associations traditionally have been relatively value-driven and setting values and missions over goals, also many new managerial approaches have started to emphasize the importance of values as basic background for management and leadership. It can be said that value-driven management is not at all outdated. The question of the best managerial approach still remains open for discussion. In real situations, the founding institutions may pose requirements and pressures to the internal management of voluntary associations. This question is doubly so as we move from the era of the New Public Management to that which has been termed the 'New Public Governance' (Osborne 2006).

Anyway, there are certain concrete issues within the management of voluntary organizations which require attention. The typical association is formed around three parts: the managerial body, the paid staff and the volunteers. The internal relations between these groups have not been much studied. Particularly the managerial role of the board seems to be often ambiguous. It is often selected from the motivated volunteers but it should also act as managerial 'motor' for the paid staff which more and more often consists of professionals in the area. Empirical research on the internal relations of voluntary organizations is needed. The diversity of voluntary associations evidently requires room for different managerial approaches according to the situational and contextual factors.

The changing contextual relations create new pressures to find sufficient balances between autonomy and dependence (see for example Osborne and McLaughlin 2004 for an example of the impact of these contextual pressures from a UK perspective). These pressures may give birth to innovative solutions, new kind of combinations among organizational forms. Innovations within the third sector are an interesting theme for research. Innovations and the innovative capacity of voluntary organizations (Osborne *et al.* 2008) can be analysed from the managerial viewpoint but also more broadly as change processes driven by several actors from different societal domains. It may be that networks of managers are coming to be the more important focus for studies than the studies of managing single organizations. Networks of managers imply the contextual relations between different societal zones. Often processes of change are only partially managed and simultaneously capable of producing unanticipated and creative solutions by combining several managerial perspectives.

The research, particularly of the last ten years, has greatly added to the knowledge about the third sector but simultaneously this achieved knowledge has revealed a lot of new challenges for the forthcoming research work.

References

Anheier, H.K. (2006). *Nonprofit Organizations. Theory, Management*, Policy. London and New York: Routledge.

Anheier, H.K., Carlson, L. and Kendall, J. (2002). Third Sector Policy at the Crossroads: Continuity and Change in the World of Nonprofit Organizations, in *Third Sector Policy at the Crossroads. An International Nonprofit Analysis*, H.K. Anheier and J. Kendall (eds). London: Routledge: 1–16.

Dekker, P. (2004). The Netherlands: From Private Initiatives to Non-Profit Hybrids and

Back? in *The Third Sector in Europe*, A. Evers and J-L. Laville (eds). Cheltenham and Northampton: Edward Elgar: 144–165.

De Hart, J. and Dekker, P. (1999). Civic Engagement and Volunteering in the Netherlands, in *Social Capital and European Democracy*, J. W. van Deth, M. Maraffi, K. Newton and P. F. Whiteley (eds). London: Routledge: 75–107.

Evers, A. and Laville, J.-L. (2004). Defining the Third Sector in Europe, in *The Third Sector in Europe*, A. Evers and J.-L. Laville (eds). Cheltenham and Northampton: Edward Elgar: 11–42.

John, P. (2001). *Local Governance in Western Europe*. London: Sage Publications.

Kiviniemi, M. (2006). Differentiation within the Third Sector: Elaboration of Dimensions and Types. Paper presented at the Annual Meeting of EGPA. Milan: 6–9 September 2006.

Knoke, D. (1999). Organizational Networks and Corporate Social Capital, in *Corporate Social Capital and Liability*, R. Leenders and S. Gabbay (eds). Boston: Kluwer.

Kramer, R.M. (2004). Alternative Paradigms for the Mixed Economy: Will Sector Matter? in *The Third Sector in Europe*, A. Evers and J.-L. Laville (eds). Cheltenham and Northampton: Edward Elgar: 219–236.

Lewis, D. (2001). *The Management of Non-Governmental Development Organizations*. London and New York: Routledge.

Lewis, J. (2004). The State and the Third Sector in Modern Welfare States: Independence, Instrumentality, Partnership, in *The Third Sector in Europe*, A. Evers and J.-L. Laville (eds). Cheltenham and Northampton: Edward Elgar: 169–187.

McGill, M.E. and Wooton, L.M. (1975). Management in the Third Sector, *Public Administration Review*, 35, 5: 444–456.

Osborne, S. (2006). The New Public Governance? in *Public Management Review*, 8, 3: 377–387.

Osborne, S., McLaughlin, K. and Chew, C. (2008). The Once and Future Kings? The Innovative Capacity of Voluntary Organisations and the Provision of Public Services: a Longitudinal Approach, *Public Management Review*, 10, 1 [in press].

Osborne, S. and McLaughlin, K. (2004). The Cross-cutting Review of the Voluntary Sector: Where next for Local Government–Voluntary Sector Relationships?, *Regional Studies*, 38, 5: 573–582.

Ruostetsaari, I. (2003). *Valta muutoksessa*. Helsinki and Porvoo: WSOY.

Salamon, L.M. and Anheier, H.K. (1992). In Search of the Non-Profit Sector: in Search of Definitions, *Voluntas*, 13, 2: 125–152.

Sbragia, A. (2000). The European Union as Coxswain: Governance by Steering, in *Debating Governance*, J. Pierre (ed.). Oxford: Oxford University Press.

Sjöstrand, S.-E. (1997). *The Two Faces of Management. The Janus Factor*. London and Boston: International Thomson Business Press.

Smith, C. and Freeman, A. (1972). *Voluntary Associations. Perspectives on the Literature*. Cambridge: Harvard University Press.

Taylor, M. (2004). The Welfare Mix in the United Kingdom, in *The Third Sector in Europe*, A. Evers and J.-L. Laville (eds). Cheltenham and Northampton: Edward Elgar: 122–143.

Vakil, A.C. (1997). Confronting the Classification Problem: Toward a Taxonomy of NGOs, *World Development*, 25, 12: 2057–2070.

Index